PRAISE FOR *BIBLICAL PRINCIPLES FOR SUCCESS IN PERSONAL FINANCE*

Finances in the Christian arena have been a topic of ferve[nt] ... has been consumed on material written about this topic. *Biblical Principles for Success in Personal Finance* is unique because it applies proven Word principles to real life. The book is clear, specific, and relevant for all of us in the trenches every day, regardless of our financial situation.

The principle-based approach of *Biblical Principles for Success in Personal Finance* has cross-cultural and international relevance irrespective of ethnic, national background or financial condition. The Father wants us all to transform the burden of individual finances into a powerful tool to enable us to reach our individual true destiny in life. This book full of scriptural references is indeed a "how to" guide to financial freedom and strength inspired by the Holy Spirit.

ALBERTO AND SILVIA SALCEDO
EKKLESIA-INTERNACIONAL, LA PAZ, BOLIVIA

Rich Brott's in-depth knowledge of finances and the strong Biblical principles he has absorbed over the years make him an authority on the subject. In his usual humorous way, Rich displays his superb communication skills in letting all, especially Christians, know that God intends for us to be debt-free and financially independent of anyone, except on Him alone.

DIVINE AND PAULINA KUMAH
C.E.O. SONLIFE PRESS, ACCRA, GHANA, W. AFRICA

Finally! A book that provides biblically sound, practical insight and tools to effectively get you from scarcity to abundance!

EMILIA LIM
DIRECTOR, CANAANLAND SDN BHD, KUALA LUMPUR, MALAYSIA

Rich Brott's book *Biblical Principles for Success in Personal Finances* begins Chapter 1 with some hard-hitting questions to help the reader face the reality of his or her financial situation. From that point on he presents clear, practical, biblical solutions for personal financial success. This book will be beneficial for pastors doing financial counseling, cell groups, and anyone interested in evaluating and adjusting their personal finances to align more with biblical principles. I'm excited about using this book and others Rich has authored to teach biblical financial management principles to our church and leaders and church members in Cambodia.

CHUCK MCCAUL
CHAIRMAN, CAMBODIA OUTREACH, CAMBODIA

Rich Brott's latest financial book, *Biblical Principles for Success in Personal Finance,* is full of sound advise and biblical principles that will help Christians in any country and culture to be successful financially and to live according to God's purpose.

JAIRO CARBAJAL DELGADO
PRESIDENT, DISTRIBUIDORA ARIEL, MEXICO

I had the privilege of meeting Rich Brott at a Cook Communications Publishing Institute held in Colorado Springs. Even after a short acquaintance, one of the things that stood out about Rich is his integrity and his compassion for people. This book *Biblical Principles for Success in Personal Finance* continues to reflect that integrity and compassion.

A people and church in so much debt cannot possibly be good for the Kingdom. Rich tackles these issues head on in such a way that it actually helps people to work through some of these issues. Some are like the ostrich, burying their heads in the sand, hoping that someday they will inherit a $1,000,000 from some distant, unknown relative. But for those of us who need to live in reality, Rich's book is thought provoking, sensitive and practical. This is a book that crosses cultures and I regard it as a great privilege to heartily recommend this book.

CLAIRE BROCKLEBANK
EDITOR, BAPTISTS TODAY, SOUTHERN AFRICA

Becoming a good steward of all God's blessings is what this book is about. It is user-friendly, yet extracts profound biblical principles to help you in your every day life. Read it with pen and notepad in hand. You will be the beneficiary of the prudent insights found within its pages.

DANIEL MANEKSHAW
EDITOR, HYDERABAD, INDIA

Rich Brott has brought us yet another indispensable book full of biblical principles, purposeful insights and sensible strategies. *Biblical Principles for Success in Personal Finance* takes the stress out of managing your personal finances and worrying about the future. Combining good stewardship behavior while practicing good lifestyle habits, the reader can relax knowing the future will be better than the past. You won't want to miss out on any of the books written by this author.

AYAD BEBAWY
C.E.O. FUTURE GENERATIONS MINISTRY, CAIRO, EGYPT

I have read several books written by Rich Brott, and have found in them invaluable principles based on the word of God and on his personal experience. I have discovered that earning a lot of money is not by itself enough to set someone free from financial bondage. Rich has explored this truth and shown us that when a Christian decides to follow God's principles as they are plainly put in the Bible, he has set his path in the right direction. We may be living extremely apart from each other on this planet earth, but only the color of our problems differ. Inside and underneath, those who violate God's principles on finance, face the same problems. I highly recommend this book to all Christians who need to seriously make changes in their lives and bring their finances into order for the glory of God.

CHARLES E. Z.NGOWI

MANAGING EDITOR, LEARN AND SHARE PUBLISHERS, ARUSHA, TANZANIA.

There are few topics that are more crucial to us than our finances. Although many would consider a topic like money to be carnal, it is actually very spiritual and greatly influences every area of our life. *Biblical Principles For Success In Personal Finance* is packed full of God-Centered, Biblical truths that are also highly practical and easily put to use in our lives. What a great resource that Rich Brott has made available to us.

STEVEN KAYLOR

SENIOR PASTOR, HOPE CHURCH, TOKYO, JAPAN

Biblical Principles for Success in Personal Finance is an outstanding and practical book for everyone who would like to understand good stewardship and wise management with their personal finances. Whether seasoned veterans or one with ongoing financial challenges, this book provides rich resources and Kingdom principles to learn from. It will assist you in discerning God's purpose for your financial world.

STANLEY HAIXIANG ZHANG

SHENZHEN CITY, CHINA

Throughout my Christian life, I have found that dealing with money has been one of the greatest difficulties the believer encounters in fully serving God. I believe it is because money is held as a material thing, dissociated from one's relationship with God. However, *Biblical Principles for Success in Personal Finance* shows us how our finances may also be a blessing to the believer alongside the other things in life.

ISAEL DE ARAUJO

EDITOR, CASA PUBLICADORA DAS ASSEMBLÉIAS DE DEUS, BRAZIL

Even if one graduated with an Accounting major, managing personal finances is a skill that we thought could be automatically learned by observation and experience during the life's journey. However, the economic situation these days is so complicated that one should take it more seriously now than before. The interesting about this book, *Biblical Principles for Success in Personal Finance,* is the encouragement given to intentionally learn the skill. It should be included in the family curriculum, church curriculum, and school curriculum.

ISHAK WONOHADIDJOJO

ACSI – ASSOCIATED CHRISTIAN SCHOOLS INTL., INDONESIA

This book is a timely, practical, and yet solid Bible-centred resource that addresses salient issues regarding our financial lifestyle. Coming at a time when 'prosperity gospel' is quite common in many teachings on finance, *Biblical Principles for Success in Personal Finance* will assist you in examining your present financial situation and go beyond just examination by giving you biblical advise on what you need to do to salvage your present as well as your future. It's a must read for those whose finances are a mess and for those who desire pearls of wisdom to help them avoid a financial mess at a later time. It is indeed your roadmap to financial independence.

BARINE, A. KIRIMI
C.E.O., EVANGEL PUBLISHING HOUSE, NAIROBI, KENYA

The author of this book really catches the need of all Christians with regard to biblical steward-ship and managing the personal finances that God trusts us with. Its content is very useful and highly readable for all people of all cultures, all countries. Everyone can be a smarter and more successful manager of the personal resources God has allowed to come through his/her life. Read this book and take actions according to the steps the author has outlined. You will learn to be wise, faithful and how to honor our Lord!

GRACE CHIAN
SENIOR EDITOR, CAMPUS EVANGELICAL FELLOWSHIP PRESS, TAIWAN

Read the book *Biblical Principles for Success in Personal Finance* and you will not only discover how to be successful in your personal finances but also how to serve God free of worry about how much money you have in your pocket. Money is a tool God uses to build His kingdom on earth and if His people are financially free they are also free to serve God with all their heart and with all of their mind. This book will unlock the door of serving God with joy while living a life of financial freedom. Financially successful people under God's standard have an edge over a person who is financially in bondage. Therefore, we should learn how to manage our finances successfully under God's standard. This book has given us Kingdom perspective regarding our personal finances. As you read this book, may you find the way to financial free-dom and usher you to your greatest height of serving God. May the book be a blessing to you as it has been a blessing to me.

ESMERALDA DIZON
MANAGING DIRECTOR, PHILIPPINE CHRISTIAN LITERATURE, INC., PHILIPPINES

Monetary issues affect every person, every city and every state without regard to country of origin. From the very poorest of the poor, to the richest of the rich, whether individual or country, financial matters must be dealt with openly, honestly, diligently and with the greatest possible attention to every detail. Every country must have economic stability. Every city must have fiscal responsibility and every individual must have personal financial accountability. In his book, *Biblical Principles for Success in Personal Finance,* Rich Brott approaches the subject from all aspects: emotional, practical, and spiritual. From broad biblical principles to the tiniest of everyday practical details, the subject of financial responsibility and independence is explored. Highly relevant for all, both the inexperienced person who is heavily in debt and the financial independent person with considerable means will gain substantial insight and assistance for every season of their financial life.

JOYCE CHACKO
EDITOR, SATHYAM LITERATURE SERVICES, INDIA

I have the privilege of knowing the author personally. From my experiences with him, I can truly say that Rich Brott lives out every biblical truth you'll find in this book, *Biblical Principles for Success in Personal Finance.* I am a fan of all his stewardship books because they have proven to be well-researched, well-grounded in the Word of God and very applicable for the reader. The books have become my favorite materials in the area of finance because every principle communicated is drawn directly from the Word of God. Rich skillfully makes essential, biblical financial principles applicable in day-to-day life. This book will bring refreshing to many readers as they discover God's pattern in the area of personal finance. God has made it clear that money matters and that He wants us to fulfill our destiny in this important area of our lives. I wholeheartedly recommend *Biblical Principles for Success in Personal Finance* to every reader who is eager to master the area of personal finance according to the Master's principles.

ISMEE WUBS
LAWYER, THE NETHERLANDS

In this book, Rich Brott has brought the truths of God's word down into practical simple steps to help you assess your own financial situation. These timeless but practical truths are sure to be a blessing to the most experienced financial steward as well as to the novice. Thank you Rich for taking the time to distill these principles for the body of Christ and bringing clarity to an area that has been complicated for so many of us for so long.

JOHN AND KARUNA BOWEN
MISSIONARIES, S.E. ASIA

Biblical Principles for Success In Personal Finance is a handy reference for every Christian. It is very practical. It is also very inspiring because it is scriptural. Many will be grateful to the author for his excellent coaching on personal finances.

CHEN HUI LIN
DIRECTOR, CAMPUS CRUSADE FOR CHRIST, SINGAPORE

In Georgia, where past Soviet Union dominated much of our thinking, we are struggling to take control of our future, knowing that the future is in our hands. After reviewing *Biblical Principles for Success in Personal Finances*, I realized the great need of our people to be good stewards of all God has entrusted us with. I am grateful that God has people like you who articulate His will and help others to be incredibly effective in their personal and professional life and ministry.

GURAM IMERLISHVILI
CEO, PARADIGM PUBLISHING, GEORGIA, ASIA

In the country of Tanzania, many people feel their todays and tomorrows are solely in God's hands and therefore will not proactively attempt to change their current situation or plan for the future. Our personal livelihood, the managing of our finances and our future depends a lot upon ourselves. As we are good stewards and actively get involved, we create the opportunity for God to bless the work of our hands. This book will help us understand that while God is in control, He expects us to be involved as partners.

MICHAEL NCHIMBI
EDITOR IN CHIEF, CENTRAL TANGANYIKA PRESS, TANZANIA

Biblical Principles for Success in Personal Finances is a book I wish I'd read, mastered and diligently applied years ago. I've gone through some traumatic, roller-coaster experiences in my finances in the past because I lacked the necessary and practical skills to manage it according to God's prescribed way. With his new book, Rich Brott has placed in our hands a must-read, a tremendous mentoring guide to help us honor God and advance His kingdom by becoming the wise stewards He wants us to be.

BISHOP JOVIE GALARAGA
CHAIRMAN, LIVING WAY MINISTRIES INTERNATIONAL
PRESIDENT, GALARAGA GROUP, INC, PHILIPPINES

While reading *Biblical Principles for Success in Personal Finances* God was speaking directly into my life and impacting my thinking. This book is destined to impact everyone who reads it and without a doubt will make a huge difference in his/her life. Rich Brott passionately leads his readers into new dimensions of God's blessings through provisional stewardship.

ANDREY BELKEVICH
EDITOR-IN-CHIEF, WORD OF LIFE PUBLISHING, MOSCOW, RUSSIA

When first reading *Biblical Principles for Success in Personal Finances* I barely got through the Preface before I wanted to read the whole book! I appreciated the way the book emphasized that personal wealth is secondary to a lifestyle of biblical stewardship! As Christians we want to live a life that honors God, and in doing so the most important is not only how well we manage our personal finances, but also how well we are able to reflect his love through our lives. But in living for Christ, we want to honor him in every way, including through our finances. The manuscript brings promises that are solidly based in Scripture, and tempered with a very practical and conditional approach. I kept thinking as I read chapter one, that few people can escape the author's observations without feeling that he has a solid grasp on reality. Knowing that the author is pointing us to God's Word for guidance, I look forward to reading the published book. The Bible provides answers to our financial and personal challenges, and this book helps to point the way.

EIVIND JATUN
DIRECTOR, SCRIPTURE MISSION, TANZANIA, AFRICA

Biblical Principles for Success in Personal Finances truly conveys God's answer to financial freedom. This is what every serious minded Christian leader has been waiting for as this book has the Bible as its basis on how to manage one's finances. It is a must read for us Third World Christian leaders where "Christianity is supposed to a mile wide and yet one inch deep!"

Rich manages to break the monotony of the text by using real life examples and communicates clearly to his readers. Whether one is a serious minded financial guru or an ordinary Christian seeking to honor God through one's finances, this book addresses all and sundry. It's right on target!

EDWARD MUTEMA
GENERAL SECRETARY, BIBLE SOCIETY OF ZIMBABWE, ZIMBABWE

There are not many spiritual leaders or churches that teach us about how to apply financial principles properly, either in our personal or in family life. Churches and spiritual leaders often emphasize more on how we should give our tithe and offerings, but less on how we should manage the 90% of the rest of our money. This book is the new breakthrough for all believers to see how the Bible clearly teaches us the true financial principles. The content of this book can be applied in detail and deeply in our daily life because it is based on God's values. The writer of this book has inspired and blessed many believers all around the world. (So,) read and enjoy the inspirations and the blessings in this book!

KUSNADI KUNAWI
EXECUTIVE DIRECTOR OF METANOIA PUBLISHING & BOOKSTORES, INDONESIA

RICH BROTT

BIBLICAL PRINCIPLES

FOR

SUCCESS

IN

PERSONAL

FINANCE

Your Road Map To Financial Independence

FOREWORD BY KEVIN J. CONNER

WWW.CITYCHRISTIANPUBLISHING.COM

Published by City Christian Publishing
9200 NE Fremont • Portland, Oregon 97220
Printed in U.S.A.

City Christian Publishing is a ministry of City Bible Church and is dedicated to serving the local church and its leaders through the production and distribution of quality materials. It is our prayer that these materials, proven in the context of the local church, will equip leaders in exalting the Lord and extending His kingdom.

For a free catalog of additional resources from City Christian Publishing
please call 1-800-777-6057.

This publication is designed to provide interesting reading material and general information with regard to the subject matter covered. It is printed, distributed, and sold with the understanding that neither the publisher nor the author is engaged in rendering religious, family, legal, accounting, investing, financial, or other professional advice. If any such advice is required, the services of a competent professional person should be sought.

Every effort has been made to supply complete and accurate information. However, neither the publisher nor the authors assume any responsibility for its use, nor for any infringements of patents or other rights of third parties that would result.

Richard A. Brott

Rich Brott holds a Bachelor of Science degree in Business and Economics and a Master of Business Administration. Rich has served as CEO of several successful businesses. He has functioned on the board of directors for churches, businesses, and charities and served on advisory boards for colleges. Formerly the Family Life Pastor at City Bible Church, Rich currently serves as the director of City Christian Publishing.

He has authored and published nine books, including his most recent CCP bestsellers: *Family Finance Handbook, Biblical Principles for Becoming Debt Free!, Family Finance Teacher Workbook, Family Finance Student Workbook, Biblical Principles for Releasing Financial Provision!, Biblical Principles for Building a Successful Business, and Biblical Principles for Success In Personal Finance.* He and his wife, Karen, have been married for thirty-five years. Rich and his wife, as well as his three children, son-in-law, and granddaughter reside in Portland, Oregon.

DEDICATION

*This book is dedicated to the most Christ-like
person I have ever met, my wife Karen. She is the reason
I continue to strive for excellence both in my personal and
professional life. My world would be empty without her.*

*Thank you, Karen, for being my faithful
partner for 35 years. I love you very much!*

CONTENTS

Rich Brott's latest text is an excellent sequel to his "Finance" series, already written and published. ***Biblical Principles for Success in Personal Finance*** is a blessed relief from so much of the world's philosophy concerning finance, i.e. 'How to get rich' in so many easy lessons. Rich's books are not like this. Instead they are biblical-based, full of spiritual principles, practical guidelines and are careful to say that financial responsibility and integrity come by living a responsible lifestyle that is pleasing to God.

Any person, be they in marketplace business or just their own personal world—after reading and answering the challenges of Section I—will find the subsequent Sections II, III, IV and V *must* reading.

This book is one that I highly recommend for its principles, purpose and practical application to real life.

—Kevin J. Conner
Best-selling Author,
Founder, CityLife Church
Melbourne, Australia

Money is an exact index to a man's true character.

—Richard C. Halverson

Would you describe yourself as successful in managing your personal finances? What does it really mean to be "successful" with one's finances? And how exactly does the Bible relate to these questions? According to the principles found in God's Word, "personal finance" involves much more than just dollars and cents. Consider three examples:

1) The biblical account of the rich, young ruler describes a man who was eager to follow Jesus, but who held too tightly to his personal possessions. His refusal to give reflected what was really most important to him in life. *Personal finance is about priorities.*

2) The gospels contain the story of a manager who entrusted his servants with different amounts of resources. He fully expected his employees to wisely manage and multiply what had been entrusted to them. *Personal finance is about taking action.*

3) Solomon's book of Proverbs directs us to consider an example in nature…ants. Small in size, yet mighty in wisdom, these creatures use their time diligently to store up resources in preparation for the harsh winter. *Personal finance is about vision for the future.*

This book is not just about making money and spending it. It's not just about getting wealthy, because true wealth is not indicated by the amount you have in the bank. *Biblical Principles for Success in Personal Finance* is about lifestyle—living according to God's Word, and enjoying the blessings that flow out of this obedience. While much of the content is related to the practical areas of your finances, it is also vitally important that you grasp the bigger picture of God's purpose for your life.

What *is* God's purpose for your life and for your finances? Thankfully, He has not left us alone in this world to figure it all out on our own! God's plan from eternity has been for man to understand his reason for existence, his purpose in this world, and the right way to live. The history-spanning, inerrant words of the Bible actually contain God-breathed principles to help us in life. Living by these principles will not only affect our checkbooks, but also our priorities, our personal goals, our vision, and our lifestyle.

Perhaps you picked up this book because you desire to become more successful in your money management. This book contains some dynamic truths to assist you, but the level of success you achieve will depend upon how you respond to the truths of God's Word. Are you willing to look at your personal finances through the penetrating lenses of Scripture? Are you willing to invest some time learning what God has to say about money management? This investment will be costly—it will mean change, discipline, and lifestyle adjustments. Yet the rewards are unspeakably worth the cost. Those who build their lives upon the truths of God's Word discover a foundation that brings peace, wisdom, and success. I encourage you to delve into these pages with a spirit of faith, believing that God knows your financial situation and is able to help you to faithfully manage that which He has entrusted to you.

In Faith,
—Rich Brott

Money management is very closely related to the biblical idea of steward-ship. For many in this generation, the word "stewardship" is perceived as old-fashioned. Let's imagine that you were given a compliment by a close friend after making a wise financial move that resulted in great success: "John, way to go! You're such a tremendous steward!" Wouldn't really make your heart swell with pride, would it?

And yet, take a look at the words of a compliment that Jesus referred to in a story he told about stewardship. After telling His disciples about a master who entrusted his servants with varying amounts of resources, Jesus then described the reaction of the master to the work performed:

> *"His master replied, 'Well done, good and faithful servant! You have been faithful with a few things; I will put you in charge of many things. Come and share your master's happiness!'" (Matthew 25:21)*

The master commended his servant, or "steward," for his excellence in management. His pleasure with the servant resulted in increased honor and responsibility. From this passage, a steward could be defined as one who manages that which has been entrusted to him or her.

This concept of stewardship forms the heart and soul of this book. God has called each one of us to be faithful managers of our time, money, and resources. If we were called to account for the management of our personal finances, what kind of praise would we earn from our Master? This book seeks to set forth principles to enable us to live our lives in a manner that is "worthy of the calling we have received" (Eph. 4:1).

Biblical Principles for Success in Personal Finances is divided into five sections which are intended to help you discover both spiritual principles and practical tips in managing your personal finances. In these sections, we will seek to answer the following questions:

SECTION I—ASSESSING YOUR FINANCIAL SITUATION

How am I doing in managing my personal finances? Am I wise when it comes to borrowing and using credit? What money traps should I be aware of? What can I do when I face times of financial difficulty?

SECTION II—UNDERSTANDING GOD'S PRINCIPLES FOR FINANCIAL FREEDOM

Why is it so important for me to understand God's principles for financial freedom? What are the financial laws of nature, and how do they affect me? How can giving and tithing bring financial blessing? Would God trust me with wealth?

How can I use prayer as a tool to strengthen my finances?

SECTION III—CREATING A SECURE FINANCIAL FRAMEWORK

How do my decision-making skills influence my finances? How can I get out of debt? How can I rebuild my credit? What is my financial vision for the future? How can I keep records that will enable me to manage my cash flow?

SECTION IV—INCORPORATING TRUTH INTO YOUR ATTITUDES AND ACTIONS

How do my daily habits of time management and communication affect my finances? How can I learn to budget my money successfully? What are some practical ways to save money? What small changes can I make that will improve my overall financial situation?

SECTION V—ANTICIPATING YOUR FINANCIAL FUTURE

What are some investing tips that will help me to multiply my money? How can I wisely save and invest my money for retirement? How can I prepare for unexpected events that would have a huge impact on my finances?

Biblical Principles for Success in Personal Finance has been designed for a broad audience of readers who are ready to accept personal financial accountability. Both single and married individuals will find the content helpful in preventing the future possibility of having to financially swim upstream. Others who have enjoyed years of successful budgeting, saving and investing will glean new tips from the financial principles which are set forth. Whether you are in a financial crisis or are just seeking to sharpen your skills, this book contains many pearls of wisdom to help you discover success in the financial arena.

Managing your personal finances successfully is truly a "balancing act." We are in this world, but not of it. We have earthly responsibilities, yet our citizenship is in heaven. We are to seek first God's kingdom, and yet we are to faithfully manage our possessions. This kind of dual management would be impossible without a good instruction manual! Thankfully, God has given us his Word to guide us, and a Wonderful Counselor to help us activate these principles. May you be blessed—spirit, soul, and body—as you partner with the Holy Spirit in applying his trustworthy principles to your personal finances.

For Your Financial Success…
— Rich Brott

ASSESSING YOUR FINANCIAL SITUATION

How am I doing in managing my personal finances? Am I wise when it comes to borrowing and using credit? What money traps should I be aware of? What can I do when I face times of financial difficulty?

"Jesus Christ said more about money than about any other single thing because, when it comes to a man's real nature, money is of first importance. Money is an exact index to a man's true character. All through Scripture, there is an intimate correlation between the development of a man's character and how he handles his money."

—RICHARD C. HALVERSON (1916-1995)
FORMER SENATE CHAPLAIN, PASTOR AND AUTHOR

A FINANCIAL CHECK-UP

What is the quickest way to check your financial well-being? If you don't like accounting, math or bank statements, you probably don't savor the thought of a financial check-up. But is there a fast and painless way to get a feel for whether you're in trouble?

Yes, there are a couple of techniques that you can use. Obviously they're not going to give you as much information as if you took the time to do a personal balance sheet and budget. But they will let you know if you're heading for serious financial trouble. So let's spend some time giving you a financial check-up to see the condition of your financial health.

One way is to take a look at your checkbook. If you were to look over all of your cancelled checks and credit card statements for the past 12 months, what story would they tell about you and your spending habits?

One biographer said that when he started to do research on a person, the first thing he wanted to know was how that person spent their money. He felt that if he could look at their checkbook, he'd learn more about that person than if he interviewed friends and relatives.

We can learn a lot about ourselves in the same way. What's the biggest check you wrote last month? If you still have a mortgage, that should be it. If the biggest check went somewhere else, you might want to ask yourself, "Why?"

Paying for college is expensive and may in fact demand a rather high monthly payment, but if your car payment is that high, you could be heading for trouble.

Maybe you don't have a mortgage payment. Perhaps you're a little older and have already paid it off. If so, the biggest check each month should be written to your retirement savings account. Or are you taking that money and using it to pay for a boat or other luxuries instead?

WHERE IS YOUR MONEY GOING?

Then take a look at the other big checks you write. How many of them are to pay monthly bills for things you bought long ago? Are you still paying for the furniture that's been in your living room for three years?

What about TV's, stereos and electronics? Making monthly payments on those types of items is a danger sign. You could be heading for trouble.

Now let's do a little rough math. Take a look at your deposits for the month. Then compare those big unavoidable monthly bills—for your mortgage, car payments and utilities. Do those payments consume more than two thirds of your deposits? If so, you are already in dangerous territory. A closer look is in order.

Don't forget about the little checks either. Are you writing a lot of smaller checks to credit card companies? How are you recording your credit card purchases? Are you deducting from your check register each time you make a credit card purchase?

Maybe you're spending too much time in the mall. What about checks for cash or ATM transactions? Are you always just a little short of cash? Time to take a look at some of that 'miscellaneous' spending. Those five and ten dollar lunches can add up over time.

What about your credit card bills? Are you among the 30 percent who pay off all their purchases every month? If so, you probably have your spending under control.

Take a quick look at the credit card statements. Can you remember what you bought with each charge? If you can't remember what you bought, there's a good chance that you didn't need it.

Think about all the ones you do remember. Were you buying things that you really needed or was it for something that you just wanted at the time? Have you used all those things since you bought them?

Here's a quick test for you. Are you just paying the minimum each month on your credit card account? Flash the warning lights! Look at it this way. For every $1,000 you owe on your account, you may be paying up to $200 each year in interest payments.

If you have a credit card balance of $5,000, that comes to about $100 every month that doesn't bring any food, clothing or anything else into your house. Do your own math to see how much is flying out your window every month in interest. Wouldn't you rather have no credit card balance? Wouldn't you rather be debt free?

Finally, how do you feel about money? Some people look at money as a pleasure pass. They think you buy stuff and happiness follows. Those are usually the people with large credit card bills.

Others view money as a measure of their success. They need to earn more than their neighbor to feel satisfied, justified or fulfilled. Their income (and what they buy with it) determines how happy they are. Since they're always on a quest for more, they can't be happy with what they have. It's a great formula for a lifetime of unhappiness.

Well, there it is. A quick check-up on your financial health. Hopefully you have found yourself in top shape! But if not, remember that we were just looking for the symptoms today. It's up to you to take a few more tests and discover how critical your situation is.

How Will I Know If I Have Too Much Debt?

Fortunately, potential debt problems can be spotted before they reach the serious stage. By knowing what danger signals to look for, you can take steps to prevent a problem before it occurs.

Go through the checklist below. If any of these danger signals looks familiar, you may be headed for financial trouble.

- You think of credit as cash, not debt.

- Your debts are greater than your assets.

- You owe more than seven creditors.

- You are an impulsive or compulsive shopper.

- You and your spouse are dishonest with each other about your use of credit.

- You don't know how much your monthly living expenses are or the amount of your total debt.

- Your expected increase in income is already committed to paying off debts.

- You depend on extra income, such as earnings by a second person or overtime by the breadwinner, to help you make ends meet.

- You have less than two months' take-home pay in cash or savings where you can get to it quickly.

- You have to pay back several installment payments that will take more than 12 months to pay off.

- You have more than 15 percent of your take-home pay committed to credit payments other than your home mortgage.

- You get behind in utility or rent payments.

- You have to consolidate several loans into one or reduce monthly payments by extending current loans to pay your debts.

- You cannot afford to pay for regular living expenses or credit payments.

- Creditors are sending overdue notices.

- The portion of your income used to pay debts is rising.

- This month's credit balances are larger than last month's.

- You are usually late paying some of your bills.

- You borrow for items you once bought with cash.

- You don't know how much installment debt you owe and you are afraid to add it up.

- You have borrowed money from a new source to pay off an older, perhaps even overdue debt.

- You have borrowed money to pay for regular household expenses such as rent, food, clothing, gas or insurance.

- You have reached your credit limits.

- You hurry to the bank on payday to cover checks already written.

- You no longer can contribute to a savings account or have no savings at all.

- You pay bills with money earmarked for other financial obligations.

- You pay minimum amounts or less on your outstanding debt.

- You use a cash advance from one credit card to make payments on others.

- You've applied for more credit cards to increase borrowing.

- You have drawn from savings to pay regular bills.

- Your liquid assets total less than your short-term debt.

    …and on and on!

This causes you to….

- ✓ Take out a loan.

- ✓ Withdraw savings.

- ✓ Skip payments.

- ✓ Pay only the minimum amount due on your charge accounts.

If you identified with two or three of these, it's time to do something about it. If at least four of the above statements applied, examine your budget and look for ways to tighten your belt.

If you identified with five or more, you are probably headed for financial trouble.

If you identified with seven or more, then your financial health is in trouble. You are in financial danger!

How Do You Handle Credit?

At some point or other, most everyone applies for some form of credit, whether it's for a new house, a new car or bank credit cards. There are very few people who can afford to pay cash for every single purchase.

This is where banks come in. There are many businesses that will not accept a personal check from a person who does not have a credit card. It is also difficult and sometimes impossible to rent a car without a credit card. The credit card has quickly become a major identification tool.

Your credit rating is very important and must be protected at all costs. Whether good or bad, your credit standing is no secret. Whenever you apply for any type of credit, you will be investigated. Your payment habits go on file at the credit bureau. Your credit file shows your credit history, income level and your payment habits. Delinquent entries on your credit report may very well result in denial of credit.

Not only is having credit a necessity, a good credit rating is just as important. However, each year, millions of well-intentioned people find themselves in financial crunches that severely jeopardize their credit standing.

These are well-meaning people, just like you, who might have lost income through illness and/or hospitalization, job loss or, more commonly, simply over-extending themselves. The reasons why you are now in a financial bind are not particularly important at this point. Your aim now is to get out of debt and re-establish your credit.

How can you tell whether or not you have a credit or debt problem? Review the following list and ask yourself these questions:

- Are you paying high interest rates?

- Are you being charged late fees?

- Are you getting calls from creditors?

- Can you afford the monthly payments but not the past-due amount?

Section I: ASSESSING YOUR FINANCIAL SITUATION

- Are you making monthly payments, but your balance never seems to go down?

- Do you worry about paying your bills?

- Would reducing your payment help?

- Are you racking up credit card debts faster than you can pay them?

- Do you feel like you're sinking in quicksand and you desperately want to get out?

- Are you always short on cash because you have to cover the past due bills?

If you answered yes to any of these questions, you have a problem.

Some of the nicest people have the worst problem handling debt and credit issues, but unfortunately by the time they realize it, it may be too late. Take these warning signs to heart and decide now to conquer debt before it conquers you.

ASSESSING THE RESULTS

Have you ever taken your car in for an annual tune-up, only to discover that there are major repairs needed? An oil-change is one thing, but a transmission overhaul is a more costly matter. Ignoring either problem will eventually cause damage to your vehicle.

As you read this first chapter, what were the results of your financial check-up? Whether you found yourself in top shape or in need of major repairs, there is hope for your situation! In the next chapter, we'll discuss further borrowing and credit issues. Though you may be tempted to give in to discouragement, don't do it! Keep reading! The first step in achieving financial success is to make an honest assessment of where you are today. This will give you the insight to recognize any changes you may need to make for the future.

"I hear, I know. I see, I remember. I do, I understand."[1]

CHAPTER 1 ▶ APPLY IT

Key Points:

➤ current spending habits ➤ debt danger signs

➤ credit concerns ➤ habits and lifestyle changes

1. **Write down** any parts of the chapter that were meaningful to you.

_____

_____

_____

_____

2. **Personal Application:** How can you personally apply these truths in your own life? Write down several long-term goals.

_____

_____

_____

_____

Section I: ASSESSING YOUR FINANCIAL SITUATION

3. **Steps to Action:** Write down one small step you could take to begin immediately applying the truths and principles of this chapter.

_____

_____

_____

_____

4. **Prayer for the Practical:** Write out a prayer to God asking Him for help in making any changes that these goals would require.

_____

_____

_____

_____

Psalm 62:8 "O my people, trust in him at all times.
Pour out your heart to him,
For God is our refuge."

"Modern man drives a mortgaged car over a bond-financed highway on credit-card gas."

—EARL WILSON
FINANCIAL EXPERT, CHRISTIAN COUNSELOR AND AUTHOR

CHAPTER TWO

THE DEBT PENALTY: THE DANGERS OF EXCESSIVE BORROWING

There is a great danger in our society of getting trapped by debt. This chapter will address a number of borrowing and credit issues. Perhaps the greatest need in families today is to understand the consequences of being trapped by debt, with limited income, creating a financial position where recovery seems impossible.

Anyone can find a wealth of information which deals with borrowing, easy credit and debt issues, but the problem counselors often encounter is failing to get people to recognize the seriousness of their actions before they make wrong decisions. All too often, people only want help after their situation has become nearly hopeless. Just know that borrowing can be very hazardous to your financial health and possibly to your mental health, spiritual health and the health of your relationships.

PUTTING THE BRAKES ON BORROWING

Too often, people are quick to borrow instead of trusting the Lord to meet their needs. After all, doesn't Scripture tell us that our God is a providing God, and that He will take care of us by meeting our needs? What if we turn to credit and take on new debt, when all along God wanted to show Himself strong on our behalf? Before you run to the bank for a loan, before you pull out the charge card, before you rush to meet your own needs, give time for the provision of God to work.

"Not that I am looking for a gift, but I am looking for what may be credited to your account. I have received full payment and even more; I am amply supplied, now that I have received from Epaphroditus the gifts you sent. They are a fragrant offering, an acceptable sacrifice, pleasing to God. And my God will meet all your needs according to His glorious riches in Christ Jesus" (Philippians 4:17-19 NIV).

We have been taught from childhood to make decisions and move quickly and decisively, so we feel compelled to hurry to fix our own problems. Yet, in spite of this need for speed, we should be patient in waiting on God. We should be cautious about always making our own way independently instead of seeking the wisdom of God.

"Let the wicked forsake his way and the evil man his thoughts. Let him turn to the LORD, and He will have mercy on him, and to our God, for He will freely pardon. 'For My thoughts are not your thoughts, neither are your ways My ways,' declares the LORD. 'As the heavens are higher than the earth, so are My ways higher than your ways and my thoughts than your thoughts'" (Isaiah 55:7-9 NIV).

CLIMBING INTO DEBT

The road into the misuse of credit is wide, broad, simple, easy, accessible, effortless, uncomplicated, painless, spacious, available and trouble-free.

> WITH DEBT, YOU ESSENTIALLY SLIDE IN AND CLIMB OUT. EASY TO GET IN, DIFFICULT TO GET OUT.

However there is no quick and easy way out from under a heavy debt load. With debt, you essentially slide in and climb out. Easy to get in, difficult to get out. If you have ever been heavily in debt and burdened down with monthly payments so steep that you could barely keep your head above water and then had to slowly and methodically climb out, then you know that it is an uphill struggle. There is no easy way out. You cannot wave a magic wand and undo in twelve months what it took twelve years to accomplish.

Living Your Life in Debt

What about a lifestyle of debt? Is a Christian to borrow? Is debt okay? Some would believe that it is wrong for a Christian to have any debt. Some will say it is alright to borrow for a house, but never to borrow for anything that would depreciate. One of the greatest challenges and hindrances to reaching the world for Christ is this. People who live in a society where there is the possibility of making significant amounts of money all too often spend their way into enormous debt. In doing so, there is little left over (above their tithing) to give to their local church, missions, and evangelism projects. If you have to borrow, learn to give while borrowing.

Do You Intend to Repay?

It is not wrong to borrow money, but it is wrong to take on debt without the ability to pay it back or with the intention of never repaying what is owed. What is meant in Romans 13:8 when it says not to owe anything to anyone?

> *"Obey the laws, then, for two reasons: first, to keep from being punished, and second, just because you know you should. Pay your taxes too, for these same two reasons. For government workers need to be paid so that they can keep on doing God's work, serving you. Pay everyone whatever he ought to have: pay your taxes and import duties gladly, obey those over you, and give honor and respect to all those to whom it is due. Pay all your debts except the debt of love for others— never finish paying that! For if you love them, you will be obeying all of God's laws, fulfilling all his requirements"* (Romans 13:5-8 TLB).

These verses simply mean that you should obey the laws, pay your taxes and repay all of your debts. That just makes good sense. Besides repaying your debts at some future date, you are to pay your creditors on time, with any interest owed. A person who borrows but does not repay is called wicked, meaning wrong, sinful, immoral, evil and depraved.

> *"The wicked borrow and do not repay, but the righteous give generously"* (Psalm 37:21 NIV).

The Value of Self-Control

If a person or family will live a restrained lifestyle, they will be able to live on thousands of dollars less each year. You should only incur debt when it makes good economic sense.

The expense of borrowing should be less than the economic benefit that you will receive.

Don't underestimate God's desire to help you in every way. Over and over the Scriptures indicate that you are to live a controlled and temperate lifestyle.

> *"Now the overseer must be above reproach.... temperate, self-controlled, respectable...." (I Timothy 3:2 NIV).*

> *"Thus says the LORD, your Redeemer, the Holy One of Israel: "I am the LORD your God, who teaches you to profit, who leads you by the way you should go" (Isaiah 48:17 NKJV).*

Easy Credit Isn't Really Easy

The problem with easy credit is that there are always banking institutions willing to give you more money than you have the ability to repay. If you need to borrow a thousand dollars for an unexpected need because you have not set aside dollars for that purpose, the lending institutions will try to give you several thousand more than you actually need. While at first blush that may give you great pride and confidence, thinking that someone really believes in you, in reality, the only way a bank makes money is to lend it out.

If you receive seven or eight thousand dollars and you only needed one thousand, rest assured—you will find a way to spend the extra. It will disappear before you know where it went. The less you borrow, the less you pay back and the more you have available to give to missions and the needs of others. Credit should always be the exception and not the rule.

One of the problems with obtaining credit is that you are presuming that nothing is going to change for the worse in the future. You are assuming you and your spouse will have adequate income for repayment, that your jobs are secure and that your income stream will be the same or more in later years.

There is a danger in making assumptions. It could be that your intended source of repayment changes. Jobs are lost; the value of stocks and bonds can decline or even disappear; assets may not appreciate as quickly as anticipated or may even lose their value.

> *"Now listen, you who say, 'Today or tomorrow we will go to this or that city, spend a year there, carry on business and make money.' Why, you do not even know what will happen tomorrow. What is your life? You are a mist that appears for a little while and then vanishes. Instead, you ought to say, 'If it is the Lord's will, we will live and do this or that'"* *(James 4:13-15 NIV).*

A Slave to Debt

A person who is deep in debt feels like he is in bondage. He is so burdened down with the heavy load of debt, he feels like he becomes a servant to his creditors. He works all day for days on end just to meet his payment obligations to his debtors. He gladly volunteers for all the overtime he can get and works a part-time job in the evenings or on weekends, all for the purpose of getting a larger paycheck so he can turn it over to someone else. Well, all of this is not breaking news. He knew about it long before he borrowed the money. He could have read about it in Scripture.

> *"The rich rule over the poor, and the borrower is servant to the lender"* *(Proverbs 22:7 NIV).*

How Dangerous is Debt?

Americans are literally trillions of dollars in debt. That is the danger of credit, which is simply the ability to borrow money. In short, it is the spending of money today that will be tomorrow's income. Most economists would say that credit is an important part of the ability of individuals, families, cities and ultimately nations to function in a financial world. Credit consists of unpaid balances on auto loans, credit cards, student loans and generally any non-mortgage debt.

One of the real dangers of excessive borrowing is that it creates high monthly payments, which often strain even well-planned budgets. The pace of borrowing often exceeds the family's growth in income and leads to a form of credit-debt bondage. The interest expense of credit debt is often very high. Banks and other lending institutions often will loan to people with a higher credit risk, but do so at the expense of the borrower.

This is a huge profit opportunity for the company. Often those that do not qualify for the terms of a regular loan still get money, but at an interest rate several points higher than normal. Of course, most individuals, families and businesses will quickly agree to this because, in reality, they need the money at any cost.

People who have high monthly credit payments often sacrifice their other financial goals just to make their payments. This is a very serious offense. By not investing in a house, savings account or other forms of investment, they seriously put their future retirement in question.

Excessive debt cannot be ignored. It will not go away. You can ignore past-due bills, but you do so at the risk of finding yourself in even worse circumstances. A chain of events is triggered when you do not pay your bills. Creditors can take action against you, the past-due bills can be turned over to a debt collector, your property can be repossessed and your wages garnished.

While debt bondage is the result of unwise decisions and excess credit purchases, there is no easy way out. The reason why people find themselves in this position is because they spend more than they earn and the only way out is to spend less and pay the difference on their debt balance. The only way out of this dangerous situation is to get control of your spending and put yourself on a budget, which we defined earlier as a written plan that provides oversight and guidance to your spending habits.

LESS IS BETTER THAN MORE

It is always wise to borrow less rather than more. Cultivate the mindset that you will only borrow for absolute necessities and that you will repay the loan at the earliest possible date. Paying back a larger amount than the required fixed payment will help you retire the debt early. What should you not be getting a loan for and what would be something worth borrowing for? In general, it all depends on your ability to repay the loan within a practical period of time.

While you could obtain credit to purchase an asset with reasonable potential to gain in value, you should not borrow for something that will continue to lose its value from the moment you buy it. Another sensible cause for which to borrow money would be for something obtained that would bring you income opportunity. If you have a skill or a trade and purchasing a particular tool or machine would generate additional income for you, then credit might be a possibility to explore.

Avoid Indulgence

Don't get in the habit of buying something before you need it or because you think you might use it at some future date. Indulgence because you feel that you owe it to yourself or it will help your self-esteem is a very bad habit to get into.

You can develop habits that will insure financial success, regardless of how much or how little your income is. Many make very little over a lifetime, yet manage to save enough for a debt free and secure retirement.

Think Twice About Credit Card Debt

Your current credit card debt represents more than just the fact that you owe money. It represents the fact that you are spending more money than you are making. It represents the fact that, depending on how much you owe, you could be out of touch with your financial situation. It represents the fact that you need to attend to paying it off now—or it will likely get worse before it gets better.

If you are going to have a credit card, pay it off in full at the time of each statement. If you cannot do that, you have no business carrying a card with you. Pay cash instead.

Track Your Spending

Record every penny spent for the past 90 days and the next 90 days. If you don't know where the money went, how can you get out of debt? Close your eyes and visualize a stress-free, debt-free lifestyle. You are on vacation…but you have paid for it all in advance. It is not more income that you need, it is less spending.

Live Within Your Means

Scripture says that the poor will always be with us, but it does not say that none of them will be Christians. If you've ever wondered, "I cannot understand why God has not made me rich yet," we have no magic formulas but this one. Live within, not above, your income!

A friend of mine had purchased a couple of fine houses, but then sold them to pay off debts, only to get into debt all over again.

> CULTIVATE THE MINDSET THAT YOU WILL ONLY BORROW FOR ABSOLUTE NECESSITIES.

Please understand this. You will never win the lottery, so quit spending money on tickets. Quit spending money as if you were about to win the lottery. God's ways are not about windfall income like the lottery. His ways are about thriftiness, staying out of debt, working hard and serving Him. How does one get out of debt? Exactly the same way it was accumulated....one step at a time.

If you give a man a fish, you can feed him for a day. If you teach him to fish, you can feed him for life. The real help comes in changed attitudes that cause you to move from a lifestyle of debt to the freedom of being debt-free and becoming financially independent.

HEADING FOR A FINANCIAL CATASTROPHE

- Are this month's credit card balances higher than previous months?

- Have you never paid more than the minimum payment required on your credit lines or credit cards?

- Are you continuing to add new cards to your pocketbook?

- Are you always seeking new ways to borrow?

- Have you been feeling anxious about your debt burden?

- Does your spouse know about all of the credit you have obtained?

The First Step: Prayer

First, go to God in repentance and forgiveness for mishandling that which He has entrusted to you. Remember that in your borrowing, you promised to repay. In essence, you made a vow when you incurred debt. While borrowing or lending for that matter is not necessarily wrong or prohibited in Scripture, it is discouraged in a number of Scriptures. When you get into trouble because of your own unwise choices and bad decisions, while God will help you find a way out, it will not be at the expense of defrauding those to whom you go. Forgiveness is always available, but the consequences of our wrong remain.

ARE YOU A CREDIT RISK?

Everyone knows that potential lenders look closely at your credit record, but did you also know that landlords and insurance companies do, too? Here are some tips for building up a clean credit record—and making sure it stays that way.

You probably already know that your credit report is all-important when it comes to qualifying for any type of loan, including a mortgage, an auto loan or a low-rate credit card, but you may not realize that having a lousy credit rating (or credit score) can impede you when it comes to getting a job, renting an apartment or even getting a decent rate on auto insurance.

Landlords, employers and insurance companies have all discovered that someone who pays their bills on time is likely to be responsible enough to pay them as well and responsible enough to drive safely on the roads. That means it's in your best interest to keep your credit report—and your credit score —in its best possible condition.

Now you probably know that your credit report is essentially your credit history. It details what sort of loans you have outstanding, how long you've had them, whether you pay your bills on time and so on. (The information is not just from credit card companies, but all your creditors including utilities, landlords, hospitals, banks, etc.)

Your credit score, however, is more complicated. It's a computer-based determination of the risk you pose to each of your creditors. In fact, it's calculated differently for each lender, using those particular parts of your credit report that are thought to be the most telling.

According to Fair, Isaac & Co., a leading supplier of credit data, these scores include up to 100 factors, including the number of times you've paid bills 60 days late, the size of your credit line (particularly the part that isn't being used), the number of recent inquiries into your credit history (an indication that you're looking for more credit) and any bankruptcies, liens and foreclosures.

> YOU WILL NEVER WIN THE LOTTERY, SO QUIT SPENDING MONEY ON TICKETS.

Fortunately, the rules were recently changed and you can now take a look at both your credit report and see your credit score. You can also improve your score (and your overall credit history) with some fairly simple maneuvers, which will be covered later.

Wise Credit Management

In the process of building our financial future, there are times when we ask another person or a financial institution to use their money for a limited period of time. This is borrowing or taking out a loan. Usually, the lender allows us to use their money in exchange for a percentage fee called interest. Our generation seems to be caught up in easy credit because of the ready money available.

There are very few people (if any) who do not worry that money may be going out the door faster than it is coming in. Most Americans have revolving credit balances from credit cards and other retail establishments and a small group are enslaved to mountainous consumer-debt burdens that eat at large parts of their income. Whether you are moderately in hock or in a deep hole—you can break that debt cycle.

At one time (a few years ago), it may have made some sense to borrow. You could deduct interest payments from your income taxes. With the cost of living running at 8 to 12 percent a year, you could repay your loans with cheaper dollars later. But now tax deductions for interest on consumer purchases have dried up. Inflation seems to be under control, meaning that expensive dollars remain expensive; and you can't count on huge raises in personal income a couple of times a year.

In spite of some lower interest rates available, credit card companies continue to charge extremely high interest on the unpaid balances. At the same time, passbook saving accounts pay so little, it is hard to see an advantage to them. Falling behind on repaying lenders will only serve to hurt your credit rating. Late payments can remain on your credit file for seven years. Even if you do pay on time, having too much installment debt compromises your ability to borrow for something important in the future. If the whole country is in a recessionary economy, the last thing you should have is a lot of debt.

In order to be free from all those creditors, admit the problem in this area and stop borrowing. You too, as others, may be a spendaholic. Do you have too many credit cards? Do you like to shop too much? Is it hard for you to resist a so-called bargain?

Limiting Your Use of Credit

How much debt is just too much? A call to a consumer credit counseling service yielded this advice. Spending more than 15 percent to 20 percent of net income on monthly debt payments, not including your payments on a home mortgage, is just too much.

Easy availability of credit is partly to blame for many problems. Creditors are not the tight-fisted people they were years ago. It is common to receive several offers for credit cards each week in the mail. All you need to do is sign the offer and return it for instant credit. Potential creditors insure consumer credit with unparalleled leniency. After all, it's hard for them not to make money with interest rates of 18 percent or more.

People who use credit cards as a receipt process and then pay their outstanding balance in full each month will avoid trouble. Credit card companies disguise potential debt problems. It is tough to spot trouble when the minimum monthly payment required reflects only 3-5 percent of the total balance. One can be dangerously in debt before any difficulties are noticed.

While it is illegal for creditors to send you unsolicited credit cards, they can increase the limits or lines of credit without asking. For people who have difficulty in controlling their spending habits, more credit means more debt, which means more trouble.

TIPS FOR SMART SPENDING

One way to break free from the spending habit is to look at the credit in terms of total outstanding balances instead of minimum monthly payments. Each month, pay off all new charges on your cards, plus interest and a portion of the previous balance. You'll reduce each month's debt balance below the previous month's. It should get easier as you go.

Another hard-to-do but effective idea is to slice the plastic. Certainly if you have more than one credit card, get rid of the one with the highest interest rate. If you pay your outstanding balance in full each month, get rid of the card that has an annual account fee of $25 to $50.

The road to financial independence comes by making hundreds of small prudent decisions over a lifetime, each seemingly insignificant, but collectively making the difference between financial dependence and financial independence.

Avoid Using Credit to Extend Your Paycheck

Many people look to credit cards as a way of extending their paycheck. But in fact, you end up with less money, not more. Never get a cash advance with a credit card.

Many checking accounts have overdraft features that can be very dangerous to the person who has difficulty in the spending control area. These accounts make it easy to borrow money by writing checks, even when you have no funds to draw on.

Pay in Cash and Record all Spending

Get in the habit of paying as you go. Paying cash for an item not only gives a person that sense of confidence and well-being, it keeps debt at a lower balance than the previous month. If you do charge for an item with the intention of paying it off when the bill comes due, keep a written tally of your purchase.

Keep a notebook to record the name of the store where new charges are made, the amount of the charge, the purpose of the purchase and a running balance of all new charges made since the last credit card statement. In this way, you are informed continuously as to what that new statement is going to say when it arrives in the mail. There are no surprises!

Credit counselors agree that most people would avoid excess debt if they budgeted their money. Remember, a budget is simply a roadmap or a snapshot of where the income is coming from and where all of the monies will go throughout the year. From this written information, one can observe patterns of buying behavior, unnecessary spending habits and learn how to improve personal finances.

In addition to a budget, one should prepare a personal balance sheet. It can be handwritten very simply. If you have a PC, there are many software programs available for both personal budgets and Statements of Financial Condition, commonly known as balance sheets.

The program called Microsoft Money works well. For under $75, you can plug in the information and let the software do its work. If you list the information by hand, list all of your assets in one column and all of your liabilities in another. Subtract total assets from total liabilities and this will give your net worth.

Quicken is another leading personal finance software that is designed to help people keep track of their day to day finances. A nice feature of Quicken is that it allows you to determine the tax implications of your financial transactions. This and other software packages can be easily purchased on-line.

COMMUNICATION IS KEY

If you find yourself in the financial position of owing more than your assets or having more monthly bills to pay than your income permits, then it is clear that borrowing has gotten out of hand. If you do not have money to pay when a debt is due, you should communicate with the creditor to work out a solution. It is your responsibility to take the initiative. Be open and honest with the creditor and most will work with you.

Don't wait for your creditors to come to you if you are going to miss a payment or you have run short of cash. Be up front about it and get them on the telephone! Don't wait for collection agencies to call. Get them on the phone as soon as you realize you can't make a payment on time. Be honest about the situation and what you can afford to pay each month.

Most creditors will try to help you work it out. The first message from a collection agency may say you must pay in full immediately. Don't give up. This is what they are trained to tell you. Keep trying. Lenders are not stupid. They would rather extend your loan term or reduce your payments than receive nothing at all. If you are a slow payer, this will show up in your credit file, but there is some flexibility between full payment and complete default.

A quick word about seeking credit. Too many inquiries for your credit report can harm your credit rating. It may look like you are applying for credit from too many sources and are over-extending yourself. One potential problem for you is that inquiries may be made without your knowledge, even when you haven't applied for credit. If you shop around for a new car, every dealer you visit may make an inquiry to see if you are a customer worth pursuing. They get the information that they need to make an inquiry from the driver's license you show to take a test drive.

When shopping around for a bank loan, your credit report can be pulled without your knowledge. And these inquiries stay on your credit record for up to two years. A bit of timely advice: avoid applying for a lot of credit at one time. Resist giving sellers personal information they need to make a credit check unless you are serious about buying.

When you have decided to change credit card companies, be sure to notify the company of your intention to cancel. Otherwise it may look like you have a lot of credit available to you and you may not get new credit if you seek it in the future. A credit report will list all your cards and your full credit line, whether you actually use them or not.

Even if you have a spotless record, a lender may reject you because you could borrow into oblivion. Just cutting up old cards with the scissors will not suffice. You need to write or call the issuer of the card, ask them to cancel your account and then ask them to notify the credit bureaus that your account has been in good standing and closed by the borrower. If you want advice or need special help, there are numerous nonprofit consumer credit counseling services available. Check the telephone book for local chapters, or go on-line to become more familiar with local services.

Section I: ASSESSING YOUR FINANCIAL SITUATION

Moving Towards Financial Victory

Perhaps the first two chapters of this book have made you more conscious of some areas that you are struggling in financially. If this is the case with you, remember that there is great value in assessing where you are at financially. As mentioned before, the first step in moving towards financial victory is realizing that there are problems that need to be faced. In chapters 12 and 13, we will include more specific information on getting out of debt and rebuilding damaged credit.

"I hear, I know. I see, I remember. I do, I understand."

Key Points:

➤ God's thoughts on debt   ➤ self-controlled lifestyle

➤ warning signs of disaster   ➤ managing credit wisely

1. **Write down** any parts of the chapter that were meaningful to you.

_____

_____

_____

_____

2. **Personal Application:** How can you personally apply these truths in your own life? Write down several long-term goals.

_____

_____

_____

_____

3. **Steps to Action:** Write down one small step you could take to begin immediately applying the truths and principles of this chapter.

_____

_____

_____

_____

4. **Prayer for the Practical:** Write out a prayer to God asking Him for help in making any changes that these goals would require.

_____

_____

_____

_____

Psalm 62:8 "O my people, trust in him at all times.
Pour out your heart to him,
For God is our refuge."

"The things that will destroy America are prosperity at any price, peace at any price, safety first instead of duty first, and love of soft living and the get-rich-quick theory of life."

—THEODORE ROOSEVELT (1858-1919)
AMERICAN 26TH US PRESIDENT

CHAPTER THREE

THE MONEY PIT REVISITED: SCHEMES, SCAMS, AND MONEY TRAPS

Are you old enough to remember watching the 1986 slapstick comedy, *The Money Pit*? Whether you've seen it or not, this movie is a classic illustration of what it means to be "financially vulnerable." When Walter (Tom Hanks), an entertainment lawyer, and Anna (Shelley Long), a musician, purchase a beautiful mansion on Long Island, the house begins to fall apart even before they move in to it. In an ensuing battle of muddy faucets, collapsing staircases, and other costly maladies, the couple soon realizes just what a "money pit" they've purchased.

You may not have purchased a fixer-up that is falling apart, but there still may be areas of your life in which you're financially vulnerable. These areas could range from minor things—like the television commercials that bombard your children—to more serious purchases, such as extended warranties and get-rich-quick offers.

THINK TWICE BEFORE CO-SIGNING

One huge area of financial vulnerability is co-signing someone else's loan. Co-signing is essentially a quick way to go into debt. People who co-sign feel that they are doing a relative or friend a favor. The potential cost of their signature is usually not explained very carefully to them. When you co-sign a note, you are taking on someone else's debt.

Rarely do you know just how much and what kind of debt that person may have. Debt is an excess of liabilities over assets.

A home, if financed conservatively, may usually be sold for more than is owed by the mortgagor. A car, furniture and almost all other depreciating items purchased on time cannot usually be sold for sufficient money to pay off the lender. This is often the kind of debt for which co-signers are asked to be involved.

There is always the possibility that what you co-sign for could be repossessed, leaving you still on the hook for most of the outstanding loan. Ask any credit union or bank how they come out financially when goods are repossessed. Repossession is usually a financial disaster for both the borrower and the lender.

In a given situation, the co-signer may feel some embarrassment at quizzing the lender about what will happen if his relative or friend does not pay as he has promised.

Understanding Co-signing

What are you doing if you co-sign a note? You need to understand the financial transaction in which you would involve yourself. Here are three factors:

1. You are borrowing the money. The lender has refused to make the loan to the person for whom you are co-signing, based on facts which reveal that the risk is too great to loan the money to your friend or relative.

> THERE IS ALWAYS SOMEONE WILLING TO SEPARATE YOU FROM YOUR MONEY!

When you sign the note, the money is really being loaned to you. The reason you have been asked to sign is that your collateral, your character, your credit and your capacity are sufficient for the loan officer to feel good about the security on the loan. Your signature is the loaner's security.

2. You are loaning the money. You are loaning the money you borrowed to a person who was too great a risk for the professional lender. You are involving yourself in a business transaction that the expert money manager would not touch.

3. You are hoping your friend will pay back the loan. There's a good chance that it will not happen. When your friend or relative defaults, then you have the privilege of paying back the money. Never co-sign a note unless you can afford to give the money away!

GUARD YOURSELF FROM IDENTITY THEFT

When it comes to vulnerability, nothing is worse than someone trying to steal your identity. Someone who gets their hands on your credit card number and personal information can charge up thousands of dollars in goods and services—and all in your name! If you want to protect yourself from credit thieves, you should start by protecting your personal information.

It seems like everywhere you go, clerks are asking for information—your social security number, your phone number and address, your date of birth, your mother's maiden name, etc. And in most cases, you probably offer this information freely. Yet, this is all it would take for an unscrupulous person to open a credit account in your name or to access your existing account(s) and charge you into financial oblivion.

Here are some strategies to make sure that the only one who uses your credit cards is you:

- Don't give out your Social Security number unnecessarily. (Only brokerages, banks and employers are required by law to take your Social Security number.) In case you're robbed, never carry your Social Security card in your wallet.

- Be mindful of dumpster divers. Destroy documents that have your information on them before tossing them in the trash. Shred or tear up any pre-approved credit offers you get in the mail, even if you don't respond to the offers.

- Demand that your credit company stop selling your personal information to credit card marketers. Stop unwittingly giving your information away yourself, which happens every time you fill out sweepstakes entries and marketing surveys.

- Contact the three big credit bureaus (information accessible on-line) and ask them to put a fraud alert on your file. This means a credit company will be required to telephone you before opening up any new accounts.

GET-RICH-QUICK SCHEMES
=
GET-POOR-QUICK REALITIES

A lot of get-rich-quick schemes prey upon unsuspecting investors. As the old proverb goes, the man who speculates is soon back to where he began—with nothing. This becomes a very serious problem, for all his or her hard work has been for nothing. It is all swept away. He or she is under a cloud—gloomy, discouraged, frustrated and angry. Get-rich schemes rarely ever pan out. That is wishful thinking. Yet, millions of dollars are lost each year to fraudulent deals because of the greed of investors.

The salesperson who pressures you to buy now should trigger a red warning flag in your mind. Consider the friend who drops by to give you an opportunity to invest in a red-hot deal. Unfortunately, you must decide today (they say) because they are going to start drilling for oil in the morning.

Now you may be thinking that you would never be seduced into buying drilling rights over the telephone. Don't be so sure! Greed will get you nowhere. Although many modern consumers have gotten more savvy and are now less easily fooled, greed is still part of human nature. People out there still keep coming up with deals that sound smart to conscientious consumers—but aren't.

Many banks and credit card companies urge their cardholders to buy protection for losses that occur if their cards are lost or stolen and used by someone else for about $25 a year. Many don't know, however, that federal law limits cardholders' liability for unauthorized charges to $50 and then only for charges made before notifying the card issuer. The protection is a waste of money.

Many lenders require borrowers to get credit life or disability insurance. It protects the lender if the borrower dies or becomes disabled before repaying a loan. For the borrower, however, it's no bargain. According to the Wall Street Journal, insurers collect over $2 billion a year in premiums, but pay out only $900 million a year.

If a lender wants you to buy this insurance, explain that your other assets or life insurance will cover the loan if you cannot pay. For example, a term life insurance policy that will pay enough to cover the loan, should you die, is much cheaper. If the lender insists, watch your balance carefully and ask your lender to let you drop the insurance when you've repaid 25 percent of the loan.

Extended Warranties

Many merchants encourage customers to buy extended warranties when they buy autos, appliances or electronic items. They're profitable for the merchants, who pocket up to 40 percent of the amount before sending the rest to the insurer. Don't buy extended warranties on appliances or electronics. While you pay for them in advance, they do not begin until the manufacturer's warranty runs out—up to three years.

These warranties do not cover normal wear and tear or rough handling—the usual reasons repairs are needed. Certainly don't finance an extended warranty. You then pay interest on a contract that won't start for up to three years. Consumers rarely benefit from extended warranties. Name-brand appliances usually don't break down during the first few years and if they do, they're covered by the original warranty. Similarly, defective electronic equipment usually breaks within the first few months and is covered by the original warranty.

Repair Your Credit Schemes

Major credit bureaus offer services that let you check your credit file. Under some programs, you get a copy of your credit file as often as you want for $30-$50 per year and receive notification every time a creditor receives a copy of your file.

Federal law already lets you see your credit file as often as you want and at least one time each year you get a copy of your report free. You may have to pay $10 or $15 each additional time, but few people need to see their file more than once a year. Being notified whenever a creditor receives a copy of your file normally tells you something you already know—after all, it's your credit, insurance, employment or housing application that triggers a credit request. In the meantime, many services sell the information to direct marketers, who clog your mailbox and call you during the most inconvenient times.

Some companies claim they can fix your credit, qualify you for a loan or get you a credit card. But even legitimate companies can't do anything for you that you can't do yourself. What they will do, however, is charge you between $250 and $2,000. A few credit repair companies have resorted to illegal practices—breaking into credit bureau computers to change a bad credit file, or stealing credit files or Social Security numbers and substituting them for the files of people with poor credit histories. You are better off avoiding them!

Pool Your Debt Schemes

Also called debt consolidation or debt pooling, budget planning or debt adjusting companies, these people end up increasing, not decreasing, your debts, once you pay their debt consolidation charges. Some of these companies charge outrageously high interest or fees that may amount to illegal loan sharking operations. If you need help paying your bills, you're better off visiting a Consumer Credit Counseling office.

Don't pay any company that offers to obtain a Social Security benefits statement, Social Security numbers for your children, or name change when you get married. You can get this information and service free from the Social Security Administration and only *you* can legally fill out the application forms, so why pay for it?

"Free" Vacations

A favorite giveaway to lure you to sales presentations, such as those peddling condos, is the promise of a dream vacation to Hawaii, the Bahamas or Mexico. In fact, what you get is a vacation certificate. To take advantage of it, you must typically deal with an out-of-state travel agency by mail, not by telephone. It is difficult to get reservations and even harder to get the name of the hotel where you are supposed to stay.

With many vacation certificates, you must get to the destination on your own, where you will get two or three nights' lodging—probably someplace you wouldn't want to stay. So remember, it's not your education, social status, money or experience that counts. It's taking the time to check it out! If a deal sounds too good to be true, you can bet that it probably is!

"Take-Their-Money" & Disappear Schemes

Most people make major financial expenditures without really looking at all the facts. This kind of action is downright dangerous and certainly not smart. The ultimate cost and alternative possibilities are seldom considered when someone is swept along in a desire to acquire a new home, car, business or other personal investment.

Beware of retail sales advertisements. Buying a $50 item that is on sale for $40 is not a $10 savings if you did not need the item in the first place. It is actually an unnecessary $40 expense!

A number of publications and 900 phone services list government surplus and different types of auctions at a cost of $30 to $100. Charging anything more than a few dollars for this information is an overcharge. And 900 calls are charged to you. Despite what you may think from these companies' ads, information on public and private auctions is free and readily available.

Classified newspaper ads like the one below are often the opening pitch for what dozens of local Better Business Bureaus report as the fastest-growing category of consumer fraud:

"Financial Problems? Bad Credit? No Credit? Loans/debt consolidations to $20K. 800-XXX-XXXX."

According to USA Today, New York City and Dallas each recently reported 4,000 complaints and inquiries; Phoenix had 6,000 and Cincinnati had 8,000. Consumers who respond are easily pre-approved for a loan. They'll receive it once they send an application fee or processing fee of several hundred dollars. The new loan, of course, never materializes.

State consumer protection agencies are finding that loan brokers are often a slippery bunch. Following thousands of complaints, Florida swiftly shut down more than 100 companies. But they soon show up in other states under different names.

Ask questions, check the answers and consider all the facts before making that purchase or investing those hard-earned dollars. Always standing close by are those with their hands out, more than willing to take your savings from you. Don't let it happen to you. Be prepared, investigate and then invest!

"I hear, I know. I see, I remember. I do, I understand."

CHAPTER
3
APPLY IT

Key Points:

➤ vulnerability in co-signing ➤ extended warranties and "credit checks"

➤ credit scams   ➤ sales schemes

1. **Write down** any parts of the chapter that were meaningful to you.

_____

_____

_____

_____

2. **Personal Application:** How can you personally apply these truths in your own life? Write down several long-term goals.

_____

_____

_____

_____

3. **Steps to Action:** Write down one small step you could take to begin immediately applying the truths and principles of this chapter.

_____

_____

_____

_____

4. **Prayer for the Practical:** Write out a prayer to God asking Him for help in making any changes that these goals would require.

_____

_____

_____

_____

Psalm 62:8 "O my people, trust in him at all times.
Pour out your heart to him,
For God is our refuge."

CHAPTER FOUR

FLYING BY YOUR INSTRUMENTS: FACING FINANCIAL STORMS WITH CONFIDENCE

"The ultimate measure of a man is not where he stands in moments of comfort, but where he stands at times of challenge and controversy."

—MARTIN LUTHER KING, JR. (1929-1968)
PASTOR, CIVIL RIGHTS LEADER AND WINNER OF 1964 NOBEL PEACE PRIZE

My friend was in desperate need of some answers. Due to reorganization of the company he worked for, he had just lost a high-paying management job. Now, with a high debt-load and little money in savings, he had no idea of how to move forward. Fear-filled questions bombarded his mind as he began the search for a new job. How could he provide for the basic needs of his wife and family? Where could he hope to find work with so few jobs available? And what was in store for his future?

Everyone is faced with seasons of financial hardship that require us to make difficult decisions. Maybe you are asking some hard questions now about a financial trial that you are going through, wondering what the future holds. These times of blurred financial vision may be compared to a pilot who encounters a sudden lack of visibility while flying. Under normal circumstances, a pilot receives assistance from the air-traffic controllers in positioning the plane for a safe landing. In this type of "precision approach," the air-traffic controllers are required to set the pilot up so that he or she doesn't need to make more than a 30 degree turn to land the plane.

In times of unexpected turbulence or in a storm, however, a pilot may be required to make a "non-precision approach" in which he or she must know how to fly by the instruments. A non-precision approach requires the pilot to make complex turns and, in some situations, be the one who is solely responsible for the airplane's positioning and landing.

Becoming an "instrumented-rated pilot" is important for the purpose of flexibility. Pilots need to know how to fly when weather conditions are optimal, but there may come a time when they encounter limited visibility and unexpected turbulence. They may even be forced to land the plane at an unfamiliar airport, or make an emergency landing without the help of air-traffic control. How essential it is to develop the necessary skills *before* the storm comes!

USING YOUR INSTRUMENTS

Do you know how to survive a financial storm? There are God-given "instruments" that you can rely upon in these times to help you endure the storms of life with confidence.[2] We'll first address four practical areas that, if built into your life, will help you when you're facing financial difficulties. These areas include 1) budgeting, 2) savings, 3) controlled spending, and 4) goal-setting. We'll then discuss several spiritual instruments which, we hope, will be great sources of strength for you in tough times. Though there are other spiritual "tools" you can apply in a trial, the ones we have mentioned include 1) the Word, 2) prayer, 3) good counsel, and 4) trust in God. It should be noted that all of these instruments are not meant for the storms alone; ideally they should become a part of our everyday lives.

Budgeting

Budgeting is a valuable instrument to help you prepare in advance for the storms. Having a financial plan is absolutely essential in enabling you to manage your money, whether in "smooth flying" or in rough times. A financial plan will be a great help to you in making realistic decisions. Decisions must be made within some kind of framework or design. That framework or design provides guideposts that mark the limitations or boundaries within which the individual or family must operate.

Sometimes people become discouraged with budgeting because an emergency arises and there is no money. The roof leaks, the front tire blows out, or some other minor or major disaster wrecks the family budget. A budget helps you cope with unexpected expenses. The more modest the income, the more important a budget is. People with a lower income have less flexibility in their spending patterns; this actually *increases* the importance of developing a good budget.

Emergencies can't be determined in advance, but provision can be made for them in the budget. No one can say for sure just how much money should be kept in this emergency fund, but many financial experts recommend three to six months' income.

How can one provide for such emergencies? What if, during a recessionary economy, sales are slow at the plant or office and the company is forced to arrange for layoffs in order to keep its budget on course for the year? Provision for emergencies such as a temporary work layoff should be made in advance by finding some extra money each week to put away for unexpected expenses. There are really only two ways to do that. You must either raise your level of income or reduce your current expenses.

If you are now in a financial trial and find yourself without a budget, don't become overwhelmed! True, it's hard to create a budget when the bills are greater than your income. Like the friend I mentioned earlier, you may find yourself without a job, not knowing where the money is going to come from. Even in times of inconsistent income, however, budgeting is a tool to help you determine where your money is going. Resolve in your heart to budget, whether income is predictable or not.

Savings

When a financial storm hits, saving money is one "instrument" you will be very grateful you learned how to use. It isn't easy to save! One must make a commitment to start saving and stick to it. There will always be something waiting to take your money. But no one else will save for you, so you've got to do it for yourself. You may have heard that a penny saved is a penny earned. But actually a penny saved is more than a penny earned. This is especially true if you invest it in an IRA or retirement plan. If your pennies earn a 7 percent interest rate, then the following applies:

> In 10 years, 1,000 pennies, or $10 a week,
>
> > would grow to $7,185.
>
> In 20 years, 1,000 pennies, or $10 a week,
>
> > would grow to $21,318.
>
> In 30 years, 1,000 pennies, or $10 a week,
>
> > would grow to $49,120.

How much should you be putting away? Professionals suggest at least ten percent of take-home pay should go into savings. This would include such investments as stocks, mutual funds and bank accounts. But this is only a guideline.

Most Americans actually save different amounts at different stages of their lives. What's important is to keep the savings habit alive by always saving something.

When should you begin? As early as you can. If you start at 25 and put away $25 a month, you could reach $300,000 by age 65. If you wait until 45, that $300,000 at 65 may cost $300 a month.

Remember the rule of 72. This tells you how long it will take to double your money at a given rate of interest. You simply divide 72 by the interest your money is earning. At six percent, your savings will double in 12 years. At nine percent, they will double in eight years.

Here's an idea. When working overtime on the job, set aside 75 percent of the extra income into a special emergency savings account. Another idea which deserves some thought is to set aside in your special savings account any company bonus dollars paid in cash. This should be done until an amount is accumulated which equals three to six months' income. After this, you can consider other timely investments with the extra cash. Resist the urge to spend the extra money. In the long run you'll be glad you did!

Controlled Spending

One fairly obvious way to save money is by developing good spending habits. Many people have never learned the art of "living below their means"—essentially, controlling their spending. Spending money to get the most out of it is something you will have to work at, just as you will work to earn it in the first place. Do you put first things first when you make purchases? Do you buy what you need most or what you want? Do you shop in more than one store to compare the price and quality of a particular item you want? Do you resist the temptation to buy something because it is on sale or just because it appeals to you at the moment, when there are other things you need more?

It is during financial storms that the value of controlled spending is fully realized. Through budgeting and setting aside money each month in savings, you can have the confidence of knowing that there will be extra should an emergency strike. If you are now in a financial crisis and realize that you have not been making use of this "instrument," don't get discouraged! Resist the urge to get into debt by paying for everything with a credit card during your time of lack. Financial trials may require you to cut back in some areas of your life. Ask the Lord for His help in this trial to spend money wisely and to begin living a life of controlled spending.

Problem-solving / Goal-setting

How would you respond if someone asked you to describe where you want to be financially in ten years? In facing financial challenges, it is vital to have a clear definition and understanding of individual and family financial goals. After all, if you don't know where you're going, how will you know when you get there? Block off some time to sit down and put on paper those personal goals that you wish to accomplish. Prioritize them, rating them as to their importance.

After you identify your goal, you are ready to state the challenge or obstacle that stands in the way of reaching it. More than one obstacle may become apparent. Possibly several solutions will have to be found. Financial challenges need to be defined carefully. If they are formulated only in vague and general terms, the solutions are apt to be vague and general, too. Also, problems can be studied more easily if they are stated in relationship to your goals. Stating the problem helps keep the goal in focus and the problem in perspective.

Perhaps you are wondering how goals relate to times of trial. Having financial vision and goals provides a much-needed compass for decision-making in a trial. Let's use the example of my friend I referred to earlier. The obvious problem is that he no longer has a job and needs to pay the bills, but let's look at the bigger picture. Is there a certain set of skills that he feels the Lord has been calling him to develop and use? Is there a debt he wants to have paid off by a certain time? Are there goals for the future that will require his funds and resources? With financial vision, you are able to respond wisely instead of reacting hastily. Financial goals will determine the immediate decisions that are made in times of hardship, and help you to remain focused, even in times of lack. Of course, your goals will need to be frequently reviewed and revised.

As you deal with one goal, you'll find it is related to other goals. In this way, an overall view is necessary; a snapshot is not enough. Seldom can a problem be dealt with in isolation. The solution to one puzzle may alter other solutions or it may introduce new problems and obstacles; the process of problem-solving goes on and on.

SPIRITUAL INSTRUMENTS FOR THE STORM

Any pilot will tell you that learning to fly by your instruments takes a lot of hard work and training. Developing the skills of budgeting, saving, controlling your spending, and setting goals will take time and energy. However, these skills alone will not help you to soar through a serious financial storm. You also must learn how to use the spiritual instruments God has given to you.

The Word

Psalm 119:105, David said, "Your Word is a lamp to guide my feet and a light for my path. I've promised it once, and I'll promise it again: I will obey your righteous regulations" (NLT). God's words, given to us in the Bible, are the ultimate instruments that we need to help us avoid a crash-landing. Through His perfect law, we can find peace and assurance for our souls, even though the circumstances around us may be less than perfect. As we read His Word, we discover principles about giving, tithing, and stewardship that help us to move from the realm of the natural into the realm of the miraculous. Remember, God's ways are not our ways! We must saturate our minds with His truth in times of trial to give us faith that He is our ultimate Helper.

Prayer

George Mueller (1805-1898) was an English evangelist who had many deep insights on prayer. Establishing orphanages in Bristol, he was also the founder of the Scriptural Knowledge Institution for Home and Abroad. In talking about prayer, Mueller once made a powerful statement: "I hope in God, I pray on, and look yet for the answer. They are not converted yet, but they will be."[3]

Mueller knew the importance of the dual weapons of prayer and the Word. In talking about their power, he made this statement: "It is a common temptation of Satan to make us give up the reading of the Word and prayer when our enjoyment is gone; as if it were of no use to read the Scriptures when we do not enjoy them, and as if it were no use to pray when we have no spirit of prayer."[4]

Maybe you aren't establishing orphanages, but you also need to rely upon prayer and the Word in your times of trial. Hearing from God (the Word) and talking to Him (prayer) are how you stay connected to God. He is your "air-traffic controller" in the midst of your trial, and will show you the steps you are to take, one day at a time.

Good Counsel

One of the most important instruments that you can rely upon in a storm is that of good counsel. There are times when a pilot becomes disoriented and off-course. It is at these times that he or she seeks out the help of someone who is "outside the fog." The air-traffic controllers can provide the radar vectors and altitudes needed to land the plane.

In Proverbs 12:15, it tells us, "The way of a fool is right in his own eyes, but a wise man is he who listens to counsel" (NKJV). There are certain times when our own eyes are too focused on our immediate situation to see the bigger picture. In these times, we will greatly benefit from going to a friend or a financial advisor for help. Do you have problems with excessive debt? Try the Consumer Credit Counseling Service, which is listed in your local yellow pages. For a small fee, you can negotiate a payment plan that will keep your creditors at bay. It would also be wise to pray with a close friend over your financial situation (see Financial Prayer Guide in Chapter 10).

Are you considering buying a used automobile at an auction? Transportation is important, but before you buy a used or a new automobile, remember to prepare and get good counsel. Consider the repair history of the vehicle, the amount of interest charged if financed, the length of time for repayment of the loan, new insurance costs, and whether or not it would be more cost effective to maintain your current one. When considering a major purchase like a new home, even more preparation and counsel are needed.

Trust God

In his book *Weather Flying,* retired pilot Robert Buck talks about the importance of the copilot during serious weather conditions:

"A copilot during serious instrument flight is a necessity—not required by regulation, but without doubt, flying instruments without a copilot is a very tough job. I've flown small aircraft in serious weather, on instruments alone, and it's much more difficult than flying a 747 with a crew"[5].

Even in financial storms, we can rest assured that God is our copilot! In Hebrews 13:5-6, we see the following command and promise: "Don't love money; be satisfied with what you have. For God has said, 'I will never fail you. I will never abandon you.' So we can say with confidence, 'The Lord is my helper, so I will have no fear...'"

If we will put our trust in God, He will teach us how to use the proper instruments to face the storms we are facing with confidence. In the next section of the book, we have included seven chapters which will enable you to understand God's principles for financial freedom. You may be tempted to skip over these chapters to get to the more practical areas of your finances. We strongly encourage you, however, to investigate these truths more carefully, which form the foundation for the rest of the book. Chapter 5 on "Kingdom economics" will help you understand some key differences between God's thoughts on money and man's limited perspective. Chapters 6-8 are filled with powerful truths on releasing your money in ways which will gain God's favor and blessing. And chapters 9 and 10 reveal some astonishing ideas about how to manage both money and time using God's supernatural principles. The final chapter in this section, Chapter 11, ties these principles together with a prayer guide to help you begin to pray over the practical areas of your finances. Whether you are in the midst of a financial storm or not, we hope these chapters will strengthen and encourage you as you discover what the Scriptures say about your finances!

"I hear, I know. I see, I remember. I do, I understand."

Key Points:

➤ times of financial trial ➤ goals / decision-making in
the midst of trials

➤ budgeting and savings ➤ prayer and the Word,
good counsel and trust

1. **Write down** any parts of the chapter that were meaningful to you.

_____

_____

_____

_____

2. **Personal Application:** How can you personally apply these truths in your own life? Write down several long-term goals.

_____

_____

_____

_____

3. **Steps to Action:** Write down one small step you could take to begin immediately applying the truths and principles of this chapter.

_____

_____

_____

_____

4. **Prayer for the Practical:** Write out a prayer to God asking Him for help in making any changes that these goals would require.

_____

_____

_____

_____

Psalm 62:8 "O my people, trust in him at all times.
Pour out your heart to him,
For God is our refuge."

UNDERSTANDING GOD'S PRINCIPLES FOR FINANCIAL FREEDOM

WHY IS IT SO IMPORTANT FOR ME TO UNDERSTAND GOD'S PRINCIPLES FOR FINANCIAL FREEDOM? WHAT ARE THE FINANCIAL LAWS OF NATURE, AND HOW DO THEY AFFECT ME? HOW CAN GIVING AND TITHING BRING FINANCIAL BLESSING? WOULD GOD TRUST ME WITH WEALTH?

HOW CAN I USE PRAYER AS A TOOL TO STRENGTHEN MY FINANCES?

"You say, 'If I had a little more, I should be very satisfied.'
You make a mistake. If you are not content with what you
have, you would not be satisfied if it were doubled."

CHARLES HADDON SPURGEON (1834-1892)
ENGLISH PREACHER, AUTHOR AND EDITOR

CHAPTER FIVE

KINGDOM ECONOMICS 101: WHAT YOUR PROFS NEVER TOLD YOU

God's economy is different than ours. His economy is based upon a system of values and principles. Ordering your life according to His values and principles will make you successful. Living a life that is void of all principles, on the other hand, will eventually lead to your downfall. The values of ethics, love, compassion, giving, caring, honesty, integrity, serving and forgiving will empower you. They have stood the test of time.

A value system built on dishonesty, lying, cheating and stealing leads only to disaster. If your desire is to measure success by the size of a check you can write, then your foundation is already shaky. God's economy measures our success by how our value system adheres to divine principles. God values whether or not we have accumulated those things which take us from this life to the next.

GOD'S VALUE SYSTEM

When we are successful in God's economy, we benefit both now and for eternity. If we have become successful by using this world's standards, we will always have to be on red alert, because thieves can steal, disasters can destroy and rust can corrode. If our possessions belong to God, nothing is powerful enough to take them away. So in the face of any natural economy or even as we face death, our success continues because we have laid up riches in heaven. Though many people of the world possess few material goods, those who live according to the principles of God can anticipate the wealth and treasures awaiting them in heaven, which far outweigh the temporal wealth of this world.

> IF OUR POSSESSIONS BELONG TO GOD,
> NOTHING IS POWERFUL ENOUGH TO TAKE THEM AWAY.

A Kingdom View of Material Possessions

Much of western culture is centered around things and possessions that money can buy. Christian culture in the West is not immune to its influence. It's not that we are necessarily in love with money, but certainly we could say that we are enticed, and maybe entrapped, by what we know that money can do for us. Of course we do live in this society and in this world's system and we should not be so unwise as to think that we are immune from it altogether. The Bible has a lot to say about material goods and our desire for them. The Apostle Paul suggests that contentment is a very powerful value to guide us. Then he reminds us that we came into this world with nothing and will depart in the same way. He suggests that we should be happy when we have food to eat and clothes to wear. He notes that people who desire to get rich quickly often fall into temptation, fulfilling harmful desires that lead to ruin and destruction.

Luke 12:15 instructs us to be on guard against every form of greed. It says that even when we have abundance, our lives are not to be caught up in our possessions. In this passage, we are told that if our priority is the gathering up of riches and treasures for ourselves, then we are not being rich toward God. And finally we are told that it is God who watches out for the raven, who neither sows nor reaps, who has neither storerooms nor barns. Yet God takes care of and feeds the birds. And He says that we are certainly more valuable than they. George Mueller has said that the beginning of anxiety is the end of faith. It is important that we live in the now, not in yesterday or in the tomorrow. Yesterday is filled with mistakes and problems, and can't be changed. It is easy to carry the burdens of tomorrow, which may not even exist when we get there. Yet they become very real diversions to our ability to be fruitful today. Tomorrow can certainly be a real distraction and it can also keep us from being productive today.

The Lord is our provider and substance. We are not to covet the wealth of the world, but we are to trust in God and in His ways. "But godliness with contentment is great gain. For we brought nothing into the world, and we can take nothing out of it. But if we have food and clothing, we will be content with that. People who want to get rich fall into temptation and a trap and into many foolish and harmful desires that plunge men into ruin and destruction. For the love of money is a root of all kinds of evil. Some people, eager for money, have wandered from the faith and pierced themselves with many griefs. But you, man of God, flee from all this, and pursue righteousness, godliness, faith, love, endurance and gentleness." (I Timothy 6:6-11 NIV).

A Kingdom Sense of Contentment

Millions of people today are on a quest to accumulate possessions and even wealth. It is hard for all of us to be content with what we have when the world's entire system is geared toward making us unhappy with everything we have and desirous of everything we don't have. From advertising to attitude, we face a discontented culture. How much money do they want to be content? Usually just a little bit more. Money cannot buy contentment or happiness. It is very hard for us to be satisfied with what we do have, but we need to strive for contentment and contend for happiness.

A lot of people today are often frustrated, confused and unhappy with their personal and professional lives. But as long as we are in Christ, we have the ability to be content. Of course the opportunity to be content, when all around you there is dissatisfaction, is of great value.

Contentment with our portion of food and clothing is good. But all of us have additional treasures of great value worth mentioning. Being well-nourished, enjoying shelter, yes. But what about the love and warmth of our family and friends? Treasures, that's what they are. Most people do not recognize what really counts in this life.

A Corrupted Worldly System

Trusting In Cash

In Acts 16:16-24, an event in the life of the apostle Paul is described. Paul and his partner Silas were being beaten with many stripes and then were thrown into jail. Listen to what brought about these terrible things—their personal crime was to cast an evil spirit out of a young woman while in the Greek city of Thyatira.

Most of the time something like this would be appreciated or even go unnoticed, but being free of this unclean spirit rendered the girl incapable of continuing her work as a fortune-teller. The bottom line was that the controllers (masters) of her life were pretty upset because their source of income from this poor child had suddenly ceased. They were so upset they even brought charges against both Paul and Silas, hence, the hard treatment. Kind of difficult to imagine!

It is obvious that the love of money was extremely important to these characters. The fact that the girl was living a horrible and wretched life of servitude while these guys made lots of money off her services made no difference to them. This brings to mind the prostitutes and pimps of our day.

Why should these unscrupulous characters care? Why did it matter if they wanted to use this poor little girl to make a coin or two off the unsuspecting people who wished to have their fortunes told for a price? After all, they weren't the ones responsible for the girl becoming demon possessed.

If certain citizens wanted to indulge a little in this and that, why not get rich off human weakness? This sounds pretty familiar to all of us even today! History does repeat itself. Even more notable is that human weakness has been around since the beginning of time. These guys were probably thinking that if they didn't collect the money, someone else would sell the same service, so it might as well go to them.

Who Are You, Really?

It's not that money is unimportant—it *is* important and sustains our livelihood. If spent in the right way, on the right things and in the right places, it can do a lot of good. But God places great importance on the methods we use to make that money. Proverbs 14:9 says, "Fools mock at making amends for sin, but goodwill is found among the upright." (NIV) Proverbs 15:6 notes, "The house of the righteous contains great treasure, but the income of the wicked brings them trouble." (NIV)

You see, what we are is far more important than what we possess. Shedding all sense of right and wrong and morals for the sake of money is the most foolish thing a person can do. Yet men and women get involved all the time in things that are not honest and respectable because of greed for material things. Yes, many people experience success based on the wrong motives.

I well remember my dear Mother once saying, "I don't want to do anything, no matter how small, that would prevent me from going to heaven." I've never forgotten that statement and it guides me every day of my life.

Matthew 25:21 says "… 'Well done, good and faithful servant! You have been faithful with a few things; I will put you in charge of many things. Come and share your master's happiness!'" (NIV) As God develops our character and sees He can trust us, He has every reason to prosper us as it says in II Corinthians 9:11, "You will be enriched in everything for all liberality." (NASU) This is no get-rich-quick scheme. Rather, it is God's reward for faithfulness and God's enabling for greater ministry through generosity.

The Love of Possessions

Lack of contentment gets a lot of people into trouble. Remember the Ten Commandments? These instructions (guidelines for good living) were etched in stone for Moses to deliver to the people. Specifically, the tenth warns of the destructive power of greedy materialism. In essence, it is telling us not to let what we don't have rob us of the joy of grateful living. Knowing just how much that discontentment can eat away at the inner man, Scripture gives us this admonition:

> *"You shall not covet your neighbor's house. You shall not covet your neighbor's wife, or his manservant or maidservant, his ox or donkey, or anything that belongs to your neighbor" (Exodus 20:17, NIV).*

New Testament characters Ananias and Sapphira tossed aside the values of honor and integrity because they also had a love of money. The resulting loss of life was quite a price to pay. Judas did so also. For a mere 30 pieces of silver he sold his soul and then felt so guilty that he committed suicide. God really is concerned about our actions, character and motives. No matter how much money a person gives to God, if it is money that comes from an origin of disrespect, it is wasted. God cannot be bought. Jesus Christ said that one could not serve two masters and that a person had to make a choice—either to serve God or mammon (money).

The Cost of Self-indulgence

But greed did not begin with our generation. One Old Testament king failed miserably because he was over committed to the profit motive. King Saul had been instructed by God to destroy all of the people and the livestock of the Amalekites. Instead of doing as commanded by God, he disobeyed by saving King Agag and the best sheep and oxen. His excuse was that he wanted to sacrifice the sheep and oxen to God. Of course this was nothing more than a flimsy excuse. It didn't fool God one bit. God rebuked him by saying in I Samuel 15:22, "To obey is better than sacrifice." (NIV)

Money, and the desire for it, can become an obsession. When it does, nothing can satisfy. Peace of mind is gone, the wonder of a new day is gone and a person's life turns into nothing more than a search for material gain. Some of the most miserable people in the world are those who seem to have everything. Money can buy a bed, but not rest. It can purchase food, but not fulfilled satisfaction. It can buy a house, but not a home. It can buy stocks, yet not security. Money is a tool, not a treasure.

Take a look at the hundreds of prominent people who have committed suicide over the past century. They seemed to enjoy everything. They had everything except a clean heart and a clear conscience.

WHICH SYSTEM WILL YOU CHOOSE?

A Kingdom Renewal of the Mind

God has promised a way to live this life without preoccupation of creating great gain. Matthew 6:31-33 tells us this. "So do not worry, saying, 'What shall we eat?' or 'What shall we drink?' or 'What shall we wear?' For the pagans run after all these things, and your heavenly Father knows that you need them. But seek first His kingdom and His righteousness, and all these things will be given to you as well. Therefore do not worry about tomorrow, for tomorrow will worry about itself. Each day has enough trouble of its own" (NIV).

The great apostle Paul addressed the believers in Philippi with this notable comment: "I am not saying this because I am in need, for I have learned to be content whatever the circumstances. I know what it is to be in need, and I know what it is to have plenty. I have learned the secret of being content in any and every situation, whether well fed or hungry, whether living in plenty or in want" (Philippians 4:11, 12 NIV).

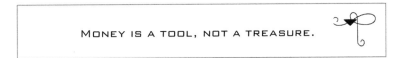

MONEY IS A TOOL, NOT A TREASURE.

But he did not stop with the contentment statement. He went on to suggest that they should always have a heart of thanksgiving, rejoicing in the Lord and living life to its fullest. He admonished them not to worry about each little thing but to instead think good thoughts, thoughts that are pure, admirable, beautiful and excellent.

A KINGDOM PERSPECTIVE ON MONEY

To desire great wealth and to spend a lifetime in search of prosperity and affluence is to abuse the time on earth that God has given to each of us. But to use money as a tool, rather than a means to accumulate material goods, is the best route to take.

You may have noticed that it is not having money itself, rather the love of money, that is said to be evil. Some people would rather ruin their health for money. Others tread on friendships and the innocence of others to enable them to accumulate the goods and riches of this world. Of course, if you stop and think about it, neither money nor fame can guarantee happiness. Countless celebrities and countless people of wealth could attest to a life of shallow existence. The Scriptures make it clear that we have brought nothing into this world and it is certain that we can carry nothing out. Any natural accumulation of money is only handed down in our wills to someone else. But one thing is sure. While earthly accumulation cannot help us in our death, it is clear that the spiritual treasures which can be accumulated while we are still on this earth will pass with us to eternity.

Lives that are chaotic with materialism are unfulfilled, but peace and contentment from above are priceless. If we know Jesus Christ, we are eternally rich. If we live only for the pleasures of this life, we are eternally poor. In Christ, all believers have been given a position of prestige, honor and privilege as heirs of God and joint-heirs with Jesus Christ. We do not have to wait for death to make our promised inheritance a reality. According to Scripture, He bestows His blessings upon us daily.

What Did Jesus Say About Money?

Jesus had some things to say about money and its effect upon our lives.

- We are definitely rewarded for the deeds done in the body. In other words, we are only rewarded for those deeds accomplished while we are alive. While we are alive, true life does not consist in the abundance of material things. (Luke 12:15)

- Prosperity is much more than acquiring personal monetary wealth! Be sure that money doesn't have you, instead of you having it. (Luke 18:18-23, Matthew 19:21-22, Mark 12:41-44)

- Give according to your income, unless you prefer that God makes your income proportionate to your giving! There is such a thing as becoming rich toward God, as one refrains from being preoccupied with materialistic concerns. (Luke 12:21)

- Giving God what is His is a parallel duty to one's faithful payment of his taxes. (Matthew 22:21, Mark 12:13-17, Malachi 3:8)

- We should not make a public show of giving. By doing so, we may have already received the only recognition that we deserve. (Matthew 6:1-4)

- Life priorities are very important to understand. What is the most important thing for you to acquire? Is it the love of your family? How about serving your loved ones, your church and your neighbor? How about your good health and honorable character? You can't serve God if you are fascinated only by money. (Matthew 6:24-34, 19:21-22)

- God uses willing people in imaginative ways. In God's eyes giving even a cup of water can bring a reward. (Matthew 10:41)

- Everything we have belongs to God. We are allowed to be temporary stewards of His wealth. Embracing kingdom treasures requires a releasing attitude toward earthly resources. (Matthew 13:44-46)

- You are either laying up treasure in heaven or upon earth. Everything you have you will ultimately lose. Gaining earthly abundance is an unworthy goal if you forfeit spiritual priorities. (Matthew 16:26)

- The Dead Sea takes in and takes in, but it never gives anything out; hence it is stagnant. Stinginess is a characteristic of those who don't understand the extent of their forgiveness. The Sea of Galilee takes in but it also gives out; for this reason it is filled with life and its water is fresh. (Matthew 18:27, Luke 19:8-9)

- Putting the needs of others first will be rewarded. Sacrifice of self-interest for the kingdom will be compensated one hundred-fold. (Matthew 19:29-30, Luke 18:28-30)

- Talent is on loan from God. We did not deserve God's love and forgiveness. Possessions and talent are responsibilities entrusted to us. We are responsible to multiply those gifts and funds entrusted to us. (Matthew 25:14-30, Luke 19:11-27)

- God so loved the world that He gave His only Son. He gave His best. Are you giving your best? Are you sharing what you have with others? What you give will be bountifully multiplied back to you. (Luke 6:38)

- What we are is far more important than what we possess. A wise handling of people and money illustrates a spiritual sensitivity in God's kingdom rules of finance. (Luke 16:1-13)

- God never promised a reward for those who give away their money after they are dead and gone. To will your material goods to charity doesn't help you in your relationship to God. Wealth is not prohibited, but this admonition points to the compassionless lifestyle it can breed. (Luke 18:24-27, Luke 16:19-31)

- The size of the gift is not so important, rather the ability of the giver. Our giving is made great in the proportion it represents and by the cheerful and generous spirit which prompts it. (Mark 12:41-44, Luke 21:1-4)

God's System Requires Faith

As noted at the very beginning, God's economy is different than ours. His economy is based upon a system of values and principles. Ordering your life according to His values and principles is what brings true success in life. Does that mean that, the instant we align our value system with His, immediately we will begin to experience great prosperity of body, soul and spirit? If this does not happen, then what? Our walk of integrity in God's economic world is one of faith.

> ORDERING YOUR LIFE ACCORDING TO HIS VALUES AND PRINCIPLES IS WHAT BRINGS RUE SUCCESS IN LIFE.

Faith is the confident belief that God takes action in our lives and that His action is for our ultimate benefit. Much of the struggle we have in the Christian life is not believing that God *can* do something, but believing that He will. One of the areas that tests our trust in God is the realm of finances.

Many of us, as a matter a fact, find it hard to believe that God is interested in such practical things as finances. Yet Bible scholars tell us that one out of four of the teachings of Jesus related to our material possessions. As Christians, we are called to be stewards and, as referred to earlier, a steward is one who has been entrusted with another person's property. Consequently, we are required to give a faithful accounting for that which God has entrusted to us.

If we are to become the kind of faithful, generous stewards that God intends for us to be, it will happen only as we come to understand how God operates in His own supernatural economy and how we, in faith, can receive His supernatural resources.

In the natural economy, we experience such things as debt, bankruptcy, recession, depression and other financial crises. But in God's economy there is no such thing as want, lack, recession or depression. Yet because most of us are not aware of God's economy and His willingness to provide financial abundance, we need to be strengthened in our faith when it comes to the area of finances.

God's System is Supernatural

God reveals His economy by taking a little and turning it into much. The most obvious example is the miracle of the feeding of the five thousand in Matthew chapter 14. This is where Jesus took the little boy's lunch of five loaves and two fishes, blessed it, broke it and distributed it to His disciples, who fed five thousand men, plus women and children.

> IN GOD'S ECONOMY THERE IS NO SUCH THING AS WANT, LACK, RECESSION OR DEPRESSION.

Another example is found in II Kings, chapter 4. This is a story from the life of Elisha the prophet, who gave instructions to a widow who had a need. Her late husband's creditors were about to take her two sons as slaves. She sought help from Elisha, who instructed her to collect empty jars from her neighbors and then go home and pour oil into the jars from the one jar of oil she had.

"She left him and afterward shut the door behind her and her sons. They brought the jars to her and she kept pouring. When all the jars were full, she said to her son, 'Bring me another one.' But he replied, 'There is not a jar left.' Then the oil stopped flowing. She went and told the man of God, and he said, "Go, sell the oil and pay your debts. You and your sons can live on what is left" (II Kings 4:5-7 NIV).

Besides the fact that God took a little and turned it into much, we should also note that the size of the widow's blessing was dependent upon her expectancy. In other words, how much oil she received depended on how many jars she collected—the more jars, the more oil. When she got to the last jar, she probably wished she had done a better job of collecting the jars.

God's Thoughts on Wealth

There is nothing wrong with being wealthy. The Bible does not condemn riches. Joseph of Arimathaea must have been rich to own the new tomb which he gave for the burial of Jesus. Barnabas, a leader in the early church, was a wealthy man who used his money for the Lord's work. Abraham was a man of faith and a friend of God, but he was also very rich. Solomon is described in the Bible as one of the wealthiest men of his day. There is no harm in possessing riches, but there can be great harm in letting riches possess you.

While the Old Testament seems to speak less about symbols of monetary value, the New Testament addresses money more specifically. James had something to say to those who let money become their God. "Now listen, you rich people, weep and wail because of the misery that is coming upon you. Your wealth has rotted, and moths have eaten your clothes. Your gold and silver are corroded. Their corrosion will testify against you and eat your flesh like fire. You have hoarded wealth in the last days. Look! The wages you failed to pay the workmen who mowed your fields are crying out against you. The cries of the harvesters have reached the ears of the Lord Almighty. You have lived on earth in luxury and self-indulgence. You have fattened yourselves in the day of slaughter" (James 5:1-3 NIV).

In His Sermon on the Mount, Jesus warned the disciples concerning the short-lived nature of wealth. "Lay not up for yourselves treasures upon earth, where moth and rust doth corrupt, and where thieves break through and steal: but lay up for yourselves treasures in heaven, where neither moth nor rust doth corrupt, and where thieves do not break through nor steal: for where your treasure is, there will your heart be also" (Matthew 6:19-21 KJV).

A KINGDOM PERSPECTIVE ON MATERIAL POSSESSIONS

Money's deception is that it can bring a false sense of security. Paul warned Timothy about just that:

> *"But godliness with contentment is great gain. For we brought nothing into the world, and we can take nothing out of it. But if we have food and clothing, we will be content with that. People who want to get rich fall into temptation and a trap and into many foolish and harmful desires that plunge men into ruin and destruction. For the love of money is a root of all kinds of evil. Some people, eager for money, have wandered from the faith and pierced themselves with many griefs"*
> *(I Timothy 6:6-10 NIV).*

Do Your Possessions Own You?

The stewardship of material goods comes to grips with the question of ownership. To whom do you belong? To whom have you surrendered your will? Who calls the shots in your life?

> *"Whoever can be trusted with very little can also be trusted with much, and whoever is dishonest with very little will also be dishonest with much. So if you have not been trustworthy in handling worldly wealth, who will trust you with true riches? And if you have not been trustworthy with someone else's property, who will give you property of your own? No servant can serve two masters. Either he will hate the one and love the other, or he will be devoted to the one and despise the other. You cannot serve both God and Money" (Luke 16:10-13 NIV).*

Most of us understand what it is that we would classify as earthly treasures. This list would include earthly possessions like cars, boats, clothes, houses, bank accounts, jewelry, portfolios, etc. In the Scripture, Jesus is warning us about protecting our heart from the love of all these things. They can seem so real, so lasting, so concrete, but in reality can disappear so quickly. They can be literally here today and gone tomorrow. Some of the ancient tombs discovered in the Middle East have been found packed with food and furniture and even slaves. Death is the great equalizer, the constant leveler. Yet all of those tombs, buried under sand for thousands of years, have done nothing for the ones who spent a lifetime of accumulation. Our stock portfolios are always at great risk to the ups and downs of the market, the wars and rumors of wars, the economy of the nation and the world, and the integrity of the company management in which we invest. Our body and our mind, which may seem so healthy and sharp, may be wasted by disease or crushed by a mishap tomorrow.

What we care about, we invest in. If we invest our money with God, our attitude will be the same. We will be interested in the ministry advance of our local church and will pray for the expansion of His kingdom locally and globally. Note that Jesus is not saying that we should have nothing or enjoy nothing. Nor does he imply any kind of a sin. Christ is saying to us not to get too tied to these things. Be a conduit, not a dam. It is not about what we have, but what has us. If we center our life around our things or base our living upon our possessions, we will surely be disappointed. Don't base your life, your future, your well-being or your happiness on the things you have accumulated. Instead, be sure that you lay up for yourself the real treasures, the ones that will be of eternal value.

> BE A CONDUIT, NOT A DAM. IT IS NOT ABOUT WHAT WE HAVE, BUT WHAT HAS US.

The Scriptures illustrate that giving of one's own things is an evidence of God's grace in a person's life (II Corinthians 8:4-7). Because 100 percent of what is received comes from God, we are responsible to use it wisely and in accordance with God's will. Like every other area of stewardship, God is interested in the whole picture, not just a percentage. What a person does with all his treasure is important to God.

Stewardship means recognizing your obligations to God because of Calvary. Stewardship means that God owns you and is counting on you to become an instrument through which He can love and save the world. It's as simple as that! If you cannot offer yourself as a channel of God's wealth, how can He bless your life? The bottom line in stewardship is not money or a block of time, but your entire life.

Trusting God with Your Money

The person who takes stewardship seriously will regard his or her life, talents, strength and money as a trust from God. Trustees have specific responsibilities. They are charged with holding property in trust for someone else.

Scriptural principles give us clues as to how we can trust God with our money and our entire lives. Four steps may help simplify the process.

Placing God First

The first step is to put God first and He will supply our basic needs. A Christian should be content with having his needs met when he learns how to surrender all control of his life to God. Then God can entrust more responsibility to him.

> *"But seek first his kingdom and his righteousness, and all these things will be given to you as well" (Matthew 6:33 NIV).*

Trusting God's Provision

A second step is to trust God to provide for financial well-being. We will probably experience both plentiful and lean times financially, for such is life; but if we will be faithful and not complain, we can be sure that God will provide.

God's Desire to Bless

Thirdly, God will care for our needs and He will even give us the desires of our hearts. According to Psalm 37:4, God enjoys giving to those He loves. We are directed to have fun (delight ourselves in the Lord) and are reminded that He loves us so much that He will just give us the principled desires of our heart.

Responsible with Finances

Jesus taught that we must be responsible in our finances. God is the source of all wealth. He is the original owner of all things, for He made all things. As Scripture has said, He owns the cattle on a thousand hills. God also gives us the ability to earn a living (Deuteronomy 8:18).

Really, all that we have or expect to obtain comes from God. Our clothes, cars, homes and jobs are ultimately all gifts from His bountiful hand. God is not stingy or tight-fisted, nor does He refuse to share with mankind what is rightfully His.

Jesus also taught us that mankind is on earth for a very, very short time and then goes to an eternal destination. If we really understand this to be true, where we place our priorities and how we deal with our finances is extremely important. Should our resources be physical and temporal or spiritual and eternal? What is a man's real treasure? Matthew gives us a very concise answer to this question.

> *"But store up for yourselves treasures in heaven, where moth and rust do not destroy, and where thieves do not break in and steal. For where your treasure is, there your heart will be also" (Matthew 6:20, 21 NIV).*

What are man's real treasures—that which thieves can steal and corrupt, or that which becomes part of our retirement plan in heaven? "For where your treasure is, there will your heart be also" (Matthew 6:21 NIV).

"I hear, I know. I see, I remember. I do, I understand."

Key Points:

➤ God's economy vs. man's economy ➤ Jesus's thoughts on money

➤ true contentment ➤ heart motives

1. **Write down** any parts of the chapter that were meaningful to you.

_____

_____

_____

_____

2. **Personal Application:** How can you personally apply these truths in your own life? Write down several long-term goals.

_____

_____

_____

_____

3. **Steps to Action:** Write down one small step you could take to begin immediately applying the truths and principles of this chapter.

_____

_____

_____

_____

4. **Prayer for the Practical:** Write out a prayer to God asking Him for help in making any changes that these goals would require.

_____

_____

_____

_____

Psalm 62:8 "O my people, trust in him at all times.
Pour out your heart to him,
For God is our refuge."

"If we were given all we wanted here, our hearts would settle for this world rather than the next."

—ELISABETH ELLIOT
MISSIONARY, AUTHOR, CONFERENCE SPEAKER

GOD'S GREEN THUMB: SOWING, REAPING, AND HARVESTING

T he Scripture has this to say about the cycle of nature. "All streams flow into the sea, yet the sea is never full. To the place the streams come from, there they return again" (Ecclesiastes 1:7 NIV).

EXAMPLES FROM NATURE

There is a cycle to the elements in nature as seen in God's great creation. Take a seed, for example. It is hidden away, ever so small, just waiting there beneath the sod of the earth. But at the appropriate time—when the earth begins to warm, the rain begins to fall and the sun begins to shine—the seed begins to grow roots. As the earth fertilizes the roots, a bud begins to form and peak out on the surface of the earth. In time, the plant grows to full blossom. Eventually it releases a fragrance, which attracts pollinators, bees and bugs. When the plant matures, it drops new seeds upon the ground. The seed, in turn, waits just below the surface until a new season begins.

Water is another example of recycling. Water constantly renews its purity by cycling itself from a liquid (or a solid) into a vapor and back again. The change to a vapor removes most impurities and allows water to return to Earth in its clean form.

The study of water or hydrology starts with the water cycle, the process by which water renews itself. Since the cycle is continuous, it doesn't really have a beginning, but a convenient place to start studying it is with precipitation (rain, snow, sleet and hail). When precipitation falls to earth, several things can happen. It can be absorbed into the soil. According to the United States Environmental Protection Agency, this is called infiltration. This process allows water to seep into the earth and be stored underground as groundwater.

Precipitation can also become runoff, flowing into rivers and streams. Water can evaporate or it can be returned to the atmosphere by transpiration through plants. Precipitation can also be stored. An ice cap is a form of storage. In temperate climates, water is found in depression storage or surface water puddles, ditches and anywhere else that runoff water can gather. This is a temporary form of storage. Water will evaporate from the surface and infiltrate into the ground. It will be absorbed by plants and transpired back into the air. It will flow to other areas. This cycling of water is continuous.

THE KINGDOM SEQUENCE OF RICHES

Money can only affect our world around us for the gospel if it is put into circulation. The Dead Sea is dead because it only takes in and gives nothing out. The law of living is giving. If money is to be useful, it must be used. When increase comes our way, we should use it, not only for our needs, but also for the good of others. Treasures on earth can become paths to building heavenly treasures if they are used and distributed for the glory of God. Jesus understood clearly that, in the consumer culture of this world, we live in a constant battleground for our affections, our heart and our soul.

There is also a cycle to money and its use. Money can be similarly compared to the cycle of water in nature. Did you know that money is only profitable when it is used? If we are to live life abundantly as Christians, we must follow the scriptural principle of giving. Our measure of giving determines the measure of how we will receive.

Luke 6:38 states, "Give, and it shall be given unto you; good measure, pressed down, and shaken together, and running over, shall men give into your bosom. For with the same measure that ye mete withal it shall be measured to you again." (KJV) The more you give, the more He gives back to you. He gives back to the giver. Giving is for your sake, because God gives to givers.

Does the receiver benefit? Yes, in the sense that needs are met. But it is the giver who benefits the most. In II Corinthians 9:6-15, Paul gives clear instructions to the church concerning giving. Verse 7 notes that God will love the giver in a special way. Verse 8 says God will provide for him. Verses 9-11 speak of his resources being multiplied and enriched. God sees to it that givers are receivers. They obtain money, prosperity, blessing and eternal rewards. And they grow in faith.

Treasures in Heaven

Giving money is so significant to God because giving money is a way to give of yourself. Matthew 6:19-21 reminds us, "Lay not up for yourselves treasures upon earth, where moth and rust doth corrupt, and where thieves break through and steal: But lay up for yourselves treasures in heaven, where neither moth nor rust doth corrupt, and where thieves do not break through nor steal: For where your treasure is, there will your heart be also" (KJV).

> GIVING MONEY IS SIGNIFICANT TO GOD BECAUSE GIVING MONEY IS A WAY TO GIVE OF YOURSELF.

In Bible times, riches often consisted of beautiful clothing and precious metals. Immense value resided in garments passed down from generation to generation. Jacob gave Joseph a coat of many colors. Joseph gave Benjamin five changes of clothing. Samson promised thirty changes of garments to the one who guessed his riddle. It was very common to place a great deal of importance in clothing. There was a cycle to the flow of wealth.

In the days of the ancient past, people of influence had treasures that consisted of fine clothing, gold, silver, gems, wine, lands, etc. Any of this in abundance was considered of great value and wealth. Today, we are still thrilled with possessions of jewelry, fine cars, boats, clothing, electronic equipment, houses, money and so on. While Jesus said that the poor would always be with us, He also made clear the obligation of the wealthy to the needy. In ancient times, there were many examples of brotherhood. Joseph gave his brothers changes of garments. Achan apparently coveted a beautiful Babylonian garment. Today, there are many food drives to feed the hungry and many clothing drives to provide warm apparel for the needy.

James said to the rich men who had hoarded up clothing and wealth, "Your riches are corrupted, and your garments are moth-eaten" (James 5:2 NKJV). In other words, your unused wealth will get you nowhere. The problem here was unused money. These men had gathered riches for riches sake. James said, "The rust of them (your wealth) shall be a witness against you" (James 5:3 KJV). Rust is a symbol of disuse. It is a sign of inactivity.

Of course, we know that rust can destroy even the best of tools and moths also attack things that we consume. Literally, rust in its destructive path will eat into and destroy nearly everything. Rust will eventually corrode all metal including silver and gold. Figuratively speaking, rust can be anything that would destroy you and your life. In short, all of your treasures, whether physical or otherwise, can be destroyed. The treasures of the kingdom, however, are eternal. When we concentrate on using our earthly possessions to bring glory to God, then we are storing up treasures in heaven.

KINGDOM PRINCIPLES OF SOWING AND REAPING

Some events seem to be a way of life. For example, you never get a busy signal when you dial a wrong number. Children never seem to spill their food on dirty floors and the line at the grocery store is always the longest when you are in a hurry.

It seems that while waiting in line at the bank, the gas station, or the grocery store, the other line next to you moves faster. I (Rich) was in a local variety store in Portland, Oregon, by the name of Fred Meyer. While headed for the 10-items-or-less line, an entire family cut just in front of me. I was in a hurry, but waited until they all crowded into the line in front of me. Their cart was filled with grocery items. As I watched in surprise, the parents passed out the money and proceeded to divide up the cart between themselves and the kids!

> THE LAW OF LIVING IS GIVING. IF MONEY IS TO BE USEFUL, IT MUST BE USED.

Additional laws might include: it always rains on the weekends, you seem to get sick on your day off, etc. Perhaps they could be called Murphy's Other Laws. Some of these laws you can live without knowing about. However, there are some laws you ignore at your own risk of potential destruction.

There are basic laws of nature. In regards to sowing and reaping, here are some things to consider.

1. *The seed we plant is the same kind of seed we reap—seed of its kind.*

One phenomenon of God's creation is that the seed we plant is from the fruit which was harvested. We see this in life. Parents often see in their children the characteristics of themselves, both good and bad. Each of us must set good examples, for life is spent planting. You have no choice but to sow. When we sow financial seeds into God's kingdom, we benefit from the same.

2. *We determine the size of the harvest at the time of planting (II Corinthians 9:6,8,11).*

The farmer who plants hundreds or thousands of acres knows that, barring some natural disaster, he is going to reap more than he planted, but always in proportion to what he planted. One who is generous with his time, talents and resources is going to reap generously. One who is generous with love, appreciation and mercy will reap in the proportion that he sows those things.

The man who gives beyond his tithe (the tithe belongs to the Lord) has just begun to give. The more one gives, the more one reaps. But don't just look for repayment in monetary measure. Good health is more important than money. A family serving the Lord is more important than dollars.

3. We will always have a harvest (Malachi 3:10; Galatians 6:9).

When you sow, you will always reap! This law is as sure as the rising and going down of the sun. The success of this harvest is not determined by natural laws, but the success is governed by the Lord Himself. Should you sow your seed into your local place of worship from which you and your family receive much benefit? Of course! Will you reap the harvest? Certainly! You and your family reap a good harvest every time your local pastor preaches the Word and sows good seed into your lives.

4. You will usually reap later than you sow.

In the American Midwest, farms are everywhere. You don't have to be around a farm too long to learn that both growth and decay take time. The same is true in our spiritual lives. Perhaps this is the reason Paul warned that we shouldn't be deceived. There's a caution in sowing to the flesh. Nothing seems to happen right away. Marriages do not collapse in an instant. People become deceived and don't realize what's happening until they are trapped.

While we receive much immediate benefit when we sow into our local church, it doesn't stop there. We continue to reap the harvest throughout our lives, because the seed continues to multiply.

5. We will always reap more than we planted (Matthew 13:8).

When we plant a kernel of corn, we reap a stalk with several ears of corn on it. On the ears of corn are hundreds of kernels of corn. So it is with a blade of wheat. Only God could design such a wonder. The law of increased return is what makes farming a workable business enterprise. But sowing to the Spirit results in eternal life. The NIV translates I Corinthians 2:9, "No eye has seen, no ear has heard, no mind conceived, what God has prepared for those who love him."

6. There is a season for planting and a season for harvesting (Ecclesiastes 3:1, 2).

Not all harvesting follows immediately. The time element is important. If the seed germinates before its proper time, a harvest can be lost. Many give as if there will not be a harvest. Some people think God has not noted what they are planting, simply because they have not experienced a harvest. But if we plant the seed, a harvest will come. For example, consider Proverbs 22:6 from the NIV: "Train a child in the way he should go, and when he is old he will not turn from it." The promise is, if we continue to plant the seed of godly training when the child is young, then in a different season of life the child will not forget their training. Thus, as parents or grandparents, we enjoy the harvest, even though it might be years later.

7. *Seed can be sown secretly; however, the harvest is always viewed by many.*

We do not see all the work, sweat and tears that a person has expended to plant the seed. It may seem to those who were not involved in the labor that the seed was just planted yesterday. When we see the lives of people who are reaping a great harvest of blessing, we should remember that it sometimes took years of faithful cultivating and sowing to bring them to the place where they are today. The harvest they are now reaping, visible and apparent to all, required hours of sacrifice, pain, and toil when nobody else was watching.

8. *We are responsible to sow and God is responsible for the harvest.*

We are laborers together with God. God does not produce failures; He is the Lord of the harvest. With these laws God has set in order, we need to sow seed that is going to bring fruit both now and for eternity. He is the Lord of the harvest. As we enter each new season, we must start by planting.

SECRETS IN SOWING THE SEED

Here are four key principles that relate to seed sowing and your personal finances:

1. God Owns the Seed

When you understand this first principle, you will be in a right position to prosper; you will be able to then make God your partner. Prospering by partnering with God is first done by accepting this fact: God owns everything! You do not own anything. You may have a business that you operate or manage, but you are only doing what God has allowed you to do. Christians don't own anything at all; they merely manage things for God. When you die, how much of your money will you leave behind? All of it! When you die, how much of your money will you take with you? None of it!

Ultimately, you don't own anything. You won't take your house with you. You won't take your land with you. You won't take any of the wealth or possessions with you that you have managed to accumulate here on earth. You won't even take your body because you don't even own it. When your spirit leaves your body, it will turn to dust. You may currently possess certain things, but mere possession is not ownership. Those things that you possess can be taken from you in an instant.

> *"The earth is the LORD's, and everything in it, the world, and all who live in it" (Psalm 24:1 NIV).*

> *"'The silver is mine and the gold is mine,' declares the LORD Almighty" (Haggai 2:8 NIV).*

> *"For every animal of the forest is mine, and the cattle on a thousand hills. I know every bird in the mountains, and the creatures of the field are mine" (Psalm 50:10,11 NIV).*

You can possess, but it is God who owns. You may earn a living, but it is God who gives you the ability to earn. How does this relate to the laws of sowing and reaping? If God is the true owner of your possessions, then your role is that of a steward. With the resources God has entrusted to you, you must seek to sow into his kingdom in order to reap a heavenly harvest.

What does this look like in everyday life? Sowing into God's kingdom means setting aside a portion of your paycheck to give into the lives of others, instead of just thinking about your own needs. It means listening and giving with compassion as missionaries describe the needs around the world. Sowing into God's kingdom means daily looking to God and asking Him, "How do you want me to spend *Your* money today?"

2. You are a Steward of the Seed

The principles upon which a person builds his financial future are very important. They can ensure security in the later years of a person's life. The manner in which finances are acquired and disbursed must be based on sound moral guidelines. The desire for money can become an obsession. When it does, nothing can satisfy. Peace of mind is gone. The joy of a new day gives way to worry about retaining what one has and gaining more and more.

Our life's stewardship should reflect God's interest in all that He has entrusted us with. Genesis 1:26 records that God made man to rule over all the earth and all life on earth, both plant and animal. In Genesis 2:15, man was made steward over the Garden in which there was gold, precious stones and rivers. In other words, man was created for more than going to heaven after a lifetime of waiting. He was created to be a faithful steward over the work of God's hands. This is a lot of trust that God places in our lives. It is more than just finances. It is our entire life and how we handle it with faithfulness, responsibility, accountability, honesty and integrity. Stewardship is bringing everything we have to offer to the Lordship of Christ. What kind of a person makes a good steward? A person who has a great respect for God and his creation.

Money and possessions, at best, only last a lifetime. At worst, they don't last at all. They are but a fleeting vapor, just like our lives. Why spend all of your life trying to accumulate something that will never last? How much better it would be for you to spend your time investing in things that are of eternal nature.

Some of the most miserable people in the world are people who literally have everything. Everything, that is, except a loving family and a clean heart! Everything except honor. Everything except the blessing of God. The Lord has better things to come for those who have been good stewards of all He has entrusted to them.

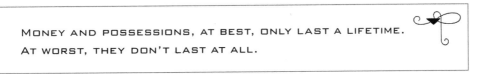

MONEY AND POSSESSIONS, AT BEST, ONLY LAST A LIFETIME. AT WORST, THEY DON'T LAST AT ALL.

Leaving all scruples and morals for the sake of money is a foolish thing to do. Yet that is just what many men and women are doing today. And their seemingly apparent success sometimes causes an infectious greed that hangs upon people who should know better. Some people don't seek to put in an honest day's work for an honest dollar, a day's work for a day's pay. They get caught up in the spirit of the fast buck. Easy money; unearned income; get rich quick!

God is concerned about our actions and motives. What we are is far more important than what we possess! The person who takes stewardship seriously handles life, talents, strength and money as a trust from God.

3. Be Careful Not to Hoard the Seed

It is important to continually invest the seed that God has given to you. This doesn't mean putting your entire paycheck in the offering basket at church! It does, however, mean that you should guard yourself from an attitude that hoards the seed God gives you.

There is nothing wrong or evil about money itself. It is just a medium of exchange for goods or services rendered. However, there is often something wrong with our attitude toward money. We always seem to want more than we have. This dissatisfaction with our current state or condition can be blamed on our Adamic human nature. Discontentment and coveting what belongs to another can cause problems with money. Paul wrote in I Timothy 6:9, "But they that will be rich fall into temptation and a snare, and into many foolish and hurtful lusts..." (KJV)

Many people who have lived for money and success have failed God. When a person's attitude is not right toward money, he or she may fall into the trap of materialism. If, on the other hand, we use the monetary blessings God has given us to finance His cause and further His kingdom, we will be blessed accordingly. I Timothy 6:7 reminds us, "For we brought nothing into this world, and it is certain we can carry nothing out." (KJV)

> *"For in him we live and move and have our being"* (Acts 17:28 KJV).

> *"But remember the LORD your God, for it is He who gives you the ability to produce wealth..."* (Deuteronomy 8:18 NIV).

> *"For every living soul belongs to me"* (Ezekiel 18:4 NIV).

> *"Therefore, I urge you, brothers, in view of God's mercy, to offer your bodies as living sacrifices, holy and pleasing to God"* (Romans 12:1 NIV).

> *"Know that the LORD is God. It is he who made us, and we are his; we are his people, the sheep of his pasture"* (Psalm 100:3 NIV).

"You are not your own; you were bought at a price. Therefore honor God with your body" (I Corinthians 6:19-20 NIV).

Because we are not our own, we should dedicate to God all that we are, all that we own and all that we will ever be. You are God's, so all you have belongs to God. You simply manage your possessions for Him. Your business belongs to God. When everything you have belongs to God, it takes all of the pressure off you. For example, let's say you are a farmer and your farm belongs to God. If the weather is dry and it doesn't rain, you don't have to worry about it because it belongs to God. If your business is dedicated to God, it becomes His problem and not yours. In business, when you partner with God, He not only will bless it, He will let you enjoy prosperity also. But there is a caution not to keep everything for yourself. Instead of trying to figure out how little we can give to God, try giving it all to Him and ask Him how much you should keep.

4. Enjoy some of the seed!

The apostle Paul realized that, although everything in the universe belongs to God, if we partner with Him, He allows us to keep some of everything He provides. The farmer who harvests the crop has a right to eat some of it. The one who plants the vineyard gets to enjoy some of its fruit.

"Give, and it shall be given unto you" (Luke 6:38 KJV).

"I hear, I know. I see, I remember. I do, I understand."

CHAPTER 6 ▶ APPLY IT

Key Points:

➤ cycle of money   ➤ laws of sowing and reaping

➤ significance of giving   ➤ ownership, stewardship, and contentment

1. **Write down** any parts of the chapter that were meaningful to you.

_____

_____

_____

_____

2. **Personal Application:** How can you personally apply these truths in your own life? Write down several long-term goals.

_____

_____

_____

_____

3. **Steps to Action:** Write down one small step you could take to begin immediately applying the truths and principles of this chapter.

_____

_____

_____

_____

4. **Prayer for the Practical:** Write out a prayer to God asking Him for help in making any changes that these goals would require.

_____

_____

_____

_____

Psalm 62:8 "O my people, trust in him at all times.
Pour out your heart to him,
For God is our refuge."

"Never worry about numbers. Help one person at a time and always start with the person nearest you."

—MOTHER TERESA (1910-1997)
MISSIONARY TO THE POOR OF CALCUTTA,
WINNER OF THE 1979 NOBEL PEACE PRIZE

CHAPTER SEVEN

THE EXTRAORDINARY POWER OF GENEROSITY

Is having a lot of money the key to everything? Does money bring happiness? Does money bring solutions to life's problems? If you had a limitless amount of money and could buy anything you wanted, what would you buy? When would you stop buying, gathering, grasping and grabbing?

Our wealth does not come from what we grab in life, but from what we give in life. Some of the wealthiest men in the world gathered in 1923 at the Edgewater Beach Hotel in Chicago. This group of seven was worth more than the entire US Treasury in their time. These were great financial men with records of success who had achieved great prosperity. But this was not the end of their story. Within twenty-five years the president of the largest steel company had died penniless. A millionaire wheat speculator had also become poor. Another, who was the president of the New York Stock Exchange, had already spent many years in prison. Yet another of the wealthy seven who was a member of the president's cabinet had spent time in prison, but was pardoned so that he could die at home. The fifth of the seven committed suicide and the sixth man, who headed one of the world's largest companies, also had taken his life. The seventh, and last, of the world's richest men took his life.

CALAMITY OR FAVOR?

Will your money become your blessing or your curse? Can money buy happiness? Can it buy contentment? How about peace of mind? Contrast the previous men of wealth with the founder of the Quaker Oats Company who gave 70 percent of his income to God. Or contrast the Chicago Seven to the wealthy father of many nations. Abraham was a great man of faith, but also a very wealthy individual. Solomon was probably the richest man of his day. Barnabas, an early New Testament local church leader, was also very wealthy but used his money and affluence to extend the kingdom of God.

James 5:1-3 speaks to the wealthy who would use their money for personal gratification. He tells them that they will weep and howl because of all the misery that is coming upon them. He boldly says that their gold and silver is plagued and their precious metals will soon rust. James points out how foolish it is to value and esteem one's riches so highly and, in doing so, how corrupt one can become.

> THERE IS NO HARM IN POSSESSING RICHES,
> SO LONG AS THE RICHES DO NOT POSSESS YOU.

There is no harm in possessing riches, so long as the riches do not possess you. Jesus recommended that we not stockpile our treasures in this life, at the expense of accumulating our treasures for the hereafter. In other words, if one is a long-term planner and visionary, it makes much more sense to accumulate wealth for the long haul in eternity. Time here on earth is the short haul, the temporary vapor of life. Life in eternity—life in heaven—is the long-term commitment.

Remember, you own nothing and God owns everything. Whatever you have, God allowed you to accumulate. When you die, you won't take your new BMW with you. You can't take diamond rings and precious jewelry with you. Neither can you take your house. You won't take any of the possessions you have managed to accumulate here on earth.

CAPABILITY TO SUCCESS IS GOD-GIVEN

Your heavenly Father allows you to possess certain things, but mere possession is not ownership. Those things that you possess can be taken from you in an instant. The scores of dishonest accounting firms and corrupt corporate CEO's of our day have seen to that. Billions of honest dollars invested by millions of wage earners have disappeared. Wage earners have seen their retirement savings disappear in a matter of mere months. You can possess, but it is God who owns. You may earn a living, but God is the one who gives you the power to get wealth.

Let's review what the Scripture says about just how much you really own:

"But remember the LORD your God, for it is he who gives you the ability to produce wealth..." (Deuteronomy 8:18 NIV)

"The earth is the LORD's, and everything in it, the world, and all who live in it" (Psalm 24:1 NIV).

"For every animal of the forest is mine, and the cattle on a thousand hills. I know every bird in the mountains, and the creatures of the field are mine" (Psalm 50:10,11 NIV).

"Know that the LORD is God. It is he who made us, and we are his; we are his people, the sheep of his pasture" (Psalm 100:3 NIV).

"For every living soul belongs to me" (Ezekiel 18:4 NIV).

"'The silver is mine and the gold is mine,' declares the LORD Almighty" (Haggai 2:8 NIV).

"For in him we live and move and have our being" (Acts 17:28 NIV).

"Therefore, I urge you, brothers, in view of God's mercy, to offer your bodies as living sacrifices, holy and pleasing to God" (Romans 12:1 NIV).

"You are not your own; you were bought at a price. Therefore honor God with your body" (I Corinthians 6:19-20 NIV).

A CHANNEL OF GOD'S BLESSING

"Don't be deceived, my dear brothers. Every good and perfect gift is from above, coming down from the Father..." (James 1:16,17 NIV)

"One man gives freely, yet grows all the richer; another withholds what he should give, and only suffers want. A liberal man will be enriched, and one who waters will himself be watered" (Proverbs 11:24 RSV).

When you understand who really owns everything, you won't always be trying to benefit yourself with possessions. You will begin to bless others.

When you collaborate with God, He will prosper you! When God becomes your source, then your well will never run dry. When we become Christians, we become children of God. And the Bible says that God wants to give good gifts to His children.

But God also wants to be sure that we are more interested in pleasing Him than pleasing ourselves. What is your motive for being in business? Is it so that you can accumulate a lot of money and possessions to hoard for yourself? Or are you in business to help bless others?

AVOIDING AN ATTITUDE OF ENVY

God is interested in your motives. Can you be trusted with prosperity? Jesus said in Matthew 6:33, "Seek ye first the kingdom of God, and his righteousness; and all these things shall be added unto you" (KJV).

Our motives and priorities must be summed up in "God first, me last." Sometimes we get jealous of the success of others who are not Christians. They seem to be happy and rich, while enjoying a life of luxury. A musician and prophet in Old Testament times by the name of Asaph said, "I was envious at the foolish, when I saw the prosperity of the wicked" (Psalm 73:3 KJV).

There are ungodly men and women who may achieve material prosperity apart from God. But they can never achieve the deep inner peace that comes from God. Riches gained without God are a snare and do not bring peace. But the prosperity that comes from God brings, not only an abundance of possessions, but also emotional peace, happiness and great joy.

Do you know why some very wicked people are rich today? The Bible gives us a very simple explanation. The wicked who are rich are simply holding the wealth that someday God will give to His children.

> *"And the wealth of the sinner is laid up for the righteous"*
> *(Proverbs 13:22 ASV).*

GOD IS YOUR PROVIDER!

"And my God shall supply all your need according to His riches..."
(Philippians 4:19 NKJ)

Notice the Scripture does not say that the company that employs you will provide for your needs. Neither does it say the local banker or loan officer will supply your needs. Nor does is say that the welfare department of your government will supply your needs. It says that God, and no one else, will supply your needs.

God is your only Source! It's not your job that provides your income. It is God that provides for your needs being met.

This story has been told through many generations. It is about a Christian family that was going through some very tough times. They were so destitute that they didn't even have food for their next meal. The father and mother got down on their knees and cried out to God for food so their children would not go hungry. A man who was not a Christian was walking by their house and heard their prayer. Instead of feeling bad for them, he decided to play a trick on them.

He went down to the grocery store and bought a huge box of groceries, put it on their front porch and rang the doorbell. When the Christian parents saw the groceries on the porch, they immediately began to thank God for it. Just then the unbeliever walked up and said, "Why are you thanking God? I'm the one who placed the groceries there." The Christian father replied, "Oh no, it was God who answered our prayer and provided the groceries. But I do want to thank you for being His delivery boy and bringing them to us!"

Don't make the mistake of thinking that your job or your business is what provides your income. God is the source of your abundant supply. Jobs disappear; even large companies cease to exist. Your clients and your customers in your business will always come and go. It is God who sees to it that your needs are being met.

> NOTHING HAPPENS IN THE ECONOMY OF GOD UNTIL YOU GIVE SOMETHING AWAY.

Everyone and everything else is just His instrument for getting it accomplished. God uses many vehicles to get the job done, but in the end, it is not our own strength, but God's blessing upon our lives.

GENEROSITY: ACTIVATION OF BLESSING & PROVISION

Giving is the trigger for God's financial miracles. When you give to the kingdom of God, it will be given back to you. But where will it come from? Who will give to you? Will God cause money to float down from heaven so that your needs will be met? No. The Bible says, "...shall men give into your ....(life)." This is how the cycle of blessing works. When you give to God, He in turn causes others to give to you. Perhaps it will be in the form of new customers to your business, new products to sell and so on. When God owns your business, He will bring success to it as you faithfully stand on the principles of His Word.

"Give, and it shall be given unto you" (Luke 6:38 KJV).

Nothing happens in the economy of God until you give something away. It is a universal law of God. Paul very appropriately reminds us:

"Remember this: Whoever sows sparingly will also reap sparingly, and whoever sows generously will also reap generously"
(II Corinthians 9:6 NIV).

OBEYING THE WORD BRINGS TRUE SUCCESS

A passage of Scripture in the Bible describes the reign of King Uzziah over the land of Judah. It gives us a clear guideline for today:

"As long as he sought the LORD, God gave him success" (II Chronicles 26:5 NIV).

Another Scripture in the Bible tells us how to be prosperous and successful:

"Do not let this Book of the Law depart from your mouth; meditate on it day and night, so that you may be careful to do everything written in it. Then you will be prosperous and successful" (Joshua 1:8 NIV).

Six Truths About Tithing

So far we have been addressing the joy of giving to those around us. When you give with joy and with all of your heart, you are not thinking about "the least amount" that you can give. You give because you want to!

Tithing, too, should be done because we want to obey the truths in God's Word. Read carefully the following principles on tithing:

1. God is training us to be faithful stewards in handling money. People who do not pay a tithe, or tenth, of their income often have poor financial habits that leave them broke soon after payday. Tithing teaches us to pay that which we owe first. Our financial obligation to God is our first priority. When He blesses us with increase, He expects us to give a minimum of ten percent as a tithe into the storehouse, which, by definition, is our local church. We should be cheerful givers! We should give out of our abundance. We should give out of our love. And we should give to meet the needs of those who find themselves in need.

> PEOPLE WHO DO NOT PAY A TITHE, OR TENTH, OF THEIR INCOME OFTEN HAVE POOR FINANCIAL HABITS THAT LEAVE THEM BROKE SOON AFTER PAYDAY.

2. Tithing is commanded. Malachi 3:10 says, "Bring ye all the tithes into the storehouse." (KJV) Tithing, as established by Abraham, involves giving 10 percent of one's earnings.

3. Abraham tithed before the Law of Moses. The first Biblical record of tithing is found in Genesis 14. Abram's nephew, Lot, was taken captive in a battle between some kings and their armies. When Abram set out to rescue him, not only was he successful, but he also brought back a large amount of spoils. Genesis 14:11-20 records this event.

This Old Testament account of the first mention of tithing indicates that the spoils belonged to Abraham by right of conquest. Abraham has been called the "father of the faithful" (Romans 4) and his life is exemplary to us today. In this passage we are told that Melchizedek was the priest of God Most High. Verse 19 notes that Abram was also "of the Most High God" (KJV). And we are told that the Most High God is "possessor of heaven and earth" (Genesis 14:19 KJV). Apparently, tithing in this context was a direct acknowledgment of the sovereignty and lordship of God over all the earth. Giving God back a tenth of what is already His anyway is acknowledging God's ownership of the entire earth's wealth. Haggai 2:8 declares, "'The silver is mine, and the gold is mine,' saith the LORD of hosts" (KJV).

> IF GOD CANNOT TRUST YOU WITH THE FIRST
> PORTION, HOW CAN HE GIVE YOU FUTURE DESTINY?

4. The New Testament recounts the first tithe. Hebrews 7:1-19 records the same story as the Genesis 14 account. This is the last direct reference to tithing in the New Testament and it seems interesting that it also refers to the first reference found in the Old Testament. Abraham gave tithes to Melchizedek long before the Mosaic Law was given by God at Mount Sinai. Abraham honored the Most High God by freely giving from a loving, grateful heart. It was a true act of worship. Abraham's giving was not based on the law but on a grateful response to God's grace. You can give without loving, but you cannot love without giving!

5. Tithing: A Tithe Is A Tenth. The tithe simply means the tenth. A tenth is 10 percent. A ratio of 1 to 10 is easy to remember and easy to figure, much like our decimal system today. It seems natural and logical to divide things into tens.

- Tithing is scriptural.

- Tithing is systematic.

- Tithing is simple.

- Tithing is successful.

- Tithing is right.

> THE ONLY WAY TO GET OUR TREASURES IN TO
> HEAVEN IS TO PUT THEM INTO SOMETHING THAT
> IS GOING TO HEAVEN.

God has ordained that the use of money is related to spiritual values. The only way to get our treasures into heaven is to put them into something that is going to heaven. Cattle, lands, stocks, bonds and houses will not make it to heaven. Only men, women, boys and girls of all color are going to heaven. By exchanging our earthly possessions and money into the saving of souls, we will take our acquired wealth with us to an eternal home.

6. Tithing does away with hit-and-miss methods of giving. If a person is truly tithing, it is a systematic giving of 10 percent of all earnings to the Lord's work. Of every $10 earned, $1 is given back to God, leaving the remaining 90 percent for living expenses. Some may think that if they gave God an occasional tenth, this would be enough. But one cannot be counted as a tither unless the tenth is given consistently. The Bible teaches that tithing is to be the minimum of one's giving, not the maximum. Just because one gives a tenth does not necessarily mean he has fulfilled his stewardship responsibility to God. We are to put God first and show that He is most important to us by tithing the first fruits of our income. Over and over, we've seen the Lord bless the nine-tenths after the tithe, until it went farther than the full amount would have, had we withheld the first tenth.

> WHEN WE GIVE GOD OUR FIRST FRUITS, HE MULTIPLIES IT BACK TO US MANY TIMES OVER.

GOD'S WORD ON TITHING

Jesus Approved the Tenth

Jesus Christ did not repeal the law concerning tithing—He endorsed it. Tithe paying was a general practice during the time of Christ. In the New Testament, the term tithe(s) is found ten times. The sect which was strictest concerning tithing was the Pharisees. In order to be admitted into the fellowship of the Pharisees, one was obligated to pay his tithe. He was obligated to tithe to the treasury what he bought, what he sold and what he ate. Three of the references are found in the gospels. Jesus faced the question of tithing. If He had not been a tither this would have been one of the first complaints of the Pharisees. They continually watched His every word and action, seeking to find fault with Him, but they never once pointed to a lack of tithing.

The fact that Jesus Christ was admitted into the homes of the Pharisees for meals is evidence that He was a tither. Luke 11:37 says, "And as He spoke, a certain Pharisee asked Him to dine with him. So He went in and sat down to eat"

(NKJV). It was definitely against the vow of a Pharisee to be the host of an outsider. In Luke 18:12, Christ did not offer disapproval to the Pharisee who said, "I give tithes of all that I possess," (NKJV) nor was He finding fault in his tithe paying. Jesus was condemning his attitude of self-righteousness and egotism.

Again in Matthew 23:23, Jesus says, "Woe unto you, scribes and Pharisees, hypocrites! For ye pay tithe of mint and anise and cummin... These ought ye to have done, and not to leave the other undone." (KJV) The Lord did not disapprove of tithing, but on the contrary, expressed His approval.

Matthew and Luke both refer to very strong statements by Jesus regarding the legalism of the Pharisees. The teachers of the Law had added all kinds of details to the practice of tithing. In doing so, they turned a beautiful principle into a heavy burden for the people. The Pharisees prided themselves in keeping the letter of the law concerning rituals. However, they failed in keeping the moral laws of love, justice, mercy and faithfulness.

The Pharisees knew that Jesus tithed. On one occasion during Christ's earthly ministry, a group of Pharisees were looking for a way to get Jesus to incriminate himself with the authorities. They attempted to entangle Christ in His own words. In Matthew 22:16, after a brief statement of insincere flattery, the Pharisees asked Christ something notable in the next verse: "Tell us therefore, What thinkest thou? Is it lawful to give tribute unto Caesar, or not" (KJV)? They were obviously baiting Christ, hoping He would say that they should not pay tribute to the Roman occupational government. But Jesus was not that easily fooled. He replied, "'Shew me the tribute money.' And they brought unto him a penny. And he saith unto them, 'Whose is this image and superscription?' They say unto him, 'Caesar's.' Then saith he unto them, 'Render therefore unto Caesar the things which are Caesar's; and unto God the things that are God's.' When they had heard these words, they marveled, and left him, and went their way" (Matthew 22:19-22 KJV).

Solomon Taught the Principle of Firstfruits

Notice that Jesus said, "... And unto God the things that are God's." God lays claim to a tenth (tithe) of our earnings. The things we render unto God are tokens of our honor for God. They demonstrate our respect and esteem for Him. Solomon caught the spirit of this principle in Proverbs 3:9-10: "Honour the LORD with thy substance, and with the firstfruits of all thine increase: So shall thy barns be filled with plenty, and thy presses shall burst out with new wine." (KJV)

Other References to Tithing

Malachi 3:8 asks the question, "Will a man rob God?" Kind of a thought-provoking question isn't it! In today's language, the question would be, "Are you a thief?" Even if you are a tither, you may still be just 1 percent short of being a thief. Malachi goes on to say in verse 10, "Bring ye all the tithes into the storehouse." (KJV) In I Corinthians 16:2, Paul says, "Let every one of you lay by him in store, as God hath prospered him." (KJV) This was an obvious reference to the tithe. Tithing and revival go hand in hand as seen throughout the Old Testament. Nehemiah, seeing the lack of support of the Levites and the house of God forsaken, contended for the tithe in Nehemiah 13:10-12. God considers giving so important that John 3:16 records , "For God so loved the world, that he gave his only begotten Son, that whosoever believeth in him should not perish, but have everlasting life." (KJV)

The apostle Paul reminded the Corinthians to pay tithes on the first day of the week (I Corinthians 16:2). Hebrews 7:5 indicates that the sons of Levi were commanded to collect tithes from the people on a regular basis. Tithing, when practiced by a congregation, will generally be sufficient to meet the needs of the congregation according to II Chronicles 31:10.

Jesus taught His disciples to give. His instruction was, "When you give..." He didn't say, "if you give." In Luke 18:22, He urged the rich young ruler to sell all his possessions and give to the poor. Not to tithe of our increase would be to do less than a Pharisee would do. Not only does Malachi 3:10 promise the blessings of tithing, Jesus commanded it.

FOUR MORE TRUTHS ON GIVING

1. Giving goes beyond your tithes. The tithing principle doesn't only apply to the person who receives a regular paycheck. It also applies to the person who does not have regular monetary income, but instead has material income which comes from herding, farming, growing, etc. Tithing is basically proportionate giving.

Giving goes beyond the tenth. Malachi 3:8 notes that we are not to rob God of tithes and offerings. It is all a matter of achieving a proper balance. God does not expect you to give what you don't have.

In giving to God, we only return a portion of whatever He has already given to us. The true spirit of giving brings on an automatic boomerang-like effect. Sowing, reaping, tithing and giving all overlap in some areas. Luke 6:38 tells us, "Give, and it shall be given unto you; good measure, pressed down, and shaken together, and running over, shall men give into your bosom. For with the same measure that ye mete withal it shall be measured to you again" (KJV).

Look at what this Scripture is really saying. It does, in fact, say that when we give, we will receive. This ties in closely with another verse found in Galatians 6:7, "Be not deceived; God is not mocked: for whatsoever a man soweth, that shall he also reap" (KJV). Giving is a seed and, if we sow it properly, God will see to it that we reap a harvest. According to Malachi 3:10, if we give properly of our tithes and offerings, God will open up the windows of heaven and pour out blessings that will be so great that we won't have room to receive them.

2. Giving expresses our love. How much money should a Christian give to the Lord? Nowhere in the New Testament is this question answered. God is not so much interested in how much we give, whether it be the minimum of 10 percent, 15 percent, 20 percent or even 50 percent of our income. He is interested in how and why we give. II Corinthians 9:6-9 notes that the one who sows sparingly shall reap the same. "Remember this: Whoever sows sparingly will also reap sparingly, and whoever sows generously will also reap generously. Each man should give what he has decided in his heart to give, not reluctantly or under compulsion, for God loves a cheerful giver. And God is able to make all grace abound to you, so that in all things at all times, having all that you need, you will abound in every good work" (NIV).

II Corinthians 9:7 tells us how we should give. "Each man should give what he has decided in his heart to give, not reluctantly or under compulsion, for God loves a cheerful giver" (NIV). We must be completely honest with ourselves. Do we honestly get a lot more enjoyment out of giving than we do out of receiving? Too many people put more emphasis on receiving than they do on giving.

> GOD'S WORD PLAINLY TEACHES THAT ALL GIVING SHOULD BE BASED UPON LOVE.

I Corinthians 13:3 tells us this truth: "If I give all I possess to the poor and surrender my body to the flames, but have not love, I gain nothing" (NIV). Some people learn part of God's laws of prosperity and give in a calculating manner, anticipating something in return. This just isn't going to work. Giving without love is of no value whatsoever. No matter what we give, if our gift isn't based upon love, it is worth nothing. Love is the key to giving and only love opens the channels for our loving Father to give back to us.

3. Giving should be done with generosity! David wrote in Psalm 112:5,9, "Good will come to him who is generous... He has scattered abroad his gifts to the poor, his righteousness endures forever; his horn will be lifted high in honor" (NIV). The true spirit and attitude of giving (helping the needy) is at the heart of Jesus' instruction in the Sermon on the Mount. In Luke 6:35 we are told not to expect a lot in return for our kindness: "...without expecting to get anything back. Then your reward will be great..." (NIV).

So should we then give just in order to get? Absolutely not! A giving person gives out of a spirit of genuine generosity. When he or she receives, it is a totally unexpected blessing. Seeking to get is disastrous to the spirit of giving! Remember it was Jesus Christ, Son of Man, Son of God, who said, "It is more blessed to give than to receive" (Acts 20:35 KJV).

Our giving must be bountiful and with the knowledge that our kindness and generosity will ultimately be of much help to those in need. It is not the amount of our gift, but it is our motive. We are not to give grudgingly or out of necessity or sorrow. Don't give large gifts if you don't feel obliged to do so. Don't give sorrowfully because you are giving out of regard for public opinion. Give out of a sense of need and a pure motive. This is the kind of giving God delights in; giving cheerfully, with laughter, delight, exuberance and joyfulness. When we manage to grasp these principles, giving really does become a blessing!

4. Giving keeps our hearts humble. Why is it more blessed to give than to receive? When we give freely and generously, we put God first, obeying His Word ahead of our own selfish interests. This obedience will cause Him to bless us. When we give freely and generously, we demonstrate our trust in God. The degree of our giving is a clear indication of our freedom from fear. Freedom from fear is always a blessing.

> FREELY GIVING PROTECTS US FROM THE PITFALLS OF GREED AND MATERIALISM.

Freely giving protects us from the pitfalls of greed and materialism. Generous giving comes from a humble and loving heart. Greed and selfishness are derived from a prideful "me first" attitude which serves to put barriers between us and the blessings of God. I Peter 5:5 says that, "God resisteth the proud, and giveth grace to the humble." (KJV) What an important verse!

"I hear, I know. I see, I remember. I do, I understand."

Key Points:

➤ God's ultimate ownership   ➤ motives in giving and in receiving

➤ collaborating with God in giving   ➤ the power of tithing / obedience to the Word

1. **Write down** any parts of the chapter that were meaningful to you.

_____

_____

_____

_____

2. **Personal Application:** How can you personally apply these truths in your own life? Write down several long-term goals.

_____

_____

_____

_____

3. **Steps to Action:** Write down one small step you could take to begin immediately applying the truths and principles of this chapter.

_____

_____

_____

_____

4. **Prayer for the Practical:** Write out a prayer to God asking Him for help in making any changes that these goals would require.

_____

_____

_____

_____

Psalm 62:8 "O my people, trust in him at all times.
Pour out your heart to him,
For God is our refuge."

CHAPTER EIGHT

KINGDOM PRINCIPLES TO RELEASE BLESSING IN AND AROUND YOU

"You're rich if you've had a meal today."

—BILLY GRAHAM

AMERICAN EVANGELIST, AUTHOR AND NATIONAL SPIRITUAL ADVISER

The heart and attitude of a blessed person are worth examining. Blessed people are set apart in many ways because they have learned how to be blessed. We all have the opportunity to receive the blessing of God and be under the shadow of the Almighty if we so desire. The blessed person gives of his or her resources freely, cheerfully and out of genuine appreciation to God. Generosity is God's antidote to greed.

This chapter will focus specifically on the heart and attitudes of a blessed person, beginning and ending with scriptural examples and the principles they expound. First, let's look at what it means to live a life that is "blessed."

BLESSING BEGINS IN THE HEART

What kind of heart does one need to receive the blessing? What theme was so important to Jesus that He talked about it more than anything else? Was it heaven? Was it repentance? Was it prayer? Was it salvation? No, to each of these questions! Jesus spoke on the subject of money more than any other topic. He must have known that, if He had our money, He would certainly have our hearts.

What is the attitude of a blessed person? Our principal attitude must be that all money and all possessions belong to God. He trusts us with the care of these things until we prove ourselves unworthy of His trust. Since it is not our money, it's not our problem to worry about it. It is our responsibility as good stewards to use it correctly.

> GENEROSITY IS GOD'S ANTIDOTE TO GREED.

BLESSING IS NOT JUST ABOUT POSSESSIONS

"Then he said to them, 'Watch out! Be on your guard against all kinds of greed; a man's life does not consist in the abundance of his possessions'" (Luke 12:15 NIV).

Many wealthy people wish they had friends. Some of the most prominent people in the world are some of the saddest people on earth. Even their money cannot hide their unhappiness and displeasure with life. It is so sad when a person spends his entire lifetime trying to get rich, only to find that when he finally strikes it rich, he is still unhappy, dissatisfied with life and sad. Jesus lets us know in Luke 12:15 that a man's life and happiness do not consist of his things, his possessions, or his money. In other words, all of the possessions in the world will not bring him contentment. They will not buy happiness.

The rich man of Luke 12:19 declared that, after working hard for many years accumulating great wealth and all of the goods this world could offer him, he could now "eat, drink and be merry." He had dedicated his whole life to accumulating great possessions to be enjoyed on earth. But God had other plans for him. After calling the man a fool for working selfishly for a lifetime, just so he could retire in pleasure and ease, God said that his last evening on earth would be that very night.

MONEY ALONE DOES NOT BRING HAPPINESS

Money and happiness are not mutually inclusive. Will Rogers said, "Too many people spend money they haven't earned to buy things they don't want, to impress people they don't like."[6]

Benjamin Franklin noted, "Money never made a man happy yet, nor will it. There is nothing in its nature to produce happiness. The more a man has, the more he wants. Instead of filling a vacuum, it makes one. If it satisfies one want, it doubles and triples that want in another way."[7]

> ARE WE A CONDUIT OR DO WE STOP THE STREAM OF GOD'S FAVOR?

Being a good steward begins with the blessing of God, but the fruit of good stewardship is how we use those blessings. Are we a conduit or do we stop the stream of God's favor? Do we allow the river to flow or do we dam God's supply? This is an issue of management, not ownership. Are we to give only a little and hoard the rest for our own pleasure? Not at all! God expects us to use what we need (He has promised to supply our need), then to multiply and return the rest. Stewardship is trusting, knowing and disbursing His blessing. The blessing of stewardship is in the giving.

30 PRINCIPLES TO RELEASE BLESSING IN AND AROUND YOU

What kind of principles do you live your life by? Blessed people do not become that way by accident. They have chosen intentionally to live according to the truths in God's Word. The following 30 principles are ones which, when put into practice, will help you to live a life that is truly blessed.

1. The Principle of Knowing That God Owns It All

*"The silver is mine and the gold is mine, declares the LORD
Almighty" (Haggai 2:8-9 NIV).*

Not only is the silver and the gold the Lord's, but *everything* belongs to
God. So why not give it all to Him? Paul says in I Corinthians 4:2 that it
is required that those who have been given a trust must prove faithful. A
steward is simply a manager of someone else's money and possessions. We
give it all back to God and manage it as He would have us to.

*"…for every animal of the forest is mine, and the cattle on a
thousand hills" (Psalm 50:10 NIV).*

A successful businessperson by the name of R.G. LeTourneau was in
the business of manufacturing earth-moving equipment. As his business
grew and prospered, he decided to increase his tithe over and above the
tenth. In time, he eventually increased his giving to ninety percent of his
income and lived on the rest. Instead of giving the tenth, he lived on the
tenth. God blessed this man bountifully and used his inventive God-
given genius and creativity to reach the world for the gospel. While there
are many great giving scriptures in the Bible, none seems more specific
than the directive that every person should give what is in his heart, not
reluctantly or under compulsion. Mr. LeTourneau certainly recognized
the value of II Corinthians 9:7 and that it was God who gave him the
power to gain wealth.

2. The Principle of Giving from the Top

*"Then Abram gave him a tenth of everything" (Genesis
14:20 NIV).*

Abraham tithed the tenth before any other commitment was made. Jacob
paid a tithe. Joseph instructed the people to prepare for years of famine
by tithing 20 percent on their current abundance of harvest. Zaccheus
gave one half of all his money. Barnabas gave a parcel of land. The widow
gave all that she had. Whatever we give, either the tenth or beyond the
tenth, it should be given from the start, off the top, before we commit to
anything else. Proverbs 3:9 directs us to honor the Lord with our wealth

by giving the first of all our produce. The Jews were told to dedicate the first-born son and the first-born beast to God. It was all to be given from the top.

3. The Principle of Supernatural Provision

> *"So she went away and did according to the word of Elijah; and she and he and her household ate for many days. The bin of flour was not used up, nor did the jar of oil run dry, according to the word of the LORD which He spoke by Elijah" (I Kings 17:15-16 NKJV).*

Supernatural provision happens when the natural is not enough. If we can make it happen on our own, there is no need for faith. No need for trusting God. And it follows that if we do not have faith and have no need for God, He will not step into areas that we have reserved for our own self-control. The principle of supernatural provision is that He is strong when flesh cannot be.

> IF WE CAN MAKE IT HAPPEN ON OUR OWN, THERE IS NO NEED FOR FAITH.

4. The Principle of Being Proactive

> *"…go to the lake and throw out your line. Take the first fish you catch; open its mouth…" (Matthew 17:27 NIV)*

We are to take action—to be pro-active. The abilities and giftings that He provides motivate us to action. Sometimes, it takes our persistence in doing the same things faithfully with the heart of a servant. Other times, it is useful to try new things or new methods and seek after new opportunities. Sometimes, it is the steady plodding that brings the success of the blessed life. Ecclesiastes 9:11 says, "The race is not to the swift or the battle to the strong, nor does food come to the wise or wealth to the brilliant or favor to the learned; but time and chance happen to them all" (NIV). Hebrews 12:1-2 advises, "…let us throw off everything that hinders and the sin that so easily entangles, and let us run with perseverance the race marked out for us. Let us fix our eyes on Jesus, the author and perfecter of our faith…" (NIV). Proverbs 21:5 instructs us that, "Steady plodding brings prosperity; hasty speculation brings poverty" (TLB).

Taking action, being proactive and not giving up are principles for living the life of a blessed person.

5. The Principle of Knowing How to Be Content

"But if we have food and clothing, we will be content with that" (I Timothy 6:8-9 NIV).

Millions of people today are on a quest to accumulate possessions and even wealth. It is hard for all of us to be content with what we have when the world's entire system is geared toward making us unhappy with everything we don't have. From advertising to attitude, we face a discontented culture. How much money is enough? Usually, just a little bit more. Money cannot buy contentment or happiness. We need to strive for contentment and contend for happiness.

There is certainly nothing wrong with making money, as long as we do not violate the laws of our land and the principles of God's Word. The all-for-me and none-for-others way of man's thinking is immoral. The person of principle who subscribes to the values of the Bible will be a good steward who obeys the law of giving. This person will find happiness in exact proportion to his giving. He will be content with his life and all that it affords.

6. The Principle of Resisting World Views

"Don't copy the behavior and customs of this world, but be a new and different person with a fresh newness in all you do and think. Then you will learn from your own experience how his ways will really satisfy you" (Romans 12:2 TLB).

We must resist the world's view of wealth, happiness and possessions. We do not have to have it all! Our culture and society have sold us a bill of goods. They teach us that in order to be happy, we have to have certain things. We must resist the world's view of wealth, happiness and possessions. We do not have to have it all! We don't have to wear just the right clothes, drive that certain brand of car, have the latest model available, buy a bigger home, own six televisions, possess the latest camera and carry a dozen credit cards in our wallet. We must not allow the world to dictate to us their view of what things our life should consist of. The world should not be allowed to determine our lifestyle. The world should not tell us what success is and what the picture of affluence should look like. Success is doing what God wants done. It is having only what you need to exist on. Wealth is more than money. It is having a local church that inspires you to draw close to God. It is having a loving spouse and the blessing of children. Wealth is enjoying great health, great relationships and friends. You can experience great success and great wealth as long as your giving is in proportion to your getting.

7. The Principle of Plenty Left Over

> *"God is able to make it up to you by giving you everything you need and more so that there will not only be enough for your own needs but plenty left over to give joyfully to others" (II Corinthians 9:8-9 TLB).*

It's not about God making you rich just because you tithe regularly. However, God has promised to meet your needs. That promise may come by way of a job so that you can work hard and provide for your family. When you give, it is with complete confidence that God is faithful to His Word. You can trust Him to take care of you. You can trust him with your whole heart and your whole mind; you can trust Him with your life. Some of us find it easier to trust God for eternity than for today's bills and tomorrow's problems. When it comes to giving, we must do so in complete confidence that our God will not only meet our needs, but allow us to have plenty left over so that we can joyfully share it with others.

8. The Principle of Feeding the Local House

> *"Bring the whole tithe into the storehouse, that there may be food in my house" (Malachi 3:10 NIV).*

> STEWARDSHIP IS THE MANAGEMENT OF OUR ENTIRE LIVES; ALL THAT WE HAVE, ALL THAT WE ARE...

We are commanded, as believers, to obey God in the area of giving tithes and offerings. God doesn't need our money. He is not broke. What He wants is us. His goal is relational, not financial. Stewardship is more than money. Stewardship is more than our talents, our giving, our tithing and our money. Stewardship is the management of our entire lives—all that we have, all that we are—for the purpose of glorifying and magnifying God. Our life management is a reflection of our relationship with Him.

9. The Principle of Obedience

"Bring the whole tithe into the storehouse, that there may be food in my house" (Malachi 3:10 NIV).

The Scripture here is very clear in its message. It does not begin with a thought or suggestion about something to consider. It simply begins with the word "bring." The word "bring" means to carry, fetch or transport. What are we instructed to bring? Not only the tithe, we are told to bring the whole tithe. Where are we to bring it? We are to bring it into the storehouse—our local church. That means the place of our worship, the storehouse that feeds us. We are not to send part of our tithe to some distant place, rather we are to bring the whole tithe into the house that feeds us. The reason is so simple, yet profound. So that there can be finances for operation and evangelism (food in the storehouse). God always blesses our obedience. He wants to bless us in the best possible way, but that can only happen as a result of our obedience.

10. The Principle of Advanced Preparation

"Joseph collected all the food produced in those seven years of abundance in Egypt and stored it in the cities. In each city he put the food grown in the fields surrounding it. Joseph stored up huge quantities of grain, like the sand of the sea; it was so much that he stopped keeping records because it was beyond measure" (Genesis 41:48-49 NIV).

Joseph told the people to pay 20 percent in preparation for the coming famine. The preparation done by the people cared for their needs during the years of want.

11. The Principle of Honesty

"'Will a man rob God? Yet you rob me. But you ask, "How do we rob you?"' 'In tithes and offerings. Bring the whole

tithe into the storehouse, that there may be food in My house. Test me in this,' says the Lord Almighty, 'and see if I will not throw open the flood gates of heaven and pour out so much blessing that you will not have room enough for it'" (Malachi 3:8,10 NIV).

Three things stand out in this reference. The first is the word "rob." In no uncertain terms, this Scripture says that, yes, we can rob God by withholding what is rightfully His. Second is the challenge to test God. The Christian walk is designed to be a walk of faith. If our hearts are right, we can take God at his Word. What He says will happen. The final thing that stands out in this verse is the blessing. God has promised that He will open heaven's storehouse and flood us with His abundance.

Billy Graham once said, "You cannot get around it; the Scripture promises material and spiritual benefits to the man who gives to God. You cannot outgive God. We challenge you to try it and see."[8]

How much should we give? No one can tell you for sure, but if you are not giving God His tenth, that is a place to begin. You must begin to give regularly a percentage of your paycheck, your bonuses, your increases, etc. Malachi 3:8 refers to tithes and offerings. This means returning ten percent of what belongs to God without question, plus offerings. He has placed in our hands the opportunity to decide how much our offerings should be. Just make sure that you give to God first. By doing so, you will never have to worry about having your needs met.

12. The Principle of Seeking the Kingdom First

"But seek first His kingdom and His righteousness, and all these things will be given to you as well" (Matthew 6:33 NIV).

Putting God first in our lives relieves us from the task of having to worry about everything else. Seeking His kingdom and righteousness first is simply making God the priority in our lives. There is always the temptation to put your money first. Do you remember the rich young ruler who came to Jesus and said that he wanted to follow Christ? Jesus' response didn't make him real happy. Jesus told him to give his money away and follow Him. It wasn't the money that was wrong, it was that this young man placed his money ahead of and above all else.

If we have too much money, there is always the danger that we can depend upon it above all else. Does your life reveal your desire to put God first? The Lord admonishes us to seek first His Kingdom, His way of doing things. We must ask God to help us develop an attitude of serving Him faithfully and a lifestyle that is free of debt and worry.

13. The Principle of Temporary Possessions

> "For we brought nothing into the world, and we can take nothing out of it" (I Timothy 6:7 NIV).

We will do well to remember the fact that money and possessions are only temporary. At best, money only lasts a lifetime. At worst, it doesn't last at all. It is very fleeting, only a vapor, just like our lives. Why spend all of your life trying to accumulate something that will never last? How much better it would be for you to spend your time investing in things that are eternal in nature.

14. The Principle of Giving to the Needy

> "If anyone has material possessions and sees his brother in need but has no pity on him, how can the love of God be in him" (I John 3:17 NIV)?

If our attitude is one of hoarding what we have, God will stop giving to us. If we are ever going to be financially free, we must allow God to use us as a conduit in which to bless others. The needs of others must be met by our generous giving. If we are open and generous with the things God has provided for us, God will bless us in a great way.

Christians must understand that the lesson of stewardship is found in returning to God all that He has provided and entrusted to our care. Failure to give back to God what He has generously given to us is to be condemned. Maturing in Christ means to develop a growing spirit of generosity and a willingness to share.

15. The Principle of Committed Giving

> "Remember this: Whoever sows sparingly will also reap sparingly, and whoever sows generously will also reap generously. Each man should give what he has decided in his heart to

give, not reluctantly or under compulsion, for God loves a cheerful giver. And God is able to make all grace abound to you, so that in all things at all times, having all that you need, you will abound in every good work" (II Corinthians 9:6-9 NIV).

The purpose in grouping this entire passage together is that there is a group message here. Commitment stands alone, but is insufficient without right attitudes. Giving freely and cheerfully is great, but insufficient in itself. There must be commitment. Overriding all is the unchangeable law of sowing and reaping. We get out what we put in. We harvest what we plant. The fruit is the same as our seed.

We must have a commitment to giving and it must be settled in our hearts and minds once and for all. If God owns it all, and he does, then our maximum part is the ninety percent. Our attitude is to be one of happiness in returning the money to its rightful owner. We are happy to give to the very Giver of life. All that we have is his. When we give, we help to further the work of His kingdom. And furthermore, when we give with commitment, right attitude, cheerfulness and right motives, His grace abounds toward us in every good work. This means that we will have all that we need and more.

16. The Principle of Systematic Giving

"On the first day of every week, each one of you should set aside a sum of money in keeping with his income, saving it up, so that when I come no collections will have to be made" (I Corinthians 16:2-3 NIV).

A godly perspective on giving is found in this scripture setting. In it, Paul gives a direction and formula for consistent, regular giving. Note Paul's appeal for consistency. He asks for regular giving on the first day of the week. He asks specifically that a sum of money be set aside. Finally, he asks them to give a proportionate amount that is in keeping with their income.

Giving—like saving—needs to be regular, and it belongs in your budget for your place of worship. Your local church has regular financial challenges that must be met with regularity.

17. The Principle of Giving Freely

"Freely you have received, freely give" (Matthew 10:8 NIV).

We have been blessed beyond measure and now it is time to return the blessing. This verse simply implies giving with a spirit of liberality. And yet, like the gospel message, it is so simple that men and women stumble over its simplicity; freely you have received, so you should freely give.

Man likes to make simple things complicated. Are we under the law or under grace? Are we to give a minimum of 10 percent or 15 percent? What should our offerings be? Do we recognize our obligation to give to the poor and downtrodden or do we ignore their plight? God has designed a wonderful program to finance the spreading of the gospel to reach the world for Jesus Christ. After all, didn't Christ die and shed righteous blood for all? Don't the many tribes and nations of the world have a right to experience salvation?

Before that can happen, missionaries have to be called, trained and sent out. Local churches have to be planted, people have to be discipled and giving has to occur. The needs of those who are called to reach the nations can only be met through partners who freely give as they have freely received.

18. The Principle of Never Withholding

> "One man gives freely, yet gains even more; another withholds unduly, but comes to poverty" (Proverbs 11:24 NIV).

We gain by giving. We lose by withholding! You may recall the story about the widow and her son who were about to eat their last meal, as noted in I Kings 17. After that, they assumed they would just starve to death, because they had no more food available and there was a famine in the land. In our culture today, this is very hard for many of us to comprehend. Some people teach that we should give to get. Others teach that we should sacrifice and withhold from our family in order to give more. Neither extreme point of view is correct. We must provide for our family. We should not give to get. Our attitude should be one of obedience and liberality. The best way to give to the Lord is to understand all that he has given to us, and then freely give back to him.

God removes His blessings from those who withhold. He cannot bless an act of disobedience. Our money becomes a curse when we think more of our money than we do of God. One of the greatest privileges God has given us is to participate in the blessings of regular tithing and the giving of our offerings.

When we freely give to God, regardless of our own personal need, we allow God to be big in our lives. We allow him to provide for us. This can only happen as we buy into the principle of giving freely. If we are stingy in our giving and withhold from the Lord, we miss the many blessings and provisions that He wants to shower upon us.

19. The Principle of the Tenth

"Then Jacob made a vow, saying, 'If God will be with me and will watch over me on this journey I am taking and will give me food to eat and clothes to wear so that I return safely to my father's house, then the LORD will be my God and this stone that I have set up as a pillar will be God's house, and of all that you give me I will give you a tenth'" (Genesis 28:20-22 NIV).

Early in biblical history we see a picture of Jacob, a man who promised God that he would return a tenth of all his increase. Jacob was beginning a journey, apparently leaving his family for a period of time, making his bed under the stars. God came to him in a dream, promising him great blessings in the future, which of course He did. Jacob promised the tenth, as he understood the principle of the tenth.

20. The Principle of Increased Measure

"Give, and it will be given to you. A good measure, pressed down, shaken together and running over, will be poured into your lap. For with the measure you use, it will be measured to you" (Luke 6:38 NIV).

Note that these verses describe a cause and an effect. In short, the principle of increased measure is that we must give if we ever hope to have a return. Secondly, the size of our return is dependent upon the size of our gift. Thirdly, our return will be bountiful, over and above our expectations.

21. The Principle of True Prosperity

"Do not let this Book of the Law depart from your mouth; meditate on it day and night, so that you may be careful to do everything written in it. Then you will be prosperous and successful" (Joshua 1:8-9 NIV).

In America and many other nations all around the world, this generation has access to untold quantities of wealth. Yet even though our wealth and blessing have increased, the world-wide needs of the poor and the hungry have never been greater. Untold millions are needed to reach the world with the Gospel. According to the above verses, the true pathway to prosperity is to read, know and obey the Word of God. As the Lord fills our treasuries with both natural and spiritual increase, we will then be able to extend these blessings to the world around us.

22. The Principle of Supply

"They are a fragrant offering, an acceptable sacrifice, pleasing to God. And my God will meet all your needs according to his glorious riches in Christ Jesus" (Philippians 4:18-20 NIV).

The Scripture is full of instructions about sacrificing, bringing offerings and giving to the Lord. Jesus was not a fundraiser, but He talked about stewardship a great deal. Jesus dealt with money matters, because money matters! Both God and Satan know that where your treasure is, there your heart will be also. That's why both are very interested in what we do with our money. Our attitude toward money is a spiritual matter! If our attitude is right, we will give as needed and, by doing so, an unending supply of provision will come our way.

23. The Principle of Sacrificial Giving

"Jesus sat down opposite the place where the offerings were put and watched the crowd putting their money into the temple treasury. Many rich people threw in large amounts. But a poor widow came and put in two very small copper coins, worth only a fraction of a penny. Calling his disciples to him, Jesus said, "I tell you the truth, this poor widow has put more into the treasury than all the others. They all gave out of their wealth; but she, out of her poverty, put in everything—all she had to live on" (Mark 12:41-44 NIV).

This verse teaches us an important truth—God is honored when we give sacrificially. The amount is not as important as the heart attitude with which we give! Jesus called attention to the poor widow's offering because, although she had only given two small copper coins, her offering was acceptable because it cost her something. In Chronicles 21:24, King David demonstrated this same principle with the following words:, "No, I insist on paying the full price. I will not take for the LORD what is yours, or sacrifice a burnt offering that costs me nothing."

Most definitely, you need God to be involved in your financial life and you need His provision and blessing. God will bless you financially if He knows that you will pass it on. God wants to bring money to you and pour out through you. He wants you to be a channel, not a reservoir.

24. The Principle of Heart Decisions

"Each man should give what he has decided in his heart to give, not reluctantly or under compulsion..." (II Corinthians 9:7 NIV)

The decision of how much to give is always left up to us. Of course we know the principle of the tenth that always belongs to God. But giving is more of an attitude than an amount. Get the heart and attitude right and the amount will be exactly as it is supposed to be. God doesn't want us to give without thinking, nor does He want our leftovers. He desires that we give out of our best resources.

OUR GIVING STARTS WITH OUR TITHING.

Our giving starts with our tithing. But it does not relieve us of our responsibility to meet other needs as they become known. When you give, give as though you are giving to God. With that attitude adjustment, you don't have to worry about your giving becoming as routine as simply paying a financial obligation. When you pay the monthly mortgage or the utility bills, you are giving under compulsion...you are not given a choice. The Scripture says to simply give as you feel in your heart, not reluctantly or under compulsion. Make your giving an act of worship! Give because He is worthy to receive. Give because you want to give. Give because you enjoy giving. Give because you have received. Give because you have been blessed. Give because your family is blessed. Give because you want to honor your Creator!

25. *The Principle of Equal Giving*

> *"And here is my advice about what is best for you in this matter: Last year you were the first not only to give but also to have the desire to do so. Now finish the work, so that your eager willingness to do it may be matched by your completion of it, according to your means. For if the willingness is there, the gift is acceptable according to what one has, not according to what he does not have"* (II Corinthians 8:10-12 NIV).

Equal giving does not equate to equal sacrifice. Our lifestyle of stewardship must reflect not only generous giving but also sacrificial giving. When we are quick to acknowledge that all of our money and possessions come from a loving God, our role as a sacrificial giver is made much easier.

The principle of equal giving directs us to assess and examine how we manage our finances, so that we can give to God according to how He has blessed us. It enables us to rethink our lifestyles and to reorder the priorities in our life. In doing so, we will reallocate our gifts and resources to the work of God. We will give over and above.

26. *The Principle of Being Faithful*

> *"Now it is required that those who have been given a trust must prove faithful"* (I Corinthians 4:2-3 NIV).

If God has blessed you with a great life, a good family and good friends, they are precious gifts entrusted to you. Not all stewards have been trustworthy. What about you? What is important to you? When you see how God has blessed you and as He becomes first in your life, you realize that He is faithful to supply all of your needs. Are you faithful to Him? Deuteronomy 5:32 warns us that we need to be careful to do what the Lord has told us to do. We are to walk in the ways of God, not turning to the right or left. When you give to God, you must ask yourself if God is directing your decision. Examine whether the amount accurately reflects who you are, how God has blessed you and the resources He has placed into your life.

27. The Principle of Laying Up Treasures

"In this way they will lay up treasure for themselves as a firm foundation for the coming age, so that they may take hold of the life that is truly life"
(I Timothy 6:19 NIV).

There is an ancient legend about a monk who found a precious stone, a precious jewel. A short time later, the monk met a traveler, who said he was hungry and asked the monk if he would share some of his provisions. When the monk opened his bag, the traveler saw the precious stone and, on an impulse, asked the monk if he could have it. Amazingly, the monk gave the traveler the stone.

The traveler departed quickly, overjoyed with his new possession. However, a few days later, he came back, searching for the monk. He returned the stone to the monk and made a request: "Please give me something more valuable, more precious than this stone. Please give me that which enabled you to give me this precious stone!" [9]

Jesus teaches us that the world in itself is not important, but how we exist in it and where it leads us is the important consideration. *This world is not an end in itself, but a stage along the way.*

Since this world is not the end of our path, we should never sell out to it, lose our hearts to it or lose our souls because of it. Richard Glover, in his Commentary on Matthew, says this: "He builds too low who builds beneath the skies."[10]

28. The Principle of Avoiding the Sluggard Lifestyle

"I went past the field of the sluggard, past the vineyard of the man who lacks judgment; thorns had come up everywhere, the ground was covered with weeds, and the stone wall was in ruins. I applied my heart to what I observed and learned a lesson from what I saw: A little sleep, a little slumber, a little folding of the hands to rest— and poverty will come on you like a bandit and scarcity like an armed man" (Proverbs 24:30-34 NIV).

The sluggard. What can we say about this kind of person. Is he self-centered? Is he lazy? Does he rest? Does he do what he wants to do without regard for others? Certainly all of these things probably describe him, but let's take a closer look at the profile of a sluggard.

At the very least, a sluggard has a major problem with procrastination. His motto would be to never do today what he can put off until tomorrow....always with good intentions;

always just about ready to start a job, but not quite. The sluggard probably gets started on a few jobs and may even get some things done, but never quite gets them finished or brought to completion.

What is his excuse? Maybe he didn't have all of the tools to finish the job. Maybe he wasn't feeling well. Maybe the rain was on its way or it could be just that the sun was not shining as bright. Perhaps his excuse was that the job became bigger than he was expecting or more time-consuming. He is always ready to set the job aside in favor of something more to his liking and more convenient.

Proverbs 12:27 says, "The lazy man does not roast his game, but the diligent man prizes his possessions" (NIV). Here is the picture of a man who is not only lazy but also wasteful. Not only does the sluggard do what he wants to, when he wants to, but he also is a great waster of resources and provision. He goes out, he hunts his game, and he kills his game. But after the fun of the hunt, the work never begins. While he could prepare the provision for his family or for the poor, he instead chooses to walk away from it, let it die and lie there. He doesn't even consider how to make the food available for the hungry.

You need to understand your calling and purpose in life and set out objectives that will allow you to live that fulfilled life.

The diligent person would never waste God's provision. They would thank God for the provision and prepare the meat for future use. They would share it with others. They would diligently continue with investing the resources available to them.

Sluggards are not interested in saving resources and helping others. To them, it is all about the fun of the sport. They are wasteful about everything. Sluggards proclaim that, when their ship comes in, they will begin to give. Herein lies the problem. If you never sent your ship out to begin with, you cannot expect it to come in. What kind of ship are you waiting for? God does not give money miracles to a lazy, slothful person. If you want to avoid living the life of a sluggard, you need to get your act together. Start working, applying godly wisdom and insight. Understand your calling and purpose in life and set out objectives that will allow you to live that fulfilled life. Then and then only will you reap with joy what you have sowed with tears.

29. *The Principle of Working Diligently*

"Go to the ant, you sluggard; consider its ways and be wise! It has no commander, no overseer or ruler, yet it stores its provisions in summer and gathers its food at harvest. How long will you lie there, you sluggard? When will you get up from your sleep? A little sleep, a little slumber, a little folding of the hands to rest— and poverty will come on you like a bandit and scarcity like an armed man" (Proverbs 6:6-11 NIV).

Here is another lesson to the lazy man—the sluggard—but given with a conscious effort to try to redeem him. The Scripture extends hope by admonishing him to look at the ant. This poem, written by Isaac Watts in his book *Divine Songs for Children*, also describes a "sluggard":

THE SLUGGARD

'Tis the voice of the Sluggard: I heard him complain,
"You have waked me too soon! I must slumber again!"
As the door on its hinges, so he on his bed
Turns his sides, and his shoulders, and his heavy head.
"A little more sleep, and a little more slumber!"
Thus he wastes half his days and his hours
    without number;
And when he gets up he sits folding his hands,
Or walks about sauntering, or trifling he stands.
I made him a visit, still hoping to find
He had took better care for improving his mind:
He told me his dreams, talk'd of eating and drinking
But he scarce reads his Bible, and never loves thinking.[11]

Check out the ant. The ant has no one to tell him what to do and yet he is a self- starter, a self-motivator. He works all summer long, gathering his food for the harvest season. The Scripture extends a wake-up call to the sluggard, hoping for some kind of response.

It says to the sluggard, have you not slept enough? Do you want to go hungry, walking through life looking for handouts because you haven't the wherewithal to earn your own keep?

The Bible is very clear on the principle of working diligently. It says that a lazy person who conveniently excuses himself from working with a little sleep, a little slumber and a little folding of the hands to rest will come to nothing. His life will be one of poverty, bankruptcy and despair. He is one who consoles himself with rest, unconcerned that others are out there getting the job done. However, the person who gets up early, gets right to work and prepares for his future will someday be honored for it. Proverbs 22:29 declares, "Do you see a man who excels in his work? He will stand before kings" (NKJV).

30. The Principle of Love, the Greatest Gift

"But whoso hath this world's good, and seeth his brother have need, and shutteth up his bowels of compassion from him, how dwelleth the love of God in him" (I John 3:17 KJV)?

A 19th-century folktale is set in a small *shtetl* in Russia, where a terrible cold front was causing extreme suffering to the poor. On one bitingly cold day, the rabbi went to solicit the only wealthy man in town, a man known to be a miser.

The rabbi knocked and the man opened the door. "Come in, Rabbi," the rich man said. Unlike everyone else in town, he was only in shirtsleeves; after all, his house was well-heated. "No," the rabbi said. "No need for me to come in. I'll just be a minute." The rabbi then proceeded to engage the rich man in a lengthy conversation, asking him detailed questions concerning each member of his family. The man was shivering, yet every time he asked the rabbi to come inside, the rabbi refused.

"And your wife's cousin, the lumber merchant, how is he?" the rabbi asked.

The rich man's cheeks were fiery red. "What did you come here for, Rabbi?"

"Oh, that," the rabbi said. "I need money from you to buy coal for the poor people in town."

"So why don't you come in and we'll talk about it?"

"Because if I come in, we will sit down by your fireplace. You will be very warm and comfortable and when I tell you how the poor are suffering from the cold, you really won't understand. You'll give me five rubles, maybe ten, and send me away. But now, out here," the rabbi went on, indicating the frozen moisture on the man's cheeks, "when I tell you how the poor are suffering from the cold, I think you'll understand better. Right?"

The man was happy to give the rabbi 100 rubles just so he could shut the door and return to his fireplace.[12]

"I hear, I know. I see, I remember. I do, I understand."

Key Points:

➤ principles involving heart attitudes

➤ blessings / miracles from giving

➤ giving to the needy, systematic giving

➤ avoiding the lifestyle of the sluggard

1. **Write down** any parts of the chapter that were meaningful to you.

_____

_____

_____

_____

2. **Personal Application:** How can you personally apply these truths in your own life? Write down several long-term goals.

_____

_____

_____

_____

3. **Steps to Action:** Write down one small step you could take to begin immediately applying the truths and principles of this chapter.

_____

_____

_____

_____

4. **Prayer for the Practical:** Write out a prayer to God asking Him for help in making any changes that these goals would require.

_____

_____

_____

_____

Psalm 62:8 "O my people, trust in him at all times.
Pour out your heart to him,
For God is our refuge."

"I have always enjoyed making money, and God knew that. Had He left me undisturbed in this area, I could have become a proud, materialistic, self-centered spiritual misfit. In asking of me the submission of the greatest drive of my life, He removed a blighting influence and replaced it with an inner peace and satisfaction such as I could never have known otherwise."

—STANLEY TAM
AUTHOR (*GOD OWNS MY BUSINESS*), BUSINESSMAN

CHAPTER NINE

MANAGING GOD'S MONEY SO THAT HE TRUSTS YOU WITH MORE

The world we live in is largely self-centered and consumer-oriented, presenting life from a selfish point of view. It can easily influence even our Christian activities. If we are not careful, it can be our tendency today to make personal satisfaction and comfort our priority. Scripture teaches us that the comfort that we receive from God will enable us to comfort others.

"Praise be to the God and Father of our Lord Jesus Christ, the Father of compassion and the God of all comfort, who comforts us in all our troubles, so that we can comfort those in any trouble with the comfort we ourselves have received from God. For just as the sufferings of Christ flow over into our lives, so also through Christ our comfort overflows. If we are distressed, it is for your comfort and salvation; if we are comforted, it is for your comfort, which produces in you patient endurance of the same sufferings we suffer. And our hope for you is firm, because we know that just as you share in our sufferings, so also you share in our comfort" (II Corinthians 1:3-7 NIV).

REDEFINING STEWARDSHIP

Throughout Scripture, the concept of a steward is introduced to us again and again. Stewardship disciplines in Scripture involve much more than the income we earn to sustain our livelihood. Certainly money is a big part of it, but not nearly all of it. The account of the rich young ruler in Mark 10:17-22 tells the story of a man and all his possessions. He thought that what he possessed belonged only to him. This story was not a lesson on tithing and giving, rather one on stewardship. When the Ten Commandments were mentioned by Jesus, the response from the wealthy young ruler was that he had honored those in his life from a very young age.

If the Lord had asked him about whether or not he was a tither, most likely the wealthy young ruler would have also replied in the affirmative. Next Jesus hones in on the real problem…the man's possessions. Jesus wanted to confront him concerning his priorities, his stewardship and where the real ownership of these things lay. But this was just too hard for the rich young ruler. He had to leave with a countenance full of dismay and a sad heart.

One of God's objectives for the church is that we would allow Him to reproduce Himself in us as good stewards of His abundant grace. A steward is not an owner, but a manager. God is always the owner and we are always the managers of the many and various stewardship roles He has given to us. But in order to fulfill these roles as extenders of His grace, we need to know all of the areas of stewardship for which we are accountable. The areas of good stewardship that He requires of us are almost limitless. They would, of course, include life itself, the gift of children and the stewardship of His creation. Additionally, we would include the stewardship of our communication, the stewardship of time, the stewardship of truth and the stewardship of talents or giftings. Discovering and developing our spiritual gifts and natural talents for the purpose of blessing others and glorifying God is our duty.

Stewardship throughout the Bible

Nearly two-thirds of the parables of Jesus deal with stewardship or the proper use of money. In the New Testament there are 38 parables, twelve of which are about money. One out of every six verses in Matthew, Mark and Luke has to do with money and individual fiscal responsibility.

As stewards, it is our responsibility to trust God to supply our needs. We have been given responsibility over the natural resources of the earth according to Genesis 1:28. Matthew 10:8 instructs us that, as we have abundantly received, we are to freely give. The rich young ruler did not understand that the possessions he had been entrusted with had been given to him for a purpose. That purpose was to include sharing his wealth with the poor and needy of the earth.

Stewardship in the Bible deals with more than finance and its proper use. The term stewardship implies that there is a steward—someone who is entrusted with material or spiritual responsibility. In the story above, the rich young ruler was a steward over great possessions, but failed to act accordingly. According to Scripture, it is required that a steward be faithful to his charge (Genesis 15:2; Genesis 24; Luke 16:1-13).

Stewardship implies a fiduciary responsibility. Fiduciary is a term that means "of, pertaining to or involving one who holds something in trust for another." A person with a fiduciary relationship is one who stands in a special position of trust, confidence or responsibility in his or her obligations to others.

Speaking to Stewardship via the Old Testament

The word steward appears only once in the Old Testament. Genesis 15:2 says, "And Abram said, 'Lord GOD, what wilt thou give me, seeing I go childless, and the steward of my house is this Eliezer of Damascus?' " (KJV) The word translated "steward" in Genesis 15:2 means "son of acquisition."

In this generation such a person would also be considered an heir. Eliezer's role was that of the number one servant or steward in Abram's house (see Genesis 24). Stewardship is delegated oversight of another's possessions. It is delegated authority coupled with accountability. Abram had Eliezer to whom he gave oversight. As a matter of fact, Eliezer was even entrusted with the task of finding a wife for Isaac (the son whom Abram and his wife later had).

The Hebrew Old Testament word for steward is one who oversees another's house. Eliezer of Damascus was Abram's slave and trusted steward; he had oversight of all his affairs and was entrusted with important duties. He had charge of the family of his master as well as his property. Jacob was a steward for Laban. Joseph was a steward for Potiphar until Potiphar's wife lied about him. Later, Joseph was Pharaoh's steward and ruled all Egypt.

Examples from the New Testament

In the New Testament, Jesus uses parables about stewards as examples of God's people and Paul refers to Christians as stewards in the epistles. Stewards in biblical times were very common. All wealthy people and rulers had stewards to whom they entrusted the oversight of personnel and property.

These responsibilities were either as a guardian of the children or administrator of the affairs of the household. According to the International Bible Encyclopedia, "every household of distinction or sufficient wealth had a steward in charge." The functions of this officer seem, at times, to have included the care of minor children as well as property. The Greek word for stewardship is *epitropos*, meaning one who oversees another's possessions, usually having to do with the supervision of personnel. The word for one who oversees another's possessions, usually in reference to property, is *oikonomos*. (ISBE)

Stewards, like many bosses today, had varying degrees of stewardship. According to Scripture, some managed property and some personnel, while others had financial oversight. As is also the case in our society, a good steward was rewarded with increased responsibility and income, while a poor steward was disgraced or fired.

In Luke 16, Jesus told the story of a certain rich man who had a steward. As the parable continues, the rich man required an accounting of his steward. Any individual in a fiduciary relationship must be held accountable to that agreement. We can manage or mismanage the Master's resources.

CHARACTER MAKES THE STEWARD

Since stewards are charged with great authority and responsibility, their character cannot be flawed. Additionally, their value systems must be ones of great integrity. Faithfulness was a fundamental virtue of a person who served as a steward. "It is required in stewards, that a man be found faithful" (I Corinthians 4:2 KJV). The steward of the rich man in Luke 16 was obviously not faithful to his lord. He was dishonest in his dealings and made it a point to look out for himself first. Consider the following responsibilities of a good steward.

Guided by Integrity

Good stewards of time and finance are not only faithful and responsible, there is an honesty and integrity about them. The word integrity means, "being complete, unimpaired, perfect condition, of sound moral principle, uprightness" (Webster's Dictionary). Proverbs 19:1 says, "Better is the poor that walketh in his integrity, than he that is perverse in his lips, and is a fool" (KJV) True riches are not determined by what a person possesses, but by his or her personal integrity. Is it more important to have or to be? Someone can take that which we have, but they cannot take that which we are.

Wholly Devoted to God

What are you controlling? What does God already own that you are trying to keep absolute control over by refusing to acknowledge God's ownership? What about your business or your house? What about your transportation vehicles, your recreational vehicles, your clothes, toys or other worldly goods? What about your body? According to Romans 12:1, your body belongs to the Lord. Does your time belong to you or to God? What about your income, your savings, your investments and your other possessions? Do these things belong to you or to God? Have you been allowed oversight of them for the purpose of showing good stewardship or have you taken them over assuming that they are yours only? Everything you say, every decision you make, every action you take must be accountable to the principles of God.

> WHAT DOES GOD ALREADY OWN THAT YOU ARE TRYING TO KEEP ABSOLUTE CONTROL OVER BY REFUSING TO ACKNOWLEDGE GOD'S OWNERSHIP?

What about your entire life—your dreams, your goals, your visions? Are they born of God or have you allowed your carnal nature to take complete control? Are you a thief or a steward? If a steward, what kind of steward are you? Are you one that God can trust with complete care or are you careless in your stewardship?

Faithful

> *"Now it is required that those who have been given a trust must prove faithful"* (I Corinthians 4:2-3 NIV).

Deuteronomy 5:32 warns us that we need to be careful to do what the Lord has told us to do. We are to walk in the ways of God, not turning to the right or left. When you give to God, you must ask yourself if God is directing your decision. Does the amount accurately reflect who you are, how God has blessed you and what resources He has blessed you with?

What about you? What is important to you? When you see how God has blessed you and as He becomes first in your life, you realize that He is faithful to supply all of your needs. Are you faithful to Him?

RESPONSIBILITIES OF A STEWARD

Faithfulness leads to responsibility. Adam is an example of the unfaithful steward. Although God had given him the oversight of the beautiful Garden of Eden, he betrayed the owner's trust. He misused His creation and that very creation (according to Romans) still groans because of the unfaithfulness of Adam, the steward God had entrusted His creation to.

The servants (stewards) in Bible times who were entrusted with a portion of the master's possessions were challenged not only to keep them, but to utilize them and multiply the property.

The thought presented in this parable of Luke 16 is that what we possess is really not our own, but God's. Because 100 percent of what is received comes from God, we are responsible to use it wisely and in accordance with God's will. The fact that God is the true owner of everything is illustrated in Psalm 50:10-11.

"For every beast of the forest is mine, and the cattle upon a thousand hills. I know all the fowls of the mountains: and the wild beasts of the field are mine" (KJV).

Carefully Maintains Possessions

How do you care for those possessions God has entrusted to you? Do your keep your house in good repair both outside and inside? Is your house clean and spotless? Do you organize and keep your yard equipment and tools in a safe dry place or do you leave them lying around in the rain to rust? God is a good caretaker. He is very organized. He created and continues to manage galaxies, the universe, billions of stars, the sun, moon and earth. He maintains His creation very well. We are to be equally as good at the organization and management of our affairs. Everything we have belongs to the Lord.

Do you keep the oil and fluids fresh in your car or do you let it go for several thousand miles before you drain and refill? Are your vehicles kept clean on the inside and outside? You see, good stewardship involves more than just having possessions and material goods; it goes to the core of how you care for them. You are caring for God's blessing. If you don't care how you treat the blessings that God has allowed you to receive, how can you expect to keep them, let alone ask for more?

Dependable in Commitments

Stewardship is about dependability, which is a virtue of the person who has learned the importance of being worthy of trust. One of the basic values or principles of dependability is to live up to one's obligations. If, for any reason, a commitment or promise cannot be fulfilled, the proper thing to do is to talk to the person with whom the commitment was made and negotiate a workable solution. The rich man's steward of Luke 16 was not dependable and apparently did not fulfill his financial responsibilities to his lord. He was about to lose his position, because he had violated his fiduciary relationship to the master of the house.

Invests in Eternity

The dishonest steward wasted his lord's goods for which he was liable and was judged by his master. We also are responsible to our Master for his creation and blessing. The scope of the parable is to suggest to us that it is important to manage our possessions and lives on earth in such a way that will benefit us in the eternal life. It's not that eternal life is our sole reason for managing our possessions judiciously. We should do so out of our obedience, appreciation and our love for God. The thought is that all of us are stewards of what has been entrusted to us and we have a responsibility to employ our wealth in acts of charity and good works. This is because we are seeking an eternal return in much the same way that the dishonest steward employed his abilities to achieve the greatest temporal profit.

The steward's lord commended him because he finally showed some ingenuity and ambition, even though it was for his own personal gain and benefit. The steward is not commended because he showed good financial sensitivity, rather because he had done wisely for himself. The steward who was about to be dismissed made every attempt to better his cause through any means available, even though that cause was self-serving.

What a person does with all his possessions is important to God. Jesus said in Luke 16:11, "If therefore ye have not been faithful in the unrighteous mammon, who will commit to your trust the true riches?" (KJV) Mammon means "gain or wealth" (Berry's Greek-English New Testament Lexicon with Synonyms).

The Scriptures present us with a staggering reality. II Peter 1:3 notes, "…His divine power hath given unto us all things that pertain unto life and godliness" (KJV). Think of all that He has given us! The gift of salvation, the gift of grace, the gift of mercy and the gift of the Holy Spirit are just a few of God's amazing gifts! These treasures are infinitely more valuable than any worldly possessions we could own.

Faithful with Finances

Christians have access to unlimited and unimaginable resources. But with this access comes accountability. If you don't take care of that old clunker of a vehicle you now own, how can you care for a new car? If you goof off during the day at your current job, why would God want to bless you with a better one? If you cannot take good care of the apartment you live in or the house you rent, how can you be trusted with your own property? There is a principle at work here. We must prove that we can be good stewards!

The Bible also indicates that one's control of the finances in his possession is a direct indication of the control he exercises in spiritual matters. If a person cannot handle God's blessing of finance, it is likely that he cannot handle too much time on his hands, promotion on the job, authority on the job, authority in the church, and probably a whole host of other spiritual matters. The unjust steward of Luke 16 had other personal problems besides just being a bad manager for his lord. His dishonesty became very apparent when he was about to lose his job. The handling of a person's financial affairs is closely akin to his or her other values. The value system of one's heart is exposed by one's relationship to money and material things. The rich young ruler is another illustration of that fact. (See Matthew 19:16-22.)

RESOURCES OF A STEWARD

Entrusted with Much

Our life's stewardship should reflect God's interest in all that He has entrusted to us. Genesis 1:26 records that God made man to rule over all the earth and all life on earth, both plant and animal. In Genesis 2:15, man was made steward over the Garden, in which there were precious stones, gold, and rivers. In other words, man was created for more than going to heaven after a lifetime of waiting. He was created to be a faithful steward over the work of God's hands. This is a great trust that God places in our lives. More than just money or finances, it is our entire life that we must handle with faithfulness, responsibility, accountability, honesty and integrity. Stewardship is bringing everything we have to offer under the Lordship of Christ. What kind of a person makes a good steward? A person who has a great respect for God and his creation.

Dominion Over Creation

Only God has the power to speak the word and cause something to happen instantly, but with man, work is necessary. Adam was the sole steward appointed over all natural resources, as well as plant and animal life; this was a substantial entrustment from God. So when Adam disobeyed and lost that leadership, it affected a lot more than his descendants; it affected the sea, the air, the earth and life, as well. When the steward went astray, that which had been entrusted to him was severely injured. According to Romans 8:22, the whole earth groans in travail. When Adam and Eve sinned, God judged them. Man was required to leave the plush Garden of Eden. God commanded this in Genesis

3:19, "In the sweat of thy face shalt thou eat bread, till thou return unto the ground" (KJV).

Unlike third world countries, in this country we do not have a lower class. Though many think otherwise, every healthy person who wants to can work, be self-supporting, have plenty to eat and shelter for sleep. There are, of course, economic cycles of employment, job availability, discomfort and limited opportunity for growth. But when compared to the poor of this world, those who lack the most in this country are far better off than almost anywhere else in the world.

In the United States, a great deal of emphasis is placed upon having fun, spending time in leisurely activity and taking care of the whims of "me." Many are content to put as little into their work as they think they can get away with. Far too many employees are receiving a full paycheck for less than a full day's work. The Scriptures note in II Thessalonians 3:10, "... If any would not work, neither should he eat" (KJV).

Use of Personal Resources

Every human being alive must be a steward of his or her own personal resources of skill, knowledge, strength, possessions and influence. We don't need to necessarily aspire for more or feel discouraged over areas of what we may perceive as lack. We just need to use what we have. Hard work, efficient use of our available resources, and a disciplined personal life will lead to prosperity and success.

In Matthew 25:14-30 the parable of the talents is recorded. This story tells of a certain man who distributed his wealth among three servants, giving to each according to his ability. As this parable would imply, our abilities vary individually, including our ability to earn money.

The parable proceeds to tell how each man invested his seed money. The first two traded theirs. That is, they used it and, in the process, they doubled the original amount. The last person, however, tried to hoard his by doing nothing with it. In the end, each had to account for his actions.

Seven Motivations of a Steward

1. Motivated by God's Word

The following Scriptures should encourage you in the knowledge that God truly owns everything!:

"... Our God, we thank Thee... for all things come of Thee, and of Thine own have we given Thee" (I Chronicles 29:13, 14 KJV).

"... The earth is the Lord's" (Exodus 9:29 KJV).

"Thus saith the Lord, 'The heaven is My throne, and the earth is My footstool... For all those things hath Mine hand made...'" (Isaiah 66:1, 2 KJV)

"Heaven is My throne, and earth is My footstool... Hath not My hand made all these things?" (Acts 7:49, 50 KJV)

"... Thou art the God... Thou hast made heaven and earth" (II Kings 19:15 KJV).

"Thou, even Thou, art Lord alone; Thou hast made heaven, the heaven of heavens, with all their host, the earth, and all things that are therein, the seas, and all that is therein, and Thou preservest them all..." (Nehemiah 9:6 KJV)

"I have made the earth, the man and the beast that are upon the ground, by My great power and by My outstretched arm, and have given it unto whom it seemed meet unto Me" (Jeremiah 27:5 KJV).

"And, Thou, Lord, in the beginning hast laid the foundation of the earth; and the heavens are the works of Thine hands" (Hebrews 1:10 KJV).

"God that made the world and all things therein, seeing that He is Lord of heaven and earth, dwelleth not in temples made with hands" (Acts 17:24 KJV).

"Who knoweth not in all these that the hand of the Lord hath wrought this? In whose hand is the soul [life] of every living thing, and the breath of all mankind?" (Job 12:9, 10 KJV)

"The heavens are Thine, the earth also is Thine: as for the world and the fullness thereof, Thou hast founded them" (Psalm 89:11 KJV).

"For the Lord is a great God... The sea is His and He made it: and His hands formed the dry land" (Psalm 95:3, 5 KJV).

"... The most High ruleth in the kingdom of men, and giveth it to whomsoever He will, and setteth up over it the basest of men" (Daniel 4:17 KJV).

"Jesus answered, 'Thou couldest have no power at all against Me, except it were given thee from above...'" (John 19:11 KJV)

"Thou art worthy, O Lord, to receive glory and honor and power: for Thou hast created all things, and for Thy pleasure they are and were created" (Revelation 4:11 KJV).

2. Motivated to Plan Ahead

The astute business person looks ahead and plans for the future. He or she manages money so as to provide benefits, not only for the present, but also for the future. Christ is suggesting that, in doing good works, we should consider our future with just as much ingenuity as the dishonest steward. For the sake of Jesus Christ, we are mandated with a responsibility to use every means at our disposal to spread the good news to mankind. In doing so, our gains will have great effect upon eternal matters.

The astute business person looks ahead and plans for the future. He or she manages money so as to provide benefits, not only for the present, but for the future.

The shrewdness with which the unjust servant negated his fiduciary responsibility to his lord was commended. He promoted his cause with the utmost care and effort. With an unprincipled passion he sought to use his master's money in securing advantage after his inevitable dismissal. Christ was simply asking those to whom he spoke to be as inventive for a better cause.

The parable of Luke 16 ends with a piece of advice for His hearers. He says to use worldly wealth to gain friends for yourselves, so that when it is gone you will be welcomed into eternal dwelling. Money, tainted as it can be, should be used in such a way that, when we die and our money is gone, we can say it went for the best use. The message is clear: in our financial stewardship to God, we should be at least as whole-hearted and energetic as was the steward in prosecuting his own interests.

3. Motivated to Give More than is Expected

As good stewards, we are required to work hard. If you work for someone else, you need to do it with everything you have. Give more than is required, go the second mile and the third and fourth.

> *"Go to the ant, you sluggard; consider its ways and be wise! It has no commander, no overseer or ruler, yet it stores its provisions in summer and gathers its food at harvest. How long will you lie there, you sluggard? When will you get up from your sleep? A little sleep, a little slumber, a little folding of the hands to rest—and poverty will come on you like a bandit and scarcity like an armed man"* (Proverbs 6:6-11 NIV).

GIVE MORE THAN IS REQUIRED, GO THE SECOND MILE AND THE THIRD AND FOURTH.

> *"Make it your ambition to lead a quiet life, to mind your own business and to work with your hands, just as we told you, so that your daily life may win the respect of outsiders and so that you will not be dependent on anybody"* (I Thessalonians 4:11-12 NIV).

> *"Lazy hands make a man poor, but diligent hands bring wealth. He who gathers crops in summer is a wise son, but he who sleeps during harvest is a disgraceful son"* (Proverbs 10:4-5 NIV).

> *"Do you see a man skilled in his work? He will serve before kings; he will not serve before obscure men"* (Proverbs 22:29 NIV).

> *"Whatever your hand finds to do, do it with all your might..."* (Ecclesiastes 9:10 NIV).

> *"A sluggard does not plow in season; so at harvest time he looks but finds nothing"* (Proverbs 20:4 NIV).

According to the above Scriptures, we should approach life and work like the ant. Although the ant has no boss, it still works extremely hard in order to provide for its needs. A lot of people today could learn a valuable lesson from the ant. Some today have the attitude that if they can get someone else to do the work for them, then why should they put themselves out? Why not let someone else do the work? Why not let the government provide for me? Many today have little or no initiative, are not able to put themselves to work and must always have someone else instruct them and supervise them into order to keep them working.

4. Motivated to be Diligent

Some people today would rather ask for a handout instead of going to work. You see them waiting at the freeway exits with a sign which reads, "Will Work for Food." After offering one person a day's work, the response was nothing more than profanity and gestures. The integrity of this person was certainly lacking.

A person's usefulness is determined to a great degree by his motivation to work. Idleness is not looked upon kindly in biblical passages nor within our society today. In Proverbs 6:6, we can learn a great lesson from the ant. He has no guide to show him how to work. He has no supervisor to make him work, yet he is self-motivated by the natural instinct of preservation to provide for future needs.

5. Motivated to be Self-Disciplined

If we are to lead prosperous and successful lives (prosperity is not to be thought of as having money), we have to apply Biblical instruction to work hard and lead a disciplined lifestyle. Clearly, we are to do the very best that we possibly can with the talents and strength that God has given to us. Many people think that the world owes them a living. It is this kind of attitude that destroys the work ethic in our society. Our country's welfare system does little to build character and establish the needy into better life-changing environments. To pass out monies year after year to those with outstretched hands without expecting any change in life-style does little to improve the society for future generations.

A steward realizes that self-discipline is an important key to prosperity and success.

6. Motivated to be Productive

Good stewardship is not merely an occupation or a profession, rather it involves being productive. In Jesus' story of the talents, the stewards reported their earnings. One servant, however, merely hid his entrustment and earned no increase. He lost his portion. The faithful ones not only had increases, but received even more because of their faithfulness. From the very beginning, God commanded creation to be fruitful. God is energetic, creative and imaginative; He is the life-giver. Stewards are also to be concerned with productivity and so cultivate God's creation to be productive.

A warning about being productive is seen in Jesus' story about the unfruitful branch of His Kingdom which He says will be cut off by the Husbandman (John 15:1-5). God wants to have a productive kingdom and stewards who will help them do so.

7. Motivated to Develop God's Gifts

Each one of us has been given access to gifts from God. Are you developing those gifts? Are you using and exercising the giftings of God? If God has blessed you with houses and lands, businesses and possessions, are you trusting in them and pursuing more or are you developing your good stewardship of them? If these things are meaningful to you and if you give all of your time and money to seeking more, then be careful because you won't have them forever. However, if you are pursuing God and the things of His Kingdom, God will probably keep trusting you with more.

If we are idle and lazy, we will be judged accordingly (Ecclesiastes 10:18). At judgment day, we will give account for every idle word that we speak (Matthew 12:36). If we must account for an idle word, what about idle time? The Apostle Paul encouraged the Ephesians to redeem the time (Ephesians 5:16). The Greek word is *exagorazo* and means "to buy up or rescue from loss" (Strong's Concordance).

There is a great lesson to be learned from the Matthew 25 parable. When God invests something into your life and allows you stewardship over it, you must use it for His glory and His Kingdom. If you do nothing with it, God will take it away and give it to another. If you do not know how to invest it into the kingdom or how to take care of it, you had better seek out some wisdom. God is very interested in our caretaking ability and what we do with our time, money, possessions and ministry giftings. What we do, where we go, and the actions we take are very important to God. Remember, we are not the owners of all that God has given to us; we are only stewards (managers) and therefore responsible for the gifts and accountable for their use.

"I hear, I know. I see, I remember. I do, I understand."

Key Points:

➤ definition of stewardship ➤ faithfulness, oversight, and dependability

➤ the character of a steward ➤ diligence, discipline, and personal resources

1. **Write down** any parts of the chapter that were meaningful to you.

_____

_____

_____

_____

2. **Personal Application:** How can you personally apply these truths in your own life? Write down several long-term goals.

_____

_____

_____

_____

3. **Steps to Action:** Write down one small step you could take to begin immediately applying the truths and principles of this chapter.

_____

_____

_____

_____

4. **Prayer for the Practical:** Write out a prayer to God asking Him for help in making any changes that these goals would require.

_____

_____

_____

_____

Psalm 62:8 "O my people, trust in him at all times.
Pour out your heart to him,
For God is our refuge."

"Don't be afraid of the enemy! Remember the Lord, who is great and glorious, and fight for your brothers, your sons, your daughters, your wives, and your homes!"

Nehemiah (4:14)
Cupbearer to the king of Persia,
of rebuilding walls of Jerusalem (445 B.C.)

CHAPTER TEN

PRAYING FOR THE PRACTICAL: STRENGTHENING YOUR PERSONAL FINANCES WITH THE NEHEMIAH STRATEGY

D o you make time to pray the truths of God's Word over your finances? Nehemiah was a man who understood the power of combining specific prayer with the practical details of his life. When he first received the report that the walls of Jerusalem had been torn down and destroyed by fire, his first reaction was to turn to God in prayer and fasting (Neh. 1:3-4). When he was later asked by the king about what he would need to rebuild the walls, we read that he first offered up a prayer to God and then asked the king for the specific materials he would need (Neh. 2: 4, 7-8). Then, when facing heavy opposition during the building project, we read that he responded in two ways. After first crying out to God in prayer (Neh. 4:4, 9), he then placed guards behind the lowest parts of the wall in the most vulnerable places (Neh. 4:13). Nehemiah's mentality for moving forward in his God-given project combined prayer with the practical.

God's Word contains powerful truths which relate to different areas of your finances, including savings, borrowing, investing, and budgeting. Throughout this book, we have described some of these practical areas of life with corresponding truths from the Word of God. Most of us have a deep desire to apply the truths of God's Word into our lives.

Even if we don't have a huge project in front of us, as Nehemiah did, we have a longing to walk in financial success, wisdom, and freedom.

THE POWER OF FOCUSED PRAYER

Desiring financial breakthrough, however, is often a far-cry from reality. When Monday morning rolls around, the kids are still asking for new clothes, the car needs to be fixed, and the bills need to be paid. Imagine that your current financial situation is like a wall that is being built. Remember that, in Nehemiah's situation, he placed guards behind the most vulnerable places in order to ward off the attacks of the enemy. Do you see any weak, vulnerable areas in your "financial wall" that are prone to attack? How can you make sure that you are moving forward in your financial vision, protected from everyday hindrances? We believe that you need a "Nehemiah mentality" that combines specific prayer with the everyday details of your life.

The financial prayer guide below is intended to help you pray over 14 specific areas of your finances (derived from key chapters in this book). While some prayer guides are intended to be prayed in full each day, we would suggest a more simple approach for this one, offering up a prayer for your finances in the morning and in the evening. It is our hope that, through adopting a Nehemiah mentality, you can move forward in the financial vision that God has for you!

WEEKLY FINANCIAL PRAYER GUIDE

SUNDAY

Giving

> Lord, I thank you for giving the ultimate Gift to me, your Son (John 3:16). Please help me today to be conscious of giving opportunities (II Cor. 8:12-15, Col. 4:3-5), obedient in my tithing (Mal. 3:10), and compassionate for those who are in need (Prov. 19:17).

Wise Decisions

Lord, you are so faithful to give wisdom to me when I ask you for it (James 1:5)! In my decision-making this week, I ask you for the courage to step out (Josh. 1:9), the discernment to weigh the costs involved (II Cor. 9:7, Lk. 14:28), and the commitment to finish what I have started (Col. 4:17, II Cor. 8:11).

MONDAY

Seeking the Kingdom

Lord, today I acknowledge your command to seek first your kingdom and your righteousness (Matt. 6:33). Help me to avoid the lust for greed and money (I Tim. 6:6-11), to be content with what I have (Heb. 13:5), and to live for eternal things (Phil. 3:19-20).

Sowing

Lord, thank you that you have called me to sow cheerfully and generously, expecting a harvest in time (II Cor. 9:6-15). Help me not to grow weary in well-doing (Gal. 6:9), sowing to please the Spirit (Gal. 6:8) with my words (Eph. 4:29), with my time (I Chron. 12:32), and with my money (II Cor. 9:6-15).

TUESDAY

Stewardship

Lord, I am amazed that you have entrusted me with talents and resources that you want me to multiply (Matt. 25:14-30)! I ask you today for help in being diligent with my time (Ps. 90:12), faithful with my responsibilities (Col. 3:23), and both wise and gracious in my communication with others (Col. 4:6, Prov. 22:11).

Self-discipline

Lord, I need your help to be self-disciplined so that, like an athlete in training, I can win the prize (I Cor. 9:24-27)! Help me to know the short-term and long-term financial goals I need to work on (Col. 1:9-10, Phil. 3:13-14). Please grant me the grace to both resist distractions (Prov. 4:25-26, Ecc. 10:16-17) and take time for creative rest (Ps. 23:2-3).

WEDNESDAY

Persevering

I thank you, Jesus, that when troubles come my way, it is an opportunity for joy (James 1:2)! In any financial challenges I am facing, I ask you for help to discern the root of the problems (I Tim. 6:10) while praising you in the midst of them (Job 1:21-22, Ps. 27:5-6). Though life is busy, help me to invest in focused prayers (Phil. 4:6) that will give birth to peace (Phil. 4:7), new direction (Acts 13:2-3), and eventual solutions (II Chron. 20:13-24).

Vision

I give you praise, Lord, that you've called me to reach forward unto those things that are before me (Phil. 3:13-14). Grant me great wisdom to lay hold of renewed financial vision for my life (Col. 1:9-10, Neh. 1:4, 2:4-8), resisting the procrastination (Prov. 6:6-11) and distractions (Gal. 5:7-9) that would stand in my way.

THURSDAY

Planning

Lord, thank you that, by the hand of your Spirit, I am able to make wise plans in how to invest my money, time, and resources (Matt. 25:14-30, I Chron 29:3-5 Zech. 4:6). Help me to be wise in my budgeting and to close the doors on unnecessary spending (Prov. 21:20). Enable me to set aside the time to seek out good counsel (Prov. 15:22), making plans that are wise, just, and ordered of You (Prov. 12:5, Jms. 4:15-16).

Savings

Thanks, Lord, for the simple example of the ants who know how to wisely store up for the future (Prov. 6:8). Help me not to spend everything I make (Prov. 21:20), but to wisely discern the amount I need to set aside for future needs, emergencies, commitments, and long-range goals (II. Cor. 8:10-11, Prov. 6:8, 31:21, 27).

FRIDAY

Debt-free

Lord, your ways are higher (Is. 55:8-9)! I ask you to renew my mind with your divine perspective about debt, credit, and borrowing (Prov. 11:15, 22:7, Rom. 13:6-8). Help me to be intentional about paying off my debts (Rom. 13:6-8), and let me be faithful in the little things of life so that you can entrust me with more (Lk. 16:10-12, 19:18-19).

Wise Lifestyle

Thank you, Lord, that you have called me to be a person who is careful and wise (Eph. 5:15). In the way that I live, help me to be resourceful and yet generous (Prov. 21:20, Prov. 11:25), led by your Spirit in both the little choices I make and in my major decisions (Lk. 16:10-12, Jms. 4:15). Let me be known as a person who is full of the Spirit and wisdom (Acts 6:3).

SATURDAY

Watchman

Lord, you have called me to diligently guard the vulnerable areas of my life that are prone to attack (Prov. 4:20-27, Neh. 4:13, I Pet. 3:11). Help me to avoid get-rich schemes (I Tim. 6:9), unwise investments (Lk 14:28-30), hasty purchases (Prov. 14:8), and any deceptions of others (Prov. 9:13-18) that would cause me to stumble and fall. Make me a diligent watchman (Neh. 4:13, Ezek. 22:30) who knows the enemy's schemes in advance (II Cor. 2:11, II Kgs. 6:10), guarding and protecting that which you've entrusted to me.

Investing

Lord, thank you that you've called me to live a life of multiplication and not mere addition (Matt. 13:23, 25:14-30). As I look to you for vision for the future, help me to consider my options for investing (Prov. 21:5, 31:16-24), discerning the proper times (Ps. 90:12, I Chron. 12:32, Ecc. 8:5-6) and sowing with wisdom (Lk 19:13-26).

"I hear, I know. I see, I remember. I do, I understand."

Key Points:

➤ Nehemiah's example   ➤ personal areas of financial vulnerability

➤ praying for the practical   ➤ focused prayer for your finances

1. **Write down** any parts of the chapter that were meaningful to you.

_____

_____

_____

_____

2. **Personal Application:** How can you personally apply these truths in your own life? Write down several long-term goals.

_____

_____

_____

_____

3. **Steps to Action**—Write down one small step you could take to begin immediately applying the truths and principles of this chapter.

_____

_____

_____

_____

4. **Prayer for the Practical**—Write out a prayer to God asking Him for help in making any changes that these goals would require.

_____

_____

_____

_____

Psalm 62:8 "O my people, trust in him at all times.
Pour out your heart to him,
For God is our refuge."

CREATING A SECURE FINANCIAL FRAMEWORK

HOW DO MY DECISION-MAKING SKILLS INFLUENCE MY FINANCES? HOW CAN I GET OUT OF DEBT? HOW CAN I REBUILD MY CREDIT? WHAT IS MY FINANCIAL VISION FOR THE FUTURE? HOW DO MY DAILY HABITS OF TIME MANAGEMENT AND COMMUNICATION AFFECT MY FINANCES?

"If you need wisdom, ask our generous God, and he will give it to you. He will not rebuke you for asking. But when you ask him, be sure that your faith is in God alone. Do not waver, for a person with divided loyalty is as unsettled as a wave of the sea that is blown and tossed by the wind."

JAMES 1:22

JAMES WAS IDENTIFIED BY MOST SCHOLARS AS THE BROTHER OF JESUS;
WRITTEN IN APPROX. A.D. 45.

CHAPTER ELEVEN

THINKING ABOUT YOUR THINKING

This section of the book focuses upon practical steps you must take to create a secure financial framework. It would be foolish to build a house out of fine materials if there was not a secure framework for the home. In section 2 of the book, we discussed the scriptural principles which form the foundation for financial excellence. Next, we will examine four areas which will enable one to securely move forward into financial success, including a) decision-making skills, b) present debt situation, c) financial goals, and d) record-keeping methods. These four areas form a framework which, when aligned with God's Word, will enable one to forward with wisdom and stability.

DECISION-MAKING

Before you even begin to think about financial stability or long-term investment strategies, you must understand the decision-making process, or risk losing what it may have taken you years to accumulate.

Decision-making is an activity that cannot be avoided. It is a process we must engage in every day in order to function effectively as individuals. Making decisions about financial affairs demands conscious attention to one's goals as well as to one's money.

> MAKING DECISIONS ABOUT FINANCIAL AFFAIRS
> DEMANDS CONSCIOUS ATTENTION TO ONE'S
> GOALS AS WELL AS TO ONE'S MONEY.

Although decisions call for some kind of action in order to be completed, not all actions are the result of decisions. For example, when you get up in the morning, you go through a series of activities: you wash your face, brush your teeth, dress, comb your hair and eat breakfast. These actions you perform out of habit.

The same can be said about many expenditures of money. Often, we spend money not as a result of a decision, but as a daily habit or even on just an impulsive purchase.

A decision occurs when a judgment is consciously made after weighing the facts and examining the alternatives and their outcomes. The decision is the choice one makes from a field of alternatives. The decision is complete when it is acted upon—that is, when we do what we have decided to do (or be or obtain or change or begin). Until some action is taken, the decision is not a decision; instead, it is still an idea or notion or unsettled problem in one's mind.

Decisions often must be lived with for some time; many times they have a way of altering lives, even when they are least expected to. Therefore, in order to see how decisions operate, it may be helpful to identify some of their characteristics.

FIVE DISTINCTIVES OF DECISIONS

1. Decisions are interrelated. A decision has a history; that is, it is related to a past and to a future. Something has occurred prior to the decision that related to it and events will occur in the future as a result. Think of a row of dominoes standing on end. When the first domino is knocked over, the entire row falls in orderly succession. Decisions work in a similar way; once a decision is made, it sets in motion a chain reaction of further decisions.

2. Making a choice involves risk. There is no way of knowing for sure how a decision will turn out. Although we may base the decision on all the facts available and obtain the best of advice, there is still the possibility that the results will not be what we anticipated. That's how most of our decisions are made—the outcome cannot always be predicted. The risks involved are often the reasons people find it very difficult to make decisions, particularly big ones.

> A DECISION HAS A HISTORY; THAT IS, IT IS RELATED TO A PAST AND TO A FUTURE.

3. Decisions cause change. Although it is true that some decisions may not involve change, decisions that require the use of resources in order to be carried out call for change.

Decisions often require one to do things differently. If one wants to lose weight, it means a change in eating habits and regular exercise. A change in attitude usually precedes the actual decision.

Often the decision cannot be made until a change in attitude occurs that will permit one to accept the results of the decision. Many people who have stopped smoking will testify to this. The decision to stop had to be preceded by a change in attitude regarding the habit, a change that finally permitted the smoker to say, "Yes, I want to stop."

4. Decisions require commitment. A commitment is a pledge we make to another person or to ourselves. This means that we make an agreement to do something or to take some course of action. It further implies that we will accept the results of what we do as well as the conditions under which we must act. Commitment, therefore, is necessary.

When the whole notion of commitment is related to decision-making, two commitments are involved:

a) the primary commitment to a goal; and

b) the commitment to carry out the decision and accept the results.

Consider first the matter of goals. Without a serious and determined commitment, one often lacks the incentive and courage to make major decisions related to the goal and to follow through on them. Without a serious commitment to one's goal, the drastic attitude and behavior changes which are sometimes needed will hinder you at every turn.

Consider the commitment involved in carrying out a decision and accepting the results. More often than not, a decision, in order to be acted upon, calls for a course of action that requires work of some kind, that alters habits, or that limits the use of certain resources (like your money). In other words, a decision makes demands that require self-discipline. Unless there is a firm commitment to the decision, you might be tempted to throw in the towel—to give up rather than follow through. If you are involved in a self-improvement program, you must accept the pattern of change necessary to achieve your goal; you must be committed to your course of action.

5. Decisions involve cost. The cost of a decision may be measured in terms of money, but not necessarily. The cost may also be measured by what has to be given up as a result of making the decision, sometimes referred to as its opportunity cost. For some people, the cost of the decision to lose weight can be measured in terms of what they can no longer eat. If one needs a second job, the cost may mean less free time for social activities.

With financial decisions, the cost in dollars and cents can be easily recognized. For families, sometimes the children will need dental work and braces. When making the decision to finance the dental work, families face the prospect of having to live on thousands of dollars less over the next 3 or 4 years. Orthodontia is usually worth the cost, however.

For the family hoping to buy their dream house, the decision is more complex and the cost far greater, because it will be felt for many years to come. After all, there is just so much money and, when some of it is used for one thing, there will be less to use for other things. This cost of the financial decision is often overlooked and yet, it is what can make the decision a difficult one to accept and to live with.

THE DECISION-MAKING PROCESS

The decision-making process basically consists of three simple steps.

1. Seek alternative solutions. "There's more than one way to skin a cat" is an old saying that means there's more than one way of doing things. To make a decision with some confidence, it is helpful to look at all the possible ways of solving the problem. Thus, one can better measure the resources against the alternatives and examine more clearly the possible solutions in terms of the particular circumstances.

2. Weigh the alternatives. Information must be gathered about costs and materials in order to make most decisions. The facts and information gathered are necessary so that one can weigh the alternatives. Compare the possible solutions, know what resources would be used in each case and have an understanding of the outcomes of each solution.

All too often, the alternatives cannot be judged very accurately unless more is known about them. It is impossible to decide from among several methods if one does not know what each method involves. Take the matter of financing a car.

The alternatives may include financing through the dealer, borrowing from the credit union or using savings to pay cash for the car. For example, what will it cost to finance the car through the dealer? What will it cost to borrow from the credit union? What will be lost in interest earnings if one uses savings? How does interest lost compare to the charges required to pay for the loan?

Unless the car buyer knows what is involved in each method, it will be difficult to weigh the choices and come to a decision best suited to his or her financial circumstances and at the same time meet personal needs.

3. Make a choice. After studying the alternatives, one is ready to make a choice. The choice is the decision one makes after carefully examining the several possible courses of action. What one chooses will be based on personal goals and the availability of resources.

These three steps which go into the making of most decisions—seeking the alternatives, weighing the alternatives and making a choice—are each important. The decision doesn't solve anything, however, until it is carried out. Now, it becomes a matter of management—managing the resources and activities necessary to put the decision into action.

Having made a decision, one must assume responsibility for it and follow through with it. Even though there may be some risk involved in whatever is chosen, a person must be ready to accept and live with the consequences of a decision.

People often spend time worrying about their choice and wonder if another decision would have been better or more to their liking. Make a habit of not worrying whether you made the right decision. Commit to a choice and accept the result of that choice, right or wrong. To spend time second-guessing your decision only hinders your effectiveness in living with a decision. The mature individual can make decisions and put them into effect without worrying about what might have been.

MEASURING THE EFFICIENCY OF A DECISION

The effectiveness of a decision is measured by whether or not it helps accomplish whatever one sets out to do. If the course of action chosen turns out to impede progress toward a goal, probably that choice will not be made again.

> THE EFFECTIVENESS OF A DECISION IS MEASURED BY WHETHER OR NOT IT HELPS ACCOMPLISH WHATEVER ONE SETS OUT TO DO.

It may be necessary to stop and find out what is hindering the desired outcome. When the course of action requires more money than anticipated, another way may have to be found. Otherwise, the expense incurred may adversely affect other areas of concern.

Financial decisions require specific knowledge and information. Any decision that involves the use of financial resources requires careful thought, particularly a decision that may affect one's life for a long period of time.

To buy Brand A or Brand B is not a very serious problem, since the expenditure probably involves just a few dollars. If the decision is a poor one, the loss will not seriously affect our day-to-day living.

SECRETS FOR SUCCESSFUL DECISION-MAKING

A decision to finance a car, to purchase a home or plan an investment program will have consequences that extend far into the future. Because of the long-range effects of so many of these decisions, you need all the advice and factual help you can get. To help make the best financial family decisions, consider the following tips:

1. **Recall past experience.** One's own experience is not foolproof, but if it is true that experience is the best teacher, then at least you can apply what has been learned and avoid making the same mistakes.

2. **Keep financial records.** Financial records may not provide answers to new problems, but they can shed light on how much money is available to work with.

Even the most elementary records can reveal a great deal about one's financial situation. In considering a venture that requires a financial commitment of some kind, it is necessary to know how it may affect commitments that have already been made. From one's records, it is possible to determine how much income has already been committed, how much is required for daily living expenses and how much will be available for new expenses.

3. **Borrow experience from people you know.** Often our own experiences and our own records do not relate to the financial problem we must solve. For example, if one wants to go about setting up a personal investment program, nothing from past experience may help in this area. Perhaps you are planning to buy your first home. It will be important to find a friend who has already done so and ask them about closet space, traffic areas, kitchen sizes, acquiring a down-payment and working with realtors. Other people's experience may not always suit your needs or situation, but it can suggest some possibilities and serve as a starting point.

4. **Look up specific information.** Investment in real estate, mutual funds or stocks might require several trips to the local public library or to the internet to seek additional information and knowledge. It is this kind of background information and understanding that is essential in choosing a course of action.

5. **Consult professionals and experts.** Sometimes experts are not in the same professional field, but have a lot of personal experience. Other professionals are far from being experts! There finally comes a time when one must consult a professional or an expert, especially when considering financial matters. Specialists in each field can give sound advice. Accountants, for example, are in the business of helping people solve critical and perplexing financial and tax problems. But seek several references before taking the advice of any one professional!

> DECISIONS NEED TO BE REVIEWED.
> THEY SELDOM REMAIN FIXED FOR ALL TIME.

Decisions need to be reviewed. They seldom remain fixed for all time. Just because a problem has been solved once and the solution seems to be functioning as planned does not mean that the problem will never have to be solved later on.

Nothing about life remains static. Things are constantly changing. It is impossible to predict accurately what we will face next week or next year and to forecast what financial problems will confront us five and ten years down the road. To keep up with the changes in our lives, financial decisions as well as a multitude of others must be reviewed regularly. They must be kept in line with one's goals and circumstances.

"I hear, I know. I see, I remember. I do, I understand."

Key Points:

➤ characteristics of decisions   ➤ measuring a decision's effectiveness

➤ the decision-making process   ➤ obtaining counsel and professional advice

1. **Write down** any parts of the chapter that were meaningful to you.

_____

_____

_____

_____

2. **Personal Application:** How can you personally apply these truths in your own life? Write down several long-term goals.

_____

_____

_____

_____

3. **Steps to Action:** Write down one small step you could take to begin immediately applying the truths and principles of this chapter.

_____

_____

_____

_____

4. **Prayer for the Practical:** Write out a prayer to God asking Him for help in making any changes that these goals would require.

_____

_____

_____

_____

Psalm 62:8 "O my people, trust in him at all times.
Pour out your heart to him,
For God is our refuge."

CHAPTER TWELVE

FACING THE DEBT GIANT HEAD-ON

"If you're having difficulty paying those you owe, keep in mind that it's always better to run toward your creditors than away from them. Creditors who've been ignored don't like to negotiate. However, most creditors will respond positively to a written plan that includes how much you owe and a copy of your budget."

—LARRY BURKETT (1939-2003)
AUTHOR, FINANCIAL ANALYST

The stakes were set for a battle of overwhelming odds. Two armies faced each other, positioned on two separate hills. In the valley between, a fierce warrior stood alone, screaming out obscenities to the opposing army. Had he been an ordinary soldier, he might have invited some ready combat. This, however, was no ordinary soldier. Over nine feet tall, this giant of a warrior was outfitted in the sleekest armor. His bronze coat of armor weighed in at 125 pounds, and his iron spearhead, a staggering 15 pounds. Opposing army…meet Goliath.

In fear, all but one warrior stood cowering in the shadows. As Goliath bellowed out his taunts again, this young soldier began running towards this towering giant with surprising speed and agility. Other soldiers saw a giant who was far too big to challenge. Yet, equipped with only a sling-shot and raw courage, this shepherd-boy saw a giant who was too big to ignore. Years in the valley had trained him well, and now he stepped forward to attack what, to him, looked no different than the bears and lions that had threatened his flocks of sheep. With one swift release of his sling, he landed a smooth stone in the unprotected forehead of his opponent. Goliath's twisted snarl of a mouth hung open in shock. With one truly giant thud, he fell to the ground. In seconds, what had once been a huge threat was no longer a threat to the armies of Israel…Goliath was dead.

Facing debt is very much like facing the towering giant described in this Old Testament story. Truly, a perspective is needed which recognizes that debt is a giant which is too big to ignore. Giants are not defeated by accident, however. We must *intentionally run towards* any giants of debt in our lives. How convenient it would be if debt could be killed with one sturdy sling of a stone! Unfortunately, debt is not usually "killed off" in one day. Facing this giant requires the use of many practical stones of wisdom, which we hope to describe in this chapter.

A PLAN FOR BECOMING DEBT FREE

The relative ease of obtaining credit enables consumers to get goods and services when cash is not readily available. It also allows them to buy things on sale, make purchases when prices are low, and pay for items at the same time they are using and enjoying them.

Unfortunately, problems and financial risks occur because consumers and creditors abuse credit. Careless use of credit by consumers can lead to financial difficulty, family problems, repossession of property, garnishment of wages and even bankruptcy.

Options are available to help you manage financial difficulties when bills stack up and you cannot pay them. This section discusses how to spot potential debt problems, how to set up a debt-payment plan, and court provisions for handling credit obligations.

Many people find themselves deep in debt at least once in their lifetime. It is not necessarily brought on by a desire to spend oneself into oblivion, but rather a lack of financial planning. In this section are the steps one can follow to get out of debt. These should help you in fighting the "debt giant."

Avid skiers delight in telling others how exhilarating it is to glide down the slopes. In their mind, there is nothing like it and they can't understand why some of their friends are not as excited about joining them on skiing trips. Skiing into debt is also very exciting. However, the price of escaping from the debt is greater than most people realize. Simply stopping the intake of new debt is not enough. A multi-faceted and financial reverse is necessary.

Look at what must happen in order to work your way out of the debt trap.

- ✓ Stop spending more than you make.
- ✓ Spend considerably less than before.
- ✓ Pay off the old debt.
- ✓ Pay interest on the old debt.

Your journey to financial freedom will be an individual one, with your own circumstances dictating much about your plan. Here are a few steps you can use as a guide to map out your own course. A brief explanation will help you understand its simplicity as well as its usefulness. George Fooshee, Jr. gives the following ten steps to getting out of debt in his book, *You Can Be Financially Free*, published in 1976 by Fleming H. Revell Company. Much in the next several pages has been adapted from what he has written. Here is a quick summary of steps that must be taken.

1. Set a goal.
2. List all you owe and all you own.
3. Have a sale of unneeded or unused assets.
4. Fix a monthly debt-payment amount.
5. Do not add new debts.

6. Establish a time goal.

7. Cut the goal in half.

8. Develop a repayment schedule.

9. Share the repayment schedule with your creditors.

10. Stick to your plan.

Examine Your Spending Behavior

One way to save cash is by not eating lunch out every day. Not only will you save substantially, you will also avoid using the credit card to run up more debt that you do not have the cash for. This chart shows the weekly and annual cost of your lunches.and the various combinations of eating out compared to making and bringing your own lunch. The dollar figure we have used for eating out is $7.00 per meal. It is fairly difficult to eat lunch anywhere for less, especially if you add the cost of a drink to the meal. Making and bringing your own lunch is much cheaper. We have used a dollar figure of $1.00 per meal.

NUMBER OF DAYS EATING OUT FOR LUNCH	NUMBER OF DAYS MAKING YOUR LUNCH	TOTAL LUNCH EXPENSE	ANNUAL LUNCH EXPENSE
5 days per week	0 days per week	$35.00	$1,750.00
4 days per week	1 day per week	$29.00	$1,450.00
3 days per week	2 days per week	$23.00	$1,150.00
2 days per week	3 days per week	$17.00	$ 850.00
1 day per week	4 days per week	$11.00	$ 550.00
0 days per week	5 days per week	$ 5.00	$ 250.00

No New Debts!

You must decide once and for all not to take on new debt and not to become a slave to your old habits. This is very important! You must decide not to borrow new money for any reason or purchase additional merchandise on credit. This would be an excellent time to have a credit-card-destruction ceremony in your home. Gather your family together, take a large pair of scissors and deliberately cut each credit card into tiny pieces.

Make a list of all charge accounts. Call or write each store and tell them to close your account. You cannot work your way out of debt if you continue to borrow for new purchases. The key to your success in avoiding new debt will be to do without. You will be amazed at all of the so-called necessities you will find that you don't need.

Manage Your Debt Obligations

If you find yourself with more bills than your monthly income can cover, one alternative is to develop a debt-management plan. Completing this plan takes patience, but it works if you really want to get out of debt. Much of the next several pages are adapted from Getting Out of Debt, How Others Can Help You Get Out of Debt and the Mississippi and Virginia Cooperative Extension. To set up a debt-management plan, follow these steps:

- ✓ Find out how much you owe and to whom.

- ✓ Decide how much you can pay back and when.

- ✓ Set up a plan for paying back your debts.

- ✓ Discuss your plan with your creditors.

- ✓ Control spending by sticking with your debt-payment plan until debts are repaid.

Occasionally look over your plan to see if you are keeping up with your debts and your daily living expenses. If there is a change in your income, you may need to raise or lower your monthly payments accordingly.

Find out to whom you owe. The first step in getting out of debt is to find out to whom you owe and how much you owe. Using your credit statements as a reference, list the following information about each debt.

- Name of creditor.

- Creditor's address.

- Creditor's telephone number.

- Your account number.

- Collateral (property or any other asset that secures a debt).

- Balance owed.

- Remaining number of payments.

- Monthly payment.

- Payment due date.

- Amount last paid.

- Date last paid.

- Type of legal action taken (e.g., garnishment or repossession).

- Collection agency or attorney.

Organize a payment schedule. Writing down your plan will help you to achieve it. Use notebook paper and allow enough space to include the number of months to fulfill your plan. With each creditor, list the payment which is planned, the amount paid and the new balance due after the payment is made.

Do this with each creditor for each month a payment is due, until the debt with that particular creditor is erased. Recording your payments will give you a sense of achievement and satisfaction. Watching the balances diminish will give you an excitement that will help you stick to your goal.

Decide how much you can pay. Once you have listed everyone you owe, determine how much you can pay each creditor and how long it will take to pay back each debt.

Generally, it is good to limit the amount of credit you owe (excluding your home mortgage) to no more than 10 percent of your monthly take-home pay.

If your family has $2,200 a month after taxes and tithe, try to keep your credit payments under $220 per month ($2,200 x 0.10 = $220). But if you already have numerous debts, figure out a way to use 25 percent of your monthly take-home pay for paying back your monthly debts. You usually need 75 percent of your income to maintain your necessary daily living expenses.

A family earning \$2,200 a month probably needs to keep \$1,650 (\$2,200 X 0.75 = \$1,650) for basic living expenses. That leaves \$ (\$2,200 X 0.25 = \$550) for debt repayment.

If the minimum monthly payments add up to \$696, for example, you must find ways to increase the money available for debt repayment.

Three Methods for Paying Back Your Debts

By now, you should have a clear picture of how much money you can manage to pay back and when you will be able to pay it back. The next step is to decide how much you will pay each creditor and how long it will take to pay off each creditor. Try to set up your plan so you pay your creditors back within three years.

The debt payment plan can be done in several ways.

1. You may choose to give each creditor an equal amount.

2. You may choose to pay a larger portion to the creditors owed the most money—a smaller amount to those you owe the least.

3. You could choose to pay back a percentage of the total monthly obligation based on the amount of money available for debt payments.

Below are examples using each of the three methods of debt repayment. Each is based on a situation in which the consumer has only \$300 each month to repay debts.

Alternative A

Pay each creditor equal amounts.

DEBTS	AMOUNT OWED	AMOUNT REQUIRED	AMOUNT CAN PAY
Auto Loan	\$1,145.39	\$180	\$60
Visa	680.30	35	60
Debt #1	525.00	170	60
Debt #2	755.00	190	60
Debt #3	275.00	25	60
	\$3,380.69	\$600	\$300

The amount available from monthly income for debt repayment is \$300. The consumer pays each creditor an equal amount: \$300 / 5 = \$60 per month.

Alternative B

Pay the percentage of total debt represented by each individual debt.

DEBTS	AMOUNT OWED	% OF TOTAL DEBT OWED	AMOUNT REQUIRED	AMOUNT CAN PAY
Auto Loan	$1,145.39	34%	$180	$102
Visa	680.30	20%	35	60
Debt #1	525.00	16%	170	48
Debt #2	755.00	22%	190	66
Debt #3	275.00	8%	25	24
	$3,380.69	100%	$600	$300

To determine the percentage of debt owed, make the following calculation: Amount Owed / Total Debt = percentage of total debt owed. Example: Debt #1 / Total Debt = $1,145.39 / $3,380.69 = 0.34 or 34 percent. To determine the amount the consumer can pay, make this calculation: (Total amount can pay) X (Percentage of total debt owed) = Amount can pay Example: $300 X .34 = $102

Alternative C

Pay a percentage of the total monthly obligation based on the amount of money available for debt payments.

DEBTS	AMOUNT OWED	AMOUNT REQUIRED	AMOUNT CAN PAY
Auto Loan	$1,145.39	$180 x .50	$90.00
Visa	680.30	35 x .50	17.50
Debt #1	525.00	170 x .50	85.00
Debt #2	755.00	190 x .50	95.00
Debt #3	275.00	25 x .50	12.50
	$3,380.69	$600.00	$300.00

Itemize and Prioritize

It is important to pay back all of the debts you owe. However, if there is not enough money to make payments on all of your loans, consider prioritizing your debts. Debts you may want to pay first include mortgage or rent, utilities, secured loans and insurance.

Second priorities may include credit cards and unsecured debts to finance companies. Some examples of third priorities are doctor, dentist and hospital bills. Family members and friends usually are willing to wait.

Set up your debt-payment plan. Write the creditor's name in the first column. Figure the percentage of total debt owed each creditor and write it in the second column.

Write the amount of the original monthly payment in the next column. Decide if you will pay the debtors in equal amounts (Method A), by proportions (Method B or C) or according to what action the creditor might take (such as garnishment or repossession).

Write the dollar amount you can pay each creditor each month in the fourth column. If the creditor accepts your plan, write the actual amount you will pay each creditor in the appropriate monthly columns.

Shrink Your Time Target

Write down the number of months that it will take to become debt-free, based on your initial plan. Now cut the goal in half. This will shock you, but just do it—cut the goal in half. If you have determined that it will take you four years, 48 months, to get out of debt, then write down a figure of half that time. You may think it's crazy, but here is a formula for cutting your debt repayment in half.

George Fooshee, Jr. gives this illustration in his book, *You Can Be Financially Free* (Fleming H. Revell Company, 1976). Assume you have set aside $111.23 monthly to repay your debt of $5,000 with an interest rate of 12 percent. It will take you five years of monthly payments to pay off this debt. In order to cut your time schedule in half, it would take a monthly payment of $193.75 for just 2 1/2 years.

Total cost to you, including all debt repayment and interest charges over a 30-month period would be $5,812.50. Taking five years (60 months) to pay the same $5,000 back at $111.23 a month would cost you a total of $6,673.80. That's $861.30 more in interest and that should give you sufficient incentive to look hard at this plan.

Here's how it works. Subtract the $111.23 monthly payment from the $193.75. Your additional monthly cost to pay off your debt in half the time is not twice the $111.23, but only $82.52. The only way to save money while paying off debts is to pay them off faster. The faster you pay, the less it costs.

"But," you ask, "how can we come up with $82.52 a month above our payment of $111.23? Haven't we cut our budget to the bone? Perhaps so. The solution to your problem will depend totally upon the creativity of your family.

What is the objective? In this case it is to cut your debt repayment time in half. Expressing this goal in positive terms would be to say that you are going to get out of debt twice as fast as you had planned. Certainly to do that you do not have to double your income or cut your expenses in half. In the illustration, you only need $82.52 more each month to pay on your debt.

One idea is to find a family in your neighborhood who wants their house cleaned and who would be willing to pay your family to do the job at a family hourly rate. Investing every Saturday to cut your debt-repayment time in half would be a worthwhile family project.

Weekend part-time work is another alternative to earning extra money. Keep your eyes open for lawns that need mowing or shrubs that need trimming, right in your own neighborhood. You'll be surprised how much you're worth if you're willing to invest a few hours a week. Imaginative ways to earn extra money are limited only by a lack of creativity and desire.

Another way to hasten your escape from debt is to agree in advance to add any extra income to debt repayment. This would include raises, bonuses, tax refunds, garage sale income, or any other extra income that comes into your family.

Stay Focused on the Plan

You may be tempted again and again to quit. Don't do it! Each missed payment will set you back in reaching your goal. Starting something is easier than finishing. More start the race than finish it. Life is littered with dropouts who quit when the going gets rough. Tough people are determined not to quit until they reach their goal. Escaping debt will require persistence. Some new attitudes about your way of living will be essential, but you can do it!

THE IMPORTANCE OF
COMMUNICATING WITH CREDITORS

In an article discussing debt and creditors, the late financial analyst Larry Burkett made the following statement: "If you're having difficulty paying those you owe, keep in mind that it's always better to run toward your creditors than away from them. Creditors who've been ignored don't like to negotiate. However, most creditors will respond positively to a written plan that includes how much you owe and a copy of your budget."[13]

They will be very impressed with the fact that you have made out a plan. They will be even more impressed as you send them the regular monthly payments you have promised. Also, tell them that if something happens to delay one of your payments, you will contact them ahead of the date when the payment is due.

Now that you have worked out a plan, make sure to minimize the use of your credit cards! Do not take out any more loans except in extreme emergencies and contact each creditor and explain your plan.

Creditors will generally be more responsive to your proposal if you take the initiative to contact them first and express a sincere desire to pay your obligations. If you cannot visit your creditor, call or write a letter. In your letter, be sure to include the following:

- Why you fell behind in your payments (such as loss of job, illness, divorce, death in the family or poor money-management skills)

- Your current income

- Your other obligations

- How you plan to bring this debt up-to-date and keep it current

- The exact amount you will be able to pay back each month

Once the creditor has agreed to your repayment plan, make every effort to uphold your end of the bargain. If you fail to follow the plan you and your creditors have agreed upon, you harm your chances of getting future credit. Tell your creditor about any changes that may affect your payment agreement.

Learn about debt-collection laws. If debt collectors are hounding you, you can do something about it. The Fair Debt Collection Practices Act, passed by Congress in 1977, prohibits certain methods of debt collection. Also, you could report your problem to your state attorney general's office. Many states have their own debt collection laws and the attorney general can help define your rights.

Remember that nothing positive will happen with your financial problems until you start taking charge of your debts.

BUILD A DISBURSEMENT STRATEGY

The following tips can help you get started in creating a plan to monitor your spending:

Determine your net worth. Calculate your net worth by subtracting your liabilities (credit card balances, auto loans and mortgages) from your assets (savings, investments and property). Early in the year is an excellent time to do this. Then you should review and update your net worth worksheet about twice a year.

Track your cash flow. Use a small notebook to record the amount and category (food, clothing, etc.) of each purchase no matter how small. Include check and credit card purchases also. Do this every day for 3 months. Total each category at the end of the month. The information will be used to help you adjust your spending.

Evaluate your monthly income sources. Record any money that you've earned (paycheck, bonuses, freelance income, tips, etc.) or received from investments. Savings and investments should not be considered as money available to spend.

Record your monthly expenses. Fixed expenses are mortgage or rent payments, auto and educational loans, and insurance. Variable expenses are utility bills, clothing, transportation, entertainment and dining.

Put it all together. Subtract your total expenses from your total income.

Keep a written account of your progress. Set financial goals. This will help increase your savings and give you peace of mind and less stress over money issues.

List all you owe first. It may be difficult to believe, but most people don't have a good grasp of what they owe. A listing of all your debts, with the monthly payment required and the annual percentage rate of interest, can be most helpful. A financial spreadsheet, like in Excel, works well for this task.

Create a payoff plan. This might be very difficult, but you will have to get this amount out of your monthly income. Divide this figure into the total amount you owe to arrive at the number of months it will take you to be debt-free. Interest will add to the time schedule, but the answer you get gives you the approximate amount of time for your debt-repayment plan. These options may help you repay debts on a monthly basis.

Assess the damage. Make a complete list of all your credit cards and loans (auto, mortgage, student loans, etc.). Include how much you owe, the monthly payment and the interest rate. If you don't receive a monthly statement for a particular loan, call the lender for all of the information.

Pay the most expensive loan first. Make the minimum monthly payments on all your debts except the one with the highest interest rate. Put as much money as you can toward this debt each month, until it is paid off. Then apply the payments you were making on that debt toward the loan with the next highest interest rate and so on. Note: Pay credit card bills promptly to reduce the average daily balance on which you're charged.

Transfer your debts to a low-interest rate credit card. The higher the interest rate, the more money the loan is costing you. Find a card with a low interest rate and then contact that credit card company to arrange transfer of your other debts to this card.

Cut up the high-rate cards you've paid off so you won't use them again. Also, call or write these credit card companies to cancel the cards. Otherwise you might continue to receive new cards as the old ones expire.

Have a yard sale. What do you own? Which items can you do without? Most people have no idea of what they can do without until they try. Don't think of how much you will lose of what you paid for the item you are selling. Think of how much you will gain which can be immediately applied to your debt reduction. Your attitude about this will determine your success in working your way out of debt.

Keep a record of your current living expenses for a month. Look for ways to reduce your expenses so you can use the extra money to clear up debts.

Consider selling assets. What assets do you own? Do you have a savings account or stocks and bonds you could cash in to help pay off your debts? Do you have a television, furniture, stereo, car, jewelry or antiques? Could you cash in or borrow against the cash value of your insurance policy?

Increase your family income. An extra paycheck will help maintain your present lifestyle while you pay back your debts. However, additional money does NOT cure poor management habits.

- ✓ Get a second part-time job.

- ✓ Work all available overtime.

- ✓ Take in a boarder or a roommate.

- ✓ Sell assets (toys, unused household items, extra vehicles, boats, property).

- ✓ Ask for a raise.

- ✓ Attend school part-time to gain new job skills.

- ✓ Take on family jobs in the neighborhood.

Borrow money as a last resort. Loan consolidation, home equity loans or refinancing your home are ways to avoid repossession or loss of income through wage garnishment. These options may reduce the amount of your monthly payment. However, the cost for borrowing is usually increased, because the borrowing time is extended and you may be borrowing at a higher interest rate. If you can manage to pay your debts without loan consolidation, home equity loans or refinancing, you probably will save yourself extra expense.

The use of these options generally does not improve poor money management habits and the reduced monthly payment may encourage you to acquire more debts.

DEBT-FREE: A CHANGE IN THINKING

Go Against the Flow

In order to get out of debt, you have to stop charging and start taking charge of your spending habits. If you use credit cards without paying the balance monthly, owe money on a loan or are paying off a home mortgage, you're a debtor. Most Americans are in debt; if you're not, some might think you're downright unpatriotic.

Many economists believe that indebtedness keeps our country financially on the move. When was the last time you saw a bank ad encouraging you to save? The theme of our consumer-driven economy is borrow and spend. It's not popular to suggest becoming debt free. However, freedom from debt speaks for itself; in a word, it is freedom.

Although not a popular theme and despite the fact that some think they're in debt so deep that they can't ever get out, becoming debt-free is a worthy, realistic and attainable goal. Getting rid of your debt isn't always easy. However, the process is actually very simple. Allow no more debt! That means no bank or family loans and tearing up the credit cards.

Develop a balanced budget that allows each creditor to receive as much as possible. Start retiring the debt now. Begin with high interest debts first. If they're all high-interest, pay the smallest balance first. Once it's paid off, put all the available money on the next and so on. Most families can be debt free in three or four years.

> LIKE BOOT CAMP, BECOMING DEBT-FREE IS NOT THE END; RATHER IT'S THE BEGINNING OF A WHOLE NEW ADVENTURE.

Be Disciplined and Determined

When your debts are high and your monthly income is not enough to cover the payments, there are ways to solve your debt problem. However, the road to financial recovery takes a total commitment.

You must decide that you want to be debt-free. You have to discipline yourself to take the necessary action to pay back your debts. Only you can determine if you are willing to make the necessary sacrifices to achieve this goal.

Getting out of debt is like getting through boot camp. It's a lot of hard work and some days you want to quit. But when graduation day arrives, memories of pain and trouble pale in the light of the pride and accomplishment you feel. You made it! You didn't quit.

Like boot camp, becoming debt-free is not the end; rather it's the beginning of a whole new adventure. To drop out at graduation and go back to your old way of living would be to turn your back on everything for which you have been preparing. It would be to close the door on your dreams of financial freedom. It would diminish the importance of what you accomplished. Who would be so foolish as to do the difficult work and then not stick around to enjoy the reward?

Realize that Debt-free is Only the Beginning

The simple truth is that getting out of debt is only the first step. That is how you get to the starting point. Staying out of debt and moving forward to financial independence is the bigger challenge. And that's where the big rewards await.

What does a debt-free life look like?

Here's a mental picture for you:

- You give.
- You save.
- You spend less than you earn.
- You invest confidently and consistently.
- Your financial decisions are purposeful.
- You turn away from impulsive behavior.
- You shun unsecured debt.
- You borrow cautiously.
- You anticipate the unexpected.
- You scrutinize your purchases.
- You reach for your goals by following a specific plan.

People who have become disciplined and paid off their existing debt have made it to the starting line. Do they continue to progress or did they mistake the starting line for the finish line? How many of them grabbed the prize and went back to their old ways of living and thinking?

Many people have repaid a boatload of debt, only to fall back into the temptation and the old ways of piling up debt. How can we encourage people not to stop, but move on to the next level and beyond? Is it possible to win over debt for a lifetime?

You have to get to the starting line, establish your long-term goal of reaching financial freedom, define that goal in terms of steps, and then change gears from debt-recovery to debt-prevention. Think specifically, not generally, about how you're going to get there and then rejoice because each step from now on will be one of progress, not repair.

In reality, you may not have a clue what you believe about money and its role in your life. Or you might firmly believe things that are not true. No matter what you've done or believed in the past about money and how to take care of it, now is the time to tie yourself to a foundation that will not change, one that will withstand the storms of life.

ABC Philosophies of Debt Management

A. Some people get out of debt and, after doing so, they toss aside the principles that served them so well in getting out of debt. They handled debt-recovery very well, but failed to kick into debt-prevention mode. They got to the starting line and then they quit.

In this whole matter of personal money management, there are three basic management styles or ways of life. First are those people who needlessly carry heavy financial loads. They carry credit card balances from one month to the next. They owe far more than they can pay and spend more than they earn—forever juggling and trying to keep their heads above water. They are every consumer credit marketing department's dream customer, because they fit a predictable profile and contribute to the huge profit margins of the credit card companies.

B. The next group live paycheck to paycheck and spend every dime possible flirting with credit cards, debit cards and ATM cards, because it is so much fun living on the edge.

C. The last group is always the smallest. They fight to maintain their financial freedom by restraining themselves. They embrace the debt-free lifestyle in that they do not live on credit nor do they mess around with credit cards. They live according to a specific plan. What they do with their money is by design. They expect the unexpected, they are prepared, and they live with exuberance—they smile at the future.

Which person are you? You may be the person who goes the wrong way on a one-way escalator carrying a heavy load. You can't even see where you are going, stuck on a treadmill living from paycheck to paycheck.

Or, with persistence, you can choose to travel on a moving sidewalk that will take you where you want to go in your financial life. We encourage you to make a decision right now to build a strong financial foundation.

If you will build a foundation based upon debt-free living principles, it will stand up under all kinds of circumstances. When the financial challenges come and, of course, they always do, your foundation will hold and you will come through unharmed.

Living without debt is about generosity, gratitude and obedience. It is about sound choices and effective decisions. To get your finances in order means knowing exactly what to do with your money and having the freedom to earn and spend it when and how you choose. Financial freedom is a way of life, a financially disciplined lifestyle that exchanges stress and bondage for a life of peace and joy.

THE LAW ON DEBT

The Federal Bankruptcy Code provides consumers with two forms of debtor relief. Chapter 7 of the code is the straight bankruptcy provision and provides for liquidation (conversion into cash) of the debtor's assets.

With bankruptcy under Chapter 7, you give up the property you put up for collateral when using credit, unless the debts are reaffirmed by court permission and you continue to pay the creditor.

Chapter 13 is the wage-earner's plan. With Chapter 13, you promise to pay existing debts with part of the income you will earn in the next few years. While paying the debts, you will be able to keep the things you bought on credit if your plan is approved by the courts.

Chapter 7 Bankruptcy

Chapter 7 allows a person overburdened with debts to make a fresh start by discharging most of the claims against him or her.

The granting of a discharge after the filing of a bankruptcy petition in federal court releases or discharges you from the legal responsibility of your debts once the petition is approved. Once the petition is filed, garnishments and lawsuits can be stopped if proper papers are filed with the court; you are protected by the automatic stay provision of the bankruptcy code.

Your attorney will file the petition with the clerk of the United States Bankruptcy Court in the area in which you have been living for the past six months. A filing fee must be paid to file. This fee is in addition to fees charged by your attorney for his or her services. You must file a list of all your debts and creditors.

A detailed list of all property you own, money owed you, insurance policies owned, and property that may be inherited within six months also must be filed. You must also file a detailed statement of your financial affairs.

Once the bankruptcy petition has been filed, a trustee will be appointed by the court. The trustee presides over the first meeting of creditors in the bankruptcy proceeding. The trustee liquidates certain non-exempted assets and non-reaffirmed debts and these proceeds are distributed to your creditors.

All your listed creditors are notified and given the option to attend a meeting, at which you will be present, to file claims on the debts you owe them. The court-appointed trustee takes administrative control of your property that is to be sold and delivers property to the secured creditors. Once property has been sold, administrative costs are paid and the remaining cash is paid proportionately to all creditors.

The bankruptcy court holds a hearing to inform you that your debts have been discharged or gives you a reason they were not discharged. You may reaffirm certain debts with the court's approval if you desire to keep the collateral and if it is in your best interest.

For instance, if you wish to keep your car, you can reaffirm the debt and continue to make payments. You do not have to reaffirm the debt; however, if you do, you become legally liable for the reaffirmed debt. The bankruptcy process takes a number of months from date of filing until date of discharge.

Bankruptcy claims may be voluntary or involuntary; most are voluntary. The only requirement for filing is that the debtor owe one or more debts.

The following debts cannot be eliminated in bankruptcy:

- State and federal taxes owed within the past two years before filing bankruptcy

- Money or items received by fraud or false pretenses

- Unlisted debts, unless creditor had knowledge of bankruptcy filing

- Child support or alimony

- Debts incurred by embezzlement, fraud or larceny

- Willful or malicious injury to another person or person's property by the debtor

- Government-imposed fines or penalties, such as tax penalties

- Student loans guaranteed by the government or a non-profit educational institution (unless paying back the loan causes undue hardship on the debtor or the debtor's dependents or if the loan came due 5 years before filing for bankruptcy)

Chapter 7 can only be declared every six years. However, if you get into financial trouble before the end of six years, you can file Chapter 13.

Chapter 13 Wage-Earner's Plan

Chapter 13, or the wage-earner's plan, is a voluntary repayment plan. When you complete the plan, you have the satisfaction of keeping your assets, paying your creditors and discharging your debts.

When filing Chapter 13, you agree to pay approximately 25 percent of your income to the court. The court appoints a trustee to handle your money and pay your debts. The trustee also provides advice and counsel when necessary.

To file Chapter 13, first contact an attorney who has experience in filing Chapter 13 petitions.

The attorney then files the petition with the federal court. A court-appointed trustee is responsible for reviewing the petition, confirming the petition, paying the debts and advising and counseling the debtor. After that, the court clerk sends notice of court action to creditors and the employer.

The employer sends a portion of your paycheck to the court trustee, who pays creditors. Secured debts are paid first, followed by unsecured debts. The debtor cannot borrow more money without approval of the court trustee.

The actual amount of money that is paid to creditors depends on the amount owed, the debtor's salary and the payback timeframe. Chapter 13 payment plans may not be proposed for longer than 36 months, unless you can show reason for extending the plan. The maximum time allowed is five years.

Administrative costs may be high. They include the court costs, filing fee, the attorney's fee and the trustee's fee for paying off the debts. The trustee also may receive a fee for expenses such as a computer and supplies.

Take time for a Reward!

After you have tackled your debts head-on and paid them off, make sure you take time to reward yourself! Here are five low-cost ways to treat yourself:

Grab a mocha from your favorite coffee shop, find a bench where there are lots of passers-by and watch people.

Rent a DVD and enjoy a quality movie!

Take a long, hot bath.

Turn off your cell phone for an hour and take a nap.

Write "PAID IN FULL" across the original loan or credit card document and put it in a simple frame. Display it in your home office or the area where you usually sit down to pay your bills.

The greatest reward, of course, is a good night's sleep—knowing your debts are paid!

"I hear, I know. I see, I remember. I do, I understand."

Key Points:

➤ analyzing your debt situation

➤ practical tips to help you get out of debt

➤ payment plan suggestions

➤ bankruptcy issues

1. **Write down** any parts of the chapter that were meaningful to you.

_____

_____

_____

_____

2. **Personal Application:** How can you personally apply these truths in your own life? Write down several long-term goals.

_____

_____

_____

_____

3. **Steps to Action:** Write down one small step you could take to begin immediately applying the truths and principles of this chapter.

_____

_____

_____

_____

4. **Prayer for the Practical:** Write out a prayer to God asking Him for help in making any changes that these goals would require.

_____

_____

_____

_____

Psalm 62:8 "O my people, trust in him at all times.
Pour out your heart to him,
For God is our refuge."

"I know many people are feeling increased financial stress in these economic times. For some, it's easier to duck their head and continue treading water than face their situation head on. Many people wait…for credit counseling until their backs are against the wall and they realize that they have no choice but to deal with the situation. Whether it's due to job loss, illness or simply poor choices, a little planning and awareness of your own situation really can make all the difference."

—Mike Sullivan
Director of Education for Take Charge America

IMPROVING YOUR CREDIT TO IMPROVE YOUR LIFE

Credit reports are compiled by credit bureaus, often called National Credit Repositories—private, for-profit companies that gather information about your credit history and sell it to banks, mortgage lenders, credit unions, credit card companies, department stores, insurance companies, landlords and even a few employers.

To create a credit file for a given person, a credit bureau searches its computer files until it finds entries that match the name, Social Security number and any other available identifying information. All matches are gathered together to make the report.

WHAT'S IN A CREDIT REPORT?

To understand the credit process, you first need to understand what information is contained in a credit report. Although the style, format and coding may be different depending on which credit reporting bureau is used, the typical consumer's credit report includes the following four types of information:

Identifying Information—includes your name, nicknames, current and previous addresses, Social Security number, date of birth, current and previous employers and/or spouses. This information comes from any credit application you have completed and its accuracy depends on your filling out forms clearly, completely and consistently each time you apply for credit.

Credit Information—includes specific information about each account including the date opened, credit limit or loan amount, balance, monthly payment and payment pattern during the past several years. The report will show if an account has been turned over to a collection agency or is in dispute. The report also states whether anyone else besides you (i.e. a spouse or cosigner) is responsible for paying the account. This information comes from companies that do business with you.

Public Record Information—includes federal district bankruptcy records, state and county court records, tax liens and monetary judgments and, in some states, overdue child support payments. This information comes from public records.

Inquiries—includes the names of those who have obtained a copy of your credit report for any reason. This information comes from the credit reporting agency and it remains available for as long as two years according to U.S. federal law.

HOW THEY USE WHAT THEY KNOW

A credit bureau score is one type of credit score. It is calculated from the information on your credit bureau file at the time that the information was requested. Consequently, a credit score is like a snapshot. It sums up, at one given point in time, what your past and current credit usage says about your future credit performance.

Credit scoring helps lenders apply one set of rules to everybody. The sophistication of today's models allows for certain behavior patterns. As a result, a 20-year-old's credit history would not be compared to a 45-year-old's credit history. One reason these scoring models are so widely used is because they can differentiate between the credit patterns of individuals.

Current Data Predicts Future Credit Performance
Scoring models and other tools analyze data only, using it to predict future credit performance.

A scoring model contains a list of questions and answers, with points given for each answer. Information proven to be predictive of future credit performance is used in the model.

Here are a few examples of what a typical model will consider:

- Information from your credit application

- How long you've lived at your address

- Your job or profession

- How much you owe

It will also consider information pulled from your credit bureau report, such as the number of late payments, the amount of outstanding credit, the amount of credit being used, the amount of time credit has been established. Credit scoring systems do not consider race, religion, gender, marital status, birthplace or current address.

YOUR CREDIT SCORE

A credit score is intended to be a snapshot or summary of your credit history. It is produced with a computer model created most often by Fair, Isaac & Co. (or FICO) leading to the somewhat generic term "FICO score." A low score can mean you won't get a credit card or loan or that, if you do, you will pay a higher interest rate. Some lenders use what is called risk-based pricing at the point of origination, which means that the lender instantly approves or denies your application using your credit score and other information to set the price for your loan.

While we don't know exactly how a credit score is determined, we do know that the following items are always considered important:

Payment History (35%)

Your score is negatively affected if you have paid bills late, had an account sent to collection or declared bankruptcy. If you charge up that already outstanding card, they figure that you may not have enough money to pay their bills. The more recent the problem, the lower your score—a 30-days late payment today hurts more than a bankruptcy five years ago.

Outstanding Debt (30%)

If the amount you owe is close to your credit limit, it is likely to have a negative effect on your score. A low balance on two cards is better than a high balance on one.

Length of Your Credit History (15%)

The longer your accounts have been open the better.

Types of Credit in Use (10%)

Loans from finance companies generally lower your credit score.

Recent Inquiries (10%)

If you have recently applied for many new accounts, this will negatively affect your score. Among the items not considered are age, race, gender, education, national origin, marital status and receipt of public assistance.

The Range of Scores

Credit scores range from 400 to 900, with the average around 700. According to the model, as your score increases, your risk of default decreases.

Industry experience shows a direct correlation between low scores and high default rates. This means that you may have a hard time convincing a creditor to make you an affordable loan (or any loan at all) if your score is far below average.

But just as your credit history can vary from credit bureau to credit bureau, so can your credit scores. It is possible to have a high score with one credit bureau and a low credit score with another, just as you might have a clean credit history with one bureau and a muddied record with another.

Wide-ranging credit scores are rare, although some lenders admit to seeing borrowers with scores that vary by 100 points or more. To combat this, a lender usually uses the middle score, but that can be of little comfort if you have scores of 550, 570 and 700 and the interest rate for a borrower with a score of 570 is two points higher than the rate for a borrower who scores 700. Narrow ranges are more typical. For example, a person with good credit might have scores something like 685, 702 and 710.

Creditors are not required to tell you your credit score, nor does your credit report show your score.

GETTING YOUR PERSONAL COPY

Your credit can determine what type of car you drive, what you can buy and even where you can live. It is important to maintain the best credit report possible. Each consumer should check his or her credit report and make sure it is correct. It makes sense to check it about once a year or three to four months prior to the time you know you'll be applying for a major loan, which will give you time to clean it up.

With recent changes, the consumer in all 52 states is now able to receive his / her own credit report one time each year at absolutely no cost. You can request this report online, by telephone, or by mail. Your request can be directed to either of the three reporting agencies—Equifax, Trans Union and Experian. The federal Fair Credit Reporting Act (FCRA) entitles everyone to a copy of your credit report. You can also get one for free if:

✓ You've been denied credit because of information in your credit report and you request a copy within 60 days of being denied credit. If you have been denied credit, you should have received a written notice of this with instructions that you can follow for requesting your credit report.

✓ You're unemployed and looking for work.

✓ You receive public assistance.

✓ You believe your file contains errors due to fraud.

If none of these apply, a report will cost you up to $15 each.

You Will Need to Provide the Following Information:

1. Your full name (including generations such as Jr., Sr., III)

2. Your birth date

3. Your Social Security number

4. Your spouse's name (if applicable)

5. Your telephone number

6. Your current address and addresses for the previous five years

MISTAKES IN YOUR CREDIT REPORT

What should you do if you find mistakes in your credit report? As you read through your report, make a list of everything out-of-date. These may include such things as lawsuits, paid tax liens, accounts sent out for collection, criminal records, late payments and any other adverse information older than seven years.

Credit bureaus often list Chapter 13 bankruptcies for only seven years, but they can stay for ten. Credit inquiries (requests by companies for a copy of your report) remain on your credit report for up to two years.

Next, look for incorrect or misleading information, such as:

✓ incorrect or incomplete name, address, phone number, Social Security number or employment information

✓ bankruptcies not identified by their specific chapter number

✓ accounts that are not yours or lawsuits in which you were not involved

✓ incorrect account histories, such as late payments when you paid on time

✓ closed accounts that are listed as open–It may look as if you have too much open credit. Any account that you have closed should say, "closed by consumer."

✓ mistakes made not by you but by your bank or creditors

✓ any companies that have been looking into your report without your permission

After reviewing your report, immediately complete the "request for reinvestigation" form that the credit bureau sent you or send a letter listing each incorrect item and explain exactly what is wrong.

Once the credit bureau receives your request, it must complete an investigation of your disputed items within 30 days and provide you written notice of the results of the investigation within five days of its completion, including a copy of your credit report if it has changed based upon the dispute. If you don't hear back within this time, send a follow-up letter. If you let them know that you're trying to obtain a mortgage or car loan, they can do a rush investigation.

If you are right or if the creditor who provided the information can no longer verify it, the credit bureau must remove the information from your report. Often credit bureaus will remove an item on request without an investigation if rechecking the item is more bother than it's worth.

Once you've found a mistake on one credit bureau's report, you'll need to request the other two and repeat the process to make sure they're all in sync.

If you don't get anywhere with the credit bureau, directly contact the creditor and ask that the information be removed. Write to the customer service department, vice president of marketing and president or CEO. If the information was reported by a collection agency, send the agency a copy of your letter, too. Creditors are forbidden by law to report information that they know is incorrect.

If you feel a credit bureau is wrongfully including information in your report or you want to explain a particular entry, you have the right to put a 100-word statement in your report. Be clear and concise; use the fewest words possible. The credit bureau must give a copy of your statement—or a summary—to anyone who requests your report. Lenders who get the full report are likely to take it into account. After all, they're in the business of trying to make as many loans as possible.

Practical Ways to Rebuild Your Credit

People who have been through a financial crisis—bankruptcy, repossession, foreclosure, history of late payments, IRS lien or levy or something similar—may think they won't ever get credit again. This is certainly not true. By following some simple steps, you can rebuild your credit in just a couple of years.

After you've cleaned up your credit report, here are some suggestions for rebuilding your credit:

Send in Positive Information for Your Report

If your credit report is missing accounts that you have paid on time, send the credit bureaus a recent account statement and copies of canceled checks showing your payment history. Ask that these be added to your report. The credit bureau doesn't have to, but often they will.

Creditors like to see evidence of stability, so send the following to the bureaus: your current employment, your previous employment (especially if you've been at your current job fewer than two years), your current residence, your telephone number, your date of birth and your checking account number. Again, the credit bureau doesn't have to add these.

Acquire New Credit and Use It Responsibly

You can use new credit to rebuild your old credit standing. The one type of positive information creditors like to see in credit reports is credit payment history. If you have a credit card, use it every month. Don't charge as much as your credit limit allows, but make small purchases and pay them off to avoid interest charges.

If you don't have a credit card, apply for one. If your application is rejected, try to find a cosigner or apply for a secured card, where you deposit some money into a savings account and then get a credit card with a line of credit around the amount you deposited. Using credit is good, because it demonstrates your ability and willingness to pay your bills. You must have some credit history to have a credit score.

Once you succeed in getting a credit card, you might be hungry to apply for many more cards, but be careful here. Having too much credit may have contributed to your debt problems in the first place. Ideally, you should carry one or two bank credit cards, maybe one department store card and one gasoline card. This should be sufficient for most families.

Your inclination may be to charge everything on your bankcard and not bother using a department store or gasoline card. Lenders view charge accounts or home equity lines of credit that you're not using as a risk that you could go on a spending jag at any time. When creditors look into your credit file, they want to see that you can handle more than one credit account at a time. You don't need to build up interest charges on these cards, but use them and pay the bill in full.

Please be aware that if your credit applications are turned down, your file will contain inquiries from the companies that rejected you. Your credit file will look like you were desperately trying to get credit, something creditors never like to see.

Close Accounts You're Not Using

Before you apply for an important mortgage or car loan, you'll want to close dormant accounts. Be careful, though, not to do it too quickly. If you close them all at once, your new lender might assume you've hit the financial skids. Close one or two a month (including department store cards) until you've closed them all.

Don't Hit All Your Credit Limits

First, make sure that your total credit limit (not including your mortgage, of course) is less than your annual income.

Next, see how much debt you have outstanding. If you're using 80 percent or more of the credit you have available, it's a sign to lenders that you're stretched. In that case, it pays to sign up for another card or ask to have your limits raised on your existing ones.

As long as you don't tap that larger reservoir, having the additional credit available should help bring your balance back into the acceptable range. Try to keep credit card balances low on all of your credit lines.

Manage Inquiries into Your Record

The more often someone asks a credit bureau about you, which happens whenever you apply for a loan or a new car, the lower your credit score will be.

Recent rules for lenders require them to count all inquiries for the same purpose during a one month period (all inquiries from mortgage lenders, for example) as one inquiry, but it's still not a good idea to apply to more than four or five places for credit in any six month period.

Automate to Be on Time

There are some months when we all goof. We forget to pay the Visa bill. We forget to write a check to AT&T. One way to stop this from happening is to automate as many payments as possible. You can now authorize everyone from your health club to your mortgage lender to your utilities company to automatically deduct funds electronically from your checking account each month.

Then your only challenge is making sure the funds are there to cover those payments. (In fact, some lenders will give you a break on your interest rate for paying this way.)

Don't Allow Delinquent Payments

This is the single most important thing you can do. How you've paid your bills in the past is usually the best indicator of how you'll pay in the future. Be sure to pay at least the minimum amount required by the date it is due on your account statement or invoice.

You can always pay more (and should!), but you should never pay less than the minimum. Remember—being late on a payment is a negative mark on your credit record, even if you make up the payments later. If you haven't always paid your bills on time, you can start today! Credit scores emphasize your most recent payment record.

If there is an instance when you are delinquent and you catch it quickly, don't immediately pay the late fee—first try to fight it to keep it from showing up on your credit report.

Call up and explain: You were out of the country. Your child was in the hospital. Often, you can get away with one of these excuses because the lender wants to keep your business.

Beware of Fraudulent Credit Cleaning Companies

Finally, many people want to know if the agencies that promise to clean up your credit rating are legitimate. The answer is a resounding no. What these organizations often practice is fraud. They swap your Social Security number or other identifying details with those of someone with cleaner credit or no credit at all to allow you to start from scratch.

Such schemes also rarely work. It's a harsh fact of life that bankruptcies and other blemishes on your credit report stay there for up to eight years without being erased. What you can do, however, is explain your lapses in good behavior right on your report using the 100-word statement we discussed earlier.

In the U.S., the Federal Trade Commission (FTC) is responsible for enforcing FCRA. The FTC also publishes consumer-related credit brochures where you can obtain additional information on credit reports.

The Final Credit Solution: A Change in Lifestyle

To avoid getting into financial problems in the future, you must understand your flow of income and expenses. Some people call this making a budget. Others find the term budget too restrictive and use the term spending plan. Whatever you call it, spend at least two months writing down every expenditure.

At each month's end, compare your total expenses with your income. If you're overspending, you have to cut back or find more income. As best you can, plan how you'll spend your money each month.

If you have trouble putting together your own budget, consider getting help from a non-profit group that provides budgeting help for free or at a nominal fee.

YOUR PERSONAL CHALLENGES WITH FINANCE

The Lender's Perspective

Why is it that some lenders say no when others say yes? Here is why. All lenders make a judgment about...

- **Character** (your willingness to repay)

- **Capacity** (your ability to pay)

- **Collateral** (the value of what you are buying)

...before deciding whether or not to grant you a fixed loan or line of credit.

There are several tools that aid lenders in making this judgment, including automated credit or risk scores. In some cases, these scores replace human decision making. As a result, separate lenders can look at the same loan and view the same credit risk differently.

If your loan application met with a negative response from one lender, there may be another lender out there whose credit risk criteria is different. If so, they may have a loan for you. But be prepared to sign on the dotted line for a higher-than-usual interest rate. The more risk you present to the lender, the higher the annual interest rate.

Are You a Credit Risk?

How you used your credit in the past and the reasons for your past financial difficulties are two factors that affect your ability to get a loan. The first step is to understand whether or not you are considered a credit risk. Most lenders will consider you a higher credit risk only if your credit report states that you have more late and slow payments than stated in the categories given below:

Revolving Credit (i.e. credit cards) No payments 60 days or more past due and no more than two payments 30 days past due.

Installment Credit (i.e. car loans) No payments 60 days or more past due and no more than one payment 30 days past due.

Housing Debt (i.e. mortgages and rent) No payments past due. This can be proven by providing (borrower's) canceled checks for the past 12 months or a loan payment history from the mortgage servicer.

In all categories, all late payments must be explained. Contrary to popular belief, good credit does not necessarily mean perfect credit. If your credit reports show any 60 to 90 day late payments you may need to seek out a lender that specializes in less than perfect credit.

Your Total Obligations

Some people would like to consolidate their debts and have either a lower monthly payment or fewer monthly payments. You probably should not consolidate your debts if...

✓ Your habits are not likely to change.

✓ The interest rate for consolidation is high.

You might want to seriously consider the possibility of debt consolidation if it would...

1. Stop creditor harassment. (Creditors are usually very happy to receive regular monthly payments and work with a 3rd party to get their debtors back on track.)

2. Lower monthly payments. (Sometimes creditors are willing to work with 3rd parties and lower your current interest rate.)

3. Reduce finance charges. (Many creditors offer assistance with your plan by lowering or eliminating interest charges and late fees.)

If you follow the steps outlined above, it will take about two years to rebuild your credit so that you won't be turned down for a major credit card or loan. After around four years, you should be able to qualify for a mortgage.

"I hear, I know. I see, I remember. I do, I understand."

Key Points:

➤ how credit reports work   ➤ detailed explanation of credit scores

➤ obtaining higher credit scores ➤ rebuilding damaged credit

1. **Write down** any parts of the chapter that were meaningful to you.

_____

_____

_____

_____

2. **Personal Application:** How can you personally apply these truths in your own life? Write down several long-term goals.

_____

_____

_____

_____

3. **Steps to Action:** Write down one small step you could take to begin immediately applying the truths and principles of this chapter.

_____

_____

_____

_____

4. **Prayer for the Practical:** Write out a prayer to God asking Him for help in making any changes that these goals would require.

_____

_____

_____

_____

Psalm 62:8 "O my people, trust in him at all times.
Pour out your heart to him,
For God is our refuge."

"Let us not be content to wait and see what will happen, but give us the determination to make the right things happen."

—Peter Marshall (1902-1949)
Chaplain to U.S. Senate, national spiritual leader

CHAPTER FOURTEEN

MAPPING OUT YOUR FINANCIAL DESTINATION

Only a foolish person would begin a long journey without knowing the destination. Have you ever seriously thought about drawing up a plan for your life and deliberately mapping out where you want life to take you? It may be that you have considered some New Year's resolutions to guide you through the coming year. It is said that there are only two things in life that are sure—death and taxes. However, there is an additional one—time flies! The future will soon be the present. You can either be ready for it or wait and let it take you by surprise.

Your financial clock is ticking and before you know it, that which you thought was a long way off will be just around the corner. The bottom line is that you need to be ready. Start now by defining your purpose, your life philosophy, your objectives and then your goals. You need a personal / family mission statement. An important element in establishing your financial goals is to determine or maybe just review your life's purpose. From there you can clearly define your financial objectives.

> START NOW BY DEFINING YOUR PURPOSE, YOUR LIFE PHILOSOPHY, YOUR OBJECTIVES AND THEN YOUR GOALS.

Yes, you can choose a new set of New Year's resolutions to improve the coming year. But isn't your life more important than just the year ahead or a long journey planned for the family vacation? Should you not then consider your journey of life worthy of your most earnest efforts at planning and preparation? We encourage you to formulate life plans, lay down a definite course to follow, and begin your journey today.

THE PREPARATION COURSE OF ACTION

In this process of defining our purpose, objectives and goals, serious thought and intense soul-searching are required for any individual, family or business structure. There are no simple answers or easy steps, but you must determine the best ways for you to deal with this subject. So what about purpose, goals, objectives and the overall planning process? How are they accomplished?

Purpose: Your purpose might be to develop and strengthen family relationships.

Objective: Your objective would be to enjoy your vacation, to relax and to have a good time.

Goal: Your goal would be your destination. Perhaps it's Disney World.

Planning: The planning process would include requesting the necessary time off work, deciding what to take along for the trip and what activities you and your family will participate in.

DEFINE YOUR PURPOSE

Why are you here? What is your purpose in life? Why are you doing what you are doing? What brought you to this profession? Why are you employed where you are?

Don't drift through life; be purposeful! Determine some objectives, define some goals and follow the planning process through measurement and feedback. Ask yourself the question, "What do I really want? What am I trying to do?" Answering basic questions will provide stimulus to determine what it will take to achieve that result. Obstacles will always present themselves, but through perseverance and determination they can and will be overcome. Your life, both personally and professionally, can be one of achievement, accomplishment, fulfillment and success.

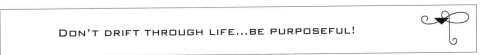

DON'T DRIFT THROUGH LIFE...BE PURPOSEFUL!

Write out a statement of purpose—a general statement of mission or vision describing the overall intent that governs your goals, objectives, strategies and activities. It represents your reason for existence, interprets your vision for others and clarifies purpose for yourself. Your purpose statement gives you direction, states the nature of your cause and gives focus and vision to your goals.

While this may seem very broad in the context of your life's purpose, let's narrow it down to the area of your financial life.

Purpose Precedes Goals

Goals are necessarily preceded by a purpose and objective. The purpose-less person who has nothing for an objective usually accomplishes it. Without purpose an individual can never rise from the mire of mediocrity.

An old story is told of an ancient king who called in the wise men of his kingdom and asked them to compile for him all the wisdom of the ages. After months of diligent research, they returned with their findings bound in twelve large volumes.

The king commended them for their work but insisted that it was too long. So the intellectuals went back to work, this time condensing the material. Many weeks later, the wise men returned with only one volume. Again they were commended by their king, but were told to make the information even briefer.

Condensing the wisdom of all the ages into less than one volume posed a very difficult problem. Not very excited, the scholars returned to their immediate responsibility. Finally the wise men brought in their findings, the results of years of research. They handed the king a small slip of paper. Yes, they had condensed all the wisdom of the ages into one sentence. This sentence was: "There ain't no free lunch!"

If you are going to discover purpose in life, define objectives and achieve personal and professional goals, you must be diligent in your personal commitment to the planning task at hand. You may not have wise men, as this king did, to help you discover a purpose statement. But you do have a Wonderful Counselor, the Holy Spirit, who wants to reveal to you God's plans and purposes for your life! (I Cor. 2:11, John 14:26)

DEFINE YOUR OBJECTIVES

What do you want to do? How do you want to fulfill yourself? What do you want to see happen? What kind of results are you looking for? What do you want your company to accomplish this year? What is your time horizon?

Objectives are simply a target or desired result. Increasing your total retirement savings might be one objective. There is a difference between goals and objectives. To increase your savings by 20 percent or a specific dollar amount is setting a goal. Whether it involves family goals or personal goals, the principles are the same. Proper discipline takes an objective (a personal or professional destination) and determines specific goals that will ultimately bring it into reality. For example, it doesn't make much sense to get the kids excited about taking a vacation, pack for it, load the family in the car, check the oil, fill the car with gas, pull out onto the highway and drive around with no destination.

DEFINE YOUR GOALS

Where do you want to go? Which direction should you be heading? What do you want to accomplish? What milestones should be reached this year? What specific things do you want to complete? What are the results you want to achieve?

In a family situation, what needs does your family have? Have you prioritized the needs and desires of your family? Your list of goals will differ from that of other families. Families set their financial goals based upon their unique family values. The following list of questions can help you to analyze your individual / family goals:

Analyze Your Goals

- What are my financial goals?

- If I had to identify my primary goal, which one would it be?

- By what criteria do I now establish my priorities?

- Is my lifestyle appropriate to my income goals?

- Which of my goals will bring the greatest value to my family?

- Which of my goals will bring the greatest value to my community?

- Which of my goals will bring the greatest value to my church?

- Which of my goals will bring the greatest value to myself?

- Are my goals realistic?

- Can I make the necessary financial provision to accomplish my goals?

- Which of my goals will bring the greatest personal satisfaction?

- Which goals will benefit the greatest number of people?

- Will my goals be able to maximize my investment returns, while minimizing the risks to other family members?

- Does each family member share in my goals?

- Since I feel all of my goals are important, how can I make sure that the action plans for one goal do not hinder or conflict with another goal?

- Do my goals match my income?

- Do my financial goals maximize tax shelters?

- Do I have clearly defined financial goals?

Achievable Goals

Achievable financial goals have the following in common.

- Direction of Activity (purpose)

- Focus on Target (objectives)

- Measurable Checkpoints (planning)

- Timeline for Results (completion)

The Motive of Your Goals

Next, ask yourself this question. "Is what I want worthwhile?" Your answer to this will determine if your want is a greed or ambition. Goal setting should bring out the best in a person, allowing him to stretch. It should be a sacrificial achievement that is matured with time, effort and service to others. Goals that do not include service to others will eventually hinder, if not destroy, the person who has set them.

Marden says it this way, "Nothing can take the place of an all absorbing purpose. Education will not, genius will not, talent will not, industry will not, will power will not. The purposeless life must ever be a failure."[14]

The Scriptures and Goal-setting

Vine's Expository Dictionary of Biblical Words has the following to say about the word goal. "GOAL …denotes 'a mark on which to fix the eye'…"

II Timothy 4:7-8 notes that after diligent efforts, one can accomplish the goals set before him and achieve significant rewards.

> *"I have fought a good fight, I have finished my course, I have kept the faith: Henceforth there is laid up for me a crown of righteousness, which the Lord, the righteous judge, shall give me at that day: and not to me only, but unto all them also that love his appearing." (KJV)*

One of the most familiar Scriptural passages which relates to the process of goal-setting is found in Philippians 3:13-14:

> *"Brethren, I count not myself to have apprehended: but this one thing I do, forgetting those things which are behind, and reaching forth unto those things which are before, I press toward the mark for the prize of the high calling of God in Christ Jesus" (KJV).*

Matthew Henry's Commentary summarizes verses 9-14 as follows: "He pressed towards the mark. As he who runs a race never takes up short of

234

the end, but is still making forwards as fast as he can… the prize we fight for, and run for, and wrestle for, what we aim at in all we do, and what will reward all our pains…"

Abraham Lincoln once noted, "If we first know where we are, and whether we are tending, we could better judge what to do and how to do it."[15]

A well-known entrepreneur by the name of J.C. Penney once declared, "Give me a stock clerk with goals and I will make history. Give me a man without goals and I will show you a stock clerk."[16]

Bottom line: You will aim where you set your goals.

ENCOUNTERING CHALLENGES

We cannot grow personally or professionally without defining our purposes and objectives. What is life without a challenge? We have to be challenged by setting goals and then listing steps we can take to reach these goals. It is told that Alexander the Great sat and cried when he determined that there were no more worlds to conquer. The Romans became soft, complacent and vulnerable at the peak of their power because there was no challenge ahead of them. It is said that many elderly people retire only to die prematurely when there is nothing to do.

Resisting Complacency

Perhaps you have read about the case of the complacent pelicans. Many years ago flocks of pelicans began to die on the California beach. Experts found no disease that contributed to the deaths. Yet many dead ones littered the beach and created a problem for the Public Health Department.

An investigation found that they had become used to eating the refuse the fishermen threw overboard when they cleaned their fish. In time, they had become lazy. They ceased to fish and were content to live a soft life. A law was passed that prohibited the fishermen from dumping their refuse into the shallow water.

These pelicans, equipped by nature to be expert fishermen, were faced with a tremendous problem. They had lived so long on the food from the fishermen that they soon forgot how to strive and seek their own food. They began to die by the hundreds.

So several hundred Alaskan Pelicans were transported to the California beach. At once they waded out into the water and began to fish. In time, the surviving pelicans of the beach caught on. They realized that if they were going to survive, they had to work. They had to be constantly challenged.

Overcoming Limitations

It is said that fleas can be captured and placed in a covered container, whereupon they will immediately attempt to jump as high as they normally do. Of course, they strike the lid. After repeating this process a few times, they finally learn to jump a little lower to keep from striking the lid. After awhile the lid can be removed and the majority of the fleas will jump no higher than they did before the lid was taken off. This is because they conditioned themselves and adjusted to their own imprisoned environment. Their desires to go any higher finally vanished.

Some people are like those fleas. They hold themselves back in relation to their circumstances, thus impeding their progress and personal growth. Some compare themselves to others who are doing worse. We need to compare ourselves with those who are doing much better than we are, so that we have something to work toward. If we are not continually progressing toward our goals, we are probably slipping back into less than we could be.

Sometimes we like to make excuses for our personal failures. It is easy to blame others, our circumstances, our environment or any convenient thing. If we fail to reach the bulls-eye, it is never the fault of the target. Most of the time a lack of success or accomplishment is not the fault of outside circumstances. The man who says, "I can," and the man who says, "I can't," are usually both right. Most of our battles are won or lost in our own imagination or mind. Some blame events, situations and, most often, others for their failures. But their real cause is failing to really define their purpose and to set goals for reaching specific objectives.

When one flea decides to risk another bump on the head and jump higher, he finds that he can do it and ultimately leaps to freedom. If one individual will strive to reach his full potential and set goals and objectives, he will reach it. Seeing this, others will be inspired to follow suit.

Deciding Who to Follow

Several years ago a scientist did an experiment with caterpillars. He placed them end-to-end around a saucer with food and water in the middle and began to watch the experiment. The caterpillars went around and around the saucer, following one another until all of them died of malnutrition.

Some people are the same way. They tend to follow each other. When one person thinks of a new idea and decides to do it, many others then jump on the bandwagon, thinking it must be the answer to their problems. Life is not fulfilled playing follow-the-leader. What if the leader is going around in circles? Or what if he is headed in the wrong direction?

FAILING TO TAKE ACTION

Fear of Failure

Goals are never set by some because of the fear of failure. By determining just what our objectives are, defining distinct goals and taking specific steps to reach those goals, we are putting into motion the very real possibility of achievement. We are placing attainment within our grasp. Taking specific action positions us for success instead of failure. But this takes time and effort. Deciding not to list our goals is the easiest way out. Our subconscious may be telling us, "no goals, no effort, thus no possibility of failure."

Lack of Determination

Another reason that many do not set goals is the lack of determination to stay with the task until it becomes a reality. Many people never accomplish above the mediocre because they lack determination. They never stay with a project long enough to see their dream come true. Upon setting their goals, if barriers appear, obstacles confront or discouragement comes, they move on to some other unfulfilled goal. The result is a life not completely fulfilled and a person who has not reached his or her fullest potential.

Procrastination

Other people are professional procrastinators. All the experts on time management agree on at least one rule for getting results: Do it now! But tackling assignments now is not always as easy as it sounds. Sometimes you're not in the mood for paperwork. Or you may be overwhelmed by the size or complexity of the project. When these tasks come up, you need the determination to forge ahead, the discipline to stay on track. Otherwise you may find yourself procrastinating and drifting toward a serious time bind.

To procrastinate means to put off doing a task—for no good reason. That last phrase, "for no good reason," is the key; because there are sometimes excellent reasons for putting off a certain task. In fact, deciding to do one thing before another is what prioritizing is all about. However, if you have organized your TO-DO list and are having trouble working through it in priority order, then procrastination may be the problem.

Most procrastination is the result of irrational thinking, occasionally called awfulizing. You talk yourself into putting off a task, not because it is simply unpleasant, but because it is awful, horrible, UNBEARABLE! Of course, none of those descriptions is accurate. Convince yourself instead that the task is worth doing. Tell yourself, "I may not enjoy paperwork, but I can certainly stand it and may even feel good when it's done."

Challenge your excuses for putting the assignment off. For example, if you generally excuse yourself by saying, "I work so well under pressure," argue that "working under pressure really leaves me frustrated and tired and I don't have the time I need to be creative."

Forcing yourself to do something uncomfortable or frightening helps to prove that it wasn't so bad after all. Don't let procrastination be a pleasant experience. If you usually procrastinate by socializing, just don't do it! If you must procrastinate, do it in unpleasant conditions. Lock yourself in your office. No coffee. No visitors. When the fun goes away, the procrastination will also. Make a written promise to yourself that states a goal and includes a reward for accomplishing the goal.

You might keep a TO-DO list on your computer. Instead of deleting the completed items, you could cut and paste them under a DONE category. This visible proof of progress reinforces your efforts to stay on track and reminds you that doing it now—not tomorrow—can make your job less stressful and much easier to manage.

Take the Procrastinator Test

Are you a procrastinator? Give yourself this test. Answer each question with one of the responses on the following continuum: never (1 point); sometimes (2); half the time (3); most of the time (4); always (5).

How often do I...

1. Put off doing something I have to get done?

2. Wait to move until someone forces or strongly encourages me to do something?

3. Look for reasons (or excuses) not to do something I should do?

4. Fail to complete projects I've started?

5. Allow myself pleasant indulgences (over-sleeping, over-eating, skipping responsibilities, etc.)?

6. Find that I've run out of time to complete a project properly because I didn't start soon enough?

7. Allow obstacles and difficulties to prevent me from completing a project?

Add up your score and see how you rate!

7-9	If you're so conscientious, why aren't you working?
10-18	You're starting to sound truthful.
19-25	With a little practice, you might never get anything done.
26-34	How did you get around to finishing this test?
35	You're a chronic procrastinator!

THE IMPORTANCE OF FINANCIAL GOALS

Earlier, we listed several components of achievable financial goals. The importance of financial goals cannot be overemphasized! The next section of the chapter will take a closer look at creating specific goals. Financial goals that last have the following in common.

- ✓ Visualized

- ✓ Achievable

- ✓ Written

- ✓ Measurable

- ✓ Manageable

- ✓ Progress Reviewed

- ✓ Deadline Oriented

- ✓ Rewarded

What kind of financial goals are you seeking? Where are you now financially? Where would you like to see yourself? How much time do you have to reach your goals? It's not only a question of whether or not you can reach your goals, but also when you will reach those goals. Your goals and time frame play a big role in your ultimate success.

Enjoying financial security in today's world takes more than simply earning a good living. Some people who have made extraordinary incomes for many years are in terrible financial shape and are not prepared for today, let alone their future. It is essential to make decisions that will help you to manage your resources if you are ever going to be financially secure. Many Americans make enough money to become wealthy by the world's standards. The problem is not our income, but our spending. Most Americans waste much of their hard-earned money on the small things, like a morning appointment with Starbucks for a latte and a bagel. Unfortunately those little expenditures add up to a very large outflow of our cash.

Setting Clear Financial Goals

The starting point for any financial objective is first setting clear financial goals. You can accomplish just about anything if you set your mind to it and outline the necessary steps to achieve it. But it will be difficult to stay on track if you do not know where you are going. By establishing clear financial goals with specific objectives in mind, you will be well on your way to obtaining the financial freedom you are looking for.

We all may be created equally in the sight of God, but we usually end up very unequal. Clearly defined goals focus our vision and channel our energy. Goals are coordinates in time and space which you plan to visit in the future. When you set goals, you are making an appointment with yourself to have specific things happen as a result of actions you take today.

Our lives will seldom be any better than our written goals. We make plans and we take action. You just can't hit a target you didn't aim at. Decide where you want to arrive and begin your journey.

Goal-setting works because:

- It focuses the mind

- It channels energy

- It gives structure to your life

- It asks for commitment to specific accomplishments

- It provides motivation

- Reaching goals becomes habit forming

- Achieving results spawns new goal-setting

Short-Term Financial Goals

Short-term financial goals are things that can be accomplished in a relatively short span when compared to your lifetime goals. Maybe you are saving for a newer car or an overseas vacation. These goals should be looked at within a 6-24 month period of time.

Maybe you have incurred $1000 in debt by the purchase of some new stereo equipment. You might want to get rid of this debt by breaking the goal into short little bites by saving $50 a week for the next five months. Money Magazine recently did a survey and found out that 29 percent of Americans picked dropping debt as their number one new year's resolution.

How bad is the problem of debt in this country? According to U.S. government statistics, revolving consumer credit in recent months totaled over $805 billion dollars. This is a huge increase when compared with just $1.4 billion in 1968, $10.2 billion in 1973 and $106 billion in 1984.

And of course this does not include the trillions of dollars in other consumer debt. In year 2000, consumer debt totaled $1.5 trillion. In 2003, that figure was $1.98 trillion. If you add in total consumer debt, that number jumps to well over $10 trillion. For a visual picture of this debt, picture a stack of bills laid flat on top of each other reaching into the sky. If each were a $1,000 bill, the stack would reach 67 miles into the galaxy.

Another startling figure is this. Back in 1971, the average car loan was financed for less than 3 years with an average of just over $3,000 financed. Today the consumer averages well over $25,000 to finance a vehicle and that amount is financed on average over a period of 5 years. Which, of course, means that the interest charge adds considerable cost to that vehicle.

Intermediate Financial Goals

Intermediate financial goals should include those that can be accomplished within a one to five year horizon. This might include the purchase of a new vehicle by paying for it in cash. It might be paying off all installment debt. Another example of this might be the children's college education coming your way in five or more years. This might be the new house you have been considering or a remodeling job in your current home.

Long-Range Financial Goals

Long-range financial goals generally include things that would take you five to fifteen or more years to accomplish. Other possibilities could be a new home or the education of a young child. This category would certainly include your retirement plans. When you set long-range financial goals, you set the stage for making sound investment decisions. Think about your goals and write them down. Then you can put together an investment opportunity aimed at reaching those desired goals.

A Hierarchy of Goals

Daily

Weekly

Monthly

Quarterly

Annual

Five-Year

Decade

Lifetime

- The accomplishment of daily goals should lead to the achievement of weekly goals.

- The accomplishment of weekly goals should lead to the achievement of monthly goals.

- The accomplishment of monthly goals should lead to the achievement of quarterly goals.

- The accomplishment of quarterly goals should lead to the achievement of annual goals.

- The accomplishment of annual goals should lead to the achievement of lifetime goals.

SEVEN BENEFITS OF SETTING FINANCIAL GOALS

Setting financial goals gives you control. As is the case with most successful people, you've probably focused more on making money than bothering with learning how to manage it. Although you have your attorney, your insurance agent, your banker, your CPA and your broker, you may not have given a lot of thought to a sound financial plan. Have you strategized in a way that will enable you to reach your financial goals? You need to. Your financial well-being and success will not come by sheer luck and inattention to your goals. In fact, that will guarantee your family economic disaster. Financial goals are reached by knowing what you want, where you are going, making informed choices and using all appropriated strategies to set out your course.

Setting financial goals takes the control from others and puts the control of your financial future into your hands. It becomes your blueprint that will guide you through the financial peaks and valleys of life. Without spending limits and preparations for your financial future by setting current goals, you, your dependents and your assets are not adequately protected against the risks of life. This can lead to needless waste of your current resources. Your daily decision making could be controlled by your current desires, not your future needs. If you do not take control of your financial possessions now, you will likely pay higher income taxes which may have been avoided with a sound financial plan.

1. Setting financial goals points you in the right direction. It helps point you toward specific family goals and gives you leverage over your financial resources.

What do you need your resources to do for you? Without setting proper financial goals, your long-term needs will not be met. Your children won't have a means to get a good education, your spouse will not be prepared in case of your disability or death, and you will be forced to a retirement income of much less than you might need.

2. Setting financial goals helps you know yourself. Financial success begins by knowing yourself. This includes knowing your objectives, determining your investment goals, your lifestyle and the type of investment goals you are comfortable with. Since your goals and needs are unique to you, making wise investment choices is very important. You will learn about yourself by taking into account your investment objectives, your tolerance for risk, your time horizon, your financial knowledge and your financial health. Another part of knowing yourself is setting realistic expectations. Are you one who can accept higher risk for higher potential returns? Conversely, will you be satisfied with lower returns by choosing conservative investments? The best way to get to know yourself and start down the path to achieving your financial goals is to get time on your side. This can only be maximized if you begin at once.

Setting financial goals keeps you on track. Living in a busy world with all sorts of demands and opportunities to spend can play havoc with our available financial resources. We all have some sort of money challenges from time to time. It's part of life and living. This is why setting financial goals is so important. How can you possibly think about the future that is ten, twenty and thirty years out there, when your checkbook is now empty and you won't get paid for another ten days!

By setting financial goals, when attempts are made to rob you of your cash, you can make the appropriate decisions based upon your previously written goals. Your money will actually seem to go further if you know where it goes. Know what you want to accomplish with your income. Know what is wise spending and where you are spending foolishly, and carefully plan your spending in advance.

Taking the time to carefully plan for your financial future is the act of accepting personal responsibility for it. Certainly, there will be times when you need information and advice from outside sources, but the ultimate decisions are yours. By staying on track with your financial goals, you will increase your ability to get what you want out of life.

3. Setting financial goals helps you to build financial assets. Whatever your choice of investment vehicle, without a goal, you are likely to just hit and miss. Your last choice for spending available income is going to be socking it away for your retirement. This means that whatever is left at the end of the week is what you will save. Your savings will not grow unless you make it your first choice of what to do with each paycheck. A definite spending goal will help you build assets. You can begin to build assets by first limiting the taxes you are currently paying. The goal of every taxpayer should be to pay your fair share and to pay everything that is legally owed. Tax evasion is both illegal and immoral. Tax avoidance through proper planning is both legal and moral.

4. Setting financial goals helps you prepare for retirement. Many uncertainties surround the subject of retirement. These include the uncertainty of your health, the economy, inflation, your age, the success of your investments and more. Because of this, it is of vital importance that you start when you are young before time becomes your enemy. Even if you are ready to retire, setting financial goals is still important. We are living longer than ever before and the uncertainty of inflation and other expenses should cause us to commit to careful planning and strategic goals. When investing, it is important to take a long-term view, giving your investments time to grow.

5. Setting financial goals helps with educational expenses. In building your overall family asset base, discuss with your family what goals they might have in mind. Of course for the parents, this would include retirement plans. For the children, it would definitely include their education. One of the greatest gifts parents can give their children is a good education. Instead of funneling large sums of money for furniture or a vehicle, let them earn their own money, but give them a head start in their earning potential by helping them get a solid education. This will cut their umbilical cord to your purse strings, enabling them to gain earning power themselves. Every family must spend according to their family values. This is how they should set their financial goals. It is not that values are right or wrong, rather that values vary from family to family.

There could be the purchase of a new house, a new business start-up in your future or an infinite list of other possibilities. Building assets for additional, yet unknown projects requires that you continue to set and consider future financial goals beginning now.

6. Setting financial goals prepares you for the unexpected. One general goal is to help you protect yourself against a number of risks. These might include the loss of income, the death of a family member, medical expenses, disability, unemployment, property and liability losses and others. At the very least, goals help you set up an emergency fund to act as a buffer for unplanned expenses.

Change is a way of life. Things happen. Life isn't always very smooth. Jobs are lost. Health problems confront. Vehicles break down. Emergencies arise. Most experts recommend setting aside anywhere from six months' to a year's salary in liquid assets, such as CD's or money market accounts. In addition, it is important to purchase disability income, life, long-term care and other types of insurance to help protect you, your family and your assets against the loss of income, illness, disability or other financial circumstances.

When you recognize the possibility of mishaps that will impact your finances, you can plan for their occurrence in advance. You may have to make slight changes or adjustments in your financial goals, but should something unforeseen come your way, the financial burden can be lessened. Your advance planning can lessen your anxiety and reduce the impact of a potentially severe blow to your finances.

7. **Setting financial goals improves family communication.** Setting financial goals, launching those goals and staying on track is a family team effort. Setting goals is full of tough choices. People who do not have a lot of extra income will have to prioritize their spending and separate their needs from their wants and desires. They may not get the house of their dreams, a new car every couple of years or an education for their children at the best private colleges available. Families have to be willing to accept trade-offs.

The entire family must come together to build a sure financial base. If one family member controls spending and promotes saving and the others do not, you will only reach a small portion of the assets you are attempting to build. Each family member should contribute to setting the goals, determining the priorities and considering the various consequences of not staying with the goals. By working together, it becomes a family project which enhances unity, creates stable relationships, and provides a method to keep each family member on track.

SEVEN STEPS TO SETTING FINANCIALS GOALS

To be successful at anything necessitates knowledge of goal setting, measuring progress, and achieving milestones. In its simplest form, goal setting includes the following steps.

1. **Write down your financial goals.** Use paper and pen or your computer to crystallize your thinking. Writing them down leads to commitment. You become open to new ideas about what you really want to accomplish. This helps you prepare and ready yourself for the future. Writing out your ideas helps you to recognize when new opportunities arise. Gather all of the information that you have related to your current financial condition as well as your assessment of where you are and where you want to be. Then, begin to gather all of the necessary paperwork.

You will need to know exactly where your income is coming from and what your spending habits are. Be very detailed. You must know about your employee benefits, insurance benefits, any insurance policies that you have purchased, your living will, a complete and detailed statement of your net worth, a personal income and expense statement, the likely cost of your child's future education, your retirement desires and, in short, a written document of your past, present and future. This will take some time, but you cannot prepare written financial goals without some intimate knowledge of your family situation. Have you analyzed your history of spending? Have you examined your spending habits? Have you investigated all future costs? Do you know where your financial leaks are coming from? Have you found the holes in your budget and identified areas requiring immediate change?

Know your purpose, your objectives and your specific goals. If your objective is to be financially sound, what specific goals will you set out for your future to obtain? Define very clearly what those goals are. Where are you going? Where do you want to be? How will you get there? Which goals are for next month and which ones are for five years from now? What are your priorities?

2. Give yourself a deadline. Specify a time for achieving your objective. Get started on your financial journey by being deadline motivated. Deadlines help get you started and keep you moving. You become a person on a mission. You have placed a target in your sights and know where it is you are aiming your life. Goals are worthless without a plan of action and some deadlines. Develop specific deadlines that will keep you on track toward meeting that goal. In the beginning, you will need to set up a family budget. Consider having automatic payroll deductions for savings or retirement purposes, a plan for contributing to your employer's 401(k) program, contributing to your own IRA account and so on. Look at those specific deadlines, prioritize them and then put them into action.

Financial goals and objectives should cover all time elements. They should anticipate changing needs as your life changes. It is never too early to understand your purpose, lay out those objectives in a clear, concise manner and then set the appropriate goals that will put you on your path to financial freedom.

3. Set your standards high. In general, the higher you set your goal, the more effort you will have to expend toward reaching it. The loftier the goal, the more motivated you will be to reach it. As you reach certain milestones in your blueprint of progress, you'll become inspired to give it all you've got to reach your desired result. It may seem strange, but it often takes just as much effort, energy and hard work to reach small goals that lead to little more than poverty and misery as it does to reach higher goals that lead to success, prosperity and abundance. So aim high! If you shoot for the moon and miss it, at least you'll be among the stars.

4. Set realistic, obtainable goals. Be level-headed and pragmatic when setting your financial goals. Goals that are set too high so that they become unattainable will be a source of never-ending frustration for you and your family members. While they might look very good on paper, if you cannot reach them, you may eventually abandon all goals and simply give up.

5. Be detailed and specific. Explicit objectives and precise family financial goals must be set. Goals that are vague might never be met. Don't ballpark your numbers or your goals. Don't say to your family, "Let's buy a small farm in the valley in a few years." Or to your spouse, "Let's set a goal of moving to Mexico when we retire." While serving in a third world country might be your purpose and retiring in Mexico might be your objective, when it comes to setting goals, the numbers must be very clear. Numbers would include your age, the year, the dollars needed and every other detail that might enter into this picture.

6. Be flexible. Each of your goals must be accommodating to whatever life brings your way. Situations change, people change, and desires and wants all change family goals. Be prepared to be flexible with however the state of your family affairs changes your course. Every pilot expects that course corrections (changes in wind direction and velocity, inclement weather, payload, etc.) will be necessary during flight. Within the family unit, changes that affect their goals and plans might include changes in health, family size or incomes.

7. Take the first step. Start now. Right now. Ask questions, do research and consult a professional. Get the advice and information that you need to create a plan today. It is important to think it all through. It's important to blueprint your strategic plan. It's also important to see the eventual result. One does not always know all of the forks in the road when beginning the journey. But if you know where you are now and where you want to be, then you can start with that knowledge and get moving to where you want to end up. You probably already have some ideas about just what kind of goals would be of interest to your family members. By setting goals, you have a direction to head in.

The best way to get started is to just start! Don't get caught up in the little things and miss the big picture! By never getting started, you are being defeated by time. If you move ahead and do not get bogged down with the daily problems and challenges of life, you can make time your friend. Time is either your greatest asset or your worst enemy.

THE FINAL PHASE— COMPLETING THE PROCESS

The final phase in mapping out your financial destination is to create plans to help you implement your objectives and goals. What is involved in the planning process? Planning is outlining a course of action in order to achieve a goal, thus fulfilling a desired objective. It is predetermining today a course of action for tomorrow. It is throwing a net over tomorrow and making something happen. It is being tomorrow-minded rather than yesterday-minded.

The only way to reach a financial goal is to work at it. The most important step in reaching the goal is to develop a plan to achieve it. That's why it is so important to plan ahead for your retirement and your financial future. While the idea of planning ahead and building a solid financial strategy for success can sometimes be intimidating and overwhelming, once you get started it will become easier.

With a little planning and a better understanding of what your investment options are, you too can successfully manage your money and pursue your financial goals. So what is planning? Planning is knowing where you are today, outlining the steps it will take to reach your financial goals, developing a sound plan and continuing to follow the pattern you outlined by pursuing your goals. Planning involves measurement and feedback. Planning is being decisive and doing work today designed to cause specified occurrences tomorrow.

Why plan? Here's why: to achieve your financial goals, to put ideas to work, to make things happen, to be prepared, to cope with change, to be in control, to decide what you want to do with your money and to decide how your money should work for you. It is essential to plan for every area of your financial future and to make sure that you are on track to meet those financial goals. Your needs will change throughout your lifetime. Review your plan every year or so to make sure that your financial goals are the same. If they have changed, your planning strategies will have to change.

Good planning is an essential step toward meeting your financial goals. Planning can be top down and bottom up. It involves communication with those concerned. Plans must be evaluated and revised from time to time.

As You Begin

1. Set specific measurements of progress. Answer questions of how much, where, when and at what cost. The progress points must be obtainable. You must consider obstacles and priorities.

2. Outline procedures. What has to be done? How will it be done? Consider equipment and materials, money and people. When will this thing be done? Make up a tentative schedule. Where will it be done?

3. Assign activities. Involve people. Involve their skills, knowledge and experience. Stimulate motivation and interest.

The planning process is no better than the goal, the goal is no better than the objective, and the objective is no better than the purpose or reason for existing.

FOUR KEYS TO QUALITY PLANNING

Like any other success in life, quality output comes from a quality plan of action. It is impossible to reach any goal without such a road map to your success. Nothing worthwhile happens by accident. It's difficult to accomplish anything important without a detailed, specific plan.

Financial planning offers you a coordinated and comprehensive approach to achieving your personal, family and financial goals. With proper planning, you will take specific steps to reach your financial goals and manage your current and future assets.

A clear, solid plan, like the blueprint for the construction of a house, can show you which steps to take. The steps, one by one, will guide you so you will not have to stop and think about each step before taking them. You'll have the benefit of systematically following ideas that you have carefully considered in advance.

Constructing the Plan

To begin, take time to think your plan completely through. Engage others in helping you with your plan. There is no such thing as too much input. And don't neglect the details. If, for example, your plan is to improve a specific part of your financial future, be sure to give some specific thought as to how exactly you plan to do it. Let's say that one of your goals is to spend less money. One of your plans must direct the family in specific ways to bring that goal to pass.

Constructing this plan might include tracking actual cash. Now of course it is relatively easy to track the big purchases, but how about the little ones? What about the pocket change that disappears so easily…the $20 dollar bill here and the $5 dollar bill there? Why not gather the family together and track for one week—seven days—exactly where every dime was spent. For the kids, you might want to track each penny.

The small stuff might not seem like a lot, but multiply it by six family members and you might be very surprised how much it adds up to in one month's time. This newly found money may just help you start saving toward that short-term goal. Long-term, it could probably fund your retirement! Actually it takes very little money saved weekly over a lifetime that, along with compounded interest, can add up to hundreds of thousands of dollars. It just takes commitment, patience and time.

Following the Plan

The ability to carry the plan with you and physically consult with it on a regular basis necessitates that it be written down and mobile. Not only will you remind yourself of tasks you should be addressing, but you will be able to regularly monitor the work you are doing according to your plan. Everyone has unique aspirations, hopes, dreams and motivations that serve as a guide for their daily life.

Those who are able to clearly identify their financial goals early in life have a very distinct advantage in achieving those goals and maintaining a commitment to their own personal values and principles they have set out to follow. In following your financial plans that you have outlined to reach your goal, be sure that you continue to unearth new facts that could necessitate any course corrections.

Evaluating the Plan

If your results don't happen according to your plan or fulfill your expectations, it may be time to reconsider your plan. Was it realistic? Was it flexible? Did it take into account unforeseeable events or circumstances? Did you follow it to the letter? Does it need some revision? Financial planning is simply drawing up a blueprint that outlines the specific steps to take that will lead you to meaningful personal and financial goals.

Some questions you need to consider again and again: Are your financial goals clear and realistic? Do you know exactly what you are desiring to accomplish and why? If these are not perfectly clear, your chances of succeeding will be hindered. In the planning stage you must be aware of some of the obstacles that may prevent you from reaching your goals.

Above all, do not see your shortcoming as a permanent failure. Instead, learn from your experiences.

Revising and Updating the Plan

Periodic updating is usually necessary. Review your planning once or twice a year or whenever your personal circumstances change. Revisions—due to unexpected changes that impact your work or reconsidered objectives—may be needed. As you progress through the months and years, your financial plans will certainly evolve to account for changes in your personal life as well as fluctuations in our economic climate.

If any of the following change, the plan must change: purpose, objectives, goals, net worth, asset allocation, liquidity, cash flow, debt, investment vehicles, risk tolerance, retirement goals, insurance needs, earnings ability, family size, tax liability, etc.

Updates in your planning will be necessary as goals and objectives change. There might be changes in your income or lifestyle. Job changes might cause a change in your financial planning. As tax laws change, you will need to adjust your planning. The bottom line is to stay flexible.

"I hear, I know. I see, I remember. I do, I understand."

CHAPTER
14

APPLY IT

Key Points:

➤ defining purpose and objectives

➤ analyzing your financial goals

➤ procrastination and other hindrances

➤ benefits of goal-setting / practical tips

1. **Write down** any parts of the chapter that were meaningful to you.

2. **Personal Application:** How can you personally apply these truths in your own life? Write down several long-term goals.

3. **Steps to Action:** Write down one small step you could take to begin immediately applying the truths and principles of this chapter.

_____

_____

_____

_____

4. **Prayer for the Practical:** Write out a prayer to God asking Him for help in making any changes that these goals would require.

_____

_____

_____

_____

Psalm 62:8 "O my people, trust in him at all times.
Pour out your heart to him,
For God is our refuge."

"Believe while others are doubting.
Plan while others are playing.
Study while others are sleeping.
Decide while others are delaying.
Prepare while others are daydreaming.
Begin while others are procrastinating.
Work while others are wishing.
Save while others are wasting.
Listen while others are talking.
Smile while others are frowning.
Commend while others are criticizing.
Persist while others are quitting."

—WILLIAM ARTHUR WARD
AMERICAN DEDICATED SCHOLAR, AUTHOR, EDITOR, PASTOR AND TEACHER

CHAPTER FIFTEEN

THE DAILY HABITS OF A SUCCESSFUL PERSON

Several years ago, a group of friends traveled to a small town to paint the house of a dying man. The house was in need of a fresh coat of paint and they had been wanting to pay him a visit. But instead of just standing around watching his pain, it was their intention to help brighten his day by painting the house. As they were saying good-bye at the end of the day, he made a profound statement they never forgot. He said, "It pays to give it all you've got while you're on stage, because you never know when your act is up." Soon afterward, he died of cancer.

The simple lesson of this short story is sobering. Time is a gift that God has loaned to us, and we never know when "our act will be up." This chapter focuses on two tools—time and communication, and how they are related to our personal finances.

GOD'S GREATEST GIFT

One of God's greatest gifts, time, is of prime importance. As stewards, we are expected to use it wisely and to our advantage in fulfilling our destiny. Time is our tool. It is a wonderful gift. We should not be enslaved by it. Put to proper use, it should be an investment for the future.

In time management, all roads lead to the management of self. Often we say, "I wish I could manage my time better." What we should really be saying is, "I wish that I could manage myself better!" The management of our time and ourselves takes perseverance and self-discipline, but no investment pays higher dividends.

Most of us would never think of going through life without budgeting and investing our finances. Yet, most of us waste a great percentage of our time. It is just as important to study the stewardship of time as it is to study the stewardship of our finances. We are accountable for both. Nothing saves more time than proper planning. How many times have you heard somebody say, "I don't have time!" What they're really saying is, "That is not important enough in my priorities to warrant taking time for it." We always seem to make enough room for the things that are important to us individually.

As our days seem to come and go swiftly, often we exclaim, "Where has the time gone?" Actually, it has gone absolutely nowhere. The clock has always ticked at the same rate of speed. Hour after hour, time continues on. Time can be lost, but never can it be retrieved. Time cannot be hoarded, but must be spent each day. It can never be borrowed. Furthermore we can only use our own.

Most people have heard of Parkinson's Law, which says, "Work expands so as to fill the time available for it." It seems that if you give somebody something to do and you want it done by 4:00 in the afternoon, you can just about be assured that you will receive it right at 4:00. Very seldom do you receive it any sooner. When there is something to be done, we always seem to wait until the last minute to accomplish the task. Yet we always make time for things that are really important to us.

It is foolish to say, "Time will tell," or "Time will heal," or even "Time will bring out the possibilities in him." Time will do nothing at all. Time will only come and go. Time does not help a person to help themselves. It is how we use the time allotted to us that really counts.

Time Can be Invested

Just as money can be spent or invested, the same is true of time. To invest either is to use them in such a way as to bring future benefits. Suppose you did not know how to type and your penmanship left much to be desired. If you decided to learn to type, just a few days or weeks of practice could eventually result in thousands and thousands of hours of time saved.

Human beings seem to be very impatient. We often like to plant today and reap tomorrow. Some impatient investors expect to invest their money today and cash in tomorrow, but it never works that way. An acorn does not grow into a mighty oak in one year. We do not mature from adolescence to adulthood in an instant. Invested dollars pay back in dollars, when they are needed, at a later date. Invested time pays back in time later when it is a scarce commodity. Time carefully planned and invested will rarely be wasted.

> "The clock of life is wound but once,
> And no man has the power
> To tell just when the hands will stop
> At late or early hour.
> To lose one's wealth is sad indeed;
> To lose one's health is more.
> To lose one's soul is such a loss
> That no man can restore.

—AUTHOR UNKNOWN

Living by Your Priorities

There is not enough time to do everything you want to do. Once you face that reality, you must then decide the degree of importance of the items on your list. By the process of establishing priority and systematic elimination, you can put the limited time available to the best possible use. Some things must always take second place or be eliminated altogether. But this plan assures that the important matters will not be among them.

Several years ago, a leading industrialist by the name of Charles Schwab said to a management expert by the name of I.V. Lee, "If you can help me get more things done in a day, I'll pay anything you charge me." Lee replied, "Tomorrow, list all of the things you want to get done. List them in order of importance by priority. Do the first job listed and stay with it until completed. If, at the end of the day, there is still time to get to job # 2 and job # 3, do so as time allows. The next day, continue to do the very same thing. Then, have all of your subordinates do it. Do this for one week and then send a check for whatever amount you think the advice is worth. At the end of the month, Schwab sent a check to Lee in the amount of $25,000.

Adlai Stevenson once said, "It's not the days in your life, but the life in your days."[17] In other words, it's not how much you do that counts, it's how much that you get done that has purpose and lasting benefit. The British author, Somerset Maugham is credited with the following statement: "The passing moment is all we can be sure of; it is only common sense to extract its utmost value from it; the future will one day be the present and will seem as unimportant as the present does now."[18]

The Bank of Time

Time is a very valuable commodity and utterly irretrievable. There is no one who has more or less of it than others. Suppose your bank credited your account each morning with $86,400.00, carried no balance from day to day, and allowed you to keep no cash in your account. Then suppose that every evening the bank canceled out whatever you failed to use during the day.

All of us have such a bank. Its name is time. Every morning it credits us with 86,400 seconds. Every night, it rules off as lost whatever time we have failed to invest for good during the day. It carries over no balance. It allows no overdrafts. Each day it opens up a new account. Each night it burns the records of the day. If you failed to use the day's deposits, the loss is yours.

Each of us has 1,440 minutes each day. We are given 168 hours each week. This makes 52 weeks each year that we must account for. In spite of its value and unique characteristics, we probably waste time more thoughtlessly than anything else. This seems to be the great paradox in life. No one feels there is enough time, yet everyone has all the time that there is. Time is not the problem—rather, how we use our allotted time.

FIVE TIPS FOR INVESTING TIME WISELY

As kingdom-minded stewards, we must realize that it is best if we spend our time wisely. For that to happen, you should make lists and plan each day. Here are some tips on how to be that good steward God desires you to be.

1. Plan your work. Long range planning for five or six days helps you to see how your work fits into the overall weekly picture. Detailed planning is absolutely necessary. With proper planning, you can gather the necessary materials, systems and procedures and utilize spare moments for preparation of coming events. This takes the rush out of life by giving you the time for fitting the whole program together.

2. List your tasks. At the end of each day, list the jobs that need to be done the very next day. Number them in the order of their importance. Then think about the materials that these jobs will require. Your mind will then begin to prepare you for the many tasks that will require your attention the following day.

3. Develop a regular work schedule. Many people hate to be tied to a regular schedule. Some may even feel that it cuts down on their spontaneity and creativity. When you dictate certain activities for regular times, your mind has already been warmed up to the task. Regardless of the activity, you will find that you have less resistance to difficult jobs and are mentally prepared for each task.

4. Do related jobs together. Each time you change to a different type of work, your mind has to change gears. Sometimes as much as 20 minutes can be required to make that mental transition. When you do jobs that have related aspects together, you cut down on mental time lag. The more related characteristics that tasks have in common, the greater the benefit of grouping them together.

5. Learn to rest creatively. The mind and body soon tire of working at one type of job or in one place or position. Fatigue begins to set in. Frequently, all that is needed is a momentary change of pace. Sometimes you can take five minutes to think through a program or read an article and then return to the task at hand.

Many people allow momentary fatigue to become an excuse for an extra cup of coffee or a talk session, thus completely breaking their work rhythm and never getting back to the task at hand. Instead of starting a gab session, take a moment to pause in silence, pray for the needs of others, or do something different from the task you had been engaged in.

A Life Well-Spent

The key to managing your time lies in developing habits that put you in control of your time. Read this section, then think how you can make the most of your daily schedule. It is estimated that, in the average life of seventy years, time is used up as follows (*USA Today*):

- 3 years - education

- 3 years - reading

- 3 years - convalescing

- 4 years - conversation

- 5 years - transportation

- 6 years - dinner table

- 8 years - amusements

- 14 years - work

- 24 years - sleeping

The following Scriptures deal with the subject of time:

> *"Before the mountains were born or you brought forth the earth and the world, from everlasting to everlasting you are God"* (Psalm 90:2 NIV).

> *"For a thousand years in your sight are like a day that has just gone by, or like a watch in the night"* (Psalm 90:4 NIV).

> *"The length of our days is seventy years—or eighty, if we have the strength; yet their span is but trouble and sorrow, for they quickly pass, and we fly away"* (Psalm 90:10 NIV).

> *"Teach us to number our days aright, that we may gain a heart of wisdom"* (Psalm 90:12 NIV).

THE BLESSING OF COMMUNICATION

Our ability to communicate with others is one of God's greatest gifts, yet it is often one of our greatest challenges. Accurate communication is one of the greatest needs today. We often say one thing, but the person to whom we are speaking hears something different. Sometimes it is the fault of the speaker, sometimes the listener, but many times neither is at fault. Communication differences vary according to our backgrounds, experiences and the various filters we use to process our thoughts and words. We talk with many, but probably communicate with only a few. Words have various meanings to different people. Here are just a few verses from the Bible which relate to communication:

> *"And he said unto them, What manner of communications are these that ye have one to another, as ye walk, and are sad" (Luke 24:17 KJV)?*

> *"But let your communication be, Yea, yea; Nay, nay: for whatsoever is more than these cometh of evil" (Matthew 5:37 KJV).*

> *"But now ye also put off all these; anger, wrath, malice, blasphemy, filthy communication out of your mouth" (Colossians 3:8 KJV).*

A Biblical Definition of Communication

Before we continue, let's get some input into the definition of the word "communication." From Strong's Greek/Hebrew Dictionary and Vine's Expository Dictionary of Biblical Words we get the following related definitions.

Nouns:

1. *koinonia*: refers to partnership, participation, social intercourse, communication, communion and fellowship. Translated in Hebrews 13:16 "to communicate, not forgetting good deeds and fellowship" (KJV, communication) in Philemon 6, RV.

2. *logos*: a word, that which is spoken (*lego*, to speak); is used in the plural with reference to a conversation; communication, (Luke 24:17). Elsewhere with this significance, the RV renders it "speech," (Matthew 5:37, Ephesians 4:29).

> *Note: In Colossians 3:8, where the KJV translates* aischrologia *as "filthy communication," the RV renders it "shameful speaking"* (aischros- *base,* lego- *to speak).*

Verbs:

1. koinoneo: used in two senses:

   (a) to have a share in (Romans 15:27; I Timothy 5:22; Hebrews 2:14; I Peter 4:13; II John 11)

   (b) to give a share to, go share with, (Romans 12:13, RV), communicating (KJV); distributing; (Galatians 6:6), communicate; (Philippians 4:15, KJV), did communicate; (RV), had fellowship with.

2. *sunkoinoneo*: to share together with; translated "communicated with" (Philippians 4:14); have fellowship with (Ephesians 5:11); be... partakers of (Revelation 18:4). The thought is that of sharing with others what one has, in order to meet their needs.

Adjectives:

koinonikos: means apt, or ready, to communicate (I Timothy 6:18).

> *"But to do good, and to communicate forget not: for with such sacrifices God is well pleased" (Hebrews 13:16 KJV).*

REFLECTIONS ON FOUR COMMUNICATION SCRIPTURES

Hebrews 13:1-17

(from Matthew Henry's Commentary, p. 44)

The sacrifice of alms-deeds, and Christian charity. To do good, and to communicate, forget not; for with such sacrifices God is well pleased, (v. 16). We must, according to our power, communicate to the necessities of the souls and bodies of men; not contenting ourselves to offer the sacrifice of our lips, mere words, but the sacrifice of good deeds; and these we must lay down upon this altar, not depending upon the merit of our good deeds, but of our great high priest; and with such sacrifices as these, adoration and alms thus offered up, God is well pleased; he will accept the offering with pleasure, and will accept and bless the offers through Christ.

> *"Let no corrupt communication proceed out of your mouth, but that which is good to the use of edifying, that it may minister grace unto the hearers" (Ephesians 4:29 KJV).*

Ephesians 4:17-32

(from Matthew Henry's Commentary, p. 15)

We are here warned against corrupt communication; and directed to that which is useful and edifying, (v. 29). Filthy and unclean words and discourse are poisonous and infectious, as putrid rotten meat: they proceed from and prove a great deal of corruption in the heart of the speaker, and tend to corrupt the minds and manners of others who hear them; and therefore Christians should beware of all such discourse. It may be taken in general for all that which provokes the lusts and passions of others. We must not only put off corrupt communications, but put on that which is good to the use of edifying. The great use of speech is to edify those with whom we converse. Christians should endeavor to promote a useful conversation, that it may minister grace unto the hearers; that it may be good for, and acceptable to, the hearers, in the way of information, counsel, pertinent reproof, or the like. Observe, it is the great duty of Christians to take care that they offend not with their lips, and that they improve discourse and converse, as much as may be, for the good of others.

> "Be not deceived: evil communications corrupt good manners" (I Corinthians 15:33 KJV).

I Corinthians 15:20-34
(from Matthew Henry's Commentary, p. 27)

A caution against the dangerous conversation of bad men, men of loose lives and principles: Be not deceived, says he; evil communications corrupt good manners, (v. 33). Possibly, some of those who said that there was no resurrection of the dead were men of loose lives, and endeavored to countenance their vicious practices by so corrupt a principle; and had that speech often in their mouths.

COMMUNICATION: A TEXTBOOK DEFINITION

Communication is defined in the textbooks as the sending and receiving of information among people. At least six messages are involved in the communication process. They can be identified in the following ways.

- What you mean to say

- What you really say

- What the other person hears

- What the other person thinks is heard

- What the other person says about what you said

- What you think the other person said about what you said

Communicating is like a contract between two or more individuals. The contract starts with talk, then must proceed through an orderly process to an agreement. There is the initial presentation of a message by one person. Second, there is the listening of that presentation by a second person. For the words to result in true communication there has to be a clarification and an understanding of the message. And finally, there must be some consensus or agreement on what that understanding is. All of this can make effective communication scary to some people because it requires trust and possibly some risk. But without communication, nothing truly effective can happen.

Miscommunication

Some words mean different things to different people. Business relationships–which include owners, executives, managers, clients, employees, associates, vendors and competitors–are the very foundation for a firm's success. These relationships require effective communication, which often means just starting a conversation. Many times relationships end with little more than just talk and the results become very expensive indeed. Instead of real communication in these relationships, talk occurs with little value.

One time, the president of a large company called his corporate finance manager on the phone looking for a particular figure. She gave him this number: two-thirty-nine-forty and he jotted the number down. What he had heard and subsequently wrote down was $239,040. Being familiar with the data, he understood what she was saying, but others may not have.

A few days later while teaching a staff gathering on the subject of communication, he asked a group of employees what these words meant to them. They came up with at least eight different answers. Two numbers given repeatedly were: 1) $230,940 and 2) $239,040. There is a significant difference in just these two numbers—a $9,000 difference!

- What did she mean to say? $239,040

- What did she really say? Two thirty nine forty

- What did he hear? $239,040

- What did others hear? Eight variations!

It is important to ask questions or restate a point for clarification of meaning. A continuous goal should be to say what we mean and be sure that what we say is what was heard. In the communication process, we spend almost all of our time thinking about sending (i.e. talking and writing), yet listening is an even more important communication skill. Listening is hard work! The brain must struggle to understand what someone is saying. One must be both objective and reflective in communication behavior.

Qualities of Communication

Being a Good Listener

The benefits of careful listening are enormous. Listening enables us to gain work-related information. Listening enables us to be more effective in interpersonal relationships. Listening enables us to gather data to make sound decisions. Finally, listening enables us to respond appropriately to the communication messages we hear.

Some ways to be a good listener include listening for the sender's central idea. This is probably the most important step in listening. To identify the sender's main idea, you must keep your own ideas in the background. If your own ideas begin to influence your listening, you may miss what the sender is trying to say. All this implies that every speaker does indeed have a central idea. This may be a lofty assumption to make about all communicators, but we should make it if we want to be a good listener.

Another point in listening is to concentrate on what the sender is saying. Good listening requires one to work very hard. This means developing a style of listening that enables one to concentrate enough to get the information he/she needs, even while doing other things. Listening should be taken seriously and one should work hard to achieve it.

The Influence of Emotion

Sometimes, we let our emotions influence our listening. Often, we hear what we want to hear and not what the sender intended to transmit. We often assign our own values to stimuli coming in. Our attitudes influence our listening behavior. It takes effort and practice to delay evaluation of the message until later.

It is often easy to reject what you hear as too familiar, unfamiliar or trivial. When we hear something that is old hat to us, it is very easy to turn off the communicator because we think we have heard it before. We may also do this if something seems too trivial for us to listen to. If we are not careful, a lot of important information may be missed.

We cannot just listen for the facts. A good listener should notice the surroundings, the reactions of others, the enthusiasm demonstrated by the sender, etc. All of these peripheral issues are part of the message being transmitted.

Avoid formulating arguments against the sender's ideas before you fully understand them. Thinking up opposition arguments takes time and energy away from our primary job as listener.

Techniques of Communication

Think of your own style of communication. Does it have a positive or negative effect upon others? If it is positive and rewarding, it will be the kind of conversation others want to have again and again. They will come back for more. On the other hand, if your communication with others is continuously negative, they will tend to interact with you as little as possible.

A good rule of thumb is to try to make most of your communications relatively positive for the other person. Of course, you can't always do this because of the nature of some kinds of problems. Some people may lack the social skills necessary to cooperate in making communication positive.

Other times, when you must take a strong position in opposition to others, positive communication may be difficult. However, over the course of your many communications with your family, co-workers and colleagues, you should be able to make the majority of your communications go easily.

Making communication positive may be difficult at times, but it comes easier with practice. Some people can keep communication constructive under pleasant circumstances, but then lose their grip on it when the pressure is on. It is an important skill to be able to put others at ease and help them stay there through the course of the communication.

We should ask ourselves this question on occasion: "To what extent do people voluntarily seek me out? To what extent do they take the initiative in contacting me, communicating with me, sharing ideas and viewpoints with me, and including me in their personal and social activities?"

Get the Most Out of Communication

Try to ignore uncomfortable surroundings. If the room is too warm or too cold, the lighting not good, the dress of the communicator not acceptable, or other things seem uncomfortable, major distractions may occur.

Try to personalize the sender's topic. Be perceptive to the sender's nonverbal communication. Do not be afraid of difficult expository messages. Experts point out that sometimes people will refuse to listen to information they feel is too difficult or complicated. One will be successful in formulating an appropriate response only after he or she has demonstrated good listening behavior.

Sometimes we communicate with people who do not seem skilled in verbal conversation. If we want to avoid potential stress for ourselves and those we're dealing with, we must consider some suggestions for handling stressful conversations.

It is always good to look for common points of interest. If you know you're going to be disagreeing with someone, start off your discussion with some area on which you both agree. Even if it requires really digging to uncover the common ground, we should do it!

Choosing your Words Wisely

When presenting a message, it is often more effective to choose words that are more positive in nature, as opposed to putting a negative spin on the communication. By doing so, a greater chance of positive reception is possible. Instead of saying, "Why not?" it's good to say, "What if?" By not saying, "I hate it when...," some conversations could be enhanced in a positive way. Try saying, "Wouldn't it be better if..."

Sometimes people use generalizations when speaking and, by doing so, sabotage their ability to communicate. To say, "He always says...," when in fact he does not always say, diminishes the speaker's ability to communicate. It becomes a matter of his or her credibility. Perhaps a way to say the same thing might be, "I've heard him say before..." I've heard employees complain, "Nobody cares about what I do around here," when in fact it might be true if they would say, "Sometimes, I feel like no one notices how hard I work around here." Instead of supervisors commanding that it must be done like this, it might be more effective to say, "Here's a good idea to consider," or, "This may prove to be more effective."

Some words do not promote good conversation and can even inhibit it. Included are the words "but" and "you." "But" acts like an eraser inside people's heads. It erases the value of anything before it with one word. Much better to use is the word "and." When responding to someone, first reiterate their statement, then say, "and," followed by your comments. It gives communication a chance and one will get a lot further by doing so. The word "you" can communicate a bad message when used in an accusatory manner. The word "I" clarifies for the other person what one thinks and feels, while "you" can make a person feel criticized. "I" reduces defensiveness and fosters communication.

It is important for everyone, especially those in leadership, to think about communication style. Reflect on the following lists of negative and positive communication behaviors. It may be useful for you to document a day's conversation. Check to see how many of these specific behaviors can be identified in your day-to-day patterns of working with others.

Negative Communication Behaviors or Styles
- Asking loaded or accusing questions
- Bragging, showing off, talking about self
- Breaking confidences, failing to keep important promises

- Complaining or excessive whining
- Criticizing excessively, fault finding
- Demanding one's own way, refusing to negotiate or compromise
- Disagreeing routinely
- Displaying frustration frequently
- Diverting conversation capriciously, breaking others' train of thought
- Flattering others insincerely
- Interrupting
- Joking at inappropriate times
- Keeping a sour facial expression
- Losing one's temper frequently or easily
- Making aggressive demands of others
- Making others feel guilty
- Monopolizing the conversation
- Not respecting the opinions of others
- Overusing "should" language, pushing others with words
- Overusing "why" questions
- Patronizing or talking down to others
- Playing games with people, embarrassing or belittling others
- Restating others' ideas for them, but with changes
- Ridiculing others
- Showing obvious disinterest
- Soliciting approval from others excessively
- Telling lies, evading honest questions, refusing to level with others
- Throwing "gotcha's" at others, embarrassing or belittling others
- Throwing verbal barbs at others
- Using nonverbal put-downs
- Verbal abuse, insulting comments
- Withholding customary social cues such as greetings, nods, etc.

Second, here's a list of preferred behaviors which are more positive and usually result in better communication.

Positive Communication Behaviors or Styles

- Affirming the feelings and needs of others
- Compromising, negotiating, helping others succeed
- Confronting others constructively on difficult issues
- Delaying automatic reactions, not flying off the handle easily
- Expressing genuine interest in the other person
- Expressing respect for values and opinions of others
- Giving one's word sparingly and keeping it
- Giving others a chance to express views or share information
- Giving positive nonverbal messages of acceptance and respect for others
- Giving suggestions constructively
- Joking constructively and in good humor
- Keeping the confidences of others
- Leveling with others, sharing information and opinions openly and honestly
- Listening attentively, hearing the other person out
- Praising and complimenting others sincerely
- Questioning others openly and honestly, asking straight-forward, non-loaded questions
- Sharing one's self with others, smiling, greeting others
- Stating agreement with others when possible
- Stating one's needs and desires honestly
- Staying on the conversational topic until others have been heard
- Talking positively and constructively
- Treating others as equals whenever possible

An honest appraisal of the preceding behaviors reveals the obvious—we all would prefer to be on the receiving end of the positive styles of communication. No one enjoys being ridiculed, put down or ignored. Thus the reaffirming, attentive listener and the uplifting, honest communicator will both reap and sow good, constructive communication experiences.

A Poetic Example

A poem by Shel Silverstein, recorded in the book, *A Light in the Attic,* summarizes what communication is all about.

"If we meet and I say, Hi, that's a salutation.
If you ask me how I feel, that's consideration.
If we stop and talk awhile, that's a conversation.
If we understand each other, that's communication.
If we argue, scream and fight, that's an altercation.
If later we apologize, that's reconciliation.
If we help each other home, that's cooperation.
And all these actions added up make civilization."[19]

What a great example of communication!

TIME, COMMUNICATION AND YOUR FINANCES

In this chapter, we have learned how the practice of wise stewardship of our allotted time and our communication with others is of utmost importance. Using our time each day to its fullest potential will have a direct effect on our other precious commodity: our money. Our stewardship of both time and communication opportunities is vital to our life's success, both temporal and in the eyes of God.

"I hear, I know. I see, I remember. I do, I understand."

CHAPTER
15

APPLY IT

Key Points:

➤ using time wisely

➤ establishing priorities

➤ developing habits to control time

➤ positive and negative communication styles

1. **Write down** any parts of the chapter that were meaningful to you.

_____

_____

_____

_____

2. **Personal Application:** How can you personally apply these truths in on: How can you personally apply these truths in your own life? Write down several long-term goals.

_____

_____

_____

_____

3. **Steps to Action:** Write down one small step you could take to begin immediately applying the truths and principles of this chapter.

_____

_____

_____

_____

4. **Prayer for the Practical:** Write out a prayer to God asking Him for help in making any changes that these goals would require.

_____

_____

_____

_____

Psalm 62:8 "O my people, trust in him at all times.
Pour out your heart to him,
For God is our refuge."

INCORPORATING TRUTH INTO YOUR ATTITUDES AND ACTIONS

HOW CAN I KEEP RECORDS THAT WILL ENABLE ME TO MANAGE MY CASH FLOW? HOW CAN I LEARN TO BUDGET MY MONEY SUCCESSFULLY? WHAT ARE SOME PRACTICAL WAYS TO SAVE MONEY? WHAT SMALL CHANGES CAN I MAKE THAT WILL IMPROVE MY OVERALL FINANCIAL SITUATION?

"Look at what's happening to you! You have planted much but harvest little. You eat but are not satisfied. You drink but are still thirsty. You put on clothes but cannot keep warm. Your wages disappear as though you were putting them in pockets filled with holes!"

—The prophet Haggai, speaking to the people of Jerusalem
Haggai 1:5-6, 520 b.c.

CHAPTER SIXTEEN

MENDING THE HOLES IN YOUR POCKET: KNOWING WHERE YOUR MONEY IS GOING

I f you are like many people, you'll find that from time to time cash flow seems to come to a screeching halt just before payday. Actually in several cases, it seems to dwindle just after the paycheck arrives. That which was a mighty river on payday, overnight seems to become a dried-up little creek. Are you anything like that? Do you regularly find yourself in a cash crunch just before payday? Do you find yourself juggling money between savings and checking because you can't maintain an adequate checking account balance? Perhaps you let one bill payment each month slide into next month. Or, even if your bills seem to be under control, you find it impossible to save any money. Does it sometimes feel like you have "holes in your pocket" that always allow the money to slip through? If so, welcome to life!

THE IMPORTANCE OF GOOD RECORD-KEEPING

Everybody needs some kind of system to account for their spending and cash flow. Spending needs to be controlled. But first you'll have to find that missing money—the income that somehow flies out of your grasp. Ultimately, it's not what you earn that gives you financial security, but what you save. Many are still trying to learn how to live within their means instead of living above their means. Yet to save more money and spend it wisely, you must first know where your money goes. And that means keeping records.

You may think the records you already keep are evidence enough. Check stubs, receipts and charge account statements do paint the big picture of your rent or mortgage, utilities, car payments, furniture and other major purchases. But the clues you really need are smaller. What about all your pocket money? How were those $50 withdrawals from automated teller machines spent? And the $45 department store charges? What do these sums tell you about your spending patterns?

It's a lot easier to tell others how to budget than it is to discipline yourself! Recognize that it's easy to stumble, to make a wrong choice and fall flat on your face in regards to personal discipline. But don't make that your last chapter! Get up, start over, get some discipline into your life and get back on track! There is always hope if you don't give up. So don't give up!

If you're like many people today, you don't know because you don't accurately keep track of spending. Yet doing so is surprisingly easy. With that accomplished, you'll be able to analyze your spending patterns, solve the case of your missing money and draw up a realistic form for accounting for the missing money.

All you really need is about $10 worth of materials. First, a daily journal. There are special daily expense logs tailored for business use, but for our purposes a $.49, spiral-bound notebook small enough to fit in your pocket or purse works fine. Second, a simple ledger book or columnar pad with one wide column on the left and at least six narrower columns ruled for entering figures. These, plus a pocket calculator and a sharp pencil, and you're ready to hunt for the missing money.

Setting Up Expense Categories

The initial step is to set up expense categories in your ledger book. They should be narrow, rather than broad, since the purpose of keeping records is to develop a detailed picture of monthly spending. Catch-all categories like household expenses aren't useful—what you want to discover is just what it is those household expenses consist of (groceries, furnishings, linens, home maintenance, gardening supplies and the like). Later on you can consolidate. For now, instead of clothes, use "his clothes," "her clothes" and "kids' clothes."

On the first ledger sheet, list spending categories down the left-hand column. Every family's spending habits will vary to some degree, but many categories are common to all households. Use a work sheet as guide, adding as many categories as you want. Each column of figures will represent one month's spending, so label them accordingly.

Expenses fall into two types: fixed and variable. Fixed expenses such as rent or mortgages, loan payments, insurance premiums and tuition are constant amounts at regular intervals. Utility bills paid on a level-payment plan are fixed expenses, while those based on each month's usage are variable. Fixed expenses will be recorded directly in the ledger. You can do the same with variable items that are paid in one monthly sum.

Don't forget to set up an expense category for savings. The primary purpose of your record keeping is to increase savings, but you can get a jump on it now. Savings should be considered a fixed expense—10 percent or more of your income, if possible. Think of it as paying yourself first.

Carefully Analyze Your Expense Categories

Determine what percentage of your net income is spent per month in each category. To calculate that percentage, simply divide each expense by your net income. (Example: If your total housing costs are $1,000 per month and your net income is $3,000 per month, you're spending $1,000/$3,000 = 33 percent of your income on housing.)

Designing a budget is more than number crunching and statistical analysis. After all, money is just a tool to help you accomplish something you want. As you work through this process, don't allow yourself to get so wrapped up in the numbers and money concerns that you forget the big picture—Everything we have is on loan from God, to use for His honor and glory.

Take the opportunity to do a little dreaming also. That might include buying a house, saving for your children's education, giving to the church or a charity, taking a vacation, paying off a debt or buying a newer car. If you're married, you need to talk this over with your spouse. And regardless of your marital status, you need to ask for God's guidance (Jeremiah 17:7-8, James 4:10).

So take a little time to ask, listen and dream. Then establish a few short and long-term goals, set priorities and adjust your budget accordingly. If you're already into deficit spending, you need to ask God's guidance in making cuts as well.

Setting up Columns

Now you're ready to set up columns in your ledger book. First, draw 15 vertical columns to the right of your expense categories. Label the tops of those columns in this way:

Column 1: Amount budgeted per month

Columns 2-13: Month (January through December). As the year progresses, you will record your actual costs for each category in these columns.

Column 14: Total cost for the year

Column 15: Average monthly cost for the year

This format is designed to be a starting place. Now you know: This month you spent $35 on coffee and bagels, $85 on lunches, $250 on groceries—whatever. You're not looking so much for precise targets here. Instead, this exercise will give you an expected spending range. That way, before the next month starts (and while your fiscal reality is fresh), you can sit down and make a spending plan.

Once you've discovered how much you have coming in, you get to decide what to spend it on. That's the key phrase: you decide. You are controlling the money, not the other way around. Start by determining how much to sock away in savings and what to pay against your credit-card debt. Then allocate leftover cash for everything else. By laying out your budget this way, you'll see opportunities to cut spending you may not have noticed before.

For example, maybe you'll find you can save $30 a month by eating out less, $50 by buying fewer clothes, $20 by carpooling and $25 by sharing a babysitter. Add these up and you'll have an extra $1,500 by the start of

Section IV: INCORPORATING TRUTH...

the new year. Invest that money—conservatively, no less—and you'll have more than $20,000 in 10 years. All thanks to some simple cutbacks.

Here are two areas to watch carefully. First, some people find it particularly hard to stick to a budget when they're addicted to credit cards. That kind of plastic is too free, flexible and—ultimately—expensive. So try to kick that habit and switch to debit cards instead. Second, it's crucial to build some free money into your budget each month—even if it's just a few dollars. That way, if there's a CD you have to have or a night you feel like going out with the girls (or guys), you can do it without feeling like a failure.

Once you see how you have been spending your money, set up a workable plan for changing your spending patterns and habits, if necessary, to accomplish your new long, medium and short-range goals.

Keeping a Journal for Recording Expenses

Use a daily journal to list out-of-pocket expenses down to the penny or nickel. It feels odd at first, but quickly becomes a habit. In the journal, label a page for each category of expenses and record every outlay under the appropriate category. This means every purchase of clothing, groceries, furniture or bark mulch; each dinner out; gasoline, oil and other auto expenses; haircuts and dry cleaning; books, records and tapes; stamps, magazine subscriptions and newspapers; baby-sitting; daily commuting expenses; and so on.

Record Keeping Basics:

Income —In this project, income is anything used to pay expenses and could include bonuses, investment gains, gifts or an inheritance. Record savings withdrawn to pay expenses as income and classify money put into your savings account as an expense.

Salary —It's simpler to include as salary only your take home pay. That way you can skip expense categories for income taxes, social security, 401(k) contributions and the like. A self-employed person, however, would record gross income and all such expenses.

Accuracy—You want to be accurate, but don't go overboard. Amounts need not add up to the penny and if you forget an outlay, it's not the end of the world. Aim for 99 percent accuracy—for $2,500 in monthly expenses to match $2,500 in income plus or minus $25. Round monthly subtotals and totals to the nearest dollar, too. Getting rid of those extra digits will make the numbers easier to analyze later.

Continuity—This system is built on the cash method of accounting—income and expenses are recorded when they are received and paid, not when they come due. So if you defer one regular monthly expense into the next month, record it in the month it was actually paid. Likewise, if you pay off a charge card bill in installments, record only the amount paid each month, remembering to allocate charges to the proper expense categories, such as "night out" or "his clothes."

Once you complete months of meticulous record keeping, you will know to within a few dollars how much you spent each month and on what. If you stick with it, keeping track of spending will become second nature.

More important, over time you will develop a realistic gut feeling about spending—a realization that when one category of expenses is higher than usual, economies are in order elsewhere. This sounds simplistic and it is. But if you have chronic money problems, a realistic gut feeling about spending may be precisely what you lack.

Keeping Good Daily Spending Records

You needn't pull the journal out of pocket or purse every half hour. Take a few minutes each evening to write down the day's expenses while they're still fresh in your mind. Receipts can help jog your memory, but remember to separate the expenses into their proper categories. The supermarket receipt, for example, may reflect, not only groceries, but also lawn chairs, medicine and other items.

Totaling the Spending Each Month

At the end of the month, sit down with your daily journal and checkbook. First, total the outlays for each category in your journal. Then allocate each check you've written into one or more categories, using credit card statements and receipts as reminders. Finally, combine the journal and checkbook numbers and record the month's total spending by category in your ledger.

Remember, a $100 check to Visa tells you nothing. Break it down into $62 for children's clothing, $17 for yard supplies and $21 for a gift. If you keep your daily journal in good order, recording total monthly expenses should take just half an hour or so.

You now have an accurate picture of one month's spending. It's early yet for analysis, but if outgo exceeded income, zero in on discretionary spending such as clothing, entertainment, gifts and purchases for the home. What can you cut down on next month?

Continuing with the Process

Now repeat the process. One month's records tell you little about spending patterns over time. To gain a full understanding of your spending patterns, you need a long-term perspective. Three months is good. Six months is better. Over and above fixed expenses and some fairly steady variable expenses, your outlays will fluctuate, perhaps widely, from month to month. There are seasonal expenses like vacation, Christmas, birthdays and anniversaries. Some fixed expenses are spaced over long intervals—insurance premiums, taxes and car-registration fees, to name a few. Then come unexpected expenses, such as big medical bills, car repairs and new appliances. All are as much a part of your overall spending profile as groceries, utilities and mortgage payments.

Tracking Minor Expenses

Keeping track of those nickels and dimes turns casual spending into a conscious, ordered process by linking the act of spending money with the act of recording the outlay. Now instead of thinking about each purchase only once, you think about it twice. This simple exercise builds discipline with your money.

After three to six months of recording monthly expenses, your ledger page will become a spreadsheet, which is a mathematical model of your finances over time. You can follow rows across the page to see how particular categories vary over time. You can calculate average amounts for variable expenses—in effect turning them into fixed expenses, which are much easier to use for planning.

At this point a home computer becomes a powerful planning and budgeting tool. With a spreadsheet program or money management program, you can ask your financial model "what if" questions, instantly manipulating income and spending categories to analyze different approaches. Some great money management programs for your computer include 'Microsoft Money Manager' and 'Quicken' or Microsoft Excel for spreadsheets. You can do the same with paper and pencil, of course. We will get to detailed budgeting in the next couple of chapters.

As you do so you'll find yourself setting goals, establishing priorities and beginning to sketch out the framework of a realistic personal financial plan. Now you're ready to budget for keeps.

DECIDING HOW TO SPEND YOUR PAYCHECK

Some financial advisors recommend a rigid approach to spending: a certain percentage of income for housing, so much for food, this much for installment debt and so on. But others take a simpler and more flexible approach, dividing expenses into needs and wants. These figures taken from *USA Today* show national averages in various spending categories.

22%   Housing (including furniture and repairs)

22%   Transportation (car, gas and oil, repairs)

15%   Food

09%   Social Security, pensions

07%   Utilities

05%   Clothing

05%   Entertainment, recreation

04%   Medical care

03%   Savings

02%   Insurance (except car and home)

06%   Miscellaneous

Your first priority is to tithe the tenth (10 percent) that belongs to God. Tithe to your local house of worship. This is the place you receive your spiritual care. Next put away 10 percent for savings and investing. Take care of yourself by setting goals, then treating those payments as fixed expenses. Suppose you have two children to put through college and you want a comfortable retirement. The first checks you write each month should be to your IRA, 401(k) and college savings plans.

Then come your living expenses. Roughly 70 percent of your money is already spoken for by needs such as rent or mortgage, utilities and taxes. Those are pretty much fixed expenses, although you can reduce taxes with proper planning.

Once needs are met, there's about 10 percent left over for debt reduction and other wants and that's where you begin making choices. You can buy new cars or used ones. Food is very discretionary—you can choose to eat very well or just a basic menu. And clothes—you need appropriate clothing for work, but after that there is a lot of leeway. Every type of expense requires similar thinking. For instance, some heavy readers stock up on books and subscriptions, but you can use the library instead and save money.

One category of wants that many people underestimate (or overspend on) is gifts. There are many more occasions to give than just Christmas and birthdays. All those baby showers, Mother's Day presents and graduation gifts can add up. Take a hard look at what you spend on gifts.

Keep an Eye on Your Spending!

Tune in to what you are spending! Write it down. Don't make it a guessing game. Most people do not even know how to tell whether they can afford something. Everyone, not just those who feel they are short of money, should use a ledger detailing all cash flow.

TUNE IN TO WHAT YOU ARE SPENDING!

Virtually every business uses a system to define the inflow and outgo of their cash and so can you. No matter how much money you think you have, it's a useful exercise to determine where it comes from and where it all should go. A more detailed discussion on budgeting follows in the next two chapters.

"I hear, I know. I see, I remember. I do, I understand."

Key Points:

➤ finding "missing money" ➤ continuing with the budgeting habit

➤ record-keeping suggestions ➤ suggested monthly allocations

1. **Write down** any parts of the chapter that were meaningful to you.

_____

_____

_____

_____

2. **Personal Application:** How can you personally apply these truths in your own life? Write down several long-term goals.

_____

_____

_____

_____

3. **Steps to Action:** Write down one small step you could take to begin immediately applying the truths and principles of this chapter.

_____

_____

_____

_____

4. **Prayer for the Practical:** Write out a prayer to God asking Him for help in making any changes that these goals would require.

_____

_____

_____

_____

Psalm 62:8 "O my people, trust in him at all times.

Pour out your heart to him,

For God is our refuge."

"A good battle plan that you act on today can be better than a perfect one tomorrow. "

—General George S. Patton
American general in World War I and II, 1885-1945

CHAPTER SEVENTEEN

WHY BUDGET?
BENEFITS YOU CAN'T AFFORD
TO LIVE WITHOUT

The word budget sounds very boring. It can even sound a little intimidating! The very word seems to spell work, details, recordkeeping—bringing up all sorts of unpleasant visual pictures. But it really isn't all that bad. In fact, budgets are a way of life for all companies and families who need to get control of their finances. Families who have everything under control and who are financially free still need a budget.

Like it or not, money is an important part of our lives. While it is true that money cannot buy happiness, it is also true that when it comes to spending more than we earn, the lack of money can contribute to much unhappiness.

If properly managed, money can enhance family relationships and can be a springboard for family discussions that will help the entire family pull together for common goals. Not properly managed, money can potentially become a real curse.

> BUDGETS AREN'T RECORDS OF EXPENSES; THEY ARE
> FORECASTS OF EXPENSES.

Budgets aren't records of expenses; they are forecasts of expenses. And preparation of a meaningful budget (as opposed to a wishful one) depends largely on that first step, keeping accurate records.

A budget is the most fundamental and most effective financial management tool available to anyone, whether you are earning thousands of dollars a year or hundreds of thousands of dollars. It is extremely important to know how much money you have to spend and where you are spending it. A budget is the first and most important step toward maximizing the power of your money.

A CLOSER LOOK AT BUDGETING

Budgeting is Scriptural

Scriptural guidelines for budgeting can be found throughout God's Word. For instance, Proverbs 27:23 says, "Know well the condition of your flocks, and pay attention to your herds." (NASU) If you don't happen to have any herds and flocks, God is probably saying, "Know well the condition of your clothing budget, your housing budget and your food budget."

Tailor-made for Your Life Situation

Each person or family has different needs. There is no one budget suitable for everyone. The single person with no family has different needs than the single parent with three kids. Money management for the 61-year-old couple planning for retirement will be very different from the 21-year-old newlyweds. And the couple with no children certainly have different expenses than the parents of children. Even greater expenses occur when the children reach college age.

Each of us has different goals, therefore a different plan and a different budget is needed. It must be customized for each individual circumstance. Each budget is neither right nor wrong—just different.

WHAT DOES A BUDGET DO?

Begins with a Statement of Income

A statement of your income tells you exactly what financial resources you have to work with. It tells you what money you will receive weekly, monthly, annually.

It should indicate any income you receive in addition to your earnings, such as interest on savings or the benefit payments a family member may receive. Once you know your total income, you know one of the limits within which to do your financial planning.

Provides for Fixed and Variable Expenses

Rent or mortgage payments, insurance premiums, contributions to church and charity, installment payments on any debt the family owes, taxes and all other payments made on a regular basis and in fixed amounts should be included in the budget.

A listing of these fixed expenses shows what you already have promised to pay and provides another set of limits within which to do further planning. Now you are in a position to plan more realistically and to use your resources to greater advantage.

Expenditures for food, clothing, personal allowances, household, automobile expenses, dry-cleaning, laundry, recreation and other needs fall under the category of variable expenses. A budget is simply a forecast of your earnings and expenses over a given period of time. This, then, is available as a guide for your future spending patterns.

Provides a Means of Directing Your Income

Too many people have given in to their desires and extended themselves beyond safety in money management. You simply cannot spend more than you have coming in.

For most people, typical long-range goals are saving for a college education for the children, a paid-off home mortgage and sufficient funds for retirement. Mid-range goals include furnishing the home, purchasing and maintaining an automobile, and perhaps a special vacation. Shorter-range expenses are for clothing, food and recreation. You should make out your own list of goals—long, medium and short range. But as you set down your goals and develop your budget, keep these points in mind:

- All goals must be based realistically on your projected budget.

- Provide for the basics first, then the comforts, and finally the luxuries.

- Set up a plan for paying off debts already accumulated.

- Plan for savings, no matter how small. Increase your savings allocation as your old debts are reduced.

- Control your spending according to your budget.

- Never give in to temptations to depart from the budget.

- If you stumble, don't give up; regroup and get on task again.

THE FINANCIAL BENEFITS OF BUDGETING

Budgeting stops unnecessary spending. Do you find yourself constantly pushing your family to new heights of debt because you want to keep up with the neighbors, your friends or the Jones family? If the answer to that question is yes, you are probably one who shops and buys impulsively, spending money both out of boredom and for other emotional reasons. Let's say that you often pass the time by visiting a variety of your favorite stores. You probably spend irrationally and when it comes to special sales at your favorite retail stores, you can always find a reason why you must buy it now.

Years ago when a family needed to purchase a major item, it may have taken months or years of saving before that purchase could be made. But times have changed. Through the world of credit financing, many families have accepted an automobile payment as a permanent part of their family budgeting.

If you ever hope to get out of debt, the first step is to bring a quick halt to credit buying, especially on common items such as clothing, appliances, furniture, food, meals out and recreation.

Budgeting opens the door to financial security. A budget is a money plan. With it, you can organize and control your financial resources, set and realize goals, and decide in advance how your money will work for you. Budgeting is a great way to assess your financial needs. It will give your family an overall picture of where your money is coming from, when it is coming in, and how you are spending the money you earn.

Many people think that preparing a budget is very complicated or that it takes up too much time. Even if you are financially free of all debt, budgeting is still an essential part of your financial life. A budget can be as simple as it is powerful. The basic idea behind budgeting is to save money up front for both known and unknown expenses. A budget is the key to making everything else work. It's your game plan, your strategy. And it has to be proactive. Knowing where you stand financially and how to control your finances is a very valuable life skill.

Budgeting will help you get in shape financially. When people ask about getting their finances in shape, they typically have very similar goals. They want to save more for emergencies today. They want to invest more for college and retirement tomorrow. They want to get out of debt. They want security for themselves and their families in case disaster strikes. And they want to know how to learn about their money—because they know that when it comes right down to it, they are responsible.

Budgeting helps you keep the money you earn. You work hard to earn the money you receive. But, once you have your paycheck in hand, do you use it wisely and efficiently? Without a spending plan it is difficult, if not impossible, to use the money in an efficient, strategic manner. Without a budget most of us will just muddle through life, trying very hard to stay one step ahead of our bills. If a budget makes you cringe, just think of the entire process in this way. First of all, you are simply summarizing how you already spend your income and, secondly, you are simply outlining some basic guidelines for your future spending. It becomes your own personal tool to develop awareness of how you are spending, where you are spending and on what things.

Budgeting will help you become debt free. If your goal is to achieve and maintain a debt free position and to use your resources in a manner that is right, you need a written budget. Trying to go without one is like trying to find your way out of a wilderness area without a map—you don't know where you are, where you are going or what lies ahead. You might get lucky and get rescued, you might wander around a long time before you get out, or you might not make it out at all.

Even if you have a budget, you still need to review it once or twice a year to make sure your spending habits are on track, to adapt to any significant changes in your life, and to make sure you are achieving the goals you established.

A budget will help you with the big-ticket purchases. When the need arises to buy things of great expense, a budget will help you in the advanced planning stages, before the need arises. Perhaps it would be for the new house or new car. It might be the children's education, a remodeled room in the house, a shed in the back yard or a fence around the property. Or perhaps it will be new blinds for the windows, new carpet on the floor, or a range or refrigerator. How about special goals? Next year's vacation, painting the kitchen, new furniture, or drapes for the living room must be provided for systematically. If the amount of money needed for a special goal or coming event can be determined in advance, it may be practical to include a regular payment for this event in "fixed expenses." Then the money will be on hand when it is needed.

Saving for what you want takes time, planning and some thought. If it is not thought out ahead of time, it is so easy just to pull out the plastic, put it on a credit account and overspend until we reach the critical stage of too much debt.

Budgeting brings you extra money. This might well be everyone's favorite. A budget will almost certainly produce extra money for you to do with as you wish. Hidden fees and lost interest paid to outsiders can be eliminated. Unnecessary expenditures, once identified, can be stripped out. Savings, no matter how small, can be accumulated and made to work for you.

BENEFITS IN YOUR DAILY LIFE AND ATTITUDES

Budgeting gives you another chance. Having a budget is what you should have been doing all along. So don't look at it as unpleasant. Setting up a budget is like getting a new lease on life. It's a way to start over. It's a way to make a success out of your finances. Remember, your plan probably will have to be long-range.

The chances are your home mortgage will be the greatest debt you have to pay. At least let's hope that is the case! Generally that is a fixed sum of money. So if you have 10, 20 or even 30 years yet to pay, your long-range budget should be set up as long as you have one outstanding debt.

Then take your debts one by one and lay out a realistic repayment plan. Your automobile may take another two years to pay. During that time, be sure to maintain your vehicle properly so that it can last several additional years.

If you unwisely went into debt for furniture, clothing and other items, then they too will have to be paid each month—you may have charged enough that your long-range plan may take two, three or even four years. But do formulate a plan. It is never too late to start and better now than never.

Make up your mind not to create any new debts while paying off the old ones. That is not going to be easy. It may take more family self-discipline than you have ever had to use before. Those debts will all have to be paid. There is no use putting it off any longer.

Budgeting helps you break bad habits. Most of us have taken many years to establish our spending habits, accumulate our debts and dig ourselves into financial holes.

Habits are indeed hard to break. It is not so easy or logical that we should be able to snap our fingers and get out of debt and onto sound financial footing by next week. Not even next month. Not even next year.

How do we get out of debt? Just like we got into debt—one step at a time.

Regardless of your past habits of money mismanagement, a sound plan, carefully thought out, can bring financial success in the future. A budget is simply an organized way to manage your finances.

Because we live in a "now" world, we are used to having everything done yesterday or today at the very latest. But some things are not this easy. Getting out of debt falls into this category. You need to sit down and pencil out a practical long-range plan. This planning period involves careful budgeting.

Budgeting will free you, not confine you. God expects us to be participants in planning budgets, not observers. As Proverbs 16:9 says, "The mind of man plans his way, but the Lord directs his steps." (NASU)

Therefore, as we apply practical concepts in handling our money, God provides godly wisdom. It should free you from worrying about whether the annual insurance payment will be made, whether you put money aside for the taxes on your home, and whether enough money will be available to buy the clothes your children need.

If those are not problems for you, you're among the fortunate few. They are problems for the majority of Americans and they may well be problems for your children when they have families. If you're not willing to live on a budget, you will not be able to help them live on budgets. So a budget can be a good teaching tool, as well as a good measure of self-discipline.

Budgeting enables you to walk in wisdom. Personal budgeting allows you to know exactly how much money you have, even down to the penny, if you so desire. Furthermore, a budget is a self-education tool that shows you how your funds are allocated, and how they are working for you; it reflects what your plans are for them and how far along you are toward reaching your goals. Knowledge is power, as the oft-quoted saying goes, and knowing about your money is the first step toward controlling it.

Budgeting offers you extra time. All your financial transactions are automatically organized for tax time, for creditor questions, or for any query that may come up about how and when you spent money. Being armed with such information saves time digging through old records.

BENEFITS IN YOUR FAMILY

Budgeting will help your family work together as a team. A budget can be used to develop good communication between husband and wife. It's one of those issues you can sit down together to discuss and then come to a reasonable compromise. A budget is really very simple. You have a given amount of money to spend. A budget helps you decide how you're going to spend it. No more will you be so quick to raise your debt to higher heights. You will be less inclined toward indiscriminate spending, discretionary purchases and impulse buying. You will stay out of the stores that provide you with the greatest opportunities for temptation.

Budgeting will give your family a spending plan. A budget is simply a family spending plan; a money makeover, if you will. You've heard of personal and physical makeovers. You know that if you diet (and don't cheat) and get yourself on an exercise plan (and stick to it), well, the pounds are going to come off. Not only will you feel better about yourself, you'll feel more in control of your physical health. Budgets are like your own personal or family business on a smaller scale. It paints the picture of all your income, minus all your expenses, and tells you what is left over. It becomes a guideline to all of your spending. When you budget your income and expenses and you see what the result is, you may either have to raise your income or reduce your spending.

Here's how it translates financially: If you make a budget (and stick to it) and put money away for short- and long-term goals (with regularity), you'll feel better about your financial health—and more in control of your financial future.

Fortunately, you don't need an MBA to get your finances in shape. You don't need hours of extra time. A few basic steps will get you where you need to go.

Budgeting encourages good communication. If you are married, have a family, or share money with anyone, having a budget that you create together is a key to resolving personal differences about money handling. The budget is a communication tool to discuss the priorities for where your money should be spent, as well as enabling all involved parties to run the system.

BENEFITS IN YOUR PLANNING AND ORGANIZATION

Budgeting encourages self-discipline. The best way to start is to keep tabs on all the money—all of it that comes in and goes out for a month. That means not only logging the checks you write to the electric and phone companies and everyone else, but also keeping track of the cash you spend. One way to get disciplined is to keep all your receipts, then jot down every penny you spent at the end of each day.

Budgeting gives you financial balance and order. The word "order" suggests balance. No one area of our financial lives should outweigh other areas to the point of weakening them or putting them out of focus. Order helps keep entertainment, for example, in line with the total budget, so that essentials like food and shelter are adequately covered.

Budgeting gives you financial control. A budget is the key to enabling you to take charge of your finances. With a budget, you have the tools to decide what is going to happen to your hard-earned money and when. It bears repeating: you can be in control of your money, instead of letting it control you!

Budgeting provides organization. Even in its simplest form, a budget divides funds into categories of expenditures and savings. Beyond that, however, budgets can provide further organization by automatically providing records of all your monetary transactions. They can also provide the foundation for a simple filing system to organize bills, receipts and financial statements.

BENEFITS IN YOUR
FINANCIAL VISION AND GOALS

Budgeting helps you attain special goals. Find out exactly where you are right now. Get all your financial bills and statements in order. It may not be very pleasant to find out how deeply you are in debt, but you might as well face it. Otherwise, you'll continue in the same old rut—digging ever deeper. Once you have noted all your debts, put down what income you realistically can expect in. Let's hope you have more income than outgo! If you find that is not the case, get in the habit of living below your means.

If you are typical, you'll find your debts cannot be paid off right away. That's where budgeting comes in. Having a budget to many people is distasteful. It's like having to go on a diet or like being a child told to go to your room. It seems like punishment for alleged wrongdoing.

A budget provides a blueprint for reaching those goals. A budget might be compared to a blueprint or map. It suggests a plan or route for getting from where we are to some other place. A financial plan shows where you are now and how you might gain what you want to accomplish.

A budget systematizes one's money affairs and aids in accomplishing goals. A budget, or plan, is a tool that is used in managing money. However the budget does not do the managing. People do.

A carpenter would never start work on a new house without a blueprint. An aerospace firm would never begin construction on a new rocket booster without a detailed set of design specifications. Yet many of us find ourselves in the circumstance of getting out on our own and making, spending and investing money without a plan to guide us. Budgeting is about planning. And planning is crucial to produce a desired result.

A budget allows you to take advantage of opportunities. Knowing the exact state of your personal monetary affairs and being in control allows you to take advantage of opportunities that you might otherwise miss. Have you ever wondered if you could afford something? With a budget, you will never have to wonder again—you will know.

"I hear, I know. I see, I remember. I do, I understand."

Key Points:

➤ defining the role of budgets   ➤ financial benefits of budgeting

➤ budgeting to secure your future   ➤ effects of budgeting on others

1. **Write down** any parts of the chapter that were meaningful to you.

_____

_____

_____

_____

2. **Personal Application:** How can you personally apply these truths in your own life? Write down several long-term goals.

_____

_____

_____

_____

3. **Steps to Action:** Write down one small step you could take to begin immediately applying the truths and principles of this chapter.

_____

_____

_____

_____

4. **Prayer for the Practical:** Write out a prayer to God asking Him for help in making any changes that these goals would require.

_____

_____

_____

_____

Psalm 62:8 "O my people, trust in him at all times.

Pour out your heart to him,

For God is our refuge."

Section IV: INCORPORATING TRUTH...

CHAPTER EIGHTEEN

BREAKING OUT OF THE BUDGETING BLUES: TIPS ON HOW TO SUCCEED

"I know how to live on almost nothing or with everything. I have learned the secret of living in every situation, whether it is with a full stomach or empty, with plenty or little. For I can do everything through Christ, who gives me strength."

—THE APOSTLE PAUL, WRITING TO THE PHILIPPIANS FROM PRISON
PHILIPPIANS 4:12-13

The most important part of making a budget work is not how the budget is set up. The most important part of the budgeting process is you! You are the only one who can make it work.

Many people say, "I just don't know where it all goes" or "I just can't seem to make ends meet." As discussed before, you should be careful to form a habit of writing down your expenses. Keep track of your outgo. It's surprising what you find when you get it all down on paper.

We also analyzed how a general budget includes the following benefits. You can...

- Review past spending and saving

- Regularly record all expenses

- Intelligently explore all expenditures and their options

- Control what you spend

- Project future spending and saving

- Enjoy including family members in the process

- Manage your money, rather than allowing it to manage you

In this chapter, we will discuss some further budgeting tips, discussing how to organize your monthly, quarterly, and annual bills. We will also address some common budgeting errors which occur, and how to avoid these mistakes.

POWERFUL HELPS IN BUDGETING

We have learned that a budget is a powerful method of gaining control, planning, communicating and fulfilling your dreams. At the very least, a budget should allow you to find extra spending money in your paycheck every month. Everyone can successfully reap the benefits of budgeting; just take it step by step. The payoff is big. It is a great life-changing experience to get and maintain control of your finances. The effects permeate every aspect of your life.

If you are new to budgeting, don't overwhelm yourself and categorize your expenses into too many little categories. Start with a few big buckets at first, until you get the rhythm; then fine-tune your budget.

If you're a parent, make this a household activity by involving all members, making sure there is some fun in it for everyone. If you never go any further than spending some time tracking your expenses for a few weeks, at least do that. The insights you'll gain from paying attention to your habits will go a long way!

- Be patient. Consider the first three months as a test period. You may have to adjust your budgeted amounts in some categories.

- Invest or save any windfall income. At the very least, treat it with care. Example: tax refunds, dividends and bonuses.

- If you have a quarterly, semiannual or annual payment (like auto licenses, insurance or taxes), calculate how much those cost you on a monthly basis. Then save that amount each month, so when the bill arrives, it doesn't throw your budget into a tailspin.

- Don't forget to pay yourself. If possible, make sure you save something each month that can go toward an investment.

- Don't try to keep track of every penny (nickels & dimes, yes!). It will drive you and everyone else nuts.

- Make impulse buying difficult. Leave your checkbook and credit cards at home.

- Make sure you set aside some money for having fun.

- Have some fun money for each family member.

- Budget for a fun item (vacation, toy).

- Don't over-categorize (too many expense categories).

- Don't divide a couple's paychecks functionally (using her check for certain categories and his for others).

- Use an interest-bearing checking account.

- Make savings an expense item.

- Create an expense item to pay off credit-card balances.

- Pay off the highest-interest rate cards first.

- Don't use credit cards again until the balance is paid off.

- After a loan is paid off, keep paying the loan amount to yourself and make a vacation or car fund.

- Set aside money monthly for bills that are due quarterly, semi-annually or yearly.

- Reconcile your budget at least once a month when balancing your checking statement.

- Make sure to mark your last reconcile point in your budget.

- Get utilities or banks to change the due dates of bills to make your work easier.

- Remember, just the act of identifying your expenses is extremely valuable.

These simple tips on budgeting can work even for those who are very young and have little income or perhaps have only the allowance given by their parents.

How to Organize Your Monthly, Quarterly and Annual Bills

✓ Paying your bills promptly will help you avoid late fees and save you money.

✓ Following basic steps will help you get rid of procrastination and keep your finances in good order.

✓ Set aside a special place to put your bills when they arrive, such as a special slot on your desk, a special section in a drawer or a bill inbox. Remember to always put your bills in this special place immediately upon their arrival.

✓ Set aside two times a month, two weeks apart, to pay bills. The middle and end of the month are good times.

✓ Call the companies that send you bills and have them revise your payment due dates to correspond with one of the two times monthly you plan to pay your bills.

✓ Mark your calendar to remind you of bill-paying dates, then pay on schedule.

✓ Pay your bills with checks or money orders, then note on the receipt portion of the bills your check number and the date and amount you paid.

- ✓ File these receipts away and keep them for up to seven years.

- ✓ Place the outgoing envelopes containing your payments next to your car or house keys, so that you remember to take them with you and mail them immediately.

- ✓ Be sure to continue your bill-paying efforts all the way to the mailbox. Nothing is more frustrating than to write your bills on time, then find them not mailed in the back seat of your car a week later.

- ✓ Some credit card companies, mortgage lenders and automobile financing companies move due dates around. Check the due dates for such bills as soon as they arrive in the mail.

Utility and phone companies are usually a little more flexible and will wait for a few days before they send you a reminder notice or charge you a late fee. Credit card companies, mortgage and automobile lenders, oil companies and landlords are not as forgiving. Many banks allow you to set up automatic bill payment with your checking account. Call your bank to find out if it offers such a service. But be careful…unpaid bills can lead to disconnected utilities, a bad credit rating and debt.

COMMON ERRORS IN BUDGETING

Don't you just hate to fail, especially when you've invested time and effort into a project? It happens all the time, especially for those who are starting to take control of their finances. Here are some common errors to watch for.

Impractical Goals

It's easy to fall into our first failure trap. In fact, in some ways it's hard to avoid it. That's because it's built right into the process. Our first step in starting a budget is to add up all our income and also all our expenses. Then we try to juggle the two until we get the income equal to the expenses. It's a game of getting the math to work out.

What's wrong with that? Well, quite often, we take the list of expenses and pick a number that just seems right. For instance, we might decide that we can live on a grocery budget of $200 per month. But, if that target is just a guess, it's probably the wrong number. And, if we reduced it to get the expenses below our income, it's probably too low.

So now we put the budget into practice. Then we get near the end of the first month. There's a week left and we've already spent our budgeted $200. Out comes the credit card and we begin to curse our budget.

But, what has really happened here? We set up a target that was unrealistic—and missed it. Now that doesn't mean our budget won't work. It just means that we need to set a more realistic target.

In fact, we're in a better position now to accomplish that, because we have a better idea of what we actually do spend on groceries. No more guesses. This is no time to quit. Rather it's an opportunity to make adjustments and keep moving toward our goal of having control of our finances.

Giving Up Too Soon

The second common cause of failure, quitting too soon, is similar. Say you've been trying to use a budget for a couple of months. You've done all the math and kept track of both the money coming into your home and where you've spent it. You've worked hard on this.

Yet you always seem to get to the end of your money before the month is over. Frustration sets in. The temptation is to throw in the towel and give up. A perfectly understandable response, but it's the wrong answer. Look at it this way. Suppose you were driving to Disneyworld and, about half way there, you realized you had made a wrong turn and had driven 50 miles off your planned route. Would you quit and go home? Of course not!

So why should we give up on a budget just because everything doesn't work perfectly the first few months? Do the same thing that you'd do on your vacation.

Look at your budget map and adjust your route to find the best way to reach your destination. Make the adjustment and move forward.

Misunderstanding the Purpose of a Budget

Our final cause for budget failure is not understanding what a budget really is. Too many people think that a budget is something to keep them from spending money. However, that is wrong. It's not a straightjacket.

A budget is a tool to provide you with information to manage your finances. The knowledge gained by tracking income and expenses will help you get the most for your money. In fact, a budget can help you find money, so you can spend where it will give you the most enjoyment.

Fortunately, all three problems can be corrected by using the budget as a management tool. Each month, your budget will show what you planned and actually earned and spent. That's valuable information. The trick is to see where the actual numbers differed from the expected numbers.

Once you've found a big difference, you can begin to analyze why it happened. Was there a big one-time expense this month? Maybe you committed our first mistake and just guessed at what you'd spend. But it could be that you've been spending carelessly on groceries. If that's the case, you'll look to find some savings this month.

Each month, work on the biggest differences until the whole process runs smoothly. Just take on one or two at a time. Month by month, you should get closer to actually having control over your finances. After awhile it's just a matter of checking to make sure that everything is roughly on target and making minor mid-course corrections.

Now that's not to say that it's easy to resolve those differences. Sometimes it's not. But it's always easier to work when you have some clues to help point you in the right direction. With the information your budget provides, you know where to look for possible savings. That is often the difference between frustration and success.

It's always a shame when you work hard and don't receive any benefit from your work. Don't let that happen to your budget. It takes much less effort to fix a budget than to start one. You've already put in the hardest work, so take the time to reap the benefits. You deserve it.

Family or Relationship Strife

Genesis 2:24 says that God created a husband and a wife to be one. That means that, in the context of a marriage relationship, a budget must work for two people and not just for one.

A common error in budgeting is to try to overcorrect previous bad habits. Crash budgets may work on paper, but not where people are involved. The husband may deem some purchases for the wife to be unnecessary, while in fact he considers his fishing supply expenditures a necessity.

In some cases the husband can make out a budget that works very well for him, but in doing so he eliminates his wife's discretionary spending, while sacrificing none of his own.

If this fits your situation perfectly, here is a Scripture for you. "The way of a fool is right in his own eyes, but a wise man is he who listens to counsel" (Proverbs 12:15 NKJV). Lesson learned? The primary counselor of any husband should be his wife.

Legalistic Budgeting

Some couples become legalistic and try to control their spending right down to the nickel. Unfortunately, many times it's the husband or the wife trying to control the other's spending.

The other extreme is that people don't maintain the discipline necessary to stay on their budgets. Many couples say, "We don't want to think about it. It's too depressing." However, thinking about how you're spending your money before you have problems is not nearly as depressing as thinking about it afterward when you're trying to climb out of a deep financial hole.

The More-Money-In, More-Money-Out Syndrome

This means you spend more simply because you have more. This is particularly dangerous if the extra money is temporary income. Although not possible for all couples, one idea is to just rely on one spouse's income, setting aside additional income in your monthly budget. Save this money and use it for one-time purchases such as a car, a down payment on a home, or vacations.

Thinking that a Little Debt Won't Hurt

Generally, the little debts come from taking a needed vacation that is more expensive than you can afford, from gifts that you just had to buy, or a car you had to have. You get the idea. A little debt will hurt, because once you've developed a cycle of debt, it grows and grows. Eventually you find yourself borrowing money just to make payments on the money you borrowed. So limit your debt right from the start.

Automatic Checking Account Overdrafts

An automatic overdraft allows you to write a check for more than you have in your account, which becomes a loan from the bank. Many couples run up thousands of dollars in debt on overdrafts before they realize it. This does two things. It encourages you to be lazy and not keep good records and it builds debt that is difficult to reduce.

Misuse of Automatic Teller Machines (ATM)

Many people fail to log ATM withdrawals in their checkbooks and end up writing bad checks. Also, it's easy to develop the habit of using the cash withdrawal to buffer your budget when you have spent what you originally allocated.

Refusing to Balance Your Checkbook

You need to make an absolute commitment to do this monthly, down to the penny. It's not difficult to do and any bank has a convenient form that shows you how to do it.

The Common Feeling of Discouragement

Remember, if your budget doesn't work the first month you try it, don't become discouraged. Developing a realistic budget takes time.

Habits change slowly, especially spending habits. It may take six months or more before your budget begins to work well. At times, your resolve will be tested by everything from a clogged sewer line to a broken arm.

Stick with it. Remember, once you have entrusted your finances to God's principles, He will be faithful to provide for your needs. Using a budget is a sign you want to employ God's wisdom in your finances.

As He says in His Word, "By wisdom a house is built, and by understanding it is established" (Proverbs 24:3 NIV).

Wrong Thinking: "I don't have enough money to budget!"

Anyone—with any amount of income—can create a simple budget that works. The belief that a person doesn't have enough money to be on a budget indicates the person does not understand the concept of budgeting. Everyone, especially every Christian, should operate with a budget in order to be the best possible steward for God. Beware of an attitude that results in the "more-money-in, more-money-out syndrome." Many people who think they don't make enough money to be on a budget believe that making more money will solve their financial problems. However, without a control vehicle (budget), the more money you take in, the more money will go out.

If you will learn to manage your budget now on a limited income, then managing your budget in the future will be much easier. Whether you make a little or a lot, living within your means on a budget can keep you on the path to being financially free.

Not Teaching Your Children

A final error in budgeting is failing to pass on budgeting skills to those who will soon need them….our children! The simple form of budget that has been presented in this book can work even for those who are very young and have little income, or perhaps have only the allowance given by their parents.

> *"Instruct them to do good, to be rich in good works, to be generous and ready to share, storing up for themselves the treasure of a good foundation for the future, so that they may take hold of that which is life indeed" (I Timothy 6:18-19 NASU).*

"I hear, I know. I see, I remember. I do, I understand."

Key Points:

➤ categorizing / writing down expenses   ➤ more tips for successful budgeting

➤ setting realistic categories / goals   ➤ common budgeting hindrances

1. **Write down** any parts of the chapter that were meaningful to you.

_____

_____

_____

_____

2. **Personal Application:** How can you personally apply these truths in your own life? Write down several long-term goals.

_____

_____

_____

_____

3. **Steps to Action:** Write down one small step you could take to begin immediately applying the truths and principles of this chapter.

_____

_____

_____

_____

4. **Prayer for the Practical:** Write out a prayer to God asking Him for help in making any changes that these goals would require.

_____

_____

_____

_____

Psalm 62:8 "O my people, trust in him at all times.
Pour out your heart to him,
For God is our refuge."

CHAPTER NINETEEN

DUSTING OFF THE PIGGY BANK

"The secret of financial success is to spend what you have left after saving, instead of saving what is left after spending."

—Author unknown

Long-term investing is your best hedge against inflation, but you need to save in order to invest. This can be tough to do. Have you ever noticed that after you pay your monthly bills, buy groceries and cover your other expenses, you have little left in your paycheck? Consider contributing to your savings plan first—not last—each month.

A Three-Part Strategy

Saving money is hard work. And the hardest part is simply getting started. If you're beginning from scratch, consider this three-part strategy:

1. Save for the unexpected—three to six month's worth of living expenses. In case you lose a job or find yourself with no steady income, this rainy-day fund will become necessary. Take no chances with this money. Keep it readily available, in a bank account or a money-market mutual fund.

2. Save for long-range expenses—a new home or college for the kids. Be more flexible with this money. Keep it in long-term certificates of deposit or in Series EE Savings Bonds. You'll earn more interest than in a conventional bank account and you can time your investment so the money is available when you need it.

3. Save for retirement. That can mean an Individual Retirement Account, a company retirement plan, or other solid financial investments. A conservative mutual fund that invests only in top-quality stocks is one possibility. Or you might risk a little more for a greater reward by investing in a mutual fund that buys growth stocks.

AUTOMATED SAVINGS

The following steps can help you make this practice automatic:

Set up an automatic payroll deduction. Thanks to payroll deduction programs, such as credit unions or 401(k) plans, part of your paycheck can go directly into your investment account.

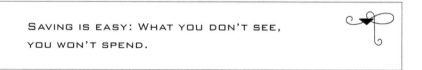

> SAVING IS EASY: WHAT YOU DON'T SEE, YOU WON'T SPEND.

Set up an automatic bank transfer. Many investment companies will transfer money automatically from your bank account to your investment account according to a schedule that you specify. Such a program can make saving for retirement as natural as paying the mortgage.

Invest all salary increases. Direct half of your next raise into an investment account before it reaches your wallet and you get used to spending the extra income.

Invest lump sum payments. Invest a portion of bonuses and tax refunds; you'll turn the extra money into added savings—not increased spending.

Section IV: INCORPORATING TRUTH...

A Few Starter Tips

Set Savings Goals

Start with 5-10 percent of every paycheck. It's easiest if your employer deducts it from your pay because you don't miss money you don't see. You could also ask your bank to move it from checking to savings every month or make automatic investments into a no-load (no sales charge) mutual fund. Saving is more certain when someone else arranges it for you. The goal may be college for the kids. It may be retirement in a few years. It could be a new car, a boat or a summer place. A real key here is that it forces you to think ahead, beyond the next paycheck. Any successful business is one that plans for the future; many times, 5 and 10 years ahead. Japanese companies project plans even longer.

Pay Yourself First

After taking care of your tithing obligations, the next person in line to be paid is you. Although this seems very hard to do with all of our other obligations, just get started by forming a regular habit. It will get easier as you progress. Use direct deposit for automatic savings. It can be much easier to save when the money goes directly into a savings account. In that way, the decision to save is out of your hands. What you don't see, you are not likely to miss as much.

Avoid Spending on Impulse

Most of us save too little because we spend too much on impulse items. Control that urge to splurge. Keep a list of all the things you really need - coats for the kids, a new refrigerator, tires for the car, etc. But wait to buy until those items go on sale. If you're drawn to something not on the list, give yourself a week to think it over.

Save All Extra Money

Once you have paid off a loan, start paying yourself by putting an equivalent amount of money directly into savings. If you have a car loan you're about to pay off and you've been paying $250 a month, keep the car for a couple more years and save that $250 each month. Some people plan so there's a tax refund each year, but most financial planners suggest handling your taxes so you don't overpay. After all, Uncle Sam doesn't pay any interest on the overpayment.

Thrift used to be a basic part of the American ethic. Before we were a nation, Ben Franklin said, "A penny saved is two pence clear."[20] All of us would benefit by returning to that thinking.

WAYS TO MAKE YOUR SAVINGS GROW FASTER!

Put cash you don't need right away in three- or five-year CD's. If you need the money and have to break into the CD before it matures, you might pay a six month interest penalty. But that's nothing compared with the penalty you're imposing on yourself by settling for today's low short term rates "just in case."

Money Market Fund

Keep the cash you use for big bills in a money market mutual fund instead of a bank account. You may get free checks and your money continues to earn interest until the check clears. As a rule, money funds pay from 0.5 to 2 percent more than the highest rate you can get with most banks.

Stock Mutual Fund

Buy a mutual fund that invests entirely in U.S. Treasury securities. These are even safer than money market mutual funds and, if you live in a high tax state, they're a better deal. Although Treasury funds often yield a little less than other money market funds, you owe no state or local income taxes on your earnings, so your return is much higher.

U.S. Treasuries

Buy Treasury securities instead of CD's if you live in a high tax state. You can buy Treasuries free through the nearest Federal Reserve bank or branch. Check your telephone book under U.S. Government or ask your own bank for the address. The minimum investment in Treasuries maturing in one year or less is $10,000; in two or three years, $5,000; in four years or more, $1,000.

Check your tax bracket carefully before buying tax-exempt mutual funds. You'll generally net more after taxes, by investing in higher yielding taxable funds if you're in the 15 percent federal tax bracket. Sometimes taxables pay for people in the 28 percent bracket too, but in the highest brackets, tax exempts are usually best.

17 Practical Ways to Save Your Money

1. Develop new habits.

Become a skillful shopper. Regional retail centers are exciting places. In supermarkets, thousands of goods line the shelves and invite attention. It takes skill and determination to pass down the aisles and resist temptation. The skillful shopper prepares a shopping list before going to market and buys only those items needed.

Learn to read labels and interpret them. Make substitutions for the higher priced items, judge the value of the week's bargain offerings and decide whether the best buys are best for the family. Careful shopping can save many dollars a week in the budget.

2. Get rid of credit card debt.

Here is a good way to save some big money fast. There is one great investment that is sure to pay off, yet we fail to recognize it, even though it's right in front of us every month. Pay off your credit cards! Let's say for example that you owe $2,000 on a Visa card. Many charge cards still have an interest rate in the neighborhood of 19 percent.

Instead of taking that $2,000 bonus check and investing it into some low-interest-paying bank account, pay off that credit card and get a great return on your money! By paying off the outstanding balance, it is the same as getting a check for $570 tax-free! And one more thing: be a real friend to yourself by cutting up the card and canceling your credit. You'll be glad you did! It's the best financial investment you can make. If you're in the 30 percent state and federal tax bracket, paying off an 18 percent credit-card debt provides the same return as an investment that yields 26 percent! If you're in the 17 percent bracket, paying off credit cards is the same as earning 22 percent. Why keep money in a 5 percent (or less) savings account when it can earn 22 percent paying off your credit cards?

3. Use installment credit sparingly.

Recognize that any installment purchase or loan means one more fixed expense in the budget. Although credit is readily available and most anything can be obtained, be wary of the low-down, low-monthly-payment offers. There may be times when installment purchases are unavoidable, but this kind of spending, if excessive, can become a costly way of providing for family needs or for achieving family goals.

4. Take good care of your assets.

Clothes last longer and remain better looking if they are kept clean and pressed. Food lasts longer when it is properly stored. Equipment lasts longer and gives better service when used according to the manufacturer's instructions. It makes sense to prolong the use of one's possessions by taking care of them. The longer we can use an article, the more we are getting for our money.

5. Update your homeowner's policy.

As a rule, you need to be covered for at least 80 percent of the cost of rebuilding your house. Otherwise you won't get full reimbursement even if a fire destroys only one room. Ask your insurance agent how to estimate the cost. If you rent, get tenant's insurance to cover furniture and other valuables. Many renters fail to do this, thinking losses will be covered by the landlord. Not so!

6. Update your life insurance policy.

You need only enough to take care of your dependents if you die. If there is a non-bread winner in the family, generally stick with low-cost term insurance; then cut it back or cancel it when the children grow up. Primary breadwinners, by contrast, often have to provide for an aging spouse, so they may need some cash value insurance whose premiums won't rise as they get older. If you have no dependents, you don't need life insurance. Put cash into retirement funds or disability insurance instead. Disability insurance is overlooked by many people.

7. Start a retirement fund.

If you work for a corporation which has one, use the 401(k) plan. If employed by a firm with no pension plan, open an Individual Retirement Account. As a rule, both the contributions to these plans and the earnings are untaxed until you withdraw the money, so tax savings help pay the cost. If you leave your job, you can take 401(k) savings with you. Do not fail to use these plans! They're the best route to independence in old age.

8. Get the best health insurance possible.

If you aren't covered at work, try to participate in a group plan through an organization you belong to or can join. Alternatively, call Blue Cross/Blue Shield or a Health Maintenance Organization (check the yellow pages). If you can't afford what they offer, talk to an insurance agent about a high deductible policy that covers only major medical costs. (You pay the small bills, but the huge ones are covered.) Today's buyers often take deductibles of $1,000 to $5,000, which greatly lowers costs. Whatever you do, never buy insurance advertised by celebrities on TV; it's not worth the cost.

9. Pay off your home mortgage faster.

All over America, homeowners are taking 15 year mortgages or making extra payments on long-term mortgages, which has the effect of shortening the term. Any homeowner who has taken a look at an amortization schedule realizes that a large part of their monthly payment merely covers the interest charges on the outstanding debt, instead of paying down on the original loan.

Faster payments do lower interest costs and allow you to own your home free and clear sooner. A paid-up home is the cheapest way to live in retirement. By making slightly larger monthly payments than your loan requires, you'll significantly reduce your total interest cost and pay off your mortgage years early. For example, send in $50 extra in advance every month on a $150,000, 30-year, ten-percent mortgage and you'll save $68,325 and reduce the term of your loan by more than five years.

While it is true that mortgage interest can offset your taxable income, this has limited value. The offset does not reduce the tax itself, rather it reduces taxable income. If you are in the twenty-eight percent tax bracket, a $100 mortgage-interest deduction will save $28 in federal taxes, $31 for you if you are in the thirty-one percent tax bracket and so on. The remaining part of that $100 mortgage ($72 or $69) interest payment is lost. Additionally, people with adjusted incomes well over $125,000 may not be allowed to deduct all of their mortgage interest.

Instead of making only the minimum payment required by a lender, many people today are repaying their loans more quickly. One way to do this is to use a fifteen-year rather than a thirty-year amortization schedule. Another way is to prepay the mortgage either by making extra payments or by increasing the size of the regularly scheduled payments and specifying that the surplus should be applied to principal. According to Spirit Magazine, adding a mere $10 a month to each payment, beginning in the third year of a $100,000 thirty-year mortgage at eight percent, can save $8,515 in interest charges and will pay off the debt sixteen months early.

David Ginsbury, president of Loantech, says, "Making just one prepayment of principal a year can make a tremendous difference over time." He goes on to note that starting with the same $100,000 loan at eight percent for thirty years, a prepayment of $500 each December will cause the mortgage to be paid off twenty-nine months early, while one-time annual prepayments of $1,000 and $2,000 will retire debt in twenty-two years, seven months and eighteen years, eight months, respectively.

These results are so dramatic that it might seem as if every homeowner should begin prepaying immediately. But don't forget to first have about six months of income set aside as an emergency fund.

10. Use non-money resources.

It is very easy to rely entirely on financial resources for all the goods one wants and needs. But this kind of thinking and living places a very heavy burden on the family income and often postpones the day when a goal can be achieved. However, by developing skills among family members and by substituting one's time, energy and skill in place of money, many services can be provided at home without dipping into the family funds. This kind of planning and achieving often provides far greater satisfaction than does the routine of shopping and buying.

11. *If you want it to last, choose quality over price.*

Do you look for quality rather than just cost or appearance when you buy something that you want to last a long time? Do you save sales slips, guarantees and other records of purchases so you know where to find them? Do you buy at reliable stores that stand behind their merchandise? Read the labels on boxes, packages or other purchases to determine the real quantity or quality you are getting for your money. Instead of purchasing your wants immediately, put money aside to save for something you want but can't afford at the moment.

12. *Pause before purchasing.*

Before spending your hard-earned resources, pause a while to ask yourself three simple questions.

A. Can I really afford it?

B. Do I really need it?

Whether or not you can afford it may be a simple matter of addition and subtraction—you either have enough money or you don't. But more often it will be a matter of deciding how important this particular purchase is compared to other purchases you may want to make.

There are many things we might like to have which would make life easier and more fun. Don't think you must always deny yourself all of these; after all, life is supposed to be fun as well as work. Many things that would have been considered luxuries in past years are now considered necessities. But you are going to have to pick and choose according to whatever your particular desires are. The more limited your budget, the more picking and choosing you are going to have to do. This is one of the harder facts of life.

C. Is it worth what I'm paying for it?

This is where spending money becomes a real skill. Worth or value is often hard to determine. Value in this case means the quality of the product itself; it also means the usefulness of the product for your particular purposes. You have to think about both. In determining value, price alone can be misleading. The lowest price may be the best value for your money, but then again it may not be. The highest price doesn't necessarily mean the best value either. Usually, you will find the best value somewhere in between.

Generally, when you are buying a product where length of service and performance are important, quality—how well it is made, how well it functions, how long it will last—is first consideration. Price is, within budget limits, a second consideration. Appearance may or may not be a consideration. If it's a suit or dress, yes; if it's an electric drill, probably not.

If you are buying a product where length of service is not so important—soap or paper plates, for instance—the lower price is usually the better value for your purposes. Quality is not as important, as long as what you buy does the job to your satisfaction. A lot of hard work and a little luck will stretch your dollars a little more. (The unit cost is most important here—how much does each paper plate cost?)

13. *You can save by putting yourself to work:*

- Always switch off the lights when you leave a room.

- Borrow books from your local public library instead of buying them.

- Buy a used car rather than a new one.

- Buy holiday cards and decorations after Christmas at half price or less and save them for next year.

- Eat out at lunchtime rather than at dinner—it is usually at least 40 percent cheaper.

- Learn to give yourself haircuts and experiment cutting your family's hair.

- Look for a package when planning a trip.

- Practice the art of trading down: one step down in suits, in travel arrangements, in size of rental cars, etc.

- Put aside gifts that can't be used or returned with the name of the giver and later on give them to someone else as a gift. Important: Catalog each gift to be sure not to give it to the person who gave it to you! (But don't save unused fruit cakes until next year!)

- Return empty bottles to the supermarket and get back your deposit.

Section IV: INCORPORATING TRUTH...

- Reuse paper clips.

- Review insurance policies to avoid overlapping coverage.

- Save the plastic or paper bags from the supermarket to use as garbage bags.

- Take advantage of all free or low-cost offers: snacks at the supermarket, free visits to try out a health club, two-for-one meals at a restaurant, etc.

- Take up walking or jogging in the park or the street and avoid the cost of joining a health club. Use free city parks and tennis courts, instead of paid recreational areas.

- Wash your car yourself instead of taking it to the car wash.

- Wear a sweater at home during cool months, so that you can keep the thermostat turned down.

- When eating out, take advantage of the special fixed-price early dinners.

- When you become tired of some article of clothing, instead of disposing of it, put it aside for a season or two, then take it out again and it will look new.

- With relatives or friends, arrange for children's hand-me-downs to be saved and passed on from child to child.

14. Understand inflation.

The rise in the price of goods and services, better known as inflation, can steadily erode the purchasing power of your income. That's why it's important to invest a portion of your savings. Inflation has been relatively tame in recent years. Since 1960, inflation has averaged 4.5 percent per year. Since 1988, it has averaged 3.5 percent per year. Still, no one can predict the direction of inflation rates, which could decline even more or return to the double-digit rates of the late 1970's and early 1980's. Even if inflation holds steady at 3.5 percent per year for 20 years, consumer prices will nearly double, as illustrated in the following table.

ITEM PURCHASED TODAY	COST IN 20 YEARS (4.5% AVERAGE ANNUAL INFLATION RATE)	COST IN 20 YEARS (3.5% AVERAGE ANNUAL INFLATION RATE)
Coffee & Scone - $7	$16.88	$13.93
Steak for 1 - $20	$48.23	$39.80
A Weekend Away - $500	$1,205.86	$994.89

15. *Understand the power of compounding.*

Inflation can steadily erode the value of your income. Long-term investing offers the best antidote to inflation through the power of compounding.

Year after year, any money that you invest may earn interest, dividends or capital gains. When you reinvest those earnings, they help generate additional earnings. Those additional earnings help generate more earnings and so on. This is called compounding.

For example, if an investment returns 8 percent per year and its earnings are reinvested annually:

- After one year, your total return will be 8 percent.

- After five years, your cumulative total return will be 47 percent.

- After ten years, your cumulative total return will be 116 percent.

Best of all, the sooner you begin investing, the greater the compounding effect.

16. *Begin saving while you are young.*

Consider the example of Dick and Jane, both 65 years old. They worked for the same company for 35 years and both invested in their employer-sponsored retirement plan. Jane started contributing at age 30. She invested $1,000 each year for ten years until the age of 40 and earned 8 percent per year. Then she stopped contributing; her investment continued to earn an 8 percent annual return. When she reached age 65, her $10,000 had grown to $107,100.

Dick postponed making contributions until age 40 and then invested $1,000 each year for 25 years. He also earned 8 percent per year. At the end of the period, his $25,000 investment was worth $79,000.

As you can see, although Jane contributed to her company plan for 15 fewer years than Dick and invested $15,000 less, she accumulated $28,100 more than Dick—simply because she started investing ten years earlier.

17. Learn how to invest.

Saving and investing are often used interchangeably, but they are somewhat different. Saving is storing money safely—such as in a bank or money market account—for short-term needs such as upcoming expenses or emergencies. Typically, you earn a low, fixed rate of return and can withdraw your money easily.

Investing is taking a risk with a portion of your savings—such as by buying stocks or bonds—in hopes of realizing higher long-term returns. Unlike bank savings, stocks and bonds over the long term have returned enough to outpace inflation, but they also decline in value from time to time.

"I hear, I know. I see, I remember. I do, I understand."

Key Points:

➤ developing new savings habits ➤ home mortgage and insurance tips

➤ spending habits to help you save ➤ understanding inflation and compounding

1. **Write down** any parts of the chapter that were meaningful to you.

_____

_____

_____

_____

2. **Personal Application:** How can you personally apply these truths in your own life? Write down several long-term goals.

_____

_____

_____

_____

Section IV: INCORPORATING TRUTH...

3. **Steps to Action:** Write down one small step you could take to begin immediately applying the truths and principles of this chapter.

4. **Prayer for the Practical:** Write out a prayer to God asking Him for help in making any changes that these goals would require.

Psalm 62:8 "O my people, trust in him at all times.
Pour out your heart to him,
For God is our refuge."

"Whenever you get a blessing from God, give it back to Him as a love gift... If you hoard a thing for yourself, it will turn into spiritual dry rot, as the manna did when it was hoarded. God will never let you hold a spiritual thing for yourself; it has to be given back to Him that He may make it a blessing to others."

—OSWALD CHAMBERS, SCOTTISH AUTHOR,
DEVOTIONAL WRITER, *MY UTMOST FOR HIS HIGHEST*

CHAPTER TWENTY

MINOR ADJUSTMENTS FOR MAJOR CHANGE

What are some of the mistakes that families make when managing their finances? Hundreds of wrong choices could be listed, including those that result from making decisions without knowledge or without taking the time to clearly think them through. Some mistakes are the result of character issues such as wrong values, selfishness, irresponsibility or lack of integrity. Other mistakes simply are the result of hastiness, lack of education or wrong priorities.

> THERE ARE ONLY FIVE THINGS YOU CAN DO WITH MONEY.
> GIVE IT, SAVE IT, INVEST IT, LEND IT AND SPEND IT.

Some are simply wrong choices made out of greed. How much is enough money? Usually just a little bit more. This kind of thinking gets people into trouble and is an indication that lifestyle changes need to occur. There are only five things you can do with money. Give it, save it, invest it, lend it and spend it. Notice where spending comes in that lineup: last. Spending should never be the first thing you do with your money. Because the proper management of money is specific and orderly, spending it first short-circuits the system with fiscal disorder and financial chaos.

People who have a spending habit that has gotten them into trouble need to make a plan, get out of debt and stop spending money they don't have. Then when they are in complete control of their money, go ahead and start saving for specific needs or for a

331

home. But you first need a written plan—a budget. A written plan stands firm whether you're on an emotional roller coaster or an even keel. Your attitude toward spending should be "no debt, no matter what."

KEYS TO FINANCIAL CHANGE

This chapter focuses on small ways that you can bring about change to your financial situation. Many of these changes initially seem very minor. When collectively integrated into your life, however, these minor adjustments in thinking and action can result in major change.

The following list of 10 financial principles were penned by the Reverend William J. H. Boetcke.[21] Part of the beauty of these remarks is that they are short, to the point, and easily understood by anyone.

- You cannot bring about prosperity by discouraging thrift.

- You cannot help small men by tearing down big men.

- You cannot strengthen the weak by weakening the strong.

- You cannot lift the wage earner by pulling down the wage payer.

- You cannot help the poor man by destroying the rich.

- You cannot keep out of trouble by spending more than your income.

- You cannot further the brotherhood of man by inciting class hatred.

- You cannot establish security on borrowed money.

- You cannot build character and courage by taking away men's initiative and independence.

- You cannot help men permanently by doing for them what they could and should do for themselves.

Bring About Change by Making Small Sacrifices

You CAN do WITHOUT these things:

- Cable TV
- Call Waiting, Call Forwarding, Conference Calling
- Gourmet coffee drinks/snacks
- Hobby acquisitions and/or expenses
- Lodging expenses at the beach, mountains or other destinations
- Massages and manicures
- Movies
- New clothes
- Restaurants
- Sports events
- Unnecessary vehicles (all new vehicles)

Bring About Change by Paying with Cash

Plastic—ATM card, debit cards and credit cards—are all stand-ins for money. They are not the real thing. They are just representatives, and often poor ones, when they represent debt.

Five reasons to pay cash!

- Paying cash means making some lifestyle changes and sacrifices, but it will keep you from drowning in a sea of red ink on your journey to financial freedom.
- Paying cash keeps you focused.
- Paying cash promotes contentment by adding meaning and value to the things you buy.
- Paying cash lets you own things, not merely acquire them.
- Paying cash makes spending difficult and uncomfortable—exactly the way it should be.

Bring About Change by Obeying God's Principles

There are certain principles which, if followed, will lead to a peaceful and prosperous life:

> *"Blessings on all who reverence and trust the Lord— on all who obey Him! Their reward shall be prosperity and happiness" (Psalm 128:1-2 TLB).*

1. You must never keep it all.

The first thing you must do when money flows into your life is give some of it away.

2. You must never spend it all.

After tithing your income, always pay yourself before anyone else. Always. Not only must you set aside a portion of all your earnings, but you need to put that money to work for you. Merely saving is not enough.

3. Remember that God is your source.

Your employer, your spouse, your investments, your trust account, your parents (or any other entity) are not the source of your money. God, who gave you the talents, intelligence and ability to think and work, is the source. Your responsibility is to be a good steward of all you receive.

> DEBT IS NOTHING MORE THAN BORROWING FROM FUTURE INCOME TO BUY NOW WHAT WE CANNOT AFFORD WITH CURRENT INCOME.

Employers, investments, spouses and parents are only the conduits in the delivery system. Grabbing onto this truth will bring a sense of peace and calm to your life. No longer will you worry about a drop in the stock market or the plunging of real estate values. No longer will you lay awake worrying about losing your job.

The way your money is delivered may change radically and frequently, but the source never changes. He is the same yesterday, today and forever.

Section IV: INCORPORATING TRUTH...

4. Remember that God knows your heart's desires!

God promises to supply all your needs and He says if you delight yourself in Him, He will also give you your desires. He is not ignorant of your needs or desires. He never falls asleep on the job or issues a due date. All He asks is that you obey His laws and trust His Word. Those who do and go on to demonstrate that they can be trusted with more are blessed beyond what they deserve or could possibly imagine.

Bring About Change by Remembering Practical Wisdom

- Americans are blessed with a lot of cash flowing through our hands. Bring a halt to some of the flow.

- Attack the problem aggressively with a plan. Your credit problems didn't just suddenly appear. It took a lot of steps to get into trouble and getting out will mean taking as much time, if not more, to draw up a financial recovery plan.

- Debt is incurred because we want something before we have the money to pay for it.

- Debt is nothing more than borrowing from future income to buy now what we cannot afford with current income.

- Getting out of debt is an attitude before it is an action.

- How do you get out of debt? Just like you got into debt…one small step at a time.

- If money isn't working for you, it's working against you and you just don't know it yet.

- If you are not content where you are, you will not be content where you want to go.

- If you don't borrow money, you can't get into debt.

- It's not what you make, it's what you spend.

- Keep track of every penny.

- Make impulse buying difficult. Leave your checkbook and credit cards at home.

- Stop spending more than you make.

- The fear of doing without in the future causes many Christians to rob God's work of the very funds He has provided.

- The only problem with borrowing money is that you have to pay it back.

- The purpose of budgeting is to free you, not confine you.

- We buy things we don't need with money we don't have to impress people we don't like.

- We should avoid debt whenever possible. In this situation, can I avoid debt?

- When you find yourself in a hole, the first thing to do is stop digging.

Debt is like cancer. At first it is not life-threatening, because it involves only a cell or two. But it never stays tiny. It begins to grow and then it takes over. It becomes the master; you become its slave. Never believe that a little debt, manageable as it may seem, is okay. It is not. Neither is a little cancer.

MINOR ADJUSTMENTS FOR MAJOR CHANGE

If your spending is out of control, it is time for a little austerity. Think of all of the minor decisions that you make in one day. What would happen if you started to make adjustments in these areas? It would eventually bring about major changes in your financial situation! Here is a comprehensive list of tips to help you analyze different aspects of your life:

- A good rule for borrowing: Never borrow to buy depreciating items. Things such as new cars, furniture, clothes, appliances, boats and luxury items should not be purchased until money is available to pay for them. Don't borrow to go on vacation, to invest in the stock market, to get married, to keep up with the Jones family, to gamble, to give the kids a head start, to bail someone else out of a jam or because you want some extra cash.

Section IV: INCORPORATING TRUTH...

- Allow no more debt. That means loans from the bank or family and no credit cards.

- As you pay off smaller debts, don't start paying less each month on your overall debt. Put that money towards another bill.

- Ask for help and seek advice about your situation. Consumer Credit Counseling Services is a good place to start.

- Assess the damage. Make a complete list of all your credit cards and loans (automobile, mortgage, student loans). Include how much you owe, the monthly payment and the interest rate. If you don't receive a monthly statement for a particular loan, call the lender for all of the information.

- Avoid cosigning or guaranteeing a loan for someone. Your signature obligates you as if you were the primary borrower. You can't be sure that the other person will pay.

- Avoid further credit and debt while you are paying off your bills.

- Avoid joint obligations with people who have questionable spending habits—even a spouse. If you incur a joint debt, you're probably liable for it all if the other person defaults.

- Avoid large rent or house payments. Obligate yourself only for what you can now afford and increase your mortgage payments only as your income increases. Consider refinancing your house if your payments are unmanageable.

- Barter your skills for someone else's skills.

- Be aware of your spending habits. Stick to the lessons you have learned about how you got into debt and how you're living to get out of it. You will probably discover along the way the things that are really important to you and what is not so important to have anymore.

- Before you purchase that must-have item, wait six months and think it through again.

- Bring your lunch to work.

- Buy used rather than new. Cars, furniture, computers, stereo equipment, televisions and appliances can all be found at substantial discounts in the want ads and at garage sales and swap meets.

- Charge items only if you can afford to pay for them now. If you don't currently have the cash, don't charge based on future income—sometimes future income doesn't materialize. An alternative is to toss all of your credit cards into a drawer (or in the garbage) and commit to living without credit for a while.

Getting out of debt is an attitude before it is an action.

- Control impulse buying.

- Clip coupons and use them. Some coupons are worth the clipping effort and others aren't. The most valuable coupons can be identified by one of the following: biggest percentage, largest dollar value or items used at least once a week.

- Create a realistic budget and stick to it. This means periodically checking it and readjusting your figures and spending habits.

- Credit cards: Don't fall into the minimum trap. If you just pay the minimum on credit-card bills, it will take you 20 years or more to pay them off. That means you'll pay more than five times the actual debt in interest.

- Credit cards: Before you spend one nickel, make sure it was pre-planned in your budget.

- Credit cards: Never use your credit cards to buy anything that is not in your budget for the month. So, of course, you should first have a budget.

- Credit cards: pay off the balance in full each month.

- Credit cards: The first month you're unable to pay the credit cards, destroy them. If you take these vows, you'll never have a problem with credit cards.

- Cut up all charge cards (department stores, gas cards, etc.).

- Cut up the high-rate cards you've paid off so you won't use them again. Also, call or write these credit card companies to cancel the cards. Otherwise you might continue to receive new cards as the old ones expire.

- Cut entertainment costs by renting DVD's rather than going to movies, eating at cheaper restaurants, eating out less frequently and brown bagging it to work. Order take-out food rather than eating at the restaurant to save on tips and drinks.

- Cut out the expensive entertainment.

- Cut your cost of transportation. Most people own more car than they really need, and the money usually goes out faster than the car anyway. Save a bundle by buying used, and maybe making public transportation a regular part of your routine, which will save even more.

- Cut your housing costs. You can do it by renting a place with fewer amenities. (Are you really using that weightlifting room anyway?) In terms of buying, you're looking at greater expense initially, but home ownership can be a good investment that grows with time.

- Deposit money in a savings account regularly and declare it off limits for withdrawals.

- Determine your net worth. Calculate your net worth by subtracting your liabilities (credit card balances, auto loans, and mortgages) from your assets (savings, investments, and property). Early in the year is an excellent time to do this. Then you should review and update your net worth worksheet about twice a year.

- Develop a balanced budget that allows each creditor to receive as much as possible.

- Develop a strategy. Without a strategic plan for getting there, reaching your goal of financial freedom will remain a dream. A plan turns a dream into a goal. Having a plan liberates you from depending on willpower. Don't depend upon your newfound willpower to curb your spending. Willpower is unreliable emotional fuel. When you have it, it can get you going at breakneck speed, but once the emotion is gone, you fizzle. Willpower is not something on which you should rely.

- Develop an awareness of the difference between wants and needs.

- Keep a written spending record. Paying attention to your spending patterns will help you in the process of paying your bills with greater control and adherence to your goals. You may then discover some holes in your budget than can be plugged up.

- Do your own chores and repairs instead of paying to have it done for you.

- Don't be so quick to pay down your mortgage. If you pour all your cash into your mortgage, you'll have no cushion to fall back on. Better to borrow as much as you can afford when you are buying a house. With today's low interest rates, you can probably get a better return on your money with other investments.

- Don't expect instant miracles - Getting out of debt will take discipline and time. You probably didn't get yourself into this situation overnight, so you won't get out of it that quickly either. Be patient and stay focused on your goals.

- Don't impulse buy. When you see something you hadn't planned to buy, don't purchase it on the spot. Go home and think it over. It's unlikely you'll return to the store and buy it.

- Don't make high-risk investments, such as in speculative real estate, penny stocks and junk bonds. Invest conservatively, opting for certificates of deposit, money market funds and government bonds.

- Drive your car an extra year or two before you replace it with a new one.

- Eat oatmeal….it's both healthy and filling.

- Eat out less and at home more. The cost of food at restaurants, especially when you add in the cost of service, really adds up. Both the food and the service are usually better at home anyway.

- Eating in: use or freeze everything you buy. When you buy the ten pound bag of potatoes and three pounds go bad, did you

Section IV: INCORPORATING TRUTH...

really get a bargain? With the exception of using those sprouting spuds for science projects, the extra three pounds you paid for is only going to make your garbage heavier.

- Extra income: peddle your skills. Whether you have a full-time job or you're not working, you always have a little bit of extra time. You can earn a considerable amount per hour if you hone and market one of your skills such as carpentry, babysitting (you can even combine it with looking after your own children), handyman tasks, painting or housekeeping. You would be surprised at how many people would rather pay you than a professional (no offense) who will inevitably charge more.

- Enjoy the city parks.

- Evaluate your monthly income sources. Record any money that you've earned (paycheck, bonuses, freelance income, tips, etc.) or received from savings and investments.

- Expect the unexpected. Build a cash cushion that you can get at quickly in case of an emergency. If you don't have such a cushion, a broken furnace or other calamity will wreck your budget and push you into a seat on the ship of credit-card slaves.

- Fast food: don't order value meals. This applies especially for those people who would have ordered the burger and a drink, but then see that for only a few cents more, you get the fries too. That timeless truth prevails—there's no such thing as a free fry. So you end up paying more than you intended and digesting the fries, which for some of us can be construed as a definite liability.

IF YOU DON'T BORROW MONEY, YOU CAN'T GET INTO DEBT.

- Find alternatives to spending money. For a friend's birthday, take him or her on a picnic rather than to an expensive restaurant. When someone suggests that you meet for lunch, propose meeting at the museum on its free day or going for a walk in the park. Instead of buying books and CD's and renting videos, borrow them for free at a library.

- Forget about buying now and paying later —costing you twice as much because it was not on sale and the interest expense is doubling the original price! Save now, buy when you have the cash and it's on sale for half price!

- Forget soda—drink water.

- Get a handle on your spending. If you are like most people, you squander away thousands of dollars without much thought to what you are buying. By making a budget, you can find out where the money goes—and start directing more of the wasted dollars to savings.

- Get at least three prices for the same item from different sources.

- Get in shape: ride your bicycle to work.

- Get medical insurance. Even a stopgap policy with a large deductible can help if a medical crisis comes up. You can't avoid medical emergencies, but living without medical insurance is an invitation to financial ruin.

- Get the most for your money. Shop for value whenever you can. Go to warehouse-type stores, buy items (ones you actually need) in bulk, wait to buy stuff on sale (especially furniture and clothing), get last year's model (car, appliance) this year. It's probably just as good and the price will be better.

- Go shopping with a list and buy only those items.

- Gifts: buy them all year long and keep a box of gifts

- Last minute gift purchases are usually more expensive since you can't shop around for a better deal. Institute a box of gifts that allows you to collect good buys as you go, then give them when an occasion arises, such as children's birthday parties, hostess gifts or anniversaries.

- Save for retirement. Make your retirement savings a sacred expense and pay it first. If you wait until the end of the month (or year!) to see what's left after you've paid other bills, usually there's nothing left.

Section IV: INCORPORATING TRUTH...

- Grow your own garden.

- If you finish paying a car loan, keep writing that check every month and invest it in mutual funds.

- Improve your gas mileage. Buy an energy-efficient car, check the air in your tires frequently and slow down on the highway.

- Incorporate a get-rid-of-it box. How often do you put something away and say to yourself, "I wonder if I'll ever use this?" What if, instead of putting those things back, you toss them into a box that only gets emptied out once or twice a year. That way, you have several months to retrieve the item if you change your mind. If it stays in the box, then you either sell it or donate it and take the write-off. This technique helps in at least three ways: it's financially smart, it reduces the amount of clutter in your house and it facilitates a happier marriage.

- Increase your insurance deductibles.

- Involve your kids and your spouse in times of crisis. If you have a family, everyone will have to participate—no one person can do all the work alone. Make sure your spouse and the kids understand that the family is having financial difficulties and agree together to take the steps that will lead to recovery.

- Keep a written account of your progress. Set financial goals. This will help increase your savings and give you peace of mind and less stress over money issues. Progress may seem very slow at first, especially if the debt load is very large. But it's a great feeling to whittle away at that list of creditors!

- Listen: A person could easily go broke saving money on good buys.

- Buying a $500 item on sale for $400 isn't a $100 savings if you didn't need the item to begin with. It's spending $400 that you didn't need to spend.

- The only way to conquer impulse buying is through self-discipline. Without discipline, no budget will help. "By what a man is overcome, by this he is enslaved" (II Peter 2:19 NASU).

- Listen: Impulse buying is another form of the get-rich-quick mentality. Scripture says, "The plans of the diligent lead surely to advantage, but everyone who is hasty comes surely to poverty" (Proverbs 21:5 NASU).

MINOR ADJUSTMENTS FOR MAJOR CHANGE

- Listen: There are no magic rules that will solve everyone's financial troubles.

- Listen: You are never going to win the lottery, so stop wasting your money.

- Live within your means. Just look at all the people who earn less than you. See how financially secure and happy they are? You can do it with just a few new habits plugged into your routine, like a spending plan.

- Look around for better insurance rates.

- Maintain an impulse list. Write down what you want, then get at least two additional prices. Never have more than one item on your list. Do you know why? Because long before you will have found two prices on the first item, you will probably find two more items that you would rather have.

- Make a plan to pay off your debts and write it down. (If it isn't in writing, it doesn't exist.) If you put your plans in writing, you are more likely to follow through on your debt management.

- Make a resolution that you will NOT overspend ever again.

- Make your gifts: birthday, Christmas, wedding, etc.

- Make long-distance calls on weekends, early in the morning and late at night. Or better yet, e-mail or write letters.

- Make one trip to the grocery store each week.

- Make plans for life after debt. Don't go crazy and run up charge cards as soon as everything is paid off. The last thing you want to do is get yourself into deep debt again. You will probably find that you need to do some things that had to be deferred while you were paying off debts. For our family, it was catching up on dental work and replacing some appliances.

- Make your own coffee.

Section IV: INCORPORATING TRUTH...

- Minimize your debt, because it's so important to your financial health. Be sure to look through it. It can turn your financial life around.

- Move in with your parents (but only if you are single).

- Never buy anything unless you have budgeted for it.

- Pare your grocery bill—eat rice and beans. (You will not starve nor die.)

- Pay your credit cards off every month with no exception.

- Pay with cash, and save your receipts.

- Pay off the most expensive loan first. Make the minimum monthly payments on all your debts except the one with the highest interest rate. Put as much money as you can toward this debt each month, until it is paid off. Then apply the payments you were making on that debt toward the loan with the next highest interest rate and so on. Note: Pay credit card bills promptly to reduce the average daily balance on which you're charged.

- Pay yourself first—well, actually second. After giving to the Lord, use 10 percent of your income for investments to build your equity. You can learn to live on less if you take the money out of your paycheck before it even gets into your hand. If cutting your salary creates a problem, make a commitment to invest any pay increases you receive so you don't have to make cuts.

- Plan for the future. Set achievable goals such as spending less than you earn each month and making regular deposits into an investment fund.

- Practice utility control. Install a water-saving shower head, buy energy-saving light bulbs, turn the temperature dial up on your refrigerator and down on your water heater and turn off the lights and television when you leave the room. Little economies add up to big savings over the course of a year.

- Know your different monthly expenses: fixed expenses (mortgage or rent payments, auto and educational loans and insurance) and variable expenses (utility bills, clothing, transportation, entertainment and dining).

- Retail Stores: Make an offer on floor models. Floor models may be discontinued or have dings that could easily be hidden with strategic plant or corner placement.

- Save any extra money that comes your way from second jobs, rebates, bonuses, medical-insurance reimbursements and tax refunds.

- Save food costs. Buy on sale, clip coupons, buy in bulk, purchase generic brands, eat less expensive cuts of meat and don't frequent convenience stores.

- Save on supplies. Use sponges rather than paper towels, use a multi-purpose cleaner rather than several specialized ones and recycle newspapers, bottles and cans.

- Save on vacations. Explore local recreational sites; ask your travel agent about special deals; visit vacation spas and resorts off season.

- Seek professional help to work your way out of debt.

- Sell the new vehicle and settle for good used reliable transportation.

- Shop around for lower auto and home insurance rates.

- Shop at thrift clothing stores.

- Some debt is bad. Don't borrow for things that you consume quickly. Instead, put aside some cash each month for these items so you can pay the bill in full.

- Some debt is good. Borrowing for a home, college or maybe a car (with zero percent financing) makes good sense. Just don't borrow more than you can afford to pay back.

- Spend less on gifts. Be creative rather than extravagant with friends and family.

- Start and maintain an emergency cash fund. This is one of those payments from your monthly spending plan that you shouldn't skip. Once you've built it up to about three to six times your monthly income, keep it there and use it when, not if, your car needs repair, a medical emergency arises, or you have to help out a loved one.

Section IV: INCORPORATING TRUTH...

- Stay at home: you'll save fuel expense.

- Stay away from the convenience stores. Buy instead from discount or outlet stores.

- Stay healthy. Eat right, exercise more, buy a few pieces of exercise equipment and drop the gym membership.

- Stay out of the malls.

- Stick to your spending plan. Have a list of needs for everyone and for your house, so that you don't find yourself buying wants and not having money for the things you truly need. Put some of your new-found extra money into savings, college or retirement funds.

- Stop incurring debt. Cut out unnecessary spending and avoid impulse buying.

THE ONLY PROBLEM WITH BORROWING MONEY IS THAT YOU HAVE TO PAY IT BACK.

- Stop spending!

- Subtract credit card purchases in your checkbook register, so you have money for the bill when it arrives.

- Take advantage of free programs for kids at local libraries or community centers.

- Take your lunch instead of eating out.

- Track your expenses. Keep a running balance sheet of every expense and pinpoint areas where you need to cut back. Use a notebook to record the amount and category of each purchase no matter how small. Include check and credit card purchases also. Do this every day for 3 months. Total each category at the end of each month and adjust your spending as needed. This is a great way to develop better spending habits.

- Transfer your debts to a low-interest rate credit card. The higher the interest rate, the more money the loan is costing you. Find a card with a low interest rate and then contact that credit card company to arrange transfer of your other debts to this card.

- Try the Consumer Credit Counseling Service, which is listed in your local yellow pages. For a small fee, you can negotiate a payment plan that will keep your creditors at bay. Don't let debt break your back. If you have more debt than you can manage, now is the time to get help.

- Turn down the thermostat in winter and turn off the air conditioner in summer. Put on a sweater in winter and use a fan in the summer to heat and cool your body inexpensively.

- Use coupons, rebates, special promotions, price-matching offers and discount shopper cards.

- Vacations: Try a home exchange. If you have friends who live in other cities or parts of the country, exchange homes for a week. It costs nothing to stay there and you get a much needed change of perspective.

- Visit your local library. There are many resources available to give you the particulars on frugal and simple living. It's a great place to check out magazines, compact discs, cassettes, etc.

- Wait at least ten days to buy non-budgeted items.

"I hear, I know. I see, I remember. I do, I understand."

Key Points:

➤ value of paying with cash

➤ controlled spending tips

➤ practical ways to decrease expenses

➤ lifestyle do's and don'ts to bring success

1. **Write down** any parts of the chapter that were meaningful to you.

_____

_____

_____

_____

2. **Personal Application:** How can you personally apply these truths in your own life? Write down several long-term goals.

_____

_____

_____

_____

3. **Steps to Action:** Write down one small step you could take to begin immediately applying the truths and principles of this chapter.

_____

_____

_____

_____

4. **Prayer for the Practical:** Write out a prayer to God asking Him for help in making any changes that these goals would require.

_____

_____

_____

_____

Psalm 62:8 "O my people, trust in him at all times.
Pour out your heart to him,
For God is our refuge."

Section IV: INCORPORATING TRUTH...

ANTICIPATING YOUR FINANCIAL FUTURE

WHAT ARE SOME INVESTING TIPS THAT WILL HELP ME TO MULTIPLY MY MONEY? HOW CAN I WISELY SAVE AND INVEST MY MONEY FOR RETIREMENT? HOW CAN I PREPARE FOR UNEXPECTED EVENTS THAT WOULD HAVE A HUGE IMPACT ON MY FINANCES?

Vision concentrates on the future. It focuses on thinking ahead rather than on dwelling upon or seeking to replicate the past.

—George Barna, Author (*The Power of Vision*),
social science researcher

CHAPTER TWENTY-ONE

UNRAVELING THE MYSTERY OF INVESTING

Investing can be very complicated or very simple. It can be very successful or disastrous. There is risk with investing and there is risk in not investing. Investing can be very enjoyable or very distasteful. So in this chapter we want to give you some overall and well-rounded investment information. Absolutely no attempt will be made to influence you to invest in a specific type of financial instrument.

We must recognize the risks involved in all investments and what you can do to minimize those risks. Next, we will look at common mistakes that lead to investment disaster, followed by several principles you need to know about investing in mutual funds. We will then present some alternatives for your investment consideration, with a discussion of their various advantages and disadvantages. The purpose of this chapter is simply to give you enough information so that you can make your own wise financial investment decisions.

UNDERSTANDING INVESTMENT RISK

First of all, it is necessary to understand investment risk. No get-rich scheme will ever bring you peace and security. No method of investing, no category of investing, and no investment vehicle will shorten the time needed to see a financial return. If someone insists that they have a way for you to easily make a greater than average return on any investment, hang up the phone or turn and run in the other direction. With regard to your money, there will always be someone more than willing to separate you from it. Just remember that hot tips lead to burnt fingers.

If you're like many investors, you want to get the highest possible return on your investments while assuming the least amount of risk. Unfortunately, finding a comfortable balance between risk and reward can be difficult.

When planning your investment strategy, you need to determine your risk tolerance level. The amount of risk you can handle in your portfolio depends on several factors—your age, family situation, your current income and your financial goals. The amount of risk you are willing to assume can help you determine the types of investments you may include in your portfolio.

There are several types of risk that every portfolio can be exposed to. Investment gains and losses can result from such factors as economic conditions and changes in the financial markets. In building your portfolio, you should be aware of some of the categories of risk.

Liquidity Risk

Liquidity risk means not being able to liquidate an investment quickly while keeping the original investment amount intact. This can occur with investing in bonds where the bond must be held to maturity in order for you to achieve a specific interest return. It can also be a risk should you invest in a particular stock, but find that the price is down at the same time you need to get your hands on the cash invested in that specific equity. For this reason, any dollars you need to access for the purpose of educational spending or maybe the purchase of a house should never be invested in the equities market.

Inflation Risk

Inflation risk is the danger that inflation will reduce the purchasing power of your investment over time. Low-yielding investments such as savings accounts and money market funds may not earn enough to outpace rising prices.

Economic Risk

Economic risk can surface due to the fact that slow economic growth will be too weak to sustain or improve the return on a particular investment. For example, the price of shares in growth companies that require a strong economy to sustain earnings may fall during an economic slowdown. Again, as in the case of liquidity risk, you would not want to invest any dollars required for education or other short-term needs into an investment that would have a substantial economic risk attached to it.

Interest Rate Risk

Interest rate risk occurs when changes in interest rates cause the value of certain investments to decrease. For example, when interest rates rise, the market value of fixed-income securities, such as bonds, declines. Bond investors hate inflation because it erodes the value of bonds' fixed interest payments. Investors are locked into the lower rate as the market rates rise. However, this type of risk may hold less potential for major financial damage.

Market Risk

Market risk is the risk associated with market fluctuations that can depress the value of particular investments. All stocks and bonds can be affected by downturns caused by fraud, war, or calamity. Additionally, certain types of investments can experience a major downturn should there be a slowdown in a specific industry or category of investments. Factors such as political developments, market cycles, changing investor sentiments or reaction to previous excessive rises or declines can all contribute to market volatility. Higher interest rates hurt stocks because they can slow the economy, which can crimp a company's revenue. They boost corporate borrowing costs and make stocks less attractive relative to interest-paying investments.

Company Risk

If a company's stock value decreases due to financial difficulties, this creates an instant company risk. Internal factors such as inefficient production and poor management or external factors such as problems with the industry, the economy, or trade can contribute to company risk.

Specific Risk

Specific risk involves any occurrences that may affect only a particular company. For example, the death of the founder, political developments, or heavy debt can affect a particular firm adversely. Some huge companies that have been around for a very long time, even with great products and unsoiled reputations, have fallen into the wrong hands and ended up worthless due to fraud and misrepresentation.

DIMINISHING YOUR INVESTMENT RISK

Risk is not something you should try to eliminate from your portfolio. However, you must manage your risk. By choosing only ultra conservative investments, you limit the potential return on your investments. Instead, minimize your risk by diversifying your portfolio and choosing investments that will bring you peace of mind as well as your desired rate of return.

You can manage your investment risk through proper diversification, also known as asset allocation. In our world of uncertainty, it makes sense to reduce your risks wherever possible. This is especially true when it comes to investing. That's what diversification does. It's a way to reduce exposure to risk without reducing your potential for return. Diversification is the spreading of your money into a variety of investments. Changes in economic conditions affect some securities differently, but the impact of any single asset category is minimized.

Through diversification, you distribute your assets among a variety of investment categories and, thus, spread your risk. Of course, your personal situation and investment goals will affect the way in which you diversify your portfolio. You need to discern your objectives based on your age, family obligations, income needs, liquidity requirements, tax considerations, and tolerance for risk.

When you're determining your asset mix, consider these four types of diversification: across asset classes, across time horizons, across industries, and among companies.

Section V: ANTICIPATING YOUR FINANCIAL FUTURE

Diversification Across Types of Securities

Investing among different categories of securities such as stocks, bonds, mutual funds, U.S. Treasuries, or money market instruments allows you to reduce your portfolio's exposure to any single part of the market. This type of diversification is also known as asset allocation.

The key to asset allocation is understanding how different categories of assets react to various market changes in relation to one another. One such correlation is that, during an economic downturn, most stocks tend to perform poorly. However, a slow economy can have just the opposite effect on the bond market. Because a sluggish economic environment is usually accompanied by lower interest rates, bonds will typically rise in value during an economic downturn. Therefore, by holding some stocks and some bonds, you can lessen the effects of economic volatility on your overall portfolio.

Diversification Across Time Horizons

While investing among different asset classes is important, proper diversification requires tailoring your portfolio to your needs. Investing across varying investment time horizons is the way to build a portfolio that is suited to your objectives, without sacrificing diversification.

For example, certificates of deposit, money market funds, and Treasury bills have relatively short time horizons. Other investments, like growth stocks, have long time horizons.

Investments with short time horizons can give your portfolio an anchor of stability. However, if your portfolio is too heavily weighted in these asset classes, you take the risk of reduced return because of declining interest rates or increased inflation.

On the other hand, investments with longer time horizons can result in significant capital appreciation in your portfolio. Stocks, for example, have historically been the best performing asset class over the long term. However, stocks require a long-term orientation in order to smooth out market volatility, the ups and downs of the market. Historically, the stock market has had up to four consecutive years of a declining market. This can devastate any portfolio immediately. If your need for money occurs during that time, not only will you lose on your investment, you may even incur substantial losses. Being too heavily weighted in investments with a long time horizon can deprive your portfolio of stability, as well as safety for emergency cash reserves over the short term. The best approach is to hold some long-term and some short-term investments to reduce overall fluctuation in your portfolio.

Diversification Across Industries

You can further diversify your portfolio by investing in companies in a variety of different industries. This reduces industry risk, the risk that an entire grouping of business will under-perform the market.

By dividing your portfolio among several industries, you ensure that its performance won't depend entirely on one type of business. Volatility in one industry will have only a negligible effect on your portfolio because you've spread your risk.

Diversification Among Different Companies

Within industries, it can make sense to diversify among stocks of different companies. This reduces what professionals call credit risk. This is the risk that any one company will experience difficulties because of factors such as poor management, a lack of market for their products or services, or the superiority of competition. It also reduces your risk should fraud and mismanagement be perpetrated by company management.

INVESTING MISTAKES TO AVOID

There are a number of mistakes that many of us make when it comes to managing our finances. While it is always very easy to make mistakes, it can be very hard to live with the consequences. One thing we should try to avoid is making the same mistake twice. Here are some very real pitfalls to be aware of.

Failing to Set Goals

Without clear targets, you will lack motivation to save and invest. But remember: all your objectives need not be high-minded or long term. Small victories pave the road to larger successes. In fact, many financial advisors find that a good way to get in the habit of moving toward goals is to establish a few near-term achievable ones with pleasurable payoffs, such as saving for a trip to Hawaii, the Caribbean, Barbados or Idaho! Small rewards and extravagances can be very nice. There can be great incentive in setting aside some cash for these personal getaways. Once you've set your aims, establish an unshakable routine for putting aside cash to keep on track.

Giving Up All Decisions to an Advisor

Yes, it's okay to hire a tax professional to handle your state and federal returns or a stockbroker to suggest investments, but no one knows as much about or is as interested in your finances as you are. Take advantage of that fact and devote the couple of hours a week or so that financial planners say is required for most people to stay on top of their money.

Failing to Find a Sensible Investment Strategy

Most people build an investment portfolio the same way they collect shells at the beach. They pick up whatever happens to strike their eye. It may be a hot tip from a friend or a friend of a friend, a slick magazine advertisement or a fancy, colored brochure. As a result, they wind up with investments that often reflect only the fashion of the moment, not their goals or their investing temperament.

Decide first how much risk you are willing to take and then hunt for investments that will let you sleep at night and provide the return you need to meet your target on time. Unless you are starting very late in working toward your major objectives, you should be able to find investments well within your comfort zone.

Remember that your investment style should reflect the time you have to devote to it and your financial expertise. If you don't know much about picking stocks or bonds or if you cannot spend a couple of hours a week researching individual equity issues, put your money in mutual funds or hire a money manager.

Failing to Understand Risk and Diversify Adequately

Investors often focus on one or two obvious risks and neglect to protect themselves against other threats. For example, if you invest the bulk of your assets in Treasury bills to avoid risks in the stock and bond markets, your returns may not keep you adequately ahead of inflation long term. Solution: a well-balanced portfolio of investments with different traits, such as stocks, bonds, money-market funds, real estate and, perhaps, precious metals.

Trying to Time the Stock Market

Few investors, professionals included, can catch a climbing stock or mutual fund just before it takes off, or can bail out at precisely the right instant. So don't try. Instead, be a buy-and-hold investor.

Driving Your Investment Strategy with Taxes

Don't allow seductive tax advantages to blind you to an investment's basic strengths and weaknesses. Before you buy a product that promises to save you taxes, compare it with taxable alternatives. To find out how much a taxable investment would have to return to edge out a tax-exempt one, use this formula.

Divide the tax-exempt yield you are considering by 1 minus your tax bracket expressed as a decimal. So if you are in the 28 percent federal tax bracket and want to find out how much you'd have to earn from a taxable asset to equal the return on a tax-exempt investment yielding 7 percent, divide 7 by 0.72 (1 - 0.28). Conclusion: to beat the return on the tax-exempt investment, you'd need to earn more than 9.72 percent on a taxable one.

Aggressively Seeking the Highest Yield

Trying to catch the highest yield is a strategy that can work well in the risk-free confines of savings accounts and CDs. Elsewhere, however, you can chase high yields down a very deep hole. That's because in more variable income investments such as bonds and bond mutual funds, the interest payments—which determine your yield—make up only part of your total return. The other part is change in the value of your principal, so a drop in a bond or a bond fund's principal value (because of rising interest rates or a default) can dent and even wipe out any higher yield it may have offered. If you only search for high yields, you may not always get high total returns—and total return is the only true measure of whether you've made money.

Relying on Past Performance Only for Investment Choices

The problem with pursuing hot performers is that last year's star all too frequently turns out to be this year's dog. Here, the lesson to be learned is to judge investments on future prospects, not past glories.

Underestimating the Effect of Commissions

High fees and commissions can shave the value of your investments and financial services very fast. Costs that sometimes sound insignificant can add up. If you are over the age of 50 and put $3,000 into an Individual Retirement Account in a mutual fund that has a no-load, low-expense policy, you'll be miles ahead of placing the same dollars in a fund with an 8.5 percent load and a 2 percent annual expense cost.

Failing to Keep Accurate Tax Records

Yes, it's a pain when you first begin this task! Accurate records can help you cut taxes by reminding you of deductible expenditures. They can also help you weed out poor investments. And, of course, they will aid your heirs after you're gone.

Not Setting Aside Adequate Cash for Emergencies

Make sure you've stashed three to six months' worth of living expenses in an account that allows fast withdrawals without penalty. The best place for the extra money is in a money-market mutual fund.

Underestimating Your Retirement Obligations

In planning for retirement, few people pay enough attention to two potential time bombs: their own life expectancy and inflation. At age 60, according to those who know, the median life expectancy is 20 years for a man and 25 for a women. But those are only medians and, for that reason, you really need to plan for 30 years or so.

And in far less time than that, inflation can make sizable savings seem insignificant. According to experts, if living costs rise at a moderate 5 percent, a pension payment of $1,000 a month when you were 60 would have only $277 of today's purchasing power when you hit 85.

Excessive Worrying about the Small Things

Be cost-conscious, but don't fret. If your neighbor's bank CD pays a quarter of a point more in interest than yours, don't worry about it. That deal will earn him or her just $2.50 more this year pretax for each $1,000 invested. Instead, focus on your goals and on carrying out a long-term strategy for reaching them.

STEPS TO SUCCESSFUL INVESTING

The following are a few guidelines and suggestions on investing that may be helpful. They represent sound ways to grow a portfolio while providing adequate built-in safeguards for long-term preservation.

Establish Investment Objectives and Stick with Them

Periodically, stock funds take a hammering. But over long spans of time, stocks as a group have consistently come up winners. Measured over 20-year periods, stretching all the way back to 1871, stocks beat bonds 94 percent of the time and cash 99 percent of the time.

Cash isn't the stuff you carry around in your wallet; rather, it refers to safe, readily-accessible assets like Treasury bills and money-market funds. Since 1926, there have been many bull and bear markets. Yet, throughout the entire period, common stocks have returned an after-inflation (the only return that really counts) average of 7 percent annually, according to Jeremy J. Siegel, a Wharton School finance professor. This compares to long-term government bond's measly 1.7 percent and Treasury bills with an after-inflation return of 0.5 percent.

For patient investors, stocks have built up an overwhelming advantage over other investments. What does that mean for the average investor? When the newspapers and networks proclaim doom and gloom with headlines about uncertainty, one needs to place them into perspective and remain committed to long-term objectives.

Invest for the Long Term

You have heard that patience is a virtue? It is especially true when it comes to investing anything of value, whether it be your time, your support, or your money. Patience is a key ingredient to investment success. Long-term investing can pay off very nicely despite fluctuations in value over the short term.

According to many financial professionals, stock investments have a long-term growth rate well in excess of bonds, Treasury securities and inflation. For any 20-year period during the last six decades, the S & P 500 has never experienced a loss on an inflation-adjusted basis.

In fact, short-term downturns often present excellent long-term investment opportunities. Historically, investors have often realized their biggest gains during market panics. So it makes sense to increase your equity positions when everyone else is selling out. If you have short-term objectives, keep investment maturities short.

Stay Invested

An investor needs to leave his/her money invested for compounding to work to its fullest. The importance of time to investment success is illustrated by the Rule of 72. This commonly used mathematical formula bears repeating here.

To estimate the amount of time it takes money to double, you divide 72 by the assumed interest rate. Assuming a 7.5 percent annual rate of return, an investment of $5,000 today will grow to $10,000 in nine and one-half years. By staying invested for the long term, you can be assured that you will not miss out on the next bull market.

Practice Dollar-Cost Averaging

How brave of an investor are you? Do you see yourself as a risk-taker? Have you ever tried to beat the market and lost? Do you have the courage to buy stocks only after prices have risen sharply, then find yourself selling them after prices have already fallen?

There is a simple way to avoid these investment pitfalls: a periodic investing technique called dollar-cost averaging. By investing a fixed amount on a regular basis, an investor can avoid the difficulty of deciding the best times to invest. Another result of investing the same dollar amount each period is that you automatically purchase fewer shares of an investment when prices are high and more shares when prices are low.

In this way, you can help lower your average cost per share over the course of your investment plan. Of course, like any investment strategy, dollar-cost averaging is not foolproof. It neither assures a profit nor protects against losses in a declining market. In addition, such a plan involves continuous investments in stocks and mutual funds regardless of fluctuating price levels. An investor should always consider his or her financial ability to continue their purchasing through periods of low price levels.

A Proverb and an Example

We can understand the principle of dollar-cost averaging by taking a look at the following biblical proverb:

> *"Steady plodding brings prosperity; hasty speculation brings poverty" (Proverbs 21:5 TLB).*

Dollar-cost averaging takes the guesswork out of timing the ups and downs of the stock and bond markets. This time-tested method for systematic investing can be a particularly good approach in today's uncertain investment environment. Dollar-cost averaging eliminates emotional investment decisions and provides a regular disciplined investment program.

Dollar-cost averaging involves investing a fixed amount of money at regular intervals, such as monthly, quarterly or annually. By investing on a dollar basis at regular intervals, rather than buying a fixed number of shares, an investor can purchase more shares when prices are low and fewer when prices are high. Short-term price decreases are viewed as buying opportunities, assuming that the investment will eventually rebound. The result... the average cost per share is typically lower.

Dollar-cost averaging also enables a person to get into the habit of investing regularly. This is one way to strive toward long-term saving targets, such as college tuition or retirement. The key to investing in anything, especially the stock market, is to set aside regular amounts for systematic investment. Market timing is not science but rather wishful thinking. In fact, some have suggested that most individual investors do not buy low and sell high. They seem to buy high and sell low. After all, it takes real courage to buy when the stock market is low, the news is bad, and the future looks bleak. That's the time when most individuals sell out.

The following illustration of dollar-cost averaging will show us its principle and its power. We will simplify this visual diagram by placing an initial per share price point of $10 per share. Let us say for example that the price of one share of a mutual fund selling at $10 a share drops by as much as 50 percent over a period of one year. Now this would obviously be a bad situation to happen after you have made an investment—actually a very devastating one and the kind that might influence you to sell out at the bottom.

But then, let's imagine that you continued to have confidence in the holdings of this mutual fund and in its management team, so you continue to invest $100 in the mutual fund every time the share price dropped another $1.00 per share. As the mutual fund share price drops all the way to $5, you continue to invest at each price point and then continue to do so as it recovers to the initial starting point of $10. This is certainly not an example of a bull market and yet, what will have happened overall will be very satisfactory.

Notice the results of $100 invested each month, at each point down the ladder and back up again to the original price.

1. Investing an additional $100 at a cost of $10 each buys 10 shares.

2. Investing an additional $100 at a cost of $9 each buys 11.111 shares.

3. Investing an additional $100 at a cost of $8 each buys 12.5 shares.

4. Investing an additional $100 at a cost of $7 each buys 14.286 shares.

5. Investing an additional $100 at a cost of $6 each buys 16.667 shares.

6. Investing an additional $100 at a cost of $5 each buys 20 shares.

7. Investing an additional $100 at a cost of $6 each buys 16.667 shares.

8. Investing an additional $100 at a cost of $7 each buys 14.286 shares.

9. Investing an additional $100 at a cost of $8 each buys 12.5 shares.

10. Investing an additional $100 at a cost of $9 each buys 11.111 shares.

11. Investing an additional $100 at a cost of $10 each buys 10 shares.

The final total of dollars you would have invested = $1,100.00

The total number of shares you would now have = 149.128.

The total value of your shares at the end of the year (149.128 X $10) = $1,491.28. The total gain on your investment at the point that the share price recovers would be 35.6 percent.

At no point did the stock ever sell above your initial buying price, but in the end you had a 35 percent profit. And this does not include whatever dividend the mutual fund may have paid. This is the value of dollar-cost averaging!

The above illustration is, of course, hypothetical. An investor should realize that no investment program can assure a profit or protect against loss in declining markets. Discontinuing the program during a period when the market value of shares is less than original cost would incur a loss.

For this reason, any investor contemplating such a program should take into account his or her ability to continue it during any such period. Keep in mind that sometimes a stock loses value and never regains its original price. This is the reason the example used a stock mutual fund. It would be less likely to stay at the lower price levels. Although dollar-cost averaging is a good investment tool, investors must realize that no method guarantees a risk-free investment. The value of holdings will only be determined by what a buyer is willing to invest.

MUTUAL FUNDS: FOUR PRINCIPLES FOR WISE INVESTING

It is a fact that a safer way to invest in a wide range of equities is to invest in them through a mutual fund holding. Achieving proper diversification is often difficult for investors purchasing individual securities. For example, many professionals recommend investing in a minimum of 15 stocks in order to have a properly diversified equity portfolio.

This can require a capital investment which simply isn't feasible for many people. Moreover, researching and monitoring a large stock portfolio can be a cumbersome chore.

That is why so many investors turn to mutual funds, which are an affordable and convenient way to diversify your portfolio. Mutual funds are designed to meet specifically stated investment goals. With such diversification, an individual may own many more issues in their particular asset class.

Many funds target a specific industry sector, investing in many stocks across that sector. For instance, there are mutual funds which invest in stocks of small, emerging companies and other funds which emphasize investments in securities of international companies.

Shareholders who invest a few hundred dollars in a mutual fund receive the same investment return, the same professional management, and the same diversification as those who invest much more.

Professional managers of the fund are able to invest the fund's assets in a variety of securities, targeting hot industries and selecting the best individual stocks within those industries. This approach to investing allows the individual to reduce risk while participating in the opportunities offered.

The Principle of Seeking Out Low Cost Funds

In the 90's, gains-hungry investors paid no more attention to fund expenses than drag racers do to gas mileage. Who cared about costs as long as stock funds were piling up average annual gains of over 15 percent and bond funds were churning out 10 percent or more a year?

In the present decade, when analysts expect yearly returns to be three to five points lower, fees and expenses will be larger, increasing losses and slowing subsequent recoveries. For instance, according to Money Magazine, a no-load fund with a 9.75 percent gross return and a low 0.75 percent annual expense ratio would build $10,000 into $23,670 over the next 10 years. A 4 percent load fund with a stiff 1.5 percent charge would knock that down to $21,210.

As a rule, avoid domestic stock funds with annual expenses that total more than 1.5 percent of assets. In evaluating international funds, in which the cost of doing business overseas increases fees, cut out any fund charging more than 2 percent a year. With bond funds, insist on expenses below 1 percent.

The Principle of Dollar-Cost Averaging

Investing a fixed amount of money at regular intervals—say, $100 to $500 a month— takes much of the risk out of stock funds, with little effort. For one thing, it prevents you from committing your total dollars available at a market peak. And if your fund's share value does drop, your next installment payment automatically picks up more of the lower-priced shares. That cuts your average cost per share and boosts your eventual gain.

The Principle of Building a Well-Balanced and Diversified Portfolio

Most investors are familiar with the don't-put-all-your-eggs-in-one-basket logic of diversification. Fewer really understand how powerful a risk-reducing tactic it is. Sensible diversification costs you relatively little in performance.

Analysts say that you should divide your money among funds with different styles. Over any investment period of 10 years or more, funds with differing investment philosophies will take turns outperforming—and being outperformed by those with other philosophies. Some experts suggest that you put 40 percent of your stockholdings into value funds. Value investing typically pays off best at the end of a bear market and in the early part of a new bull market.

By diversifying among funds, you acknowledge the unpredictability of markets and lessen the damage if you're wrong. In an uncertain market, diversification is king. Whatever happens, if your money is spread among assets and investment styles, you should be able to sleep at night.

The Principle of Understanding Market Indexes

Index funds allow individual investors to do what many corporate pension fund managers have accomplished successfully for years: invest passively in diversified stock portfolios that closely match the performance of major market yardsticks. In general, the funds that track indexes of larger capitalization stocks (such as the S&P 500) provide moderate growth with relatively low risk. In contrast, indexes of smaller capitalization stocks (for example, the Russell 2000) should demonstrate faster growth but greater volatility.

The index fund approach has two distinct advantages. First, it provides a high degree of performance predictability relative to the market as a whole and second, it does this at low cost. Expenses are low because management advisory fees generally are modest. And since fund holdings are turned over infrequently, capital gains distributions, commissions costs and operating expenses are low, enhancing net returns to shareholders.

Index funds have their drawbacks. In a slumping market, a passive strategy may fare worse than that of a conventional fund whose manager builds up a large cash reserve. However, index funds represent a relatively conservative investment option for those who are willing to ride out unpredictable market swings in expectation of long-term appreciation.

Various indexes that measure the performance of the U.S. Market range from the broadest perspective to a narrow look at a single industry. Still other indexes track foreign stock markets. Several major domestic indexes are profiled below with information from Standard and Poor's.

S & P COMPOSITE INDEX: When investment professionals want a proxy for the general market, they usually turn to the S&P 500. As the name indicates, the index consists of 500 U.S. issues, which represent about 70 percent of the total market value of American stocks. The 500 is capitalization-weighted, meaning that stocks influence the index in proportion to their importance in the market. The S&P 100 is simply the top 20 percent of the 500.

DOW JONES INDUSTRIAL AVERAGE: The oldest measure of market performance, the DJIA took its modern form of 30 large-capitalization stocks in 1928. The original version of Charles Dow's average, which consisted of only 11 stocks (nine of them railroads), first appeared in 1884. Originally the average price of a set of stocks, calculation of the DJIA has been changed over the years to reflect stock splits and substitutions. To make historical comparisons valid, the sum of the stocks in the Dow is no longer simply divided by 30. Today, the divisor is 0.559.

Two other market averages from Dow Jones track specific sectors. The Transportation average is composed of 20 airline, railroad and trucking companies, while the Utility average consists of 15 gas and electric companies. All three averages are included in the Dow Jones 65 Stocks Composite. None of the Dow averages is capitalization-weighted and each has its own divisor.

NYSE COMPOSITE INDEX: This index measures the aggregate change in the value of all common stocks listed on the New York Stock Exchange. The base value was set at 50 as of year-end 1965. (That value was chosen because it was close to the average price of a NYSE-listed share at the time.) Four sub-indexes of NYSE-listed stocks are also tracked: Industrial, Transportation, Utility and Finance.

AMEX MARKET VALUE INDEX: Established in September 1973, the AMEX Market Value Index measures the change in value of roughly 1,000 issues traded on the American Stock Exchange. Included are common shares, ADRs and warrants. The Amex index has eight industry subgroups and another eight geographic subgroups, the latter reflecting corporate headquarters locations. The Market Value Index treats cash dividends as reinvested, thereby providing a picture of the total return for Amex stocks.

NASDAQ COMPOSITE INDEX: This is a measure of all OTC (Over The Counter) issues (except warrants) traded on the NASDAQ National Market System (NMS) and all domestic non-NMS common stocks traded in the regular NASDAQ market. The composite and its six sub-indexes (Industrial, Banks, Insurance, Other Finance, Transportation and Utilities) are market-value weighted. (Large companies move them more than smaller companies.) Cash dividends are not counted in the indexes. The NASDAQ Composite and its sub-indexes were established in 1971.

RUSSELL 1000, 2000, 3000: These indexes were developed by the Frank Russell Company to track the 3000 most actively traded U.S. shares. The Russell 3000 contains all of the issues, is capitalization-weighted and represents about 99 percent of the stocks held in institutional portfolios. The 1000 is the top tier of the domestic market and the 2000 represents the second tier.

WILSHIRE 5000: Although called the Wilshire 5000, this index actually tracks the value of more than 6,000 domestic stock issues. Established in 1974 by Wilshire Associates, this capitalization weighted index is designed to represent the total value of the U.S. market.

S & P MIDCAP 400: The newest addition to the index universe is the S&P MidCap 400, which was launched in recent years. Designed to track that segment of the market just below the 500, the S&P MidCap

400 is a market-weighted index. Unlike the 500, the S&P MidCap 400 has no industry sub-indexes.

ALTERNATIVES FOR YOUR INVESTMENT CONSIDERATION

Investment in Cash

Cash investments are short-term debt instruments that you can convert into cash easily, with little or no cost or penalty. They are sometimes called short-term reserves, cash reserves or cash. Examples include money market mutual funds, bank checking accounts, certificates of deposit (CD's) and Treasury bills (T-bills). The advantages of cash investments are their stability of principal and liquidity. Disadvantages include inflation risk and income risk.

Investment in Bonds

Bonds are debt securities issued by corporations or governments in exchange for money you lend them. In most instances, bond issuers agree to repay their loans by a specific date and to make regular interest payments to you until that date. That's why bonds are often referred to as fixed-income investments.

Bonds vary according to different criteria. One is the issuer. Bonds are issued by the U.S. Treasury, U.S. government agencies, corporations, and state or local governments. Another criteria is the bond maturity. The maturity date is the date when the bond issuer agrees to repay you the principal or face value of the loan. Bonds can be short-term (less than 5 years), intermediate-term (5–10 years) or long-term (more than 10 years). Yet another criteria of bonds is their credit quality. A bond's quality is measured by the issuer's ability to pay interest and repay principal in a timely manner. Treasury bonds have the highest credit quality because they are backed by the full faith and credit of the U.S. government. Corporate high-yield "junk" bonds have the lowest credit quality.

Advantages of investing in bonds include both current income and broad diversification possibilities. Disadvantages include interest rate risk, credit risk and call risk.

Interest rate risk means that the market value of your bonds could decline due to rising interest rates. (In general, bond prices fall when interest rates rise—and rise when interest rates fall.)

Credit risk can also affect the value of your bond investment. You could lose money if a bond issuer defaults, fails to make timely payments of principal and interest, or if a bond's credit rating is reduced.

Another possible disadvantage of investing in bonds is what is termed call risk. During periods of falling interest rates, corporate and municipal bond issuers may prepay or call their loans before maturity in order to reissue the loans at a lower rate. You as lender, then, must reinvest this prepaid principal sooner than you had anticipated—and possibly at a lower interest rate.

The last two possible disadvantages to investing in bonds are inflation risk and event risk. The danger of inflation risk is that the interest income you earn from a bond investment remains the same over the life of the bond. The value of that income could be eroded by inflation. With event risk, the credit quality or market value of your bonds could suffer in response to an event such as a merger, leveraged buyout or other corporate restructuring.

The list below explains some ratings for various levels of bonds and a description of their risks. As noted these come from both Standard & Poor's and Moody's. When purchasing any kind of bond, always check the risk and rating. The actual return should be your last consideration.

STANDARD & POOR'S	MOODY'S	DESCRIPTION
AAA	Aaa	Best quality, smallest degree of risk
AA	Aa	High quality, slightly more risk
A	A	Upper medium grade, possible risk
BBB	Baa	Medium grade, but not well-secured
BB	Ba	Speculative issues, moderate protection
B	B	Very Speculative, little protection
CCC	Caa	Issues in poor standing, may default
CC	Ca	Highly speculative, marked shortcomings
D	C	Lowest quality, in default

Investment in Treasury Securities

Treasury securities are negotiable debt obligations issued by the U.S. government for a specific amount and maturity. The government issues three types of Treasuries:

- Treasury bills (T-bills), with a maturity of 1 year or less.

- Treasury notes (T-notes), with a maturity of 1 to 10 years.

- Treasury bonds (T-bonds), with a maturity of 10 to 30 years.

There is safety in the purchase of U.S. Treasury Securities. They are backed by the full faith and credit of the U.S. Government and are considered ideal for safeguarding and preserving capital.

If held to maturity, Treasuries are guaranteed to repay your original investment. No matter how volatile the market may be, you never risk your principal if you hold the security until the date of maturity.

Since Treasuries are a fixed-rate security, you'll know exactly what your income will be and when you will receive interest payments. When purchasing Treasury Notes or Bonds, you will receive a steady stream of income from the semiannual interest payments. Although Treasuries are federally taxable, the interest is exempt from both state and local taxes. Therefore, your after-tax return may be higher than the same yields on fully taxable investments, especially if you live in a high-tax state.

There is an active secondary market for Treasuries which trades billions of dollars every day. This enables you to trade your Treasury securities before maturity should you need to raise some quick cash. Of course, should you sell before maturity, you may realize either a gain or a loss on your investment, depending on market value when you sell. If interest rates have fallen, the value of the securities goes up and you'll most likely get back more than you anticipated. However, if the reverse is true, your return will probably fall short.

When buying Treasuries you have a lot of flexibility as to when you want the principal back. Whether you are saving for the children's education or your own retirement, you can target the exact date that you want the security to mature to meet your individual investment goals. T-Bills are short-term instruments and have maturities of three and six months and one year. T-Notes mature in two, three, five, seven and ten years. T-Bonds have maturities of 11 to 30 years. STRIPS have maturities of six months to 30 years.

So what are Treasury Bills? Short-term Treasury Bills are sold at a discount and return their full face value at maturity. The interest you earn is the difference between the face value and the price you actually pay. The discount rate simply indicates the trading price and does not refer to the actual yield, which is always higher. For example, if a one-year T-Bill is quoted at 7.72, the security is selling at a discount of 7.72 percent of $10,000, or $9,228. At maturity, you'd receive your original investment plus $772 in interest earned, for a yield of 8.37 percent. Treasury Bills can be an excellent investment alternative to savings accounts or CDs. Exempt from both state and local taxes, T-Bills not only protect your capital, but may also provide a better return than fully taxable alternatives.

Treasury Notes and Bonds

These securities pay interest semiannually and can provide the investor with a steady source of income. If held to maturity, intermediate T-Notes and T-Bonds both lock in a fixed rate of return that is guaranteed regardless of changes in market conditions.

Zero Coupon Bonds

Zero-Coupon Treasuries, or STRIPS, is another outstanding investment vehicle. The prospect of having to have a specific sum of money at a set point in time can be a worrisome dilemma. Whether it's your children's college tuition, your retirement, a wedding, dream vacation or a second home you are looking forward to, U.S. Treasury Zero Coupon Bonds can help to offer you an assured way to take what you have today and turn it into what you need for tomorrow.

They are sold at deep discounts and cost substantially less than their face value. Your return is the difference between what you pay for your STRIPS and what you receive at maturity. Zero Coupon Bonds make no regular interest payments. The interest on the STRIPS accrues over the life of the bond and is automatically reinvested so that you earn interest on both the interest and the principal. This compounding locks in a rate of return and enables a small initial investment to achieve dramatic growth if held to maturity.

You buy Zero Coupon Bonds at a small fraction of their $1,000 face amount—then redeem them at full value at maturity. For example, if you buy approximately $8,500 worth of 10 year Zero Coupon Bonds that pay 8.75 percent compounded semiannually, your $8,500 will grow to $20,000 at maturity. This investment vehicle is thought to be just about the best way of knowing exactly how much a certain sum of money will grow to in a given number of years. And because there are so many maturity dates to pick from, you can select the maturity that matches the time you'll need the money and know precisely how much you'll have on that date.

Since STRIPS do offer a wide choice of maturities they are popular for investors who need a large lump sum at a specific future time, such as for college or retirement. Although interest isn't paid until the STRIPS mature, it is taxable the year it's credited to you. It is because of this that STRIPS are favored for tax-deferred accounts such as IRA's.

The predictability of zeros depends on your holding them until maturity. That's why they may be ideal for your IRA. All interest (if in an IRA account) accumulates tax-deferred until withdrawn at retirement, when your tax bracket is usually much lower.

Many individuals use zeros as a long-term savings tool. With some planning, you can purchase zeros that will mature during your retirement years. At that time, the return on your zeros will supplement other sources of retirement income (pensions, profit sharing plans and Social Security benefits).

Here is a quick look at different types of zeros. You can choose from a variety of zero coupon bonds. Many IRA investors opt for Treasury zeros or STRIPS. They offer the highest degree of safety because they are backed by the full faith and credit of the United States government and your return is guaranteed if held to maturity. They are also exempt from state and local taxes.

Corporate zeros tend to offer higher yields than Treasury zeros, but safety may be compromised. They are backed only by the issuing corporation. Corporates are rated by independent agencies, such as Moody's or Standard & Poor's, to indicate their level of credit risk at the time of purchase. In addition, corporate zeros may be called or bought back by the issuing company prior to the bond's stated maturity date, putting your principal at risk.

There are some tax issues to consider. In non-retirement accounts, zero-coupon bonds are subject to tax on so-called phantom income. This means the annual buildup of interest from most zeros is taxed even though you do not actually receive any payment until maturity. The amount taxed each year starts low and increases as the bond moves closer to maturity. In the case of an Individual Retirement Account, however, you avoid having the phantom interest included with your taxable income. You bypass paying yearly taxes on the accumulating interest and you only pay taxes when you withdraw your retirement funds.

As with all other types of investment opportunities and possibilities, there are both advantages and disadvantages to investing in treasury securities, but the overall benefits are substantial. First is the stability of principal. Next is the liquidity factor. Treasuries are considered to have the highest credit quality of all debt instruments and are therefore easily sold and converted to cash. Not to be lost in the discussion of benefits is the call protection factor. Treasuries generally are not callable, which means the issuer cannot redeem the security before its scheduled maturity date. This feature locks in your interest rate until maturity. And one final benefit is the tax advantage. Income from treasury securities is exempt from state and local taxes (but not from federal income tax).

Every investment alternative has its particular downside. With treasuries, it is the interest rate risk. You are guaranteed only to receive timely payment of interest and repayment of principal upon maturity. Before maturity, however, the market value of your securities could decline due to rising interest rates. There is also the possibility of less current income. Because they have high credit quality, treasuries provide less interest income than bonds with comparable maturities and lower credit quality. One final reminder is that bonds of all types are subject to inflation risk. The interest income you earn from a bond investment remains the same over the life of the bond, so the value of that money could be eroded by inflation.

Investment in Agency Securities

Agency securities are issued by agencies that are owned, backed or sponsored by the U.S. government. The most common agency securities are as follows:

> GNMA–known as Ginnie Maes. GNMA securities are issued by the Government National Mortgage Association.

FNMA–known as Fannie Maes. FNMA securities are issued by the Federal National Mortgage Association.

FHLMC–known as Freddie Macs. FHLMC securities are issued by the Federal Home Loan Mortgage Corporation.

FHLB - These securities are issued by the Federal Home Loan Bank.

These sponsored agencies, as in the case of all investments, have both benefits and risks. The benefits include the stability of principal. Some agency securities are backed by the full faith and credit of the U.S. government while others carry less formal guarantees, but all are considered to have high credit qualities. Disadvantages include the risk of pre-payment. Prepayment risk is the possibility that, as interest rates fall, homeowners will refinance their mortgages. You, then, must reinvest this prepaid principal sooner than you had anticipated and possibly at a lower interest rate.

Additional risks include interest rate risk. The market value of your securities could decline due to rising interest rates. Then there's the risk of less current income. Because they have high credit quality, agency securities provide less interest income than bonds with comparable maturities and lower credit ratings. Finally comes inflation risk. The interest income you earn from a bond investment remains the same over the life of the bond. The value of that money could be eroded by inflation.

Investment in Corporate Bonds

Corporate bonds are debt instruments of varying credit quality issued in a range of maturities by corporations. Corporate bonds vary according to both credit quality and maturity or length of the term. Consider first the maturity variances. Corporate bonds range from short-term (less than 5 years) to intermediate-term (5–10 years) to long-term (more than 10 years).

Now let's take a look at the credit quality factor. Most corporate bonds are assigned a let-ter-coded rating by independent bond-rating agencies such as Moody's Investors Service, Inc. and Standard & Poor's Corporation. The rating indicates the likelihood that the issuer will pay interest and repay the principal in full and on time.

Bonds rated BAA or higher by Moody's or BBB or higher by Standard & Poor's are called investment-grade bonds. Bonds rated BA or lower by Moody's or BB or lower by Standard & Poor's are known as high-yield bonds (because of the higher interest rates they must pay to attract investors) or junk bonds (because of the possibility that the issuer will default).

When deciding whether or not to invest in corporate bonds, also consider the benefits of having current income. Corporate bonds generally provide higher interest income than Treasuries and agency bonds because they are considered to be less safe than government securities and the market rewards investors for assuming even a small amount of additional risk.

When considering whether or not to invest in corporate bonds, also consider the potential disadvantages. First, consider the possibility of a call risk. Again, during periods of falling interest rates, corporate bond issuers may prepay or call their loans before maturity in order to reissue the loans at a lower rate so that you as the lender must reinvest this prepaid principal sooner than you had anticipated and possibly at a lower interest rate.

There is always a great possibility of credit risk. You could lose money if a bond issuer (corporation) defaults, that is, fails to make timely payments of principal and interest or a bond's credit rating is reduced. There is event risk as there would also be in buying equities. The credit quality or market value of your bonds could suffer in response to an event such as a merger, leveraged buyout, or other corporate restructuring. There can be tax consequences. The interest income on your corporate bonds (unlike the interest income on treasuries and some agency securities) is taxable at the federal, state and local levels.

You also have to consider the interest rate risk. The market value of your bonds could decline due to rising interest rates. And finally there is the risk of inflation. The interest income you earn from a bond investment remains the same over the life of the bond. The value of that money could be eroded by inflation.

Investment in Municipal Bonds

Municipal bonds (often referred to as "munis") are issued by state and local governments to finance public projects or support other financial needs. These bonds are attractive to investors in higher tax brackets because their interest income generally is exempt from federal and state taxes. Municipal bonds also known as tax-exempt or tax-free bonds are available in two main types. Revenue bonds are used to finance municipal projects that generate revenue (a toll road, for example). This revenue is used to make interest and principal payments to the bond holders.

Another municipal bond is classified as a general obligation bond. These are issued for municipal projects that do not generate revenue (such as a government office building). These bonds are backed by the full faith and credit of the issuer and are repaid with taxes assessed by the issuer. Municipal bonds, like other bonds, can vary widely in credit quality and maturity. There are certain tax advantages when purchasing municipal bonds. You should consult your CPA for information about them. Disadvantages include less than current income, interest rate risk, call risk, credit risk and inflation risk.

Investment in Common Stocks

Common stocks represent part ownership or equity in a public corporation. Companies issue stock as a way to raise money to expand or build their business.

When you buy stock, you hope that the value of your investment will grow. Market value is determined by such factors as a company's current earnings and long-term growth prospects, overall trends in the securities markets, and economic conditions. Many companies also distribute a portion of their profits to stock owners in the form of regular dividends. If a company encounters difficulties, however, the value of your investment could decline. The company could stop paying dividends or the market value of the stock could decrease. Because stock prices tend to fluctuate suddenly and sometimes sharply, stocks are considered riskier than bonds or cash investments.

The strong stock market of the 1990's lulled many investors into a false sense of security. If there's one thing you should know about stocks, it's that the stock market is unpredictable. The value of your stock could rise one day and decline the next. So, while stocks offer the potential for regular dividends and significant capital growth, they also present substantial risks.

Of course, there are many potential benefits to owning stocks. One is the possibility of long-term growth. Over the long haul, stocks tend to offer you the greatest potential return on your investment. Since 1926, according to experts, common stocks have returned an average of 11.2 percent annually—more than bonds or cash investments and well ahead of inflation. There is also the potential for current income through stocks that pay regular dividends, which you can receive as cash or reinvest in more shares. Companies differ, however, in how much of their profits they distribute to shareholders and how much they put back into the company.

The long list of disadvantages begins with a huge one—market risk. The price of your stock could decline over short or even extended periods. Stock markets tend to move in cycles, with periods when prices rise and other periods when prices fall. (Price declines can be dramatic: On October 19, 1987, the Standard & Poor's® 500 Composite Stock Price Index fell 20 percent. And, in the worst bear market since World War II, the S&P 500 Index declined by 48 percent from January 1973 to October 1974.) In the years 2000, 2001 and 2002, the market had consecutive declining years.

Another very real consideration is the risk of losing your principal. You could lose money by investing in stocks. There is also industry risk. The price of your stock could decline due to developments affecting its company's industry. And of course, as in many investment alternatives, there is event risk. The price of your stock could decline in response to an event such as a merger, leveraged buyout or other corporate restructuring. Because of their short-term volatility, stocks should be considered a long-term investment.

Investment in Money Market Funds

Money market funds seek income, liquidity and a stable share price by investing in high-quality, short-term cash investments (that mature in 13 months or less), including certificates of deposit (CD's), Treasury bills, banker's acceptances and commercial paper.

Because cash investments are considered to be the safest of the three primary asset classes, these funds are ideal for stashing emergency money or cash that you plan to use in two years or less. Money market funds are low-risk investments that offer low returns in exchange for providing peace of mind.

The benefits of investing in money market funds include stability of principal. Cash investments are viewed as safe because your money generally is invested with reliable borrowers for only a brief period. In addition, the Securities and Exchange Commission requires that all taxable money market funds invest at least 95 percent of their assets in securities of the highest grade, as rated by Moody's Investors Service, Inc. or Standard & Poor's Corporation.

Of course there is the benefit of current income streams. Dividends, distributed monthly by the funds, typically are higher than the dividends paid by a bank savings account or CD. Another very good benefit is liquidity. Most of the funds offer free check-writing privileges and you can redeem your money at any time.

Disadvantages include inflation risk and income risk. Let's begin with inflation risk. Because cash investments are considered safe, the interest rates they pay are low and, over time, their returns have only slightly exceeded the rate of inflation. From 1926 through most of the nineties, cash investments returned an average of 3.9 percent per year while inflation averaged 3.1 percent, leaving a return after inflation of only 0.8 percent per year.

Therefore, if you have a long-term time horizon, money market funds should not be your primary choice, although they can play a smaller role in a diversified investment portfolio. Last is income risk. Money market funds hold short-term investments that must be reinvested by the fund manager when they mature and possibly at a lower rate of return.

Investment in Bond Mutual Funds

Bond mutual funds emphasize current income by investing in corporate, municipal, U.S. government debt obligations, or some combination. Bond funds can have average maturities that are short-term (less than 5 years), intermediate-term (5–10 years), or long-term (more than 10 years).

The primary types of bond funds are as follows:

U.S. Government Bond Funds Invest in securities issued by the U.S. Treasury or agencies of the U.S. government.

Mortgage-Backed Securities Funds. Invest in securities representing pools of residential mortgages.

Corporate Bond Funds. Invest in the debt obligations of U.S. corporations.

Municipal Bond Funds. Invest in tax-exempt bonds issued by state and local governments.

There are many benefits in choosing bond mutual funds as a part of your overall investment portfolio:

Current Income—While most individual bonds pay interest twice a year, most bond funds distribute interest monthly. You may choose to receive those distributions as cash or reinvest them in additional fund shares.

Diversification—A bond fund may hold bonds from hundreds of different issuers, so a default by one bond issuer would have only a slight effect on your investment.

Stability—In addition, because bond returns tend to fluctuate less sharply than stock returns, a bond fund could help reduce your portfolio's overall volatility.

Professional Management—Few investors have the time or expertise to compare the thousands of bonds available. With a bond or stock fund, an experienced manager makes sure the fund's investments remain consistent with its investment objective—whether that's to track a market index or use research and market forecasts to actively select securities.

Liquidity—You can buy or sell shares of a bond fund whenever you want. It's easy and there is no penalty for early withdrawal (although there may be a redemption fee, depending on the fund).

Convenience—With most bond funds, you can buy and sell shares, change distribution options and obtain information by telephone, by mail or online.

There are, however, some specific disadvantages to be aware of with bond funds, compared with individual bonds.

Tax Consequences—Unlike an individual bond, a bond fund has no fixed maturity date but maintains a rolling maturity by selling off older bonds and buying newer ones. These trades could create taxable capital gains (or losses) for you if you hold your shares in a taxable account. You could also realize a capital gain (or loss) if you sell your shares at a higher or lower price than you paid for them.

Income Fluctuation—While your interest payments from an individual bond are fixed, income from a bond fund could fluctuate moderately as the fund buys and sells individual bonds. In addition, bond funds face the same risks as individual bonds, including interest rate risk, call risk, credit risk, income risk, inflation risk and event risk.

Investment in Stock Mutual Funds

The primary objective of nearly all common stock funds is to provide long-term capital growth. Some conservative stock funds may include dividend income as a secondary consideration. Stock funds (also known as equity funds) vary based on whether they invest in companies emphasizing capital growth or consistent dividends and on the market value of those companies (known as market capitalization).

There are three primary types of stock funds, which vary in investment style:

Growth Funds invest in stocks of companies that have above-average growth potential.

Value Funds invest in stocks of companies that are attractively priced; these companies frequently produce above-average dividend income.

Blend Funds invest in both growth and value stocks.

There are also three categories of market capitalization (though a fund may hold stocks in multiple categories).

Small-Cap invest in stocks of small, emerging companies (defined by Vanguard as having a total market value of less than $1 billion).

Mid-Cap invest in stocks of medium-sized companies (market value of $1 billion to $12 billion).

Large-Cap invest in stocks of large, established companies (market value of more than $12 billion).

Choosing to invest in stock mutual funds brings great potential to the table. The first is that of long-term growth. Over the long haul, stocks tend to offer you the greatest potential return on your investment. Remember, since 1926, common stocks have returned an average of 11.2 percent annually, more than bonds or cash investments and well ahead of inflation.

There is the very real benefit of diversification. A stock fund may invest in the stocks of hundreds of different companies. This helps to reduce your overall investment risk, because losses from some stocks are offset by gains from others. Mutual funds offer professional management. Few investors have the time or expertise to compare the thousands of stocks available.

Other benefits include convenience and dividend reinvestment. With most stock funds, you can buy and sell shares, change distribution options, and obtain information by telephone, by mail or online. Most stock funds allow you to reinvest dividends automatically in more fund shares.

And, of course, there are always a number of disadvantages to every investment alternative. Let's begin again with what is called market risk. Stock prices could decline over short or even extended periods. Stock markets tend to move in cycles with periods when prices rise and other periods when prices fall.

Then there is the disadvantage of investment style risk. If your fund's investment style is out of favor, its returns could trail the overall stock market or the returns of stock funds with different investment styles. For example, growth funds may do poorly when value funds do well and vice versa. You can add to this management risk and principal risk. In an actively managed fund, poor stock selection by the investment adviser could cause your fund to lag comparable funds. You could lose money by investing in stock funds.

Investment in Balanced Mutual Funds

Balanced funds invest in a mix of stocks, bonds and cash investments. These funds provide a convenient way to achieve your desired asset allocation with a single investment. There are two basic types: Traditional balanced funds invest in a stable mix of assets (such as 60 percent common stocks and 40 percent corporate bonds) or maintain asset allocations that fall within a predetermined range (such as 60-70 percent stocks, 30-40 percent bonds). The funds periodically rebalance their portfolios to maintain the desired asset mix. Asset allocation funds periodically shift their desired mix of assets in pursuit of maximum return when the market is strong and minimum risk when the market is down.

Traditional balanced funds are middle-of-the-road investments that seek growth, income and preservation of capital. Though they vary in asset allocation, a typical mix is 60 percent stocks and 40 percent bonds. Balanced funds offer the benefits of diversification in a single investment—with the accompanying risks of each asset class the funds hold.

> THE GREATEST BENEFIT FOR THE INVESTOR IS THAT OF DIVERSIFICATION.

The greatest benefit for the investor is that of diversification. The fund enables you to create a diversified portfolio through a single investment. There is also less volatility. Because stock and bond prices don't move in lockstep, the price of a balanced fund is likely to fluctuate less widely than a fund holding stocks alone.

Balanced funds also enjoy potential tax advantages. The fund may be able to achieve periodic rebalancing by purchasing assets with money from new shareholders, instead of by selling assets, which could trigger a taxable capital gain. In contrast, if you hold stocks and bonds in separate funds, you might have to rebalance by selling shares of the fund in the better-performing asset class to buy more shares of the other fund.

Now it is time to consider the disadvantages. First comes market risk. The price of your fund's stock investments could decline over short or even extended periods. Stock markets tend to move in cycles, with periods when prices either rise or fall. With interest risk, the market value of your fund's bond investments could decline due to rising interest rates. And management risk occurs with poor stock or bond selection by the investment adviser.

CREATING A PORTFOLIO STRATEGY

There are numerous ways to allocate an investment portfolio. Every investment advisor has special favorites. The following represent a very basic opportunity to grow a portfolio over the long term within your personal choice of risk level.

Risk Level I: Preservation of Capital

20% Money Market Funds
20% High Quality Bonds
40% U.S. Treasury Bonds
10% Growth and Income Funds
10% Growth Funds

Risk Level II: Conservative Growth & Income

5% Money Market Funds
20% U.S. Treasury Bonds
40% Income Funds
25% Growth and Income Funds
10% Growth Funds

Risk Level III: Aggressive Growth

10% Money Market Funds
30% Income Funds
30% Growth and Income Funds
30% Aggressive Growth Funds

"I hear, I know. I see, I remember. I do, I understand."

Key Points:

➤ types of investment risks   ➤ understanding market indexes

➤ principles for success, minimizing risk   ➤ investment pro's and con's

1. **Write down** any parts of the chapter that were meaningful to you.

_____

_____

_____

_____

2. **Personal Application:** How can you personally apply these truths in your own life? Write down several long-term goals.

_____

_____

_____

_____

NOTES

3. **Steps to Action:** Write down one small step you could take to begin immediately applying the truths and principles of this chapter.

_____

_____

_____

_____

4. **Prayer for the Practical:** Write out a prayer to God asking Him for help in making any changes that these goals would require.

_____

_____

_____

_____

Psalm 62:8 "O my people, trust in him at all times.
Pour out your heart to him,
For God is our refuge."

CHAPTER TWENTY-TWO

LONG-TERM SECURITY BEYOND SOCIAL SECURITY

"Preparation for old age should begin not later than one's teens. A life which is empty of purpose until 65 will not suddenly become filled on retirement."

—DWIGHT L. MOODY (1837-1899)
FOUNDER OF THE NORTHFIELD SCHOOLS, MOODY CHURCH, AND MOODY BIBLE INSTITUTE

Financial security does not just happen. It takes a lot of planning, a heavy dose of commitment, and money. It is a fact, according to government statistics, that less than half of Americans have put aside money specifically for retirement. One third of those who have had 401(k) coverage available to them do not participate in the plan. You can't retire with security unless you really prepare for it, and this means more than just Social Security Benefits. Long-term security requires us to live up to reality and to begin to take action for tomorrow as well as today. Putting away money for retirement is like giving yourself a raise. It's money that gives you freedom when you want it and when you deserve it.

SECURING YOUR RETIREMENT FUTURE: HOME OWNERSHIP

We should not begin a discussion about planning for retirement without first talking about home ownership. This is the first step toward securing your retirement future.

Buying a home is far more expensive than somebody who has never owned a home could possibly imagine. Too many people make the mistake of thinking that if they find a house with a mortgage payment equivalent to their rent payment, they'll come out ahead. In reality, it can cost as much as 50 percent more per year in addition to the mortgage payment for expenses like insurance premiums, property taxes and maintenance. This does not include the money it will take to move, furnish and decorate.

Historically, in many areas of the country, housing has appreciated faster than inflation. Home ownership seems more difficult to afford. Many people think the biggest stumbling block to home ownership is qualifying for a mortgage. But far and away the greatest difficulty for most first-time homebuyers is accumulating enough money for the down payment and closing costs.

Many lenders require an initial down payment of 10 to 20 percent of the cost of the house, although some permit a lower percentage. A down payment is the difference between the purchase price and the mortgage that is taken out on the home. Closing costs can add another 5 percent or more, particularly if you will be required to pay points to the lender.

Points are an upfront fee charged by the mortgage lender. One point is equal to 1 percent of the principal amount of the loan. Points are also called loan origination fees. Closing costs are expenses normally incurred by the buyer when purchasing real estate. They are typically 1-4 percent of the purchase price and may include fees for recording the deed and mortgage, escrow fees, attorney fees, title insurance, appraisal and inspection fees, and survey costs.

If you are tempted to resign yourself to a life of ever-increasing monthly rent payments, don't! It is possible to own your own home and it isn't as difficult as it may appear. By saving regularly and investing those savings wisely, you'll be that much closer to making the dream come true.

Planning for a House and a Home

There is no secret to saving. It's really just a matter of living beneath your means. Some people are very good at it, but many of us have difficulty saving regularly. Many prospective first-time homeowners are able to increase their rate of saving substantially once they set their minds to buying a house. The short-term sacrifice of foregoing some pleasant, but unnecessary luxuries, is certainly worth the long-term benefits of being a homeowner.

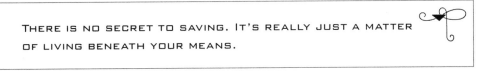

THERE IS NO SECRET TO SAVING. IT'S REALLY JUST A MATTER OF LIVING BENEATH YOUR MEANS.

The most painless way to save is to pay yourself first. Over time, you may be able to increase the amount you save each week or month, helping you reach your dream a little faster. You'll be surprised at how much you can save once your spending habits are under control. As you are building your savings, you should also contact a few potential lenders to determine the size of mortgage you will qualify for. This will help you to estimate how much of a down payment you will need and it will give you an idea of the kind of home you will be able to qualify for.

Invest your savings wisely and avoid the temptation to choose those risky investments in hopes of reaping enormous gains quickly. Money earmarked for purchasing a home should be invested more conservatively, although you may be able to assume more risk if your home purchase is still several years away.

Appropriate investments may include U.S. Government securities, CDs, Zero Coupon Treasury bonds and low-risk mutual equity funds. A mutual fund is an investment that pools the funds of its shareholders in equities or securities. It offers participants more diversification, liquidity and professional management service than would normally be available to them as individuals and at a lower cost.

Mutual funds are often appropriate, because their diversification and professional management can lead to a greater peace of mind and less volatility than you could obtain by purchasing individual securities on your own. In addition, you can have interest and dividend income as well as capital gains automatically reinvested. This very convenient option may allow you to achieve even greater growth through compounding.

Home ownership has many economic as well as psychological benefits. Real estate has always been a solid investment, especially over the last few inflationary decades. If the value of your home increases, you benefit—not your landlord.

There are tax advantages to home ownership as well. Interest on a first mortgage is deductible on your federal income tax return, as are property taxes. Within certain limits, interest on home equity loans is also deductible.

Buying a house at a relatively young age can be a potential help at retirement. More and more retirees are choosing to stay in their homes, which by retirement age are either paid off or have very low mortgage payments. They are able to use their retirement income to enjoy life rather than to make ever-increasing rent payments. Other retired persons opt to sell their homes, thereby unlocking substantial equity that can be used to purchase a less expensive home outright or provide additional funds to assure a comfortable retirement.

A high monthly mortgage payment now may turn out to be a bargain in the future, because, as your earnings increase, your mortgage payment usually doesn't. If you doubt this, just ask someone who has owned a home for 20 years about their mortgage payments. Rent payments, however, will continue to grow each year with no end in sight.

12 CONSIDERATIONS BEFORE APPROACHING RETIREMENT

Increasing numbers of people are finding that retirement is staring them in the face before they are ready to leave the work force. The job that they had counted on to sustain them in their later years may have been a victim of company layoffs. Many are facing employment which pays less and, more importantly, the loss of pension or retirement plans that they thought would be theirs. It is so important to invest personal money and adequately prepare for the golden years.

Retirement planning is taking on greater importance these days as more and more people face involuntary termination because of corporate downsizing and changes in the American economy. The following 12 strategies can help you in the retirement planning process:

1. Know your retirement needs.

Retirement living is very expensive. How much are you saving for the future? Most financial planners recommend that you save 10 to 15 percent of your income. But many of us fall short of that goal. How much will you need to retire? How much will you need to save by the time you are 62, 65 or 66? Experts estimate that you will need at least 70 percent of your pre-retirement income to maintain your standard of living. If you are not making a moderately good living now, you may need as much as 90 percent of your current income in order to live comfortably in your retirement years.

2. Know your future financial needs.

According to the government figures on aging, only one-third of people now employed have attempted to learn how much they must save to achieve a comfortable retirement. Of those who have investigated it, still 42 percent remain unsure about how much money they will need to save in order to retire. How much do you need to retire on? The answer to this depends on the lifestyle you foresee during retirement. It depends upon how long you live and how long your family members historically have lived. The answer to this also depends upon your retirement goals. Do you plan to travel around the world? Do you plan to live just as you do now? How much money will you be passing on to your heirs? Some expenses will go down just because of your age. You won't be paying social security taxes, work expenses or contributing to retirement plans. However some expenses, like health care and travel may increase dramatically.

3. Anticipate your future housing needs.

When it comes to living arrangements, most older people prefer to remain in their own home during their later years, even if it means some remodeling in order to accommodate their health concerns. Even when frail and vulnerable or when afflicted with a chronic illness, people want to stay in familiar surroundings. This can mean hiring expensive health care professionals to come into their home to provide proper care. But often this is not possible when people have failed to save enough to meet such needs. Adequate income and assets are critically important to enable-well being in virtually all dimensions of life in our later years.

4. *Know your physical condition and potential needs.*

A wealth of information is available on maintaining physical and mental health, as well as achieving an adequate level of economic security to remain as independent as possible. You can live an active life in retirement. You can lead a productive life and enjoy retirement. The longevity of life in our day provides us with new opportunities for our retirement years. The aging of the American population presents us with both new challenges and new opportunities. Of course, this also heaps more responsibility upon us right now to prepare for that lengthened span of life. With long life becoming increasingly common, we realize that our retirement plans must address special needs that arise over a longer life span.

5. *Learn about your employer's pension or profit-sharing plan.*

Employment retirement plans are the most common sources of income that people have for retirement. Most employers do offer retirement plans for their employees. These plans are an excellent way to invest money for retirement. If your employer offers a plan, check to see what your benefits are. Find out about their plan and the details as to when and how you are vested. If you have changed jobs, go back to previous employers and ask whether or not you had any plan with them. Find out about any plans your spouse may have access to. Know what is available to you.

Also, you should know what vesting is. Vesting is a designated point at which you receive both employer's and employee's contributions if you need to leave the retirement plan due to a change in jobs. Once you are vested you receive both portions. Prior to that point in your time of job service, you will only receive back from the retirement plan the amount of money that you personally contributed and you will lose the amount that your employer contributed. This is a very important factor to consider before you make any job change.

Section V: ANTICIPATING YOUR FINANCIAL FUTURE

6. Contribute to a tax-sheltered savings plan.

If your company offers a tax sheltered savings plan, such as a 401(k), sign up and contribute all that you can. Maximize your contributions starting now. Your taxes will be lower, your company might kick in a greater amount to match your contributions, and you can probably begin with automatic deductions from your paycheck. Over time, deferral of taxes and compounding on interest make a huge difference in the amount of money you will accumulate. For income during retirement, employees need to participate fully in these plans. If your employer matches your contribution to the plan, be sure to contribute as much as you possibly can.

If you change jobs and leave your current employer, consequently leaving your retirement plan, you may be able to roll over your retirement benefits into an IRA. However, you'll need some good professional advice to avoid making errors in this transfer of your money. The check to transfer your retirement money should be made out directly to the IRA account, which is often referred to as a direct transfer. If the check is mistakenly made out to you, you run the risk of taxes and a penalty for early withdrawal, which may be deducted from the check.

7. Find out about your Social Security benefits.

Generally, employers are required to withhold Social Security taxes for their employees. This amounts to 7.65 percent from paychecks and contributes a matching 7.65 percent from the employee's income for Social Security. If you have been married for ten years, you may be entitled to a spousal benefit when reaching age 62. Check with the Social Security Administration for your eligibility to this benefit.

Social Security benefits are a foundation on which people can build a secure retirement. For most retired Americans, Social Security is the largest source of income and may serve to keep them out of poverty. Call or go online (http://www.ssa.gov/) to contact the Social Security Administration about your specific account. You can get all the numbers and estimated projections about your retirement benefits. However, Social Security benefits were never meant to be the only source of retirement income. It needs to be supplemented with income from a company sponsored retirement plan, savings or income from other investments.

8. *Put money into an IRA–Individual Retirement Account.*

If you have earned income, you can set up an IRA. Earned income is the money you make from an employer or through self-employment. Unemployed spouses who do not work can also establish IRA's as long as their spouse has earned income. There are several IRA's, including traditional deductible IRA's, traditional non-deductible IRA's, education IRAs and Roth IRA's.

You can sock away thousands of dollars and delay paying taxes on the money until retirement with a traditional IRA. Or you can choose a Roth IRA, pay the taxes up front and not have to pay taxes at all on the accrued interest, dividends and appreciation when you retire. The earlier you begin, the more you will have for retirement. If you begin at age 30 to put aside only $2000 each year, by the time you are only age 60, you will have an accumulation of $112,170 using a very conservative return on your investment of just 4 percent. As of this writing, you are eligible to contribute $3,000 each year, $3,500 if you are over the age of 50.

9. *Protect your savings.*

Don't be tempted to dip into your retirement savings. Not only will you lose your principal and future interest, you may also face stiff penalties and lose tax benefits. If you change jobs, roll over your retirement benefits directly into an IRA or into your new employer's retirement plan.

10. *Follow basic investment principles.*

How you save and put money aside for retirement is as important as what and how much you save. Inflation and the types of investment vehicles play a very important role in how much you will have accumulated at retirement. Know how your funds are invested. Read books and understand what is going on with your money. Become knowledgeable. Trust yourself, instead of others for that final decision. Know what is going on in your financial world. Financial security and basic knowledge go hand in hand.

11. Remember the Rule of 72.

Let's take a minute to review the Rule of 72. This is an investing rule of thumb that calculates how long it takes to double your savings, given a certain rate of return. To use the rule, simply start with the number 72, then divide it by the rate of return that you expect to earn. The result becomes your investment horizon or the number of years it takes you to double your savings. For example, if the interest rate that you earn is 7.2 percent, it would take you 120 months or ten years to double your money. You must be aware, however, that the Rule of 72 does not include adjustments for income taxes or inflation. The Rule of 72 also assumes that you compound your interest yearly.

12. Be informed!

When you don't know about some investment vehicles or you don't understand the process, get help! Ask questions! When kids are growing up, they continually bombard you with questions, sometimes to the point of driving you nuts! When it comes to financial knowledge, drive someone else nuts! Not just one person. Ask the same question to several different people, so you can be sure of the correct answer. Get advice, read books, gather information, take care of yourself.

Bring order to your financial world by being informed. There are many investment options and opportunities available to people today. Investment opportunities that help an individual plan for retirement include buying a personal home, setting aside funds in an Individual Retirement Account, and contributing to deferred income plans such as a 401(k).

The variety of investment opportunities makes the decision for proper investment of finances very complex if an individual is not willing to do his own homework and learn about proper investing himself. A CPA, a Financial Planner, or any other professional won't be of much help. A person needs to trust only himself or herself when it comes to final investment decisions. Don't even trust your banker who wants to sell you CDs, mutual funds and annuities. Guess what? Your banker is a commissioned salesperson whose office happens to be at the bank! Just remember, no investments in equity issues are without risk.

FIVE MYTHS ABOUT
RETIREMENT PLANNING

Myth #1: "It's too early to plan for my retirement."

Whether you are close to retirement or many years away, it is never too early or too late to plan for retirement. You control your financial future by identifying your retirement needs, setting money aside and making wise investment decisions now. Tell some young family to start now to prepare for retirement and they stare in disbelief. They feel that they are still young and have lots of time before they need to save for retirement.

But the earlier a family starts, the more they will be able to salt away some great savings. That is because time is money and the power of compound interest is enormous. Assume you want to build a $100,000 nest egg by age 65 and that you can earn 10 percent on your money. You need to contribute only $16 per month if you start saving at age 25. If you wait till you're 35, you need to contribute $44 per month. The necessary contribution rises to $131 per month if you wait till 45 and skyrockets to $484 per month if you wait till 55.

Here is another example for you. Suppose you are a young person twenty years old. You start saving or investing just $21.40 each week and attain an average of 10 percent on your investment over a 45 year period. By the time you reach the retirement age of 65, your account would be worth $1,001,711.36. Over one million dollars! This shows you the power of investing just a little bit over the long haul.

On the other hand, some older couples excuse their lack of saving by thinking that they are too old to start saving for retirement. While it is very true that you can't make up for lost time and opportunity, it's never too late to start saving. Someone who takes early retirement at age 55 may still be going strong 30 years later. You'll have to contribute more to your retirement savings account than if you started it decades ago, but the time to start saving seriously is now.

Myth #2: "I Don't Need a Specific Plan"

No one actively plans to fail in providing for a comfortable old age. They simply fail to plan. Our grandparents faced different problems with money than we do. They were frightened by bank failures and the depression and tended to put their money into just three places—a home, a bank and insurance. Today, we have to be prepared for the havoc that inflation can play on our investments over the long term, as well as corporate fraud or an up-and-down economy.

> NO ONE ACTIVELY PLANS TO FAIL IN PROVIDING FOR A COMFORTABLE OLD AGE. THEY SIMPLY FAIL TO PLAN.

Working men and women of all ages need to have a greater understanding of how to prepare for retirement. Increasing numbers of people are finding that retirement is staring them in the face before they're ready to leave the work force and that it's harder than ever to amass the nest egg they thought they'd have in their golden years. There are a number of common misunderstandings that could be dangerous to the future financial health of any working individual.

One common misunderstanding is that the conservation of principal should be a person's main priority. This is not always the case. Inflation is the deadliest money-killer over time and can result in a guaranteed loss of principal. It's not simply what you make on your money that counts; it's what you make over and above inflation that really matters. So your goal should be to conserve purchasing power, not just principal.

Myth #3: "I'll be able to live on a lot less when I retire."

One real misunderstanding is that many people think that, upon retirement, they will be able to live on a lot less than they do now. While it is a nice little myth to tell oneself, it is hardly the truth. The only bills that will stop are your mortgage payments (only if you plan ahead for this to happen) and any educational costs you may now be paying. Your medical bills will almost certainly rise. Expect higher costs of food, fuel, clothing, transportation and insurance, too. This does not even include new taxes and upkeep on your home, even if it has been paid in full.

With the federal deficit continuing to balloon beyond our country's ability to finance its expenditures out of current receipts, higher taxes will be necessary to pay for the future health and retirement costs of our aging population. The only way you'll be in a lower tax bracket will be if you wind up living on a lot less money than you are today and that will mean you'll wind up in worse financial shape and be subjected to a more humble lifestyle.

Myth #4: "Social Security is all I'll need."

Although Social Security benefits may indeed be there, don't put a lot of faith into the system if you are 40 years of age and younger. Even company pensions are rapidly disappearing. As the downsizing of American business continues, many companies are folding their retirement plans or replacing them with less generous ones. And when the current generation of middle-aged workers retires, there probably won't be enough people left in the work force to fund Social Security benefits at the level to which today's retirees are accustomed.

Some people argue that living costs will be less because there will only be the two of them. Don't be too sure. These days, more and more adult children are moving back home because of economic setbacks or divorce. Many times the grandkids come with them.

It is even common for children to go to college and then move back home. The result? More food to buy, more utilities to pay, etc. The greatest service you can do for your kids is to raise them to be independent, to live within their means and to develop an appreciation for the value of hard work.

Myth #5: "I just need to live for the moment."

Some people seem to live only for the moment. They figure that, when they get old, someone will have to take care of them. Besides, they want to have fun now and enjoy life. They think that saving and investing will cramp their lifestyle. Well certainly it will cut back on the amount of cash flow available for fun things, but if a person will save just 10 percent of their current disposable income for retirement after taxes and tithing, they will still have 90 percent left for today.

An inability to live comfortably on 90 percent of your disposable income now means there is a problem with overspending. Saving and spending are not conflicting goals. Saving is merely not spending today so you can spend more tomorrow. And if you don't die young, you'll have plenty of time to savor the fruits of your frugality later on in retirement years.

Everyone needs a clearer vision of their retirement needs and the peace of mind that comes with knowing they are initiating an investment plan. Certainly, you should do a lot of reading from a variety of sources before making any kind of life-changing decisions. A person needs to read and become familiar with their personal retirement needs as well as pinpoint their goals and identify investment strategies. This information is not designed to take the place of a tax advisor or financial planner, but is simply a means to help you begin thinking about how to approach the basic planning process.

THREE RETIREMENT QUESTIONS

1. *"How much will I need for retirement?"*

The basic rule of thumb used by many financial planners is that a person will need about 60-90 percent of their final income before retirement to maintain their lifestyle during the non-working years. Of course, this rule will vary with everyone's situation. But the best way to address this issue of expenses during retirement is to sit down and plan a budget.

To identify future expenses there are some key questions to consider. How much traveling do you want to do in retirement? Will your medical expenses and insurance costs increase once you leave your company? Will your mortgage expense change because you plan to sell your house and relocate?

After considering the kind of retirement expenses you will be faced with, consider next the income needed to cover these expenses. In doing so, be sure to consider inflation as a factor in your retirement planning. Living expenses are likely to be greater in the future because inflation increases the cost of goods and services. It will require more dollars in the future to enjoy the comparable lifestyle you have today.

2. *"How can I account for inflation in my planning?"*

To address the issue of inflation, the easiest approach is to look at everything in today's dollars and then adjust income and return with an inflation factor. For example, if you want to assume an average return on hypothetical investments of 7 percent and an average inflation factor over the years of 4 percent, then in your calculations, you would use a net 3 percent return (7 percent minus 4 percent). This approximates the inflation factor by placing all numbers in current dollars.

Do you know what a gallon of milk will cost in twenty years? How about a loaf of bread? The answer of course, we cannot know, but we do know that it will in fact cost more than today. Because of inflation, a dollar today will not be worth as much in the future.

Don't worry too much about inflation, because incomes generally keep up, more or less, with prices. The key is to plan for a retirement income which will keep you up with, or better still, ahead of inflation. If your after-tax return on savings and investments exceeds the inflation rate over the long run, you'll come out ahead and retain your purchasing power.

A simple formula for determining the investment return needed just to break even after taxes and inflation is to divide the current inflation rate by 100 minus your marginal tax bracket. You must exceed the result in order for your retirement savings to grow. Let's say for example that inflation jumps to 5 percent and that you remain in the 15 percent tax bracket. Given this scenario the rate of return needed for you to breakeven is 5.9 percent. Should you be in the 28 percent tax bracket, your breakeven rate is 6.9 percent. When it comes to investing, a realistic after-tax/after-inflation goal is around 1-4 percent above the breakeven rate. In the previous scenario, the 28 percent bracket investor should seek a taxable investment product yielding 8-11 percent.

Estimating income begins with the basics of most retirement savings plans. These basics include both Social Security, 401(k)'s and IRA's. Social Security provides only a base level of income. You can affect the amount of your Social Security benefit by the age at which you decide to collect. Age 62 is the earliest you can collect. But if you begin collecting before age 65, your benefits will be reduced. And, if you delay until after age 65, benefits are increased. Your Social Security benefit can also be reduced if your retirement earnings exceed a certain level of income while drawing Social Security.

3. *"How will my retirement be funded?"*

For many people, their own 401k's or IRA's will provide a major portion of retirement income. If you are fortunate enough to have a company pension plan, then all the better. A lot of pensions are provided in the form of an annuity (equal periodic payments over a lifetime), although some will give you the option to take a lump sum distribution at retirement. To identify your pension benefits, you should request an estimate of your expected annual pension from your Employee Benefits department.

Pension payouts during retirement depend on various factors, such as the length of time you stay at a company, whether or not a pension has an inflation adjustment, and your salary. Many people do not realize the impact frequent job changes may have on future retirement benefits.

RETIREMENT INVESTMENT PRODUCTS

Investment products for your retirement years should be chosen with your objectives, financial resources, and risk tolerance in mind. Another consideration is your marginal tax bracket. If you are in a higher tax bracket, you may earn a far greater return using tax-exempt investment products such as municipal bonds or bond mutual funds. An additional important strategy in picking products for your retirement investments is to diversify your investments among several types of products. This reduces the risk of making a poor selection or other considerations beyond your control.

According to one investment firm (T. Rowe Price), a diversified portfolio (evenly divided among money market instruments, bonds, stocks and real estate) earned an average annual return of 12 percent between the years 1978 and 1987. This was the result compared to no diversity returns of 15.3 percent for stocks during this same period, 13.5 percent for real estate, 9.7 percent for bonds and 9.4 percent for money market funds. Of course, over the past ten years these numbers have changed dramatically.

Diversification is the number one consideration for all portfolios. A well-balanced portfolio will, over time, produce greater yields more consistently than any one area alone. You will enjoy less risk, less volatility, more consistent yields, and less stress about the ups and downs of any one investment product or the nation's economy.

Retirement nest eggs can be accumulated through a number of investment possibilities reviewed below. To understand the investment options, see the chapter on Investing For Your Future.

Tax-Advantaged Retirement Products

For anyone saving for the future, there are certain kinds of tax-advantaged products that must be emphasized for retirement savings. "Tax-advantaged" means that earnings will grow on a tax-deferred basis and in some cases you may also take a tax deduction when you initially invest. If you are saving for the future, the longer you can defer taxes, the larger your ultimate nest egg will be due to compounding.

Employer-Sponsored Retirement Plans

One of the simplest ways to set aside tax-deferred savings for your retirement is through an employer-sponsored retirement plan. Through automatic payroll deductions, the plans allow you to make voluntary contributions to the plan by setting aside part of your before-tax salary. Not only are the earnings tax-deferred until withdrawal, but the contributions reduce your taxable income.

Cash Equivalents / Money Markets

Basically, investments can be divided into four major groups, ranging from the more conservative to the more aggressive. Cash equivalents and money markets can be a conservative option for the investor. These are short-term, high-quality securities that pay dividend income with principal value remaining stable.

Income Investments

These are primarily taxable corporate and government bonds or tax-free bonds which can generate high, current dividend yields, but are subject to price fluctuations with interest rate changes.

Growth Investments

Considered more aggressive, these funds typically invest in stocks with the objective of showing growth in assets over the long term. They have greater upside appreciation potential, but also present much more risk. Your particular retirement investment strategy will depend on a few personal choices. What kind of risk are you willing to take? Are you a conservative, moderate or aggressive investor? How much time do you have until retirement? Are you close to retirement or many years away? What kind of investment vehicle are you interested in? Are you seeking income, growth or a combination of both?

Annuities

These may be purchased as a single investment or a series of investments over a period of time. Earnings are tax-deferred until withdrawn and annuities may provide the additional guarantee of a stream of income over your lifetime. There is no limit on the amount you can invest.

Mutual Funds

Mutual funds are diversified portfolios of stocks, bonds or money market instruments. Managed by investment specialists, mutual funds are available with objectives to meet most levels of risk and investment strategies.

Since most investors should diversify their portfolios, mutual funds provide an easy way to buy shares in diversified pools of investment instruments—without having to purchase high-cost, individual securities.

Here are a couple of basic guidelines. The closer you are to retirement, the more conservative and income-oriented you are likely to be. The longer you have until retirement, the more aggressive you may want to be in investing for long-term growth, because you have more time to ride out the ups and downs of the stock market.

"I hear, I know. I see, I remember. I do, I understand."

Key Points:

➤ home ownership and your future

➤ the importance of planning now

➤ retirement planning strategies

➤ inflation, retirement investment products

1. **Write down** any parts of the chapter that were meaningful to you.

_____

_____

_____

_____

2. **Personal Application:** How can you personally apply these truths in your own life? Write down several long-term goals.

_____

_____

_____

_____

3. **Steps to Action:** Write down one small step you could take to begin immediately applying the truths and principles of this chapter.

_____

_____

_____

_____

4. **Prayer for the Practical:** Write out a prayer to God asking Him for help in making any changes that these goals would require.

_____

_____

_____

_____

Psalm 62:8 "O my people, trust in him at all times.
Pour out your heart to him,
For God is our refuge."

"If I always appear prepared, it is because before entering an undertaking, I have meditated long and have foreseen what might occur. It is not genius where reveals to me suddenly and secretly what I should do in circumstances unexpected by others; it is thought and preparation."

—NAPOLEON BONAPARTE (1769-1821)
FRENCH GENERAL, POLITICIAN AND EMPEROR

CHAPTER TWENTY-THREE

AVOIDING TITANIC FOLLY

It was the ship that was proclaimed unsinkable. One of the largest luxury ships in the world at the time, the Titanic, when fully laden, weighed 66,000 tons. Just before midnight on April 14, 1912, however, this British passenger liner collided with a huge iceberg en route to New York City from Southampton, England. The "unsinkable ship" sank, killing almost 1500 passengers.

Some blame the catastrophe on the ship's design and manufacturing defects; others point to unfavorable weather conditions and the high sailing speed of the vessel. More concerning, however, were the errors and oversights of the crew. Even with the presence of icebergs, the radio operators failed to quickly report messages to the ship officers. The watchmen observing from the crow's nest of the ship did not have the surveillance binoculars which they should have been using to detect potential dangers. Worst of all, when the ship collided with the iceberg, the seriousness of the event was downplayed, resulting in the first lifeboats leaving almost empty. Clearly, the Titanic's personnel and crew members had failed to prepare for the unexpected. Their folly resulted in unspeakable loss.

Most of us would like to think that we are prepared for the unexpected. And in many ways, we do prepare. We think ahead, we address the what ifs; but all too often, it's that one event that we never thought could happen to us that catches us off our guard.

PREPARING FOR THE UNEXPECTED

Natural (or other) disasters can strike suddenly, at any time, anywhere. Your first priority, of course, would be to protect your family and your property. A natural disaster can damage or destroy your family, force you to temporarily live somewhere else, cut the flow of wages and other income, and ruin valuable financial records.

Inventory your belongings

You need to have an inventory of your belongings. You may want to list each item, its value and condition. There are several computer software programs designed to make the task easier.

The process of inventorying your possessions not only helps you to receive a fair settlement from your insurance company should you encounter losses, it will also speed up the process. Of course it will provide proof that you owned these possessions as well as proof of their value. Any losses not covered by your insurance company can be taken as deductions from your taxes.

Use a digital camera or video camera

Video tape the contents of your home. Slowly go from room to room. Describe each item, when you bought it, and how much it cost. Whether you're photographing each item or videotaping them, have someone open the closet doors and hold up each item. Open the drawers in your office, bedroom and kitchen. Open those kitchen doors and videotape what is inside. Don't forget to inventory your basement, the attic, the closets and garage. Include your outdoor sheds, patio, yard, trees, fencing, landscaping and the exterior of the house. When photographing, note the quality of the building materials, the type of wood and any expensive extras, such as fancy plumbing fixtures.

After you have inventoried your entire house, be sure to make several copies. Send one to a trusted friend, another to a relative, and place yet another in your safe deposit box. You might even try sending a copy to the office of your insurance agent, with a label affixed as to its purpose and the date.

Record make, model and serial numbers

When it comes to camera, equipment and other possessions, where available, be sure to record the make, model and serial numbers. Make copies of all your receipts and store them in a separate place. Get professional appraisals of jewelry, collectibles, artwork and any other items that are difficult to value. Update those appraisals every couple of years.

The location of all your original documents, including receipts to birth and marriage certificates, wills, deeds, tax returns, insurance polices, stock certificates and so on should be recorded and accessible.

Preparing for Loss of Income

Here is a question for you to think seriously about. As has happened many times in the past, if the economy went into a recession and many major companies began to lay off thousands of employees, what would you do if you missed a paycheck? What would you do if you lost a month of paychecks? Three months of paychecks?

If you don't like this question, here's another one. What would life be like for you if you lost your job tomorrow? Your paychecks would stop immediately, so what would you do?

If you are like most people who live paycheck to paycheck with credit-card debt, a car payment and a mortgage, you'd probably panic. If you had some money in savings, it could tide you over for a while, but for how long?

Now think about this question for a while. If you have no debt, no car payment, no mortgage and no credit card balances, how much money would you need each month to live on? If you were to lose your job and you were debt-free, how would you feel? Not nearly as bad. You could probably get a minimum wage job anywhere and at least get by.

What is that worth to you? Is it worth getting out of debt? Is it worth it for you to have financial freedom and peace of mind that only a debt-free lifestyle can give? If so, we challenge you to establish a debt elimination plan for yourself, follow it, and achieve the success you desire.

Yes, there are people who want to keep their mortgage and invest their extra payments for a higher return in the stock market. And yes, that many people are hanging on to their mortgage because they think it is their last tax deduction. But what about the peace of mind that comes from knowing that what's yours is yours and that you are debt free? Just when you think that the unexpected will never happen to you—get ready. Your number is probably up next.

CASH FOR THE UNEXPECTED

Once you've got your budget in place, everything else starts falling into place. The next step is to earmark some money to put away for emergencies. You can call it saving for a rainy day, but sometimes, the emergency becomes a hurricane with genuine gale winds. We've stressed before how crucial it is to have a rainy-day fund: 3 to 6 months' living expenses put away in safe, liquid cash investments, in case you're unable to work. It may be due to a layoff, a health problem, a vehicle or appliance that stops working, or even a sudden death.

Yet a lot of people out there have absolutely no money saved. None. This is a very dangerous position to be in, and it puts your family at great risk.

What is the emergency fund for? Emergency funds are a stash of cash that you can get your hands on when the need arises. How much money do I need to keep on hand? Where should I keep it? These two great questions often get asked.

The best way to determine how much money you need for emergency purposes is to do some planning. Some things to think about would include:

✓ Travel expenses to family or relatives for illness or death

✓ Deductibles or co-pays on medical expenses

✓ Automobile deductibles or temporary replacements in case of an accident

✓ Auto repairs, tires and other mechanical issues

✓ Family or friends' weddings, travel expenses and gifts involved

✓ Replacement of old appliances you know are on their last leg

When you plan your budget each year, generate some numbers for any of these examples that might be applicable to you. Try to keep some money available for use in an emergency. If you can't save the money from your regular paycheck, then sell some assets. You might have some stocks to sell, some collectibles, or, at the very least, have a multi-week garage or yard sale. Unload some stuff that's been taking up way too much room in your garage.

Some places to keep your emergency funds are:

- a savings account,

- bank money market deposit accounts,

- certificates of deposit or

- money market funds.

Just remember that when you have an emergency, you are going to need the cash and need it fast.

Automatic Savings

The way to get your emergency cushion where you need it—especially if you're starting at zero—is to build it automatically. Build it into your budget.

Have $100 taken out of your checking account or paycheck each month and put into a money market fund—more if you can afford it, less if that feels like too big a burden. Trust me, if you don't see the money, you won't miss it.

And what about compounding? At 6 percent a year, that $100 monthly stake will grow to $1,339.72 just in time to start year #2 of your new budget. That may not feel like a lot, but this is money you don't plan to touch unless you absolutely have to, so it will just continue to grow.

Five years down the road, you'll have $7,500. And if you can boost your monthly contributions, your emergency stake will soar even faster. (One way to do so without feeling pinched is to increase your savings by the amount of any raise you get at work.)

VITAL DOCUMENTS

Keeping Track of Your Will

Without a will, you or your loved ones might have to spend months—and many dollars in legal fees—locating bank accounts, safe deposit boxes and other particulars of the financial life of a deceased relative.

If you are a parent, do your children know where your will is? Do you know where your parents' wills or their bank accounts are? How about their attorney's name and phone number? Every family needs to prepare a document which provides a detailed list of everything a survivor needs to know but is too polite to ask.

This document should be updated semi-annually. At least one copy should be kept at home, another in your safe-deposit box and, if children are under twelve, a third in the hands of their potential guardian. The following information should be included.

Keeping Track of Your Personal Papers

State the location of your will, recent income tax returns, Social Security cards, marriage certificate, military discharge papers, passports, business partnership agreements, house deed, mortgage, leases and car titles.

Keeping Track of Your Advisors

List the names, addresses and telephone numbers of your accountant or tax preparer, insurance agents, stockbroker, attorney, financial planner, bank trust officer, employer and employee-benefits counselor, executor, potential guardian for your children and any other key financial players in your life.

KEEPING TRACK OF YOUR DEBTS

Write down the names of your credit-card issuers, their addresses, phone numbers and your card number. Also, furnish information on your mortgage, auto and personal loans, including the phone numbers and addresses of lenders, the loan numbers, terms and approximate balances.

Keeping Track of Your Insurance

Specify the amount, company names and addresses, policy numbers, beneficiaries and location of policies for all coverage. Don't forget to include the same information for your group plans.

Keeping Track of Your Savings and Investment Records

List the names and addresses of all the financial institutions where you have savings or investment accounts. For each account, specify the name or names on it, the number, the type, the date it was opened, and the approximate balance. Also, put down the location of account statements and passbooks, as well as stock, bond, mutual fund or other investment documents.

Keeping Track of Your Safe-Deposit Box

Note where it is, who has access, where the keys are, and in whose name the box is registered. Also provide a complete inventory of its contents. In your safe deposit box should be all of your original paperwork for the following documents:

- Certificates for your stocks, bonds and all other investments
- Passports and any military or veteran papers
- All trust and contract agreements
- A copy of your living wills (Generally, the original should be with your attorney, since safe deposit boxes can be sealed temporarily after a death.)
- Power of attorney papers
- Insurance policies
- List of household inventory & videos
- Marriage license
- Appraisals of valuables
- Deeds to property
- Titles to autos, RVs and boats
- Household improvement papers
- Tax records
- Naturalization records if applicable
- Cash for one month's living expenses
- Traveler's checks

EVALUATING YOUR INSURANCE POLICIES

Assessing Your Renters and Homeowners Insurance

Should a natural disaster occur, will you be underinsured or not insured at all? If you are a renter, you'd better have great renter's insurance. Make sure that it pays for damaged, destroyed or stolen personal property. Be clear about what the policy does and does not cover. Make sure that it covers you should you have to live somewhere else temporarily. In some areas you may want to add special coverage like earthquake or flood insurance.

If you require homeowner's insurance, buy guaranteed replacement cost coverage. Every few years, have your home reappraised to be sure that the policy reflects the true replacement cost. Update the policy to include any home improvements. Purchase a policy that covers the replacement cost of your possessions. Understand policy deductibles. Update your inventory list annually.

Assessing Your Umbrella Insurance

Umbrella insurance provides additional coverage, usually through your home or auto insurance policies, in the event that you face an unfortunate lawsuit.

Huge lawsuits are almost commonplace these days. It's not unusual for newspapers to carry stories of million-dollar judgments against people involved in tragic accidents. For many, such a lawsuit could threaten their most important assets—home, retirement funds, future earnings and other valuable property.

One way to gain added liability protection from a devastating lawsuit is with a personal umbrella policy. An umbrella serves as a backup to auto and homeowner insurance. For instance, when the home, auto or boat policy's limits have been used up, a personal umbrella will step in to add liability limits of $1 million or more. Not everyone needs a personal umbrella, but it can offer real peace of mind for people whose assets have grown significantly over the years.

Assessing Your Disability Insurance

Contrary to what life insurance agents may tell you, the coverage you need most isn't whole life, universal life, variable life, or even universal variable life. It's disability income insurance. This often overlooked coverage pays you a monthly income if you are unable to work because of injury or illness.

You are more likely to miss at least three months of work before you reach age 65 because of a disability than you are to die. Social Security Disability Insurance can pay you and your family benefits if you are severely disabled and are expected to be so for at least 12 months.

Statistics show that disability is far more probable than death, especially if you are young or middle-aged. In fact, disability is sometimes called living death, since our family's financial needs continue, but we can't meet them unless we have insurance.

Unfortunately, there are plenty of temptations to put off obtaining coverage. It is expensive. Also, you may mistakenly think you are fully protected by Social Security and possibly by your employer's group disability policy.

How much coverage do you need? In general, insurance experts recommend that disability insurance equal 60 to 70 percent of your before-tax earnings, with benefits starting 90 days after you become disabled and continuing, if necessary, until you reach age 65.

To avoid attracting phony claims, most insurers will cover you only to the point at which your disability income from all sources, including Social Security and company benefits, would equal 70 percent of your current before-tax earnings. Still, that's better than it sounds. Benefits from a policy you buy with after-tax dollars—in contrast to income from a policy paid by your employer—are tax-free.

Equally important as the amount of coverage is the way your policy defines disability. Under the most generous definition, insurers agree to pay full benefits if you can't work in your own occupation as long as you are under a physician's care. In contrast, a policy using the narrower definition would pay only if you are unable to work in any occupation for which you are clearly suited.

The most expedient way to minimize the cost of your coverage is to prolong the so-called elimination period—the time you have to wait for benefits to begin after you become disabled. To change from a 90-day waiting period to a 30-day period would be extremely costly.

Finally, you should insist upon a policy that is at least guaranteed renewable, which means that the insured cannot cancel your coverage as long as you pay your premiums or raise your premium unless it boosts premiums in general. A preferable alternative is a non-cancelable policy, which guarantees that your policy cannot be revoked and that your premium cannot be increased at all.

In just two years, disability insurers lost more than $586 million, in part because their policies didn't charge enough to cover promised benefits. These losses have resulted in many insurers drastically scaling back their disability polices and increasing their costs.

Assessing Your Life Insurance

Life insurance protects those who depend on you in the event of an untimely death. It frees them from financial disaster and the stress of trying to survive. There are many types of life insurance, often with huge sales commissions attached. Term insurance is a low-cost, efficient way to protect your family's financial well-being. If you are looking for the best deal in term life insurance, there are many solid companies to choose from. Check online by using a search engine. You will find plenty of quotes to compare.

Assessing Your Auto Insurance

You may qualify for lower rates if your car has seat belts, air bags, anti-lock brakes or an anti-theft device or alarm. Other deductions are given if you own more than one car, you drive your second car only occasionally, or you've had no accidents or moving violations in three years. Also, you benefit if you or another covered driver are over age 50, have completed a driver training course, are a student with good grades, or are away at college without a car.

LEAVE IT IN GOD'S HANDS

Once you have taken the time to really think it over, you should realize how much there is that you can actually do to prepare yourself and your family for the crises that life inevitably brings along from time to time. Set up the best savings plan you can manage, then review and adjust it periodically. Organize all the important documents that pertain to your legal and financial matters. Then, when you have enrolled in the necessary insurance plans discussed above, you can take a deep breath and feel a sense of accomplishment.

Of course, no one can foresee every situation, but with the proactive planning above, you have at least done the responsible things and the rest is in God's hands.

An Unshakeable Foundation

Preparing for the unexpected is just one more way of exercising the stewardship principles found in God's Word. According to one author, "stewardship is the act of organizing your life so that God can spend you."[22] As you faithfully organize your life and finances, never forget the ultimate goal—God wants to spend you! When God finds men and women who have faithfully set their personal finances in order, there is no limit to what He can accomplish through them! Winds may blow and storms may come, but the one whose finances are anchored in the principles of the Word of God will remain standing:

> *"Therefore everyone who hears these words of mine and puts them into practice is like a wise man who built his house on the rock. The rain came down, the streams rose, and the winds blew and beat against that house; yet it did not fall, because it had its foundation on the rock"* (Matthew 7:24, 25, NIV).

God doesn't want you to just survive the storm, however. He wants you to be a blessing to those around you who are going through the storms of life! As we build our finances on the truths of God's Word, let us believe for Him to use our time, talents, and resources for His glory.

"I hear, I know. I see, I remember. I do, I understand."

Key Points:

➤ inventorying your possessions   ➤ keeping track of important papers

➤ saving for emergencies   ➤ reviewing your insurance policies

1. **Write down** any parts of the chapter that were meaningful to you.

_____

_____

_____

_____

2. **Personal Application:** How can you personally apply these truths in your own life? Write down several long-term goals.

_____

_____

_____

_____

3. **Steps to Action**—Write down one small step you could take to begin immediately applying the truths and principles of this chapter.

_____

_____

_____

_____

4. **Prayer for the Practical**—Write out a prayer to God asking Him for help in making any changes that these goals would require.

_____

_____

_____

_____

Psalm 62:8 "O my people, trust in him at all times.
Pour out your heart to him,
For God is our refuge."

21 Unbreakable Laws of Success, Max Anders, Thomas Nelson, 1996

A Christian Guide to Prosperity; Fries & Taylor, California: Communications Research, 1984

A Look At Stewardship, Word Aflame Publications, 2001

American Savings Education Council (http://www.asec.org)

Anointed For Business, Ed Silvoso, Regal, 2002

Avoiding Common Financial Mistakes, Ron Blue, Navpress, 1991

Baker Encyclopedia of the Bible; Walter Elwell, Michigan: Baker Book House, 1988

Barrons

Becoming The Best, Barry Popplewell, England: Gower Publishing Company Limited, 1988

Bloomberg.com (http://www.bloomberg.com)

Bureau of the Public Debt Online (http://www.publicdebt.treas.gov)

Business Proverbs, Steve Marr, Fleming H. Revell, 2001

Business Week

BusinessWeek (http://www.businessweek.com)

Charles Schwab & Co., Inc. (http://www.schwab.com)

Cheapskate Monthly, Mary Hunt

Commentary on the Old Testament; Keil-Delitzsch, Michigan: Eerdmans Publishing, 1986

Consumer Federation of America (http://www.consumerfed.org)

Consumer Reports

Crown Financial Ministries, various publications

Customers As Partners, Chip Bell, Texas: Berrett-Koehler Publishers, 1994

Cut Your Bills in Half; Pennsylvania: Rodale Press, Inc., 1989

Debt Advice.org (http://www.debtadvice.org)

Debt-Free Living, Larry Burkett, Dimensions, 2001

Die Broke, Stephen M. Pollan & Mark Levine, HarperBusiness, 1997

Double Your Profits, Bob Fifer, Virginia: Lincoln Hall Press, 1993

Eerdmans' Handbook to the Bible, Michigan: William B. Eerdmans Publishing Company, 1987

Eight Steps to Seven Figures, Charles B. Carlson, Double Day, 2000

Everyday Life in Bible Times; Washington DC: National Geographic Society, 1967

Federal Reserve System (http://www.federalreserve.gov/)

Fidelity Investments (http://www.fidelity.com)

Financial Dominion, Norvel Hayes, Harrison House, 1986

Financial Freedom, Larry Burkett, Moody Press, 1991

Financial Freedom, Patrick Clements, VMI Publishers, 2003

Financial Peace, Dave Ramsey, Viking Press, 2003

Financial Planning Association (http://www.fpanet.org)

Financial Self-Defense; Charles Givens, New York: Simon And Schuster, 1990

Flood Stage, Oral Roberts, 1981

Forbes

Forbes (www.forbes.com)

Fortune Magazine (http://www.fortune.com)

Generous Living, Ron Blue, Zondervan, 1997

Get It All Done, Tony and Robbie Fanning, New York:Pennsylvania: Chilton Book, 1979

Getting Out of Debt, Howard Dayton, Tyndale House, 1986

Getting Out of Debt, Mary Stephenson, Fact Sheet 436, University of Maryland Cooperative Extension Service, 1988

Giving and Tithing, Larry Burkett, Moody Press, 1991

God's Plan For Giving, John MacArthur, Jr., Moody Press, 1985

God's Will is Prosperity, Gloria Copeland, Harrison House, 1978

Great People of the Bible and How They Lived; New York: Reader's Digest, 1974

How Others Can Help You Get Out of Debt; Esther M. Maddux, Circular 759-3,

How To Make A Business Plan That Works, Henderson, North Island Sound Limited, 1989

How To Manage Your Money, Larry Burkett, Moody Press, 1999

How to Personally Profit From the Laws of Success, Sterling Sill, NIFP, Inc., 1978

How to Plan for Your Retirement; New York: Corrigan & Kaufman, Longmeadow Press, 1985

Investing For Your Future (http://www.investing.rutgers.edu)

Investors Business Daily

Is God Your Source?, Oral Roberts, 1992

It's Not Luck, Eliyahu Goldratt, Great Barrington, MA: The North River Press, 1994

Jesus CEO, Laurie Beth Jones, Hyperion, 1995

John Avanzini Answers Your Questions About Biblical Economics, Harrison House, 1992

Kiplinger Magazine (http://www.kiplinger.com/)

Kiplinger's Personal Finance

Living on Less and Liking It More, Maxine Hancock, Chicago, Illinois: Moody Press, 1976

Making It Happen; Charles Conn, New Jersey: Fleming H. Revell Company, 1981

Master Your Money Or It Will Master You, Arlo E. Moehlenpah, Doing Good Ministries, 1999

Master Your Money; Ron Blue, Tennessee: Thomas Nelson, Inc. 1986

Miracle of Seed Faith, Oral Roberts, 1970

Mississippi State University Extension Service

Money

Money Magazine (http://money.cnn.com)

Money, Possessions, and Eternity, Randy Alcorn, Tyndale House, 2003

More Than Enough, David Ramsey, Penguin Putnam Inc, 2002

MorningStar (http://www.morningstar.com/)

Moving the Hand of God, John Avanzini, Harrison House, 1990

MSN Money (http://moneycentral.msn.com)

Multiplication, Tommy Barnett, Creation House, 1997

Muriel Siebert (http://www.siebertnet.com)

National Center on Education and the Economy (http://www.ncee.org)

National Foundation for Credit Counseling (http://www.nfcc.org)

NebFacts, Nebraska Cooperative Extension

New York Post NF91-6

One Up On Wall Street; New York: Peter Lynch, Simon And Schuster, 1989

Personal Finances, Larry Burkett, Moody Press, 1991

Portable MBA in Finance and Accounting; Livingstone, Canada: John Wiley & Sons, Inc., 1992

Portland Oregonian

Principle-Centered Leadership, Stephen R. Covey, New York: Summit Books, 1991

Principles of Financial Management, Kolb & DeMong, Texas: Business Publications, Inc., 1988

Quicken (http://www.quicken.com)

Rapid Debt Reduction Strategies, John Avanzini, HIS Publishing, 1990

Real Wealth, Wade Cook, Arizona: Regency Books, 1985

See You At The Top, Zig Ziglar, Louisianna: Pelican Publishing Company, 1977

Seed-Faith Commentary on the Holy Bible, Oral Roberts, Pinoak Publications, 1975

Sharkproof, Harvey Mackay, New York: HarperCollins Publishers, 1993

Smart Money

Smart Money (http://www.smartmoney.com)

Smart Money, Ken and Daria Dolan, New York: Random House, Inc., 1988

Social Security Online (http://www.ssa.gov)

Standard & Poor's (http://www2.standardandpoors.com)

Strong's Concordance, Tennessee: Crusade Bible Publishers, Inc.,

Success by Design, Peter Hirsch, Bethany House, 2002

Success is the Quality of your Journey, Jennifer James, New York: Newmarket Press, 1983

Swim with the Sharks Without Being Eaten Alive, Harvey Mackay, William Morrow , 1988

The Almighty and the Dollar; Jim McKeever, Oregon: Omega Publications, 1981

The Challenge, Robert Allen, New York: Simon And Schuster, 1987

The Dollar Stretcher, Gary Foreman, (http://www.stretcher.com)

The Family Financial Workbook, Larry Burkett, Moody Press, 2002

The Management Methods of Jesus, Bob Briner, Thomas Nelson, 1996

The Millionaire Next Door, Thomas Stanley & William Danko, Pocket Books, 1996

The Money Book for Kids, Nancy Burgeson, Troll Associates,1992

The Money Book for King's Kids; Harold E. Hill, New Jersey: Fleming H. Revell Company, 1984

The Seven Habits of Highly Effective People, Stephen Covey, ew York: Simon And Schuster, 1989

The Vanguard Group (http://flagship.vanguard.com/)

The Wealthy Barber, David Chilton, California: Prima Publishing, 1991

Theological Wordbook of the Old Testament, Chicago, Illinois: Moody Press, 1981

Treasury of Courage and Confidence, Norman Vincent Peale, New York: Doubleday & Co., 1970

True Prosperity, Dick Iverson, Bible Temple Publishing, 1993

Trust God For Your Finances, Jack Hartman, Lamplight Publications, 1983

U.S. Securities and Exchange Commission (http://www.sec.gov)

University of Georgia Cooperative Extension Service, 1985

US News and World Report

USA Today

Virginia Cooperative Extension

Wall Street Journal

Washington Post

Washington Times

Webster's Unabridged Dictionary, Dorset & Baber, 1983

What Is an Entrepreneur; David Robinson, MA: Kogan Page Limited, 1990

Word Meanings in the New Testament, Ralph Earle, Michigan: Baker Book House, 1986

Word Pictures in the New Testament; Robertson, Michigan: Baker Book House, 1930

Word Studies in the New Testament; Vincent, New York: Charles Scribner's Sons, 1914

Worth

Yahoo! Finance (http://finance.yahoo.com)

You Can Be Financially Free, George Fooshee, Jr., 1976, Fleming H. Revell Company.

Your Key to God's Bank, Rex Humbard, 1977

Your Money Counts, Howard, Dayton, Tyndale House, 1997

Your Money Management, MaryAnn Paynter, Circular 1271, University of Illinois Cooperative Extension Service, 1987.

Your Money Matters, Malcolm MacGregor, Bethany Fellowship, Inc., 1977

Your Road to Recovery, Oral Roberts, Oliver Nelson, 1986

Comments On Sources

Over the years I have collected bits and pieces of interesting material, written notes on sermons I've heard, jotted down comments on financial articles I've read, and gathered a lot of great information. It is unfortunate that I didn't record the sources of all of these notes in my earlier years. I gratefully extend my appreciation to the many writers, authors, teachers and pastors from whose articles and sermons I have gleaned much insight. —*Rich Brott*

1. Confucius, retrieved August 16, 2005:
   www.reflectionsoftruth.org/archive/quotearchive/confucious/confucious-quotesVZ.html.

2. Wendell Smith (sermon topic), "Are You Instrument Rated?," June 25, 1999.

3. George Mueller, retrieved July, 2005: www.kingdombiblestudies.org/savor/SOW3.htm.

4. George Mueller, retrieved July, 2005: sermonsearch.com/content.aspx?id=25269.

5. Robert Buck, *Weather Flying* (McGraw Hill, 1998), p. 91, 102.

6. Will Rogers, retrieved July, 2005: www.word-works.com/others.htm.

7. Benjamin Franklin, retrieved July 2005:
   www.quotations.about.com/cs/inspirationquotes/a/Money2.htm.

8. Billy Graham, retrieved July 2005: www.prairieviewcc.org/about/money.htm.

9. James W. Moore, *Some Things are Too Good Not to be True* (Dimensions, 1994), p. 101.

10. Richard Glover, *A Teacher's Commentary of the Gospel on Matthew* (Grand Rapids: Zondervan Publishing House, 1956).

11. Isaac Watts, "The Sluggard," *Divine and Moral Songs for Children* (New York: Hurd and Houghton, 1866).

12. *Bits and Pieces,* November 2000, (Fairfield, NJ: The Economics Press, Inc.) p. 20.

13. Larry Burkett, "Becoming Debt-free is Just That—Freedom," BP News, October 17, 2001 www.bpnews.net/printcolumn.asp?ID=350), retrieved August, 2005.

14. Orison Swett Marden, *Pushing to the Front,* (St. Petersburg, NY: The Success Company), www.arfalfa.com/PushToTheFront/Volume2_HTM/PushingToTheFront2.htm, retrieved August, 2005.

15. Abraham Lincoln, retrieved September 2005: usinfo.state.gov/usa/infousa/facts/democrac/22.htm.

16. J.C. Penney, retrieved September 2005: www.wisdomquotes.com/--1551.html.

17. Adlai Stevenson, retrieved July 2005: www.en.wikiquote.org/wiki/Adlai_Stevenson.

18. W. Somerset Maugham, retrieved August 17, 2005: www.livinglifefully.com/how.html.

19. Shel Silverstein, *A Light in the Attic,* (New York: HarperCollins, 1981).

20. Ben Franklin, retrieved July 2005: www.worldofquotes.com/author/Benjamin-Franklin/1/.

21. William J.H.Boetcke, retrieved August, 2005: quotes.liberty-tree.ca/quotes.nsf/.

22. Lynn A. Miller, retrieved August, 2005: www.generousgiving.org/page.asp?sec=80&page=289.

APPENDIX TABLE OF CONTENTS

STATEMENT OF PERSONAL FINANCIAL CONDITION (Personal Balance Sheet)

Prepared by the _____ Family   as of _____ (mm/dd/yy)

ASSETS (WHAT YOU OWN)		
CURRENT ASSETS		
Cash—(checking accounts)		
Cash—(savings accounts, money markets, CDs)		
Personal Property—Market Value (auto, jewelry, etc)		
Other Assets (itemize)		
TOTAL CURRENT ASSETS		$
LONG-TERM ASSETS		
Certificates of deposit		
Debt Owed to You (notes, contracts)		
Life Insurance (cash values)		
Partial Interest in Real Estate		
Real Estate (net market value)		
Retirement Accounts (IRAs, SEPs, 401(k)s, etc.)		
Securities (stocks, bonds, mutual funds, etc.)		
Vehicles (market value)		
Other Long-Term Assets (itemize)		
TOTAL LONG-TERM ASSETS		$
TOTAL ASSETS		$
LIABILITIES (WHAT YOU OWE)		
CURRENT LIABILITIES		
Charge Accounts (itemize)		
Credit Cards (itemize)		
Current Monthly Unpaid Bills		
Personal Debts (short-term)		
Unpaid Taxes and Interest		
Unsecured Loans (short-term)		
Other Short-Term Debts (itemize)		
TOTAL CURRENT LIABILITIES		$
LONG-TERM LIABILITIES		
Home Equity Loans		
Loans—(You Owe)		
Mortgages on Real Estate $		
Notes Cosigned, etc.		
Student Loans		
Taxes—(You Owe)		
TOTAL LONG-TERM LIABILITIES		
TOTAL LIABILITIES		$
NET WORTH (OWNER'S EQUITY)		
(Total Assets–Total Liabilities)		$

SPENDING/BUDGETING WORKSHEET					
My Spending	**Monthly**	**Yearly**	**Budget**	**Actual**	**Diff (+ or -)**
ALLOWANCES					
Parents					
Children					
CHARITY					
My Local Home Church (10-15%)					
Local Church Special Project #1					
Local Church Special Project #2					
Charity #3					
Charity #4					
Other					
DEBT REPAYMENT					
Student Loan					
Home Equity Loan					
Credit Card #1					
Credit Card #2					
Personal Line of Credit					
ENTERTAINMENT					
Movies/Videos/Sporting Events					
Recreation/Parks					
Weekend Trips					
Vacations					
Other					
FOOD					
Groceries					
Restaurants					
School Lunches					
Work Lunches					
HOUSING					
Mortgage or Rent					
Real Estate Taxes					
Gas					
Electric					
Water					
Sewer					
Phone - Landline					
Phone - Internet					
Phone - Cell/Pager					
Cable/Satellite					
Garbage/Sanitation					
Home Repairs					

Home/Appliance Maintenance				
Yard Upkeep				
KIDS' SPECIAL EXPENSES				
School				
Lessons #1				
Lessons #2				
Camp/Sports				
INSURANCE				
Vehicle #1				
Vehicle #2				
Life #1				
Life #2				
House #1				
House #2				
Disability				
Long Term Care				
MEDICAL/DENTAL				
Premiums				
Co-payments				
Prescriptions/Vitamins				
PERSONAL				
Haircut/Beauty				
Dry Cleaning/Laundry				
Clothes				
Gifts				
Subscriptions				
SAVINGS PROGRAM				
Emergency Fund				
401(k)/Retirement				
College Fund				
Investment Fund				
Christmas/Birthday				
TRANSPORTATION				
Car Loan/Lease Payment				
Gasoline				
License Plates				
Maintenance				
Repairs				
Other				

TOPICAL REFERENCES IN SCRIPTURE

Accounting
Daniel 6:1-3
Matthew 18:23
Matthew 25:14-30
Romans 14:12

Against the Unfortunate
Deuteronomy 24:14
Psalm 10:2
Psalm 12:5
Proverbs 14:20-21, 31
Proverbs 21:13
Proverbs 22:16
Proverbs 24:23
Proverbs 28:8
Matthew 18:23, 34
Luke 11:42
Luke 16:19-25

Attitudes, Viewpoints and Actions
Psalm 112
Proverbs 10:4
Proverbs 13:4, 11
Proverbs 24:10
Proverbs 28:27
Ecclesiastes 5:12
Malachi 3:5
Luke 6:35a
Romans 12:11
Ephesians 4:28
Blamelessness
Psalm 1:1, 2
Psalm 37:37
Psalm 112:6
Proverbs 10:16
Proverbs 11:4
Proverbs 12:12
Proverbs 16:8, 11
Proverbs 19:1
Proverbs 21:3
Proverbs 22:1
Proverbs 28:6, 13
Matthew 7:20

Luke 3:12-14
Luke 8:15
Luke 12:57, 58
Luke 20:22-25
Romans 13:7
Galatians 6:9

Borrowing
Exodus 22:14
Deuteronomy 15:1-11
Psalm 37:25
Proverbs 3:27, 28
Proverbs 22:7
Matthew 5:25, 26, 40
Matthew 18:23-35
Luke 12:58, 59

Budgeting
Proverbs 16:9
Proverbs 19:21
Proverbs 22:3
Proverbs 24:3, 4
Proverbs 27:12
Luke 12:16-21
Luke 14:28-30
Luke 16:1-8
1 Corinthians 16:1, 2

Caution
Proverbs 8:12
Proverbs 12:16, 23
Proverbs 13:16
Proverbs 14:8, 15, 18
Proverbs 15:5
Proverbs 16:21
Proverbs 18:15
Proverbs 22:3
Proverbs 27:12
Hosea 14:9
Amos 5:13

Contentment
Joshua 7:7
Proverbs 30:7-9
Matthew 20:1-16
Luke 3:14

Luke 12:15-21
2 Corinthians 6:10
Philippians 4:11, 12
Colossians 3:2
1 Thessalonians 5:16-18
1 Timothy 6:6-10
Hebrews 13:5

Counsel
Proverbs 3:13
Proverbs 12:5, 15
Proverbs 13:20
Proverbs 14:7
Proverbs 15:22
Proverbs 19:20
Proverbs 24:3, 6
Proverbs 27:9

Cosigning Notes
Proverbs 6:1-5
Proverbs 11:15
Proverbs 17:18
Proverbs 20:16
Proverbs 22:26
Proverbs 27:13

Debt
Deuteronomy 15:6
Deuteronomy 28:12, 13
2 Kings 4:1-7
Psalm 37:21
Proverbs 3:27, 28
Proverbs 6:1-3
Proverbs 11:15
Proverbs 17:18
Proverbs 22:7
Proverbs 27:13
Matthew 5:25, 26
Matthew 18:23
Luke 12:58, 59
Romans 13:8

Diligence
Proverbs 6:4
Proverbs 12:11, 24
Proverbs 13:11

Proverbs 14:4
Proverbs 16:3
Proverbs 21:5
Proverbs 24:3, 4, 7
Matthew 20:13
Romans 12:11
2 Timothy 2:6
1 Thessalonians 4:11

Dishonesty
Psalm 37:37
Psalm 15:5
Psalm 62:10-12
Proverbs 10:15, 16
Proverbs 11:1, 16, 18
Proverbs 12:3, 12
Proverbs 13:7, 11
Proverbs 15:6, 27
Proverbs 16:2, 11
Proverbs 17:2
Proverbs 20:21
Proverbs 22:28
Proverbs 24:16, 19, 20
Proverbs 28:6, 18
Jeremiah 9:4
Matthew 18:7
Matthew 27:5
Luke 9:25
Luke 11:42
Luke 16:1, 10-14
Luke 19:8
Luke 20:46, 47
Romans 2:21, 22

Ego
Psalm 75:4
Psalm 107:40
Proverbs 11:2
Proverbs 12:9
Proverbs 15:25
Proverbs 16:18, 19
Proverbs 18:12, 23
Proverbs 19:1
Proverbs 28:11
Proverbs 29:23
Jeremiah 9:23
Jeremiah 22:21
Matthew 23:12
Luke 14:11
Philippians 2:3
1 Timothy 6:17

Envy
Psalm 73:2
Proverbs 23:17
Proverbs 24:19
Excellence
Proverbs 18:9
Proverbs 22:29
Colossians 3:17, 23
1 Peter 4:11

Getting the Facts
Proverbs 14:8, 15
Proverbs 18:13
Proverbs 19:2
Proverbs 23:23
Proverbs 27:23, 24
Luke 14:28-32
James 1:5

Giving
Isaiah 66:20
Psalm 96:7, 8
Psalm 112:5
Proverbs 3:9, 10
Proverbs 11:24-26
Proverbs 28:22
Mark 4:24
Mark 12:41-44
Luke 6:38
Acts 2:45
1 Corinthians 16:1, 2

Greed
Psalm 73:2, 3, 17, 20
Proverbs 23:4, 5
Proverbs 28:25
Luke 12:15
Luke 18:24
Ephesians 5:5

Helping the Unfortunate
Psalm 69:33
Psalm 72:1, 4-15, 17
Psalm 109:31
Proverbs 14:21
Proverbs 14:31
Matthew 5:42
Matthew 6:19, 20
Matthew 10:42
Luke 3:11
Luke 9:48
Luke 10:35
Luke 12:33

Luke 19:8, 9
1 Timothy 5:3, 8, 15, 16
1 John 3:17
Hoarding
Psalm 49:11, 16, 17
Proverbs 13:22
Proverbs 28:22
Malachi 1:7, 9
Malachi 3:8
Matthew 6:24
Matthew 19:23
Luke 12:16-20
Luke 12:21, 33

Honesty
Deuteronomy 25:14, 15
Psalm 112:1-3, 5
Proverbs 10:3, 9
Proverbs 13:5, 11, 21
Proverbs 16:8
Proverbs 20:7
Proverbs 24:27
Proverbs 27:1
Proverbs 28:18
Proverbs 30:7, 8

Honesty versus Unmerited Gain
Deuteronomy 25:15
Proverbs 11:1
Proverbs 16:8
Proverbs 22:16
Proverbs 28:8
Jeremiah 22:13
Luke 16:10
Romans 12:17

Humility
Proverbs 22:4
Jeremiah 9:24
Matthew 6:1-3
Luke 17:3
Luke 19:8
1 Corinthians 1:26-31

Inheritance
Proverbs 13:22
Proverbs 17:2
Proverbs 20:21
Ecclesiastes 2:18, 19, 21
Ezekiel 46:16-18
Luke 15:11-31

Investing

Psalm 62:10
Proverbs 11:24, 28
Proverbs 16:1-9
Proverbs 21:5
Proverbs 23:4, 5
Investments
Proverbs 21:20
Proverbs 24:27
Ecclesiastes 6:3
Matthew 6:19-21

Matthew 13:22
Matthew 25:14-30, 45
Luke 14:28, 29
Luke 19:13-26
2 Peter 2:20
2 Peter 3:10

Laziness

Proverbs 6:6-11
Proverbs 12:24
Proverbs 13:11
Proverbs 14:4
Proverbs 19:15
Proverbs 21:17
Proverbs 22:13
Proverbs 26:13
2 Thessalonians 3:6, 10

Lending

Exodus 22:25, 26
Deuteronomy 23:19, 20
Deuteronomy 24:10, 11
Nehemiah 5:7, 10
Psalm 15:5
Psalm 37:26
Proverbs 28:8
Ezekiel 18:8
Luke 6:34, 35
Luke 7:41

Needs

Psalm 37:25
Matthew 6:8, 25-33
Philippians 4:19
Planning
Proverbs 16:1
Prosperity
Genesis 39:3
Deuteronomy 28:11
Deuteronomy 29:9

2 Chronicles 31:21
Psalm 1:3
Psalm 35:27
Luke 15:13
John 6:12

Retirement

Psalms 37:25
Proverbs 16:31
Proverbs 20:29
Saving
Proverbs 6:6-8
Proverbs 21:20
Proverbs 30:24, 25

Sharing

Exodus 16:18-20
Acts 4:32
Romans 12:13
1 Corinthians 9:7-11, 14
2 Corinthians 8:8-15
2 Corinthians 9:6-13
Galatians 6:6

Self-control

Matthew 7:13, 14
2 Corinthians 8:11
2 Thessalonians 3:11
Hebrews 12:11
Slothfulness
Proverbs 18:9
Proverbs 24:30, 31
Ecclesiastes 10:18
2 Thessalonians 3:11
Hebrews 6:12

Suing

Matthew 5:42
Matthew 6:3
Matthew 10:42
Matthew 13:12
Luke 6:30-36
Luke 12:57, 58
1 Corinthians 6:1-7

Supporting the Wealthy

Deuteronomy 1:17
Deuteronomy 16:19
Proverbs 14:20
Proverbs 28:21

Taxes

Matthew 17:24-27
Mark 12:14-17
Luke 20:22-25

Romans 13:6, 7

Tithing

Genesis 14:20, 22, 28
Malachi 3:10
Matthew 23:23
Luke 11:42
Hebrews 7:1-10
Waste
Genesis 41:36

Trust

Jeremiah 17:7, 8
Mark 6:9
Mark 8:34
Philippians 4:19
Wealth
Deuteronomy 8
Proverbs 10:22
Proverbs 28:13
Jeremiah 17:8-10
Luke 6:38
John 10:10
2 Corinthians 8:9
Philippians 4:19
3 John 2

Wives

Proverbs 31:10-31

Work

Deuteronomy 24:14, 15
Proverbs 6:6-10
Proverbs 10:4, 5
Proverbs 12:11, 24
Proverbs 14:23
Proverbs 16:26
Proverbs 28:19
Ephesians 4:28

Worry

Psalm 50:14, 15
Proverbs 12:25
Matthew 6:27-34
Philippians 4:6
1 John 4:18

SCRIPTURE REFERENCES ON FINANCE TOPICS

Accounting

DANIEL 6:1–3

It pleased Darius to appoint 120 satraps to rule throughout the kingdom, with three administrators over them, one of whom was Daniel. The satraps were made accountable to them so that the king might not suffer loss.

MATTHEW 18:23

"Therefore, the kingdom of heaven is like a king who wanted to settle accounts with his servants."

MATTHEW 25:14–30

"Again, it will be like a man going on a journey, who called his servants and entrusted his property to them. To one he gave five talents of money, to another two talents, and to another one talent, each according to his ability. Then he went on his journey. The man who had received the five talents went at once and put his money to work and gained five more. So also, the one with the two talents gained two more. But the man who had received the one talent went off, dug a hole in the ground and hid his master's money.

"After a long time the master of those servants returned and settled accounts with them. The man who had received the five talents brought the other five. 'Master,' he said, 'you entrusted me with five talents. See, I have gained five more.'

"His master replied, 'Well done, good and faithful servant! You have been faithful with a few things; I will put you in charge of many things. Come and share your master's happiness!'

"The man with the two talents also came. 'Master,' he said, 'you entrusted me with two talents; see, I have gained two more.'

"His master replied, 'Well done, good and faithful servant! You have been faithful with a few things; I will put you in charge of many things. Come and share your master's happiness!'

"Then the man who had received the one talent came. 'Master,' he said, 'I knew that you are a hard man, harvesting where you have not sown and gathering where you have not scattered seed. So I was afraid and went out and hid your talent in the ground. See, here is what belongs to you.'

"His master replied, 'You wicked, lazy servant! So you knew that I harvest where I have not sown and gather where I have not scattered seed? Well then, you should have put my money on deposit with the bankers, so that when I returned I would have received it back with interest.

"'Take the talent from him and give it to the one who has the ten talents. For everyone who has will be given more, and he will have an abundance. Whoever does not have, even what he has will be taken from him. And throw that worthless servant outside, into the darkness, where there will be weeping and gnashing of teeth.'"

ROMANS 14:12

So then, each of us will give an account of himself to God.

Against the Unfortunate

DEUTERONOMY 24:14

Do not take advantage of a hired man who is poor and needy, whether he is a brother Israelite or an alien living in one of your towns.

PSALM 10:2

In his arrogance the wicked man hunts down the weak, who are caught in the schemes he devises.

PSALM 12:5

"Because of the oppression of the weak and the groaning of the needy, I will now arise," says the LORD. "I will protect them from those who malign them."

PROVERBS 14:20–21, 31

The poor are shunned even by their neighbors, but the rich have many friends. He who despises his neighbor sins, but blessed is he who is kind to the needy. He who oppresses the poor shows contempt for their Maker, but whoever is kind to the needy honors God.

PROVERBS 21:13

If a man shuts his ears to the cry of the poor, he too will cry out and not be answered.

PROVERBS 22:16

He who oppresses the poor to increase his wealth and he who gives gifts to the rich—both come to poverty.

PROVERBS 24:23

These also are sayings of the wise: To show partiality in judging is not good.

PROVERBS 28:8

He who increases his wealth by exorbitant interest amasses it for another, who will be kind to the poor.

MATTHEW 18:23, 34

Therefore, the kingdom of heaven is like a king who wanted to settle accounts with his servants. In anger his master turned him over to the jailers to be tortured, until he should pay back all he owed.

LUKE 11:42

"Woe to you Pharisees, because you give God a tenth of your mint, rue and all other kinds of garden herbs, but you neglect justice and the love of God. You should have practiced the latter without leaving the former undone."

LUKE 16:19–25

"There was a rich man who was dressed in purple and fine linen and lived in luxury every day. At his gate was laid a beggar named Lazarus, covered with sores and longing to eat what fell from the rich man's table. Even the dogs came and licked his sores.

"The time came when the beggar died and the angels carried him to Abraham's side. The rich man also died and was buried. In hell, where he was in torment, he looked up and saw Abraham far away, with Lazarus by his side. So he called to him, 'Father Abraham, have pity on me and send Lazarus to dip the tip of his finger in water and cool my tongue, because I am in agony in this fire.'

"But Abraham replied, 'Son, remember that in your lifetime you received your good things, while Lazarus received bad things, but now he is comforted here and you are in agony."

Attitudes, Viewpoints, and Actions

PSALM 112:2–3

His children will be mighty in the land; the generation of the upright will be blessed. Wealth and riches are in his house, and his righteousness endures forever.

PSALM 112:9

He has scattered abroad his gifts to the poor, his righteousness endures forever; his horn will be lifted high in honor.

PROVERBS 10:4

Lazy hands make a man poor, but diligent hands bring wealth.

PROVERBS 13:4, 11

The sluggard craves and gets nothing, but the desires of the diligent are fully satisfied. Dishonest money dwindles away, but he who gathers money little by little makes it grow.

PROVERBS 24:10

If you falter in times of trouble, how small is your strength!

PROVERBS 28:27

He who gives to the poor will lack nothing, but he who closes his eyes to them receives many curses.

ECCLESIASTES 5:12

The sleep of a laborer is sweet, whether he eats little or much, but the abundance of a rich man permits him no sleep.

MALACHI 3:5

"So I will come near to you for judgment. I will be quick to testify against sorcerers, adulterers and perjurers, against those who defraud laborers of their wages, who oppress the widows and the fatherless, and deprive aliens of justice, but do not fear me," says the LORD *Almighty.*

LUKE 6:35A

But love your enemies, do good to them, and lend to them without expecting to get anything back.

ROMANS 12:11

Never be lacking in zeal, but keep your spiritual fervor, serving the Lord.

EPHESIANS 4:28

He who has been stealing must steal no longer, but must work, doing something useful with his own hands, that he may have something to share with those in need.

Blamelessness

PSALM 1:1–2

Blessed is the man who does not walk in the counsel of the wicked or stand in the way of sinners or sit in the seat of mockers. But his delight is in the law of the LORD, *and on his law he meditates day and night.*

PSALM 37:37

Consider the blameless, observe the upright; there is a future for the man of peace.

PSALM 112:6

Surely he will never be shaken; a righteous man will be remembered forever.

PROVERBS 10:16

The wages of the righteous bring them life, but the income of the wicked brings them punishment.

PROVERBS 11:4

Wealth is worthless in the day of wrath, but righteousness delivers from death.

PROVERBS 12:12

The wicked desire the plunder of evil men, but the root of the righteous flourishes.

PROVERBS 16:8, 11

Better a little with righteousness than much gain with injustice. Honest scales and balances are from the LORD; *all the weights in the bag are of his making.*

PROVERBS 19:1

Better a poor man whose walk is blameless than a fool whose lips are perverse.

PROVERBS 21:3

To do what is right and just is more acceptable to the LORD *than sacrifice.*

PROVERBS 22:1

A good name is more desirable than great riches; to be esteemed is better than silver or gold.

PROVERBS 28:6, 13

Better a poor man whose walk is blameless than a rich man whose ways are perverse. He who conceals his sins does not prosper, but whoever confesses and renounces them finds mercy.

MATTHEW 7:20

Thus, by their fruit you will recognize them.

LUKE 3:12–14

Tax collectors also came to be baptized. "Teacher," they asked, "what should we do?" "Don't collect any more than you are required to," he told them. Then some soldiers asked him, "And what should we do?" He replied, "Don't extort money and don't accuse people falsely—be content with your pay."

LUKE 8:15

"But the seed on good soil stands for those with a noble and good heart, who hear the word, retain it, and by persevering produce a crop."

LUKE 12:57–58

"Why don't you judge for yourselves what is right? As you are going with your adversary to the magistrate, try hard to be reconciled to him on the way, or he may drag you off to the judge, and the judge turn you over to the officer, and the officer throw you into prison."

LUKE 20:22–25

"Is it right for us to pay taxes to Caesar or not?" He saw through their duplicity and said to them, "Show me a denarius. Whose portrait and inscription are on it?" "Caesar's," they replied. He said to them, "Then give to Caesar what is Caesar's, and to God what is God's."

ROMANS 13:7

Give everyone what you owe him: If you owe taxes, pay taxes; if revenue, then revenue; if respect, then respect; if honor, then honor.

GALATIANS 6:9

Let us not become weary in doing good, for at the proper time we will reap a harvest if we do not give up.

Borrowing

EXODUS 22:14

If a man borrows an animal from his neighbor and it is injured or dies while the owner is not present, he must make restitution.

DEUTERONOMY 15:1–11

At the end of every seven years you must cancel debts. This is how it is to be done: Every creditor shall cancel the loan he has made to his fellow Israelite. He shall not require payment from his fellow Israelite or brother, because the LORD's time for canceling debts has been proclaimed. You may require payment from a foreigner, but you must cancel any debt your brother owes you. However, there should be no poor among you, for in the land the LORD your God is giving you to possess as your inheritance, he will richly bless you, if only you fully obey the LORD your God and are careful to follow all these commands I am giving you today. For the LORD your God will bless you as he has promised, and you will lend to many nations but will borrow from none. You will rule over many nations but none will rule over you. If there is a poor man among your brothers in any of the towns of the land that the LORD your God is giving you, do not be hardhearted or tightfisted toward your poor brother. Rather be openhanded and freely lend him whatever he needs. Be careful not to harbor this wicked thought: "The seventh year, the year for canceling debts, is near," so that you do not show ill will toward your needy brother and give him nothing. He may then appeal to the Lord against you, and you will be found guilty of sin. Give generously to him and do so without a grudging heart; then because of this the Lord your God will bless you in all your work and in everything you put your hand to. There will always be poor people in the land. Therefore I command you to be openhanded toward your brothers and toward the poor and needy in your land.

Psalm 37:25

I was young and now I am old, yet I have never seen the righteous forsaken or their children begging bread.

Proverbs 3:27–28

Do not withhold good from those who deserve it, when it is in your power to act. Do not say to your neighbor, "Come back later; I'll give it tomorrow"—when you now have it with you.

Proverbs 22:7

The rich rule over the poor, and the borrower is servant to the lender.

Matthew 5:25–26, 40

"Settle matters quickly with your adversary who is taking you to court. Do it while you are still with him on the way, or he may hand you over to the judge, and the judge may hand you over to the officer, and you may be thrown into prison. I tell you the truth, you will not get out until you have paid the last penny. And if someone wants to sue you and take your tunic, let him have your cloak as well."

Matthew 18:23–35

"Therefore, the kingdom of heaven is like a king who wanted to settle accounts with his servants. As he began the settlement, a man who owed him ten thousand talents was brought to him. Since he was not able to pay, the master ordered that he and his wife and his children and all that he had be sold to repay the debt.

"The servant fell on his knees before him. 'Be patient with me,' he begged, 'and I will pay back everything.' The servant's master took pity on him, canceled the debt and let him go.

"But when that servant went out, he found one of his fellow servants who owed him a hundred denarii. He grabbed him and began to choke him. 'Pay back what you owe me!' he demanded.

"His fellow servant fell to his knees and begged him, 'Be patient with me, and I will pay you back.'

"But he refused. Instead, he went off and had the man thrown into prison until he could pay the debt. When the other servants saw what had happened, they were greatly distressed and went and told their master everything that had happened.

"Then the master called the servant in. 'You wicked servant,' he said, 'I canceled all that debt of yours because you begged me to. Shouldn't you have had mercy on your fellow servant just as I had on you?' In anger his master turned him over to the jailers to be tortured, until he should pay back all he owed.

"This is how my heavenly Father will treat each of you unless you forgive your brother from your heart."

Budgeting

Proverbs 16:9

In his heart a man plans his course, but the Lord determines his steps.

Proverbs 19:21

Many are the plans in a man's heart, but it is the Lord's purpose that prevails.

Proverbs 22:3

A prudent man sees danger and takes refuge, but the simple keep going and suffer for it.

Proverbs 24:3–4

By wisdom a house is built, and through understanding it is established; through knowledge its rooms are filled with rare and beautiful treasures.

PROVERBS 27:12

The prudent see danger and take refuge, but the simple keep going and suffer for it.

LUKE 12:16–21

And he told them this parable: "The ground of a certain rich man produced a good crop. He thought to himself, What shall I do? I have no place to store my crops.

"Then he said, 'This is what I'll do. I will tear down my barns and build bigger ones, and there I will store all my grain and my goods. And I'll say to myself, You have plenty of good things laid up for many years. Take life easy; eat, drink and be merry.

"But God said to him, 'You fool! This very night your life will be demanded from you. Then who will get what you have prepared for yourself?'

"This is how it will be with anyone who stores up things for himself but is not rich toward God."

LUKE 14:28–30

"Suppose one of you wants to build a tower. Will he not first sit down and estimate the cost to see if he has enough money to complete it? For if he lays the foundation and is not able to finish it, everyone who sees it will ridicule him, saying, 'This fellow began to build and was not able to finish.'"

LUKE 16:1–8

Jesus told his disciples: "There was a rich man whose manager was accused of wasting his possessions. So he called him in and asked him, 'What is this I hear about you? Give an account of your management, because you cannot be manager any longer.'

"The manager said to himself, 'What shall I do now? My master is taking away my job. I'm not strong enough to dig, and I'm ashamed to beg—I know what I'll do so that, when I lose my job here, people will welcome me into their houses.'

"So he called in each one of his master's debtors. He asked the first, 'How much do you owe my master?'

"'Eight hundred gallons of olive oil,' he replied.

"The manager told him, 'Take your bill, sit down quickly, and make it four hundred.'

"Then he asked the second, 'And how much do you owe?'

"'A thousand bushels of wheat,' he replied.

"He told him, 'Take your bill and make it eight hundred.'

"The master commended the dishonest manager because he had acted shrewdly. For the people of this world are more shrewd in dealing with their own kind than are the people of the light."

1 CORINTHIANS 16:1–2

Now about the collection for God's people: Do what I told the Galatian churches to do. On the first day of every week, each one of you should set aside a sum of money in keeping with his income, saving it up, so that when I come no collections will have to be made.

Caution

PROVERBS 8:12

I, wisdom, dwell together with prudence; I possess knowledge and discretion.

PROVERBS 12:16, 23

A fool shows his annoyance at once, but a prudent man overlooks an insult. A prudent man keeps his knowledge to himself, but the heart of fools blurts out folly.

PROVERBS 13:16

Every prudent man acts out of knowledge, but a fool exposes his folly.

PROVERBS 14:8, 15, 18

The wisdom of the prudent is to give thought to their ways, but the folly of fools is deception. A simple man believes anything, but a prudent man gives thought to his steps. The simple inherit folly, but the prudent are crowned with knowledge.

PROVERBS 15:5

A fool spurns his father's discipline, but whoever heeds correction shows prudence.

PROVERBS 16:21

The wise in heart are called discerning, and pleasant words promote instruction.

PROVERBS 18:15

The heart of the discerning acquires knowledge; the ears of the wise seek it out.

PROVERBS 22:3

A prudent man sees danger and takes refuge, but the simple keep going and suffer for it.

PROVERBS 27:12

The prudent see danger and take refuge, but the simple keep going and suffer for it.

HOSEA 14:9

Who is wise? He will realize these things. Who is discerning? He will understand them. The ways of the LORD are right; the righteous walk in them, but the rebellious stumble in them.

Contentment

JOSHUA 7:7

And Joshua said, "Ah, Sovereign LORD, why did you ever bring this people across the Jordan to deliver us into the hands of the Amorites to destroy us? If only we had been content to stay on the other side of the Jordan!"

PROVERBS 30:7–9

"Two things I ask of you, O LORD; do not refuse me

before I die: Keep falsehood and lies far from me; give me neither poverty nor riches, but give me only my daily bread. Otherwise, I may have too much and disown you and say, 'Who is the LORD?' Or I may become poor and steal, and so dishonor the name of my God."

MATTHEW 20:1–16

"For the kingdom of heaven is like a landowner who went out early in the morning to hire men to work in his vineyard. He agreed to pay them a denarius for the day and sent them into his vineyard.

"About the third hour he went out and saw others standing in the marketplace doing nothing. He told them, 'You also go and work in my vineyard, and I will pay you whatever is right.' So they went.

"He went out again about the sixth hour and the ninth hour and did the same thing. About the eleventh hour he went out and found still others standing around. He asked them, 'Why have you been standing here all day long doing nothing?'

"'Because no one has hired us,' they answered. "He said to them, 'You also go and work in my vineyard.'

"When evening came, the owner of the vineyard said to his foreman, 'Call the workers and pay them their wages, beginning with the last ones hired and going on to the first.'

"The workers who were hired about the eleventh hour came and each received a denarius. So when those came who were hired first, they expected to receive more. But each one of them also received a denarius. When they received it, they began to grumble against the landowner. 'These men who were hired last worked only one hour,' they said, 'and you have made them equal to us who have borne the burden of the work and the heat of the day.'

"But he answered one of them, 'Friend, I am not being unfair to you. Didn't you agree to work for a denarius? Take your pay and go. I want to give the man who was hired last the same as I gave you. Don't I have the right to do what I want with my own money? Or are you envious because I am generous?'

"So the last will be first, and the first will be last."

SCRIPTURE REFERENCES ON FINANCE TOPICS

2 CORINTHIANS 6:10

Sorrowful, yet always rejoicing; poor, yet making many rich; having nothing, and yet possessing everything.

PHILIPPIANS 4:11–12

I am not saying this because I am in need, for I have learned to be content whatever the circumstances. I know what it is to be in need, and I know what it is to have plenty. I have learned the secret of being content in any and every situation, whether well fed or hungry, whether living in plenty or in want.

COLOSSIANS 3:2

Set your minds on things above, not on earthly things.

1 THESSALONIANS 5:16–18

Be joyful always; pray continually; give thanks in all circumstances, for this is God's will for you in Christ Jesus.

1 TIMOTHY 6:6–10

But godliness with contentment is great gain. For we brought nothing into the world, and we can take nothing out of it. But if we have food and clothing, we will be content with that. People who want to get rich fall into temptation and a trap and into many foolish and harmful desires that plunge men into ruin and destruction. For the love of money is a root of all kinds of evil. Some people, eager for money, have wandered from the faith and pierced themselves with many griefs.

HEBREWS 13:5

Keep your lives free from the love of money and be content with what you have, because God has said, "Never will I leave you; never will I forsake you."

Counsel

PROVERBS 3:13

Blessed is the man who finds wisdom, the man who gains understanding,

PROVERBS 12:5, 15

The plans of the righteous are just, but the advice of the wicked is deceitful. The way of a fool seems right to him, but a wise man listens to advice.

PROVERBS 13:20

He who walks with the wise grows wise, but a companion of fools suffers harm.

PROVERBS 14:7

Stay away from a foolish man, for you will not find knowledge on his lips.

PROVERBS 15:22

Plans fail for lack of counsel, but with many advisers they succeed.

PROVERBS 19:20

Listen to advice and accept instruction, and in the end you will be wise.

PROVERBS 24:3, 6

By wisdom a house is built, and through understanding it is established; for waging war you need guidance, and for victory many advisers.

PROVERBS 27:9

Perfume and incense bring joy to the heart, and the pleasantness of one's friend springs from his earnest counsel.

Cosigning Notes

PROVERBS 6:1–5

My son, if you have put up security for your neighbor, if you have struck hands in pledge for another, if you have been trapped by what you said, ensnared by the words of your mouth, then do this, my son, to free yourself, since you have fallen into your neighbor's hands: Go and humble yourself; press your plea with your neighbor! Allow no sleep to your eyes, no slumber to your eyelids. Free yourself, like a gazelle from the hand of the hunter, like a bird from the snare of the fowler.

PROVERBS 11:15

He who puts up security for another will surely suffer, but whoever refuses to strike hands in pledge is safe.

PROVERBS 17:18

A man lacking in judgment strikes hands in pledge and puts up security for his neighbor.

PROVERBS 20:16

Take the garment of one who puts up security for a stranger; hold it in pledge if he does it for a wayward woman.

PROVERBS 22:26

Do not be a man who strikes hands in pledge or puts up security for debts.

PROVERBS 27:13

Take the garment of one who puts up security for a stranger; hold it in pledge if he does it for a wayward woman.

Debt

DEUTERONOMY 15:6

For the LORD your God will bless you as he has promised, and you will lend to many nations but will borrow from none. You will rule over many nations but none will rule over you.

DEUTERONOMY 28:12–13

The LORD will open the heavens, the storehouse of his bounty, to send rain on your land in season and to bless all the work of your hands. You will lend to many nations but will borrow from none. The LORD will make you the head, not the tail. If you pay attention to the commands of the LORD your God that I give you this day and carefully follow them, you will always be at the top, never at the bottom.

2 KINGS 4:1–7

The wife of a man from the company of the prophets cried out to Elisha, "Your servant my husband is dead, and you know that he revered the LORD. But now his creditor is coming to take my two boys as his slaves." Elisha replied to her, "How can I help you? Tell me, what do you have in your house?" "Your servant has nothing there at all," she said, "except a little oil." Elisha said, "Go around and ask all your neighbors for empty jars. Don't ask for just a few. Then go inside and shut the door behind you and your sons. Pour oil into all the jars, and as each is filled, put it to one side." She left him and afterward shut the door behind her and her sons. They brought the jars to her and she kept pouring. When all the jars were full, she said to her son, "Bring me another one." But he replied, "There is not a jar left." Then the oil stopped flowing. She went and told the man of God, and he said, "Go, sell the oil and pay your debts. You and your sons can live on what is left."

PSALM 37:21

The wicked borrow and do not repay, but the righteous give generously;

PROVERBS 3:27–28

Do not withhold good from those who deserve it, when it is in your power to act. Do not say to your neighbor, "Come back later; I'll give it tomorrow"—when you now have it with you.

PROVERBS 6:1–3

My son, if you have put up security for your neighbor, if you have struck hands in pledge for another, if you have been trapped by what you said, ensnared by the words of your mouth, then do this, my son, to free yourself, since you have fallen into your neighbor's hands: Go and humble yourself; press your plea with your neighbor!

PROVERBS 11:15

He who puts up security for another will surely suffer, but whoever refuses to strike hands in pledge is safe.

SCRIPTURE REFERENCES ON FINANCE TOPICS

PROVERBS 17:18

A man lacking in judgment strikes hands in pledge and puts up security for his neighbor.

PROVERBS 22:7

The rich rule over the poor, and the borrower is servant to the lender.

PROVERBS 27:13

Take the garment of one who puts up security for a stranger; hold it in pledge if he does it for a wayward woman.

MATTHEW 5:25–26

"Settle matters quickly with your adversary who is taking you to court. Do it while you are still with him on the way, or he may hand you over to the judge, and the judge may hand you over to the officer, and you may be thrown into prison. I tell you the truth, you will not get out until you have paid the last penny."

MATTHEW 18:23

"Therefore, the kingdom of heaven is like a king who wanted to settle accounts with his servants."

ROMANS 13:8

Let no debt remain outstanding, except the continuing debt to love one another, for he who loves his fellowman has fulfilled the law.

Diligence

PROVERBS 6:4

Allow no sleep to your eyes, no slumber to your eyelids.

PROVERBS 12:11, 24

He who works his land will have abundant food, but he who chases fantasies lacks judgment. Diligent hands will rule, but laziness ends in slave labor.

PROVERBS 13:11

Dishonest money dwindles away, but he who gathers money little by little makes it grow.

PROVERBS 14:4

Where there are no oxen, the manger is empty, but from the strength of an ox comes an abundant harvest.

PROVERBS 16:3

Commit to the LORD whatever you do, and your plans will succeed.

PROVERBS 21:5

The plans of the diligent lead to profit as surely as haste leads to poverty.

PROVERBS 24:3–4, 7

By wisdom a house is built, and through understanding it is established; through knowledge its rooms are filled with rare and beautiful treasures. Wisdom is too high for a fool; in the assembly at the gate he has nothing to say.

MATTHEW 20:13

"But he answered one of them, 'Friend, I am not being unfair to you. Didn't you agree to work for a denarius?'"

2 TIMOTHY 2:6

The hardworking farmer should be the first to receive a share of the crops.

1 THESSALONIANS 4:11

Make it your ambition to lead a quiet life, to mind your own business and to work with your hands, just as we told you.

Dishonesty

PSALM 37:37

Consider the blameless, observe the upright; there is a future for the man of peace.

PSALM 15:5

Who lends his money without usury and does not accept a bribe against the innocent. He who does these things will never be shaken.

PSALM 62:10–12

Do not trust in extortion or take pride in stolen goods; though your riches increase, do not set your heart on them. One thing God has spoken, two things have I heard: that you, O God, are strong, and that you, O LORD, are loving.Surely you will reward each person according to what he has done.

PROVERBS 10:15–16

The wealth of the rich is their fortified city, but poverty is the ruin of the poor. The wages of the righteous bring them life, but the income of the wicked brings them punishment.

PROVERBS 11:1, 16, 18

The LORD abhors dishonest scales, but accurate weights are his delight. A kindhearted woman gains respect, but ruthless men gain only wealth. The wicked man earns deceptive wages, but he who sows righteousness reaps a sure reward.

PROVERBS 12:3, 12

A man cannot be established through wickedness, but the righteous cannot be uprooted. The wicked desire the plunder of evil men, but the root of the righteous flourishes.

PROVERBS 13:7, 11

One man pretends to be rich, yet has nothing; another pretends to be poor, yet has great wealth. Dishonest money dwindles away, but he who gathers money little by little makes it grow.

PROVERBS 15:6, 27

The house of the righteous contains great treasure, but the income of the wicked brings them trouble. A greedy man brings trouble to his family, but he who hates bribes will live.

PROVERBS 16:2, 11

All a man's ways seem innocent to him, but motives are weighed by the LORD. Honest scales and balances are from the LORD; all the weights in the bag are of his making.

PROVERBS 17:2

A wise servant will rule over a disgraceful son, and will share the inheritance as one of the brothers.

PROVERBS 20:21

An inheritance quickly gained at the beginning will not be blessed at the end.

PROVERBS 22:28

Do not move an ancient boundary stone set up by your forefathers.

PROVERBS 24:16, 19–20

For though a righteous man falls seven times, he rises again, but the wicked are brought down by calamity. Do not fret because of evil men or be envious of the wicked, for the evil man has no future hope, and the lamp of the wicked will be snuffed out.

PROVERBS 28:6, 18

Better a poor man whose walk is blameless than a rich man whose ways are perverse. He whose walk is blameless is kept safe, but he whose ways are perverse will suddenly fall.

JEREMIAH 9:4

Beware of your friends; do not trust your brothers. For every brother is a deceiver, and every friend a slanderer.

MATTHEW 18:7

Woe to the world because of the things that cause people to sin! Such things must come, but woe to the man through whom they come!

MATTHEW 27:5

So Judas threw the money into the temple and left. Then he went away and hanged himself.

LUKE 9:25

What good is it for a man to gain the whole world, and yet lose or forfeit his very self?

LUKE 11:42

Woe to you Pharisees, because you give God a tenth of your mint, rue and all other kinds of garden herbs, but you neglect justice and the love of God. You should have practiced the latter without leaving the former undone.

LUKE 16:1, 10–14

Jesus told his disciples: "There was a rich man whose manager was accused of wasting his possessions.

"Whoever can be trusted with very little can also be trusted with much, and whoever is dishonest with very little will also be dishonest with much. So if you have not been trustworthy in handling worldly wealth, who will trust you with true riches? And if you have not been trustworthy with someone else's property, who will give you property of your own?

"No servant can serve two masters. Either he will hate the one and love the other, or he will be devoted to the one and despise the other. You cannot serve both God and Money."

The Pharisees, who loved money, heard all this and were sneering at Jesus.

LUKE 19:8

But Zacchaeus stood up and said to the Lord, "Look, Lord! Here and now I give half of my possessions to the poor, and if I have cheated anybody out of anything, I will pay back four times the amount."

LUKE 20:46–47

"Beware of the teachers of the law. They like to walk around in flowing robes and love to be greeted in the marketplaces and have the most important seats in the synagogues and the places of honor at banquets. They devour widows' houses and for a show make lengthy prayers. Such men will be punished most severely."

ROMANS 2:21–22

You, then, who teach others, do you not teach yourself? You who preach against stealing, do you steal? You who say that people should not commit adultery, do you commit adultery? You who abhor idols, do you rob temples?

Ego

PSALM 75:4

To the arrogant I say, "Boast no more," and to the wicked, "Do not lift up your horns."

PSALM 107:40

He who pours contempt on nobles made them wander in a trackless waste.

PROVERBS 11:2

When pride comes, then comes disgrace, but with humility comes wisdom.

PROVERBS 12:9

Better to be a nobody and yet have a servant than pretend to be somebody and have no food.

PROVERBS 15:25

The LORD tears down the proud man's house but he keeps the widow's boundaries intact.

PROVERBS 16:18–19

Pride goes before destruction, a haughty spirit before a fall. Better to be lowly in spirit and among the oppressed than to share plunder with the proud.

PROVERBS 18:12, 23

Before his downfall a man's heart is proud, but humility comes before honor. A poor man pleads for mercy, but a rich man answers harshly.

PROVERBS 19:1

Better a poor man whose walk is blameless than a fool whose lips are perverse.

PROVERBS 28:11

A rich man may be wise in his own eyes, but a poor man who has discernment sees through him.

PROVERBS 29:23

A man's pride brings him low, but a man of lowly spirit gains honor.

JEREMIAH 9:23

This is what the LORD says: "Let not the wise man boast of his wisdom or the strong man boast of his strength or the rich man boast of his riches."

JEREMIAH 22:21

I warned you when you felt secure, but you said, "I will not listen!" This has been your way from your youth; you have not obeyed me.

MATTHEW 23:12

"For whoever exalts himself will be humbled, and whoever humbles himself will be exalted."

LUKE 14:11

"For everyone who exalts himself will be humbled, and he who humbles himself will be exalted."

PHILIPPIANS 2:3

Do nothing out of selfish ambition or vain conceit, but in humility consider others better than yourselves.

1 TIMOTHY 6:17

Command those who are rich in this present world not to be arrogant nor to put their hope in wealth, which is so uncertain, but to put their hope in God, who richly provides us with everything for our enjoyment.

Envy

PSALM 73:2

But as for me, my feet had almost slipped; I had nearly lost my foothold.

PROVERBS 23:17

Do not let your heart envy sinners, but always be zealous for the fear of the LORD.

PROVERBS 24:19

Do not fret because of evil men or be envious of the wicked,

Excellence

PROVERBS 18:9

One who is slack in his work is brother to one who destroys.

PROVERBS 22:29

Do you see a man skilled in his work? He will serve before kings; he will not serve before obscure men.

COLOSSIANS 3:17, 23

And whatever you do, whether in word or deed, do it all in the name of the Lord Jesus, giving thanks to God the Father through him. Whatever you do, work at it with all your heart, as working for the Lord, not for men,

1 PETER 4:11

If anyone speaks, he should do it as one speaking the very words of God. If anyone serves, he should do it with the strength God provides, so that in all things God may be praised through Jesus Christ. To him be the glory and the power for ever and ever. Amen.

Getting the Facts

PROVERBS 14:8, 15

The wisdom of the prudent is to give thought to their ways, but the folly of fools is deception. A simple man believes anything, but a prudent man gives thought to his steps.

PROVERBS 18:13

He who answers before listening—that is his folly and his shame.

SCRIPTURE REFERENCES ON FINANCE TOPICS

PROVERBS 19:2

It is not good to have zeal without knowledge, nor to be hasty and miss the way.

PROVERBS 23:23

Buy the truth and do not sell it; get wisdom, discipline and understanding.

PROVERBS 27:23–24

Be sure you know the condition of your flocks, give careful attention to your herds; for riches do not endure forever, and a crown is not secure for all generations.

JAMES 1:5

If any of you lacks wisdom, he should ask God, who gives generously to all without finding fault, and it will be given to him.

Giving

ISAIAH 66:20

And they will bring all your brothers, from all the nations, to my holy mountain in Jerusalem as an offering to the LORD—on horses, in chariots and wagons, and on mules and camels," says the LORD. "They will bring them, as the Israelites bring their grain offerings, to the temple of the LORD in ceremonially clean vessels.

PSALM 96:7–8

Ascribe to the LORD, O families of nations, ascribe to the LORD glory and strength. Ascribe to the LORD the glory due his name; bring an offering and come into his courts.

PSALM 112:5

Good will come to him who is generous and lends freely, who conducts his affairs with justice.

PROVERBS 3:9–10

Honor the LORD with your wealth, with the firstfruits of all your crops; then your barns will be filled to overflowing, and your vats will brim over with new wine.

PROVERBS 11:24–26

One man gives freely, yet gains even more; another withholds unduly, but comes to poverty. A generous man will prosper; he who refreshes others will himself be refreshed. People curse the man who hoards grain, but blessing crowns him who is willing to sell.

PROVERBS 28:22

A stingy man is eager to get rich and is unaware that poverty awaits him.

MARK 4:24

"Consider carefully what you hear," he continued. "With the measure you use, it will be measured to you—and even more."

MARK 12:41–44

Jesus sat down opposite the place where the offerings were put and watched the crowd putting their money into the temple treasury. Many rich people threw in large amounts. But a poor widow came and put in two very small copper coins, worth only a fraction of a penny. Calling his disciples to him, Jesus said, "I tell you the truth, this poor widow has put more into the treasury than all the others. They all gave out of their wealth; but she, out of her poverty, put in everything-all she had to live on."

LUKE 6:38

"Give, and it will be given to you. A good measure, pressed down, shaken together and running over, will be poured into your lap. For with the measure you use, it will be measured to you."

ACTS 2:45

Selling their possessions and goods, they gave to anyone as he had need.

Greed

PSALM 73:2–3, 17, 20

But as for me, my feet had almost slipped; I had nearly lost my foothold. For I envied the arrogant when I saw the prosperity of the wicked. Till I entered the sanctuary of God; then I understood their final destiny. As a dream when one awakes, so when you arise, O Lord, you will despise them as fantasies.

PROVERBS 23:4–5

Do not wear yourself out to get rich; have the wisdom to show restraint. Cast but a glance at riches, and they are gone, for they will surely sprout wings and fly off to the sky like an eagle.

PROVERBS 28:25

A greedy man stirs up dissension, but he who trusts in the Lord will prosper.

LUKE 12:15

Then he said to them, "Watch out! Be on your guard against all kinds of greed; a man's life does not consist in the abundance of his possessions."

LUKE 18:24

Jesus looked at him and said, "How hard it is for the rich to enter the kingdom of God!"

EPHESIANS 5:5

For of this you can be sure: No immoral, impure or greedy person—such a man is an idolater—has any inheritance in the kingdom of Christ and of God.

Helping the Unfortunate

PSALM 69:33

The Lord hears the needy and does not despise his captive people.

PSALM 72:1, 4–15, 17

Endow the king with your justice, O God, the royal son with your righteousness. He will defend the afflicted among the people and save the children of the needy; he will crush the oppressor. He will endure as long as the sun, as long as the moon, through all generations. He will be like rain falling on a mown field, like showers watering the earth. In his days the righteous will flourish; prosperity will abound till the moon is no more. He will rule from sea to sea and from the River to the ends of the earth. The desert tribes will bow before him and his enemies will lick the dust. The kings of Tarshish and of distant shores will bring tribute to him; the kings of Sheba and Seba will present him gifts. All kings will bow down to him and all nations will serve him. For he will deliver the needy who cry out, the afflicted who have no one to help. He will take pity on the weak and the needy and save the needy from death. He will rescue them from oppression and violence, for precious is their blood in his sight. Long may he live! May gold from Sheba be given him. May people ever pray for him and bless him all day long. May his name endure forever; may it continue as long as the sun. All nations will be blessed through him, and they will call him blessed.

PSALM 109:31

For he stands at the right hand of the needy one, to save his life from those who condemn him.

PROVERBS 14:21

He who despises his neighbor sins, but blessed is he who is kind to the needy.

PROVERBS 14:31

He who oppresses the poor shows contempt for their Maker, but whoever is kind to the needy honors God.

MATTHEW 5:42

"Give to the one who asks you, and do not turn away from the one who wants to borrow from you."

MATTHEW 6:19–20

"Do not store up for yourselves treasures on earth, where moth and rust destroy, and where thieves break

in and steal. But store up for yourselves treasures in heaven, where moth and rust do not destroy, and where thieves do not break in and steal."

MATTHEW 10:42

"And if anyone gives even a cup of cold water to one of these little ones because he is my disciple, I tell you the truth, he will certainly not lose his reward."

LUKE 3:11

John answered, "The man with two tunics should share with him who has none, and the one who has food should do the same."

LUKE 9:48

Then he said to them, "Whoever welcomes this little child in my name welcomes me; and whoever welcomes me welcomes the one who sent me. For he who is least among you all—he is the greatest."

LUKE 10:35

"The next day he took out two silver coins and gave them to the innkeeper. 'Look after him,' he said, 'and when I return, I will reimburse you for any extra expense you may have.'"

LUKE 12:33

"Sell your possessions and give to the poor. Provide purses for yourselves that will not wear out, a treasure in heaven that will not be exhausted, where no thief comes near and no moth destroys."

LUKE 19:8-9

But Zacchaeus stood up and said to the Lord, "Look, Lord! Here and now I give half of my possessions to the poor, and if I have cheated anybody out of anything, I will pay back four times the amount." Jesus said to him, "Today salvation has come to this house, because this man, too, is a son of Abraham."

1 TIMOTHY 5:3, 8, 15–16

Give proper recognition to those widows who are really in need. If anyone does not provide for his relatives,

and especially for his immediate family, he has denied the faith and is worse than an unbeliever. Some have in fact already turned away to follow Satan. If any woman who is a believer has widows in her family, she should help them and not let the church be burdened with them, so that the church can help those widows who are really in need.

1 JOHN 3:17

If anyone has material possessions and sees his brother in need but has no pity on him, how can the love of God be in him?

Hoarding

PSALM 49:11, 16–17

Their tombs will remain their houses forever, their dwellings for endless generations, though they had named lands after themselves. Do not be overawed when a man grows rich, when the splendor of his house increases; for he will take nothing with him when he dies, his splendor will not descend with him.

PROVERBS 13:22

A good man leaves an inheritance for his children's children, but a sinner's wealth is stored up for the righteous.

PROVERBS 28:22

A stingy man is eager to get rich and is unaware that poverty awaits him.

MALACHI 1:7, 9

You place defiled food on my altar. "But you ask, 'How have we defiled you?'

"By saying that the LORD's table is contemptible.

"Now implore God to be gracious to us. With such offerings from your hands, will he accept you?" says the LORD Almighty.

MALACHI 3:8

"Will a man rob God? Yet you rob me. But you ask, 'How do we rob you?' In tithes and offerings."

MATTHEW 6:24

"No one can serve two masters. Either he will hate the one and love the other, or he will be devoted to the one and despise the other. You cannot serve both God and Money."

MATTHEW 19:23

Then Jesus said to his disciples, "I tell you the truth, it is hard for a rich man to enter the kingdom of heaven."

LUKE 12:21, 33

"This is how it will be with anyone who stores up things for himself but is not rich toward God. Sell your possessions and give to the poor. Provide purses for yourselves that will not wear out, a treasure in heaven that will not be exhausted, where no thief comes near and no moth destroys."

Honesty

DEUTERONOMY 25:14–15

Do not have two differing measures in your house— one large, one small. You must have accurate and honest weights and measures, so that you may live long in the land the LORD your God is giving you.

PSALM 112:1–3, 5

Praise the LORD. Blessed is the man who fears the LORD, who finds great delight in his commands. His children will be mighty in the land; the generation of the upright will be blessed. Wealth and riches are in his house, and his righteousness endures forever. Good will come to him who is generous and lends freely, who conducts his affairs with justice.

PROVERBS 10:3, 9

The LORD does not let the righteous go hungry but he thwarts the craving of the wicked. The man of integrity walks securely, but he who takes crooked paths will be found out.

PROVERBS 13:5, 11, 21

The righteous hate what is false, but the wicked bring shame and disgrace. Dishonest money dwindles away, but he who gathers money little by little makes it grow. Misfortune pursues the sinner, but prosperity is the reward of the righteous.

PROVERBS 16:8

Better a little with righteousness than much gain with injustice.

PROVERBS 20:7

The righteous man leads a blameless life; blessed are his children after him.

PROVERBS 24:27

Finish your outdoor work and get your fields ready; after that, build your house.

PROVERBS 27:1

Do not boast about tomorrow, for you do not know what a day may bring forth.

PROVERBS 28:18

He whose walk is blameless is kept safe, but he whose ways are perverse will suddenly fall.

PROVERBS 30:7–8

Two things I ask of you, O LORD; do not refuse me before I die: Keep falsehood and lies far from me; give me neither poverty nor riches, but give me only my daily bread.

Honesty Versus Unmerited Gain

DEUTERONOMY 25:15

You must have accurate and honest weights and measures, so that you may live long in the land the LORD your God is giving you.

PROVERBS 11:1

The LORD abhors dishonest scales, but accurate weights are his delight.

PROVERBS 16:8

Better a little with righteousness than much gain with injustice.

PROVERBS 22:16

He who oppresses the poor to increase his wealth and he who gives gifts to the rich—both come to poverty.

PROVERBS 28:8

He who increases his wealth by exorbitant interest amasses it for another, who will be kind to the poor.

JEREMIAH 22:13

Woe to him who builds his palace by unrighteousness, his upper rooms by injustice, making his countrymen work for nothing, not paying them for their labor.

LUKE 16:10

Whoever can be trusted with very little can also be trusted with much, and whoever is dishonest with very little will also be dishonest with much.

ROMANS 12:17

Do not repay anyone evil for evil. Be careful to do what is right in the eyes of everybody.

Humility

PROVERBS 22:4

Humility and the fear of the Lord bring wealth and honor and life.

JEREMIAH 9:24

"But let him who boasts boast about this: that he understands and knows me, that I am the Lord, who exercises kindness, justice and righteousness on earth, for in these I delight," declares the Lord.

MATTHEW 6:1–3

"Be careful not to do your 'acts of righteousness' before men, to be seen by them. If you do, you will have no reward from your Father in heaven.

"So when you give to the needy, do not announce it with trumpets, as the hypocrites do in the synagogues and on the streets, to be honored by men. I tell you the truth, they have received their reward in full. But when you give to the needy, do not let your left hand know what your right hand is doing."

LUKE 17:3

"So watch yourselves. If your brother sins, rebuke him, and if he repents, forgive him."

LUKE 19:8

But Zacchaeus stood up and said to the Lord, "Look, Lord! Here and now I give half of my possessions to the poor, and if I have cheated anybody out of anything, I will pay back four times the amount."

1 CORINTHIANS 1:26–31

Brothers, think of what you were when you were called. Not many of you were wise by human standards; not many were influential; not many were of noble birth. But God chose the foolish things of the world to shame the wise; God chose the weak things of the world to shame the strong. He chose the lowly things of this world and the despised things-and the things that are not—to nullify the things that are, so that no one may boast before him. It is because of him that you are in Christ Jesus, who has become for us wisdom from God—that is, our righteousness, holiness and redemption. Therefore, as it is written: "Let him who boasts boast in the Lord."

Inheritance

PROVERBS 13:22

A good man leaves an inheritance for his children's children, but a sinner's wealth is stored up for the righteous.

PROVERBS 17:2

A wise servant will rule over a disgraceful son, and will share the inheritance as one of the brothers.

PROVERBS 20:21

An inheritance quickly gained at the beginning will not be blessed at the end.

ECCLESIASTES 2:18–19, 21

I hated all the things I had toiled for under the sun, because I must leave them to the one who comes after me. And who knows whether he will be a wise man or a fool? Yet he will have control over all the work into which I have poured my effort and skill under the sun. This too is meaningless. For a man may do his work with wisdom, knowledge and skill, and then he must leave all he owns to someone who has not worked for it. This too is meaningless and a great misfortune.

EZEKIEL 46:16–18

This is what the Sovereign Lord says: "If the prince makes a gift from his inheritance to one of his sons, it will also belong to his descendants; it is to be their property by inheritance. If, however, he makes a gift from his inheritance to one of his servants, the servant may keep it until the year of freedom; then it will revert to the prince. His inheritance belongs to his sons only; it is theirs. The prince must not take any of the inheritance of the people, driving them off their property. He is to give his sons their inheritance out of his own property, so that none of my people will be separated from his property."

LUKE 15:11–31

Jesus continued: "There was a man who had two sons. The younger one said to his father, 'Father, give me my share of the estate.' So he divided his property between them.

"Not long after that, the younger son got together all he had, set off for a distant country and there squandered his wealth in wild living. After he had spent everything, there was a severe famine in that whole country, and he began to be in need. So he went and hired himself out to a citizen of that country, who sent him to his fields to feed pigs. He longed to fill his stomach with the pods that the pigs were eating, but no one gave him anything.

"When he came to his senses, he said, 'How many of my father's hired men have food to spare, and here I am starving to death! I will set out and go back to my father and say to him: Father, I have sinned against heaven and against you. I am no longer worthy to be called your son; make me like one of your hired men.' So he got up and went to his father.

"But while he was still a long way off, his father saw him and was filled with compassion for him; he ran to his son, threw his arms around him and kissed him.

"The son said to him, 'Father, I have sinned against heaven and against you. I am no longer worthy to be called your son.'

"But the father said to his servants, 'Quick! Bring the best robe and put it on him. Put a ring on his finger and sandals on his feet. Bring the fattened calf and kill it. Let's have a feast and celebrate. For this son of mine was dead and is alive again; he was lost and is found.' So they began to celebrate.

"Meanwhile, the older son was in the field. When he came near the house, he heard music and dancing. So he called one of the servants and asked him what was going on. 'Your brother has come,' he replied, 'and your father has killed the fattened calf because he has him back safe and sound.'

"The older brother became angry and refused to go in. So his father went out and pleaded with him. But he answered his father, 'Look! All these years I've been slaving for you and never disobeyed your orders. Yet you never gave me even a young goat so I could celebrate with my friends. But when this son of yours who has squandered your property with prostitutes comes home, you kill the fattened calf for him!'

"'My son,' the father said, 'you are always with me, and everything I have is yours.'"

Investing

PSALM 62:10

Do not trust in extortion or take pride in stolen goods; though your riches increase, do not set your heart on them.

PROVERBS 11:24, 28

One man gives freely, yet gains even more; another withholds unduly, but comes to poverty. Whoever trusts in his riches will fall, but the righteous will thrive like a green leaf.

PROVERBS 16:1–9

To man belong the plans of the heart, but from the LORD comes the reply of the tongue. All a man's ways seem innocent to him, but motives are weighed by the LORD. Commit to the LORD whatever you do, and your plans will succeed. The LORD works out everything for his own ends—even the wicked for a day of disaster. The LORD detests all the proud of heart. Be sure of this: They will not go unpunished. Through love and faithfulness sin is atoned for; through the fear of the LORD a man avoids evil. When a man's ways are pleasing to the LORD, he makes even his enemies live at peace with him. Better a little with righteousness than much gain with injustice. In his heart a man plans his course, but the LORD determines his steps.

PROVERBS 21:5

The plans of the diligent lead to profit as surely as haste leads to poverty.

PROVERBS 23:4–5

Do not wear yourself out to get rich; have the wisdom to show restraint. Cast but a glance at riches, and they are gone, for they will surely sprout wings and fly off to the sky like an eagle.

Investments

PROVERBS 21:20

In the house of the wise are stores of choice food and oil, but a foolish man devours all he has.

PROVERBS 24:27

Finish your outdoor work and get your fields ready; after that, build your house.

ECCLESIASTES 6:3

A man may have a hundred children and live many years; yet no matter how long he lives, if he cannot enjoy his prosperity and does not receive proper burial, I say that a stillborn child is better off than he.

MATTHEW 6:19–21

"Do not store up for yourselves treasures on earth, where moth and rust destroy, and where thieves break in and steal. But store up for yourselves treasures in heaven, where moth and rust do not destroy, and where thieves do not break in and steal. For where your treasure is, there your heart will be also."

MATTHEW 13:22

"The one who received the seed that fell among the thorns is the man who hears the word, but the worries of this life and the deceitfulness of wealth choke it, making it unfruitful."

MATTHEW 25:14–30, 45

"Again, it will be like a man going on a journey, who called his servants and entrusted his property to them. To one he gave five talents of money, to another two talents, and to another one talent, each according to his ability. Then he went on his journey. The man who had received the five talents went at once and put his money to work and gained five more. So also, the one with the two talents gained two more. But the man who had received the one talent went off, dug a hole in the ground and hid his master's money.

"After a long time the master of those servants returned and settled accounts with them. The man who had received the five talents brought the other five. 'Master,' he said, 'you entrusted me with five talents. See, I have gained five more.'

"His master replied, 'Well done, good and faithful servant! You have been faithful with a few things; I will put you in charge of many things. Come and share your master's happiness!'

"The man with the two talents also came. 'Master,' he said, 'you entrusted me with two talents; see, I have gained two more.'

"His master replied, 'Well done, good and faithful servant! You have been faithful with a few things; I will put you in charge of many things. Come and share your master's happiness!'

"Then the man who had received the one talent came. 'Master,' he said, 'I knew that you are a hard man, harvesting where you have not sown and gathering where you have not scattered seed. So I was afraid and went out and hid your talent in the ground. See, here is what belongs to you.'

"His master replied, 'You wicked, lazy servant! So you knew that I harvest where I have not sown and gather where I have not scattered seed? Well then, you should have put my money on deposit with the bankers, so that when I returned I would have received it back with interest.

"'Take the talent from him and give it to the one who has the ten talents. For everyone who has will be given more, and he will have an abundance. Whoever does not have, even what he has will be taken from him. And throw that worthless servant outside, into the darkness, where there will be weeping and gnashing of teeth.' He will reply, 'I tell you the truth, whatever you did not do for one of the least of these, you did not do for me.'"

LUKE 14:28–29

"Suppose one of you wants to build a tower. Will he not first sit down and estimate the cost to see if he has enough money to complete it? For if he lays the foundation and is not able to finish it, everyone who sees it will ridicule him."

LUKE 19:13–26

"So he called ten of his servants and gave them ten minas. 'Put this money to work,' he said, 'until I come back.'

"But his subjects hated him and sent a delegation after him to say, 'We don't want this man to be our king.'

"He was made king, however, and returned home. Then he sent for the servants to whom he had given the money, in order to find out what they had gained with it.

"The first one came and said, 'Sir, your mina has earned ten more.'

"'Well done, my good servant!' his master replied. 'Because you have been trustworthy in a very small matter, take charge of ten cities.'

"The second came and said, 'Sir, your mina has earned five more.'

"His master answered, 'You take charge of five cities.'

"Then another servant came and said, 'Sir, here is your mina; I have kept it laid away in a piece of cloth. I was afraid of you, because you are a hard man. You take out what you did not put in and reap what you did not sow.'

"His master replied, 'I will judge you by your own words, you wicked servant! You knew, did you, that I am a hard man, taking out what I did not put in, and reaping what I did not sow? Why then didn't you put my money on deposit, so that when I came back, I could have collected it with interest?'

"Then he said to those standing by, 'Take his mina away from him and give it to the one who has ten minas.'

"'Sir,' they said, 'he already has ten!'

"He replied, 'I tell you that to everyone who has, more will be given, but as for the one who has nothing, even what he has will be taken away.'"

2 PETER 2:20

If they have escaped the corruption of the world by knowing our Lord and Savior Jesus Christ and are again entangled in it and overcome, they are worse off at the end than they were at the beginning.

2 PETER 3:10

But the day of the Lord will come like a thief. The heavens will disappear with a roar; the elements will be destroyed by fire, and the earth and everything in it will be laid bare.

Laziness

PROVERBS 6:6–11

Go to the ant, you sluggard; consider its ways and be wise! It has no commander, no overseer or ruler, yet it stores its provisions in summer and gathers its food at harvest. How long will you lie there, you sluggard? When will you get up from your sleep? A little sleep, a little slumber, a little folding of the hands to rest—and poverty will come on you like a bandit and scarcity like an armed man.

PROVERBS 12:24

Diligent hands will rule, but laziness ends in slave labor.

PROVERBS 13:11

Dishonest money dwindles away, but he who gathers money little by little makes it grow.

PROVERBS 14:4

Where there are no oxen, the manger is empty, but from the strength of an ox comes an abundant harvest.

PROVERBS 19:15

Laziness brings on deep sleep, and the shiftless man goes hungry.

PROVERBS 21:17

He who loves pleasure will become poor; whoever loves wine and oil will never be rich.

PROVERBS 22:13

The sluggard says, "There is a lion outside!" or, "I will be murdered in the streets!"

PROVERBS 26:13

The sluggard says, "There is a lion in the road, a fierce lion roaming the streets!"

2 THESSALONIANS 3:6, 10

In the name of the Lord Jesus Christ, we command you, brothers, to keep away from every brother who is idle and does not live according to the teaching you received from us. For even when we were with you, we gave you this rule: "If a man will not work, he shall not eat."

Lending

EXODUS 22:25–26

If you lend money to one of my people among you who is needy, do not be like a moneylender; charge him no interest. If you take your neighbor's cloak as a pledge, return it to him by sunset.

DEUTERONOMY 23:19–20

Do not charge your brother interest, whether on money or food or anything else that may earn interest. You may charge a foreigner interest, but not a brother Israelite, so that the LORD your God may bless you in everything you put your hand to in the land you are entering to possess.

DEUTERONOMY 24:10–11

When you make a loan of any kind to your neighbor, do not go into his house to get what he is offering as a pledge. Stay outside and let the man to whom you are making the loan bring the pledge out to you.

NEHEMIAH 5:7, 10

I pondered them in my mind and then accused the nobles and officials. I told them, "You are exacting usury from your own countrymen!" So I called together a large meeting to deal with them. I and my brothers and my men are also lending the people money and grain. But let the exacting of usury stop!

PSALM 15:5

Who lends his money without usury and does not accept a bribe against the innocent. He who does these things will never be shaken.

PSALM 37:26

They are always generous and lend freely; their children will be blessed.

PROVERBS 28:8

He who increases his wealth by exorbitant interest amasses it for another, who will be kind to the poor.

EZEKIEL 18:8

He does not lend at usury or take excessive interest. He withholds his hand from doing wrong and judges fairly between man and man.

LUKE 6:34–35

"And if you lend to those from whom you expect repayment, what credit is that to you? Even 'sinners' lend to 'sinners,' expecting to be repaid in full. But love your enemies, do good to them, and lend to them without expecting to get anything back. Then your reward will be great, and you will be sons of the Most High, because he is kind to the ungrateful and wicked."

LUKE 7:41

"Two men owed money to a certain moneylender. One owed him five hundred denarii, and the other fifty."

Needs

PSALM 37:25

I was young and now I am old, yet I have never seen the righteous forsaken or their children begging bread.

MATTHEW 6:8, 25–33

"Do not be like them, for your Father knows what you need before you ask him.

"Therefore I tell you, do not worry about your life, what you will eat or drink; or about your body, what you will wear. Is not life more important than food, and the body more important than clothes? Look at the birds of the air; they do not sow or reap or store away in barns, and yet your heavenly Father feeds them. Are you not much more valuable than they? Who of you by worrying can add a single hour to his life?

"And why do you worry about clothes? See how the lilies of the field grow. They do not labor or spin. Yet I tell you that not even Solomon in all his splendor was dressed like one of these. If that is how God clothes the grass of the field, which is here today and tomorrow is thrown into the fire, will he not much more clothe you, O you of little faith? So do not worry, saying, 'What shall we eat?' or 'What shall we drink?' or 'What shall we wear?' For the pagans run after all these things, and your heavenly Father knows that you need them. But seek first his kingdom and his righteousness, and all these things will be given to you as well."

PHILIPPIANS 4:19

And my God will meet all your needs according to his glorious riches in Christ Jesus.

Planning

PROVERBS 16:1

To man belong the plans of the heart, but from the LORD comes the reply of the tongue.

Prosperity

GENESIS 39:3

When his master saw that the LORD was with him and that the LORD gave him success in everything he did.

DEUTERONOMY 28:11

The LORD will grant you abundant prosperity—in the fruit of your womb, the young of your livestock and the crops of your ground—in the land he swore to your forefathers to give you.

DEUTERONOMY 29:9

Carefully follow the terms of this covenant, so that you may prosper in everything you do.

2 CHRONICLES 31:21

In everything that he undertook in the service of God's temple and in obedience to the law and the commands, he sought his God and worked whole-heartedly. And so he prospered.

PSALM 1:3

He is like a tree planted by streams of water, which yields its fruit in season and whose leaf does not wither. Whatever he does prospers.

PSALM 35:27

May those who delight in my vindication shout for joy and gladness; may they always say, "The LORD be exalted, who delights in the well-being of his servant."

LUKE 15:13

"Not long after that, the younger son got together all he had, set off for a distant country and there squandered his wealth in wild living."

JOHN 6:12

When they had all had enough to eat, he said to his disciples, "Gather the pieces that are left over. Let nothing be wasted."

Retirement

PSALM 37:25

I was young and now I am old, yet I have never seen the righteous forsaken or their children begging bread.

PROVERBS 16:31

Gray hair is a crown of splendor; it is attained by a righteous life.

PROVERBS 20:29

The glory of young men is their strength, gray hair the splendor of the old.

Saving

PROVERBS 6:6–8

Go to the ant, you sluggard; consider its ways and be wise! It has no commander, no overseer or ruler, yet

it stores its provisions in summer and gathers its food at harvest.

PROVERBS 21:20

In the house of the wise are stores of choice food and oil, but a foolish man devours all he has.

PROVERBS 30:24–25

Four things on earth are small, yet they are extremely wise: Ants are creatures of little strength, yet they store up their food in the summer;

Sharing

EXODUS 16:18–20

And when they measured it by the omer, he who gathered much did not have too much, and he who gathered little did not have too little. Each one gathered as much as he needed. Then Moses said to them, "No one is to keep any of it until morning." However, some of them paid no attention to Moses; they kept part of it until morning, but it was full of maggots and began to smell. So Moses was angry with them.

ACTS 4:32

All the believers were one in heart and mind. No one claimed that any of his possessions was his own, but they shared everything they had.

ROMANS 12:13

Share with God's people who are in need. Practice hospitality.

1 CORINTHIANS 9:7–11, 14

Who serves as a soldier at his own expense? Who plants a vineyard and does not eat of its grapes? Who tends a flock and does not drink of the milk? Do I say this merely from a human point of view? Doesn't the Law say the same thing? For it is written in the Law of Moses: "Do not muzzle an ox while it is treading out the grain." Is it about oxen that God is concerned? Surely he says this for us, doesn't he? Yes, this was written for us, because when the plowman plows and the thresher threshes, they ought to do so in the hope of sharing in the harvest. If we have sown spiritual seed among you, is it too much if we reap a material harvest from you? In the same way, the Lord has commanded that those who preach the gospel should receive their living from the gospel.

2 CORINTHIANS 8:8–15

I am not commanding you, but I want to test the sincerity of your love by comparing it with the earnestness of others. For you know the grace of our Lord Jesus Christ, that though he was rich, yet for your sakes he became poor, so that you through his poverty might become rich. And here is my advice about what is best for you in this matter: Last year you were the first not only to give but also to have the desire to do so. Now finish the work, so that your eager willingness to do it may be matched by your completion of it, according to your means. For if the willingness is there, the gift is acceptable according to what one has, not according to what he does not have. Our desire is not that others might be relieved while you are hard pressed, but that there might be equality. At the present time your plenty will supply what they need, so that in turn their plenty will supply what you need. Then there will be equality, as it is written: "He who gathered much did not have too much, and he who gathered little did not have too little."

2 CORINTHIANS 9:6–13

Remember this: Whoever sows sparingly will also reap sparingly, and whoever sows generously will also reap generously. Each man should give what he has decided in his heart to give, not reluctantly or under compulsion, for God loves a cheerful giver. And God is able to make all grace abound to you, so that in all things at all times, having all that you need, you will abound in every good work. As it is written: "He has scattered abroad his gifts to the poor; his righteousness endures forever." Now he who supplies seed to the sower and bread for food will also supply and increase your store of seed and will enlarge the harvest of your righteousness. You will be made rich in every way so that you

can be generous on every occasion, and through us your generosity will result in thanksgiving to God. This service that you perform is not only supplying the needs of God's people but is also overflowing in many expressions of thanks to God. Because of the service by which you have proved yourselves, men will praise God for the obedience that accompanies your confession of the gospel of Christ, and for your generosity in sharing with them and with everyone else.

GALATIANS 6:6

Anyone who receives instruction in the word must share all good things with his instructor.

Self-Control

MATTHEW 7:13–14

Enter through the narrow gate. For wide is the gate and broad is the road that leads to destruction, and many enter through it. But small is the gate and narrow the road that leads to life, and only a few find it.

2 CORINTHIANS 8:11

Now finish the work, so that your eager willingness to do it may be matched by your completion of it, according to your means.

HEBREWS 12:11

No discipline seems pleasant at the time, but painful. Later on, however, it produces a harvest of righteousness and peace for those who have been trained by it.

Slothfulness

PROVERBS 18:9

One who is slack in his work is brother to one who destroys.

PROVERBS 24:30–31

I went past the field of the sluggard, past the vineyard of the man who lacks judgment; thorns had come up

SCRIPTURE REFERENCES ON FINANCE TOPICS

everywhere, the ground was covered with weeds, and the stone wall was in ruins.

ECCLESIASTES 10:18

If a man is lazy, the rafters sag; if his hands are idle, the house leaks.

2 THESSALONIANS 3:11

We hear that some among you are idle. They are not busy; they are busybodies.

HEBREWS 6:12

We do not want you to become lazy, but to imitate those who through faith and patience inherit what has been promised.

Speculation

ECCLESIASTES 5:15–17

Naked a man comes from his mother's womb, and as he comes, so he departs. He takes nothing from his labor that he can carry in his hand. This too is a grievous evil: As a man comes, so he departs, and what does he gain, since he toils for the wind? All his days he eats in darkness, with great frustration, affliction and anger.

Suing

MATTHEW 5:42

"Give to the one who asks you, and do not turn away from the one who wants to borrow from you."

MATTHEW 6:3

"But when you give to the needy, do not let your left hand know what your right hand is doing."

MATTHEW 10:42

"And if anyone gives even a cup of cold water to one of these little ones because he is my disciple, I tell you the truth, he will certainly not lose his reward."

MATTHEW 13:12

"Whoever has will be given more, and he will have an abundance. Whoever does not have, even what he has will be taken from him."

LUKE 6:30–36

"Give to everyone who asks you, and if anyone takes what belongs to you, do not demand it back. Do to others as you would have them do to you. "If you love those who love you, what credit is that to you? Even 'sinners' love those who love them. And if you do good to those who are good to you, what credit is that to you? Even 'sinners' do that. And if you lend to those from whom you expect repayment, what credit is that to you? Even 'sinners' lend to 'sinners,' expecting to be repaid in full. But love your enemies, do good to them, and lend to them without expecting to get anything back. Then your reward will be great, and you will be sons of the Most High, because he is kind to the ungrateful and wicked. Be merciful, just as your Father is merciful."

LUKE 12:57–58

"Why don't you judge for yourselves what is right? As you are going with your adversary to the magistrate, try hard to be reconciled to him on the way, or he may drag you off to the judge, and the judge turn you over to the officer, and the officer throw you into prison."

1 CORINTHIANS 6:1–7

If any of you has a dispute with another, dare he take it before the ungodly for judgment instead of before the saints? Do you not know that the saints will judge the world? And if you are to judge the world, are you not competent to judge trivial cases? Do you not know that we will judge angels? How much more the things of this life! Therefore, if you have disputes about such matters, appoint as judges even men of little account in the church! I say this to shame you. Is it possible that there is nobody among you wise enough to judge a dispute between believers? But instead, one brother goes to law against another-and this in front of unbelievers! The very fact that you have lawsuits among you means you have been completely defeated already. Why not rather be wronged? Why not rather be cheated?

Supporting the Wealthy

DEUTERONOMY 1:17

Do not show partiality in judging; hear both small and great alike. Do not be afraid of any man, for judgment belongs to God. Bring me any case too hard for you, and I will hear it.

DEUTERONOMY 16:19

Do not pervert justice or show partiality. Do not accept a bribe, for a bribe blinds the eyes of the wise and twists the words of the righteous.

PROVERBS 14:20

But any winged creature that is clean you may eat.

PROVERBS 28:21

To show partiality is not good—yet a man will do wrong for a piece of bread.

Taxes

MATTHEW 17:24–27

After Jesus and his disciples arrived in Capernaum, the collectors of the two-drachma tax came to Peter and asked, "Doesn't your teacher pay the temple tax?"

"Yes, he does," he replied.

When Peter came into the house, Jesus was the first to speak. "What do you think, Simon?" he asked. "From whom do the kings of the earth collect duty and taxes-from their own sons or from others?"

"From others," Peter answered. "Then the sons are exempt," Jesus said to him. "But so that we may not offend them, go to the lake and throw out your line. Take the first fish you catch; open its mouth and you will find a four-drachma coin. Take it and give it to

them for my tax and yours."

MARK 12:14–17

They came to him and said, "Teacher, we know you are a man of integrity. You aren't swayed by men, because you pay no attention to who they are; but you teach the way of God in accordance with the truth. Is it right to pay taxes to Caesar or not? Should we pay or shouldn't we?" But Jesus knew their hypocrisy. "Why are you trying to trap me?" he asked. "Bring me a denarius and let me look at it." They brought the coin, and he asked them, "Whose portrait is this? And whose inscription?" "Caesar's," they replied. Then Jesus said to them, "Give to Caesar what is Caesar's and to God what is God's." And they were amazed at him.

LUKE 20:22–25

Is it right for us to pay taxes to Caesar or not?" He saw through their duplicity and said to them, "Show me a denarius. Whose portrait and inscription are on it?" "Caesar's," they replied. He said to them, "Then give to Caesar what is Caesar's, and to God what is God's."

ROMANS 13:6–7

This is also why you pay taxes, for the authorities are God's servants, who give their full time to governing. Give everyone what you owe him: If you owe taxes, pay taxes; if revenue, then revenue; if respect, then respect; if honor, then honor.

Tithing

GENESIS 14:20, 22

And blessed be God Most High, who delivered your enemies into your hand." Then Abram gave him a tenth of everything. But Abram said to the king of Sodom, "I have raised my hand to the LORD, God Most High, Creator of heaven and earth, and have taken an oath."

SCRIPTURE REFERENCES ON FINANCE TOPICS

MALACHI 3:10

"Bring the whole tithe into the storehouse, that there may be food in my house. Test me in this," says the LORD *Almighty, "and see if I will not throw open the floodgates of heaven and pour out so much blessing that you will not have room enough for it."*

MATTHEW 23:23

"Woe to you, teachers of the law and Pharisees, you hypocrites! You give a tenth of your spices-mint, dill and cummin. But you have neglected the more important matters of the law-justice, mercy and faithfulness. You should have practiced the latter, without neglecting the former."

LUKE 11:42

"Woe to you Pharisees, because you give God a tenth of your mint, rue and all other kinds of garden herbs, but you neglect justice and the love of God. You should have practiced the latter without leaving the former undone."

HEBREWS 7:1–10

This Melchizedek was king of Salem and priest of God Most High. He met Abraham returning from the defeat of the kings and blessed him, and Abraham gave him a tenth of everything. First, his name means "king of righteousness"; then also, "king of Salem" means "king of peace." Without father or mother, without genealogy, without beginning of days or end of life, like the Son of God he remains a priest forever. Just think how great he was: Even the patriarch Abraham gave him a tenth of the plunder! Now the law requires the descendants of Levi who become priests to collect a tenth from the people-that is, their brothers-even though their brothers are descended from Abraham. This man, however, did not trace his descent from Levi, yet he collected a tenth from Abraham and blessed him who had the promises. And without doubt the lesser person is blessed by the greater. In the one case, the tenth is collected by men who die; but in the other case, by him who is declared

to be living. One might even say that Levi, who collects the tenth, paid the tenth through Abraham, because when Melchizedek met Abraham, Levi was still in the body of his ancestor.

Trust

JEREMIAH 17:7–8

But blessed is the man who trusts in the LORD, *whose confidence is in him.*
He will be like a tree planted by the water that sends out its roots by the stream. It does not fear when heat comes; its leaves are always green. It has no worries in a year of drought and never fails to bear fruit.

MARK 6:9

Wear sandals but not an extra tunic.

MARK 8:34

Then he called the crowd to him along with his disciples and said: "If anyone would come after me, he must deny himself and take up his cross and follow me."

PHILIPPIANS 4:19

And my God will meet all your needs according to his glorious riches in Christ Jesus.

Truthfulness

PSALM 1:1–2

Blessed is the man who does not walk in the counsel of the wicked or stand in the way of sinners or sit in the seat of mockers. But his delight is in the law of the LORD, *and on his law he meditates day and night.*

PSALM 37:37

Consider the blameless, observe the upright; there is a future for the man of peace.

PSALM 112:6

Surely he will never be shaken; a righteous man will be remembered forever.

PROVERBS 10:16

The wages of the righteous bring them life, but the income of the wicked brings them punishment.

PROVERBS 11:4

Wealth is worthless in the day of wrath, but righteousness delivers from death.

PROVERBS 12:12

The wicked desire the plunder of evil men, but the root of the righteous flourishes.

PROVERBS 13:22

A good man leaves an inheritance for his children's children, but a sinner's wealth is stored up for the righteous.

PROVERBS 16:8, 11

Better a little with righteousness than much gain with injustice. Honest scales and balances are from the Lord; all the weights in the bag are of his making.

PROVERBS 19:1

Better a poor man whose walk is blameless than a fool whose lips are perverse.

PROVERBS 21:3

To do what is right and just is more acceptable to the Lord than sacrifice.

PROVERBS 22:1

A good name is more desirable than great riches; to be esteemed is better than silver or gold.

PROVERBS 28:6, 13

Better a poor man whose walk is blameless than a rich man whose ways are perverse. He who conceals his sins does not prosper, but whoever confesses and renounces them finds mercy.

MATTHEW 7:20

"Thus, by their fruit you will recognize them."

MATTHEW 17:24

After Jesus and his disciples arrived in Capernaum, the collectors of the two-drachma tax came to Peter and asked, "Doesn't your teacher pay the temple tax?"

LUKE 3:12–13

Tax collectors also came to be baptized. "Teacher," they asked, "what should we do?" "Don't collect any more than you are required to," he told them.

LUKE 8:15

"But the seed on good soil stands for those with a noble and good heart, who hear the word, retain it, and by persevering produce a crop."

LUKE 12:58

"As you are going with your adversary to the magistrate, try hard to be reconciled to him on the way, or he may drag you off to the judge, and the judge turn you over to the officer, and the officer throw you into prison."

ROMANS 13:7

Give everyone what you owe him: If you owe taxes, pay taxes; if revenue, then revenue; if respect, then respect; if honor, then honor.

ROMANS 13:9

The commandments, "Do not commit adultery," "Do not murder," "Do not steal," "Do not covet," and whatever other commandment there may be, are summed up in this one rule: "Love your neighbor as yourself."

GALATIANS 6:9

Let us not become weary in doing good, for at the proper time we will reap a harvest if we do not give up.

Waste

GENESIS 41:36

This food should be held in reserve for the country, to be used during the seven years of famine that will come upon Egypt, so that the country may not be ruined by the famine.

Wealth

PROVERBS 10:22

Hatred stirs up dissension, but love covers over all wrongs.

PROVERBS 28:13

He who conceals his sins does not prosper, but whoever confesses and renounces them finds mercy.

JEREMIAH 17:8–10

He will be like a tree planted by the water that sends out its roots by the stream. It does not fear when heat comes; its leaves are always green. It has no worries in a year of drought and never fails to bear fruit." The heart is deceitful above all things and beyond cure. Who can understand it? "I the LORD search the heart and examine the mind, to reward a man according to his conduct, according to what his deeds deserve."

LUKE 6:38

"Give, and it will be given to you. A good measure, pressed down, shaken together and running over, will be poured into your lap. For with the measure you use, it will be measured to you."

JOHN 10:10

"The thief comes only to steal and kill and destroy; I have come that they may have life, and have it to the full."

2 CORINTHIANS 8:9

For you know the grace of our Lord Jesus Christ, that though he was rich, yet for your sakes he became poor, so that you through his poverty might become rich.

PHILIPPIANS 4:19

And my God will meet all your needs according to his glorious riches in Christ Jesus.

Wives

PROVERBS 31:10–31

A wife of noble character who can find? She is worth far more than rubies. Her husband has full confidence in her and lacks nothing of value. She brings him good, not harm, all the days of her life. She selects wool and flax and works with eager hands. She is like the merchant ships, bringing her food from afar. She gets up while it is still dark; she provides food for her family and portions for her servant girls. She considers a field and buys it; out of her earnings she plants a vineyard. She sets about her work vigorously; her arms are strong for her tasks. She sees that her trading is profitable, and her lamp does not go out at night. In her hand she holds the distaff and grasps the spindle with her fingers. She opens her arms to the poor and extends her hands to the needy. When it snows, she has no fear for her household; for all of them are clothed in scarlet. She makes coverings for her bed; she is clothed in fine linen and purple. Her husband is respected at the city gate, where he takes his seat among the elders of the land. She makes linen garments and sells them, and supplies the merchants with sashes. She is clothed with strength and dignity; she can laugh at the days to come. She speaks with wisdom, and faithful instruction is on her tongue. She watches over the affairs of her household and does not eat the bread of idleness. Her children arise and call her blessed; her husband also, and he praises her: "Many women do noble things, but you surpass them all." Charm is deceptive, and beauty is fleeting; but a woman who fears the LORD is to be praised. Give her the reward she has earned.

Work

DEUTERONOMY 24:14–15

Do not take advantage of a hired man who is poor and needy, whether he is a brother Israelite or an alien living in one of your towns. Pay him his wages each day before sunset, because he is poor and is counting on it. Otherwise he may cry to the LORD against you, and you will be guilty of sin.

PROVERBS 6:6–10

Go to the ant, you sluggard; consider its ways and be wise! It has no commander, no overseer or ruler, yet it stores its provisions in summer and gathers its food at harvest. How long will you lie there, you sluggard? When will you get up from your sleep? A little sleep, a little slumber, a little folding of the hands to rest.

PROVERBS 10:4–5

Lazy hands make a man poor, but diligent hands bring wealth. He who gathers crops in summer is a wise son, but he who sleeps during harvest is a disgraceful son.

PROVERBS 12:11, 24

He who works his land will have abundant food, but he who chases fantasies lacks judgment. Diligent hands will rule, but laziness ends in slave labor.

PROVERBS 14:23

All hard work brings a profit, but mere talk leads only to poverty.

PROVERBS 16:26

The laborer's appetite works for him; his hunger drives him on.

PROVERBS 28:19

He who works his land will have abundant food, but the one who chases fantasies will have his fill of poverty.

EPHESIANS 4:28

He who has been stealing must steal no longer, but must work, doing something useful with his own hands, that he may have something to share with those in need.

Worry

PSALM 50:14–15

Sacrifice thank offerings to God, fulfill your vows to the Most High, and call upon me in the day of trouble; I will deliver you, and you will honor me.

PROVERBS 12:25

An anxious heart weighs a man down, but a kind word cheers him up.

MATTHEW 6:27–34

"Who of you by worrying can add a single hour to his life? And why do you worry about clothes? See how the lilies of the field grow. They do not labor or spin. Yet I tell you that not even Solomon in all his splendor was dressed like one of these. If that is how God clothes the grass of the field, which is here today and tomorrow is thrown into the fire, will he not much more clothe you, O you of little faith? So do not worry, saying, 'What shall we eat?' or 'What shall we drink?' or 'What shall we wear?' For the pagans run after all these things, and your heavenly Father knows that you need them. But seek first his kingdom and his righteousness, and all these things will be given to you as well. Therefore do not worry about tomorrow, for tomorrow will worry about itself. Each day has enough trouble of its own."

PHILIPPIANS 4:6

Do not be anxious about anything, but in everything, by prayer and petition, with thanksgiving, present your requests to God.

1 JOHN 4:18

There is no fear in love. But perfect love drives out fear, because fear has to do with punishment. The one who fears is not made perfect in love.

SCRIPTURE REFERENCES
ON GOD'S PROVISION
& ABUNDANCE

GENESIS 27:28

May God give you of heaven's dew and of earth's richness—an abundance of grain and new wine.

GENESIS 41:29

Seven years of great abundance are coming throughout the land of Egypt.

GENESIS 41:30–32

But seven years of famine will follow them. Then all the abundance in Egypt will be forgotten, and the famine will ravage the land. The abundance in the land will not be remembered, because the famine that follows it will be so severe.

GENESIS 41:47

During the seven years of abundance the land produced plentifully.

GENESIS 41:48

Joseph collected all the food produced in those seven years of abundance in Egypt and stored it in the cities. In each city he put the food grown in the fields surrounding it.

GENESIS 41:53

They will summon peoples to the mountain and there offer sacrifices of righteousness; they will feast on the abundance of the seas, on the treasures hidden in the sand.

NUMBERS 24:7

Water will flow from their buckets; their seed will have abundant water. "Their king will be greater than Agag; their kingdom will be exalted."

DEUTERONOMY 6:3

Listen obediently, Israel. Do what you're told so that you'll have a good life, a life of abundance and bounty, just as GOD promised, in a land abounding in milk and honey. (THE MESSAGE)

DEUTERONOMY 28:11

The LORD will grant you abundant prosperity—in the fruit of your womb, the young of your livestock and the crops of your ground—in the land he swore to your forefathers to give you.

DEUTERONOMY 32:2

Let my teaching fall like rain and my words descend like dew, like showers on new grass, like abundant rain on tender plants.

1 CHRONICLES 29:16

O LORD our God, as for all this abundance that we have provided for building you a temple for your Holy Name, it comes from your hand, and all of it belongs to you.

1 CHRONICLES 29:21

The next day they made sacrifices to the LORD and presented burnt offerings to him: a thousand bulls, a thousand rams and a thousand male lambs, together with their drink offerings, and other sacrifices in abundance for all Israel.

2 CHRONICLES 11:23

He acted wisely, dispersing some of his sons throughout the districts of Judah and Benjamin, and to all the fortified cities. He gave them abundant provisions and took many wives for them.

2 CHRONICLES 29:35

There were burnt offerings in abundance, together with the fat of the fellowship offerings and the drink offerings that accompanied the burnt offerings. So the service of the temple of the LORD was reestablished.

NEHEMIAH 5:18

Each day one ox, six choice sheep and some poultry were prepared for me, and every ten days an abundant supply of wine of all kinds. In spite of all this, I never demanded the food allotted to the governor, because the demands were heavy on these people.

NEHEMIAH 9:25

They captured fortified cities and fertile land; they took possession of houses filled with all kinds of good things, wells already dug, vineyards, olive groves and fruit trees in abundance. They ate to the full and were well-nourished; they reveled in your great goodness.

NEHEMIAH 9:37

Because of our sins, its abundant harvest goes to the kings you have placed over us. They rule over our bodies and our cattle as they please. We are in great distress.

ESTHER 1:7

Wine was served in goblets of gold, each one different from the other, and the royal wine was abundant, in keeping with the king's liberality.

JOB 36:28

The clouds pour down their moisture and abundant showers fall on mankind.

JOB 36:31

This is the way he governs the nations and provides food in abundance.

PSALM 36:8

They feast on the abundance of your house; you give them drink from your river of delights.

PSALM 65:11

You crown the year with your bounty, and your carts overflow with abundance.

PSALM 66:12

You let men ride over our heads; we went through fire and water, but you brought us to a place of abundance.

PSALM 68:9

You gave abundant showers, O God; you refreshed your weary inheritance.

PSALM 73:10

Therefore their people turn to them and drink up waters in abundance.

PSALM 78:15

He split the rocks in the desert and gave them water as abundant as the seas.

PSALM 132:15

I will bless her with abundant provisions; her poor will I satisfy with food.

PSALM 144:13

Our barns will be filled with every kind of provision.

PSALM 145:7

They will celebrate your abundant goodness and joyfully sing of your righteousness.

PROVERBS 12:11

He who works his land will have abundant food, but he who chases fantasies lacks judgment.

PROVERBS 13:23

A poor man's field may produce abundant food, but injustice sweeps it away.

PROVERBS 14:4

Where there are no oxen, the manger is empty, but from the strength of an ox comes an abundant harvest.

PROVERBS 20:15

Gold there is, and rubies in abundance, but lips that speak knowledge are a rare jewel.

PROVERBS 28:19

He who works his land will have abundant food, but the one who chases fantasies will have his fill of poverty.

ECCLESIASTES 5:12

The sleep of a laborer is sweet, whether he eats little or much, but the abundance of a rich man permits him no sleep.

ISAIAH 7:22

And because of the abundance of the milk they give, he will have curds to eat. All who remain in the land will eat curds and honey.

ISAIAH 23:18

Yet her profit and her earnings will be set apart for the LORD; they will not be stored up or hoarded. Her profits will go to those who live before the LORD, for abundant food and fine clothes.

ISAIAH 30:23

God will provide rain for the seeds you sow. The grain that grows will be abundant. Your cattle will range far and wide. (THE MESSAGE)

ISAIAH 30:33

Topheth has long been prepared; it has been made ready for the king. Its fire pit has been made deep and wide, with an abundance of fire and wood; the breath of the LORD, like a stream of burning sulfur, sets it ablaze.

ISAIAH 33:23

Your rigging hangs loose: The mast is not held secure, the sail is not spread. Then an abundance of spoils will be divided and even the lame will carry off plunder.

ISAIAH 66:11

"For you will nurse and be satisfied at her comforting breasts; you will drink deeply and delight in her overflowing abundance."

JEREMIAH 2:22

"Although you wash yourself with soda and use an abundance of soap, the stain of your guilt is still before me," declares the Sovereign LORD.

JEREMIAH 31:14

"I will satisfy the priests with abundance, and my people will be filled with my bounty," declares the LORD.

JEREMIAH 33:6

"Nevertheless, I will bring health and healing to it; I will heal my people and will let them enjoy abundant peace and security."

JEREMIAH 33:9

"Then this city will bring me renown, joy, praise and honor before all nations on earth that hear of all the good things I do for it; and they will be in awe and will tremble at the abundant prosperity and peace I provide for it."

JEREMIAH 40:12

They all came back to the land of Judah, to Gedaliah at Mizpah, from all the countries where they had been scattered. And they harvested an abundance of wine and summer fruit.

EZEKIEL 17:5

He took some of the seed of your land and put it in fertile soil. He planted it like a willow by abundant water.

EZEKIEL 17:8

It had been planted in good soil by abundant water so that it would produce branches, bear fruit and become a splendid vine.

EZEKIEL 19:10

Your mother was like a vine in your vineyard planted by the water; it was fruitful and full of branches because of abundant water.

EZEKIEL 31:5

So it towered higher than all the trees of the field; its boughs increased and its branches grew long, spreading because of abundant waters.

EZEKIEL 31:7

It was majestic in beauty, with its spreading boughs, for its roots went down to abundant waters.

EZEKIEL 31:9

I made it beautiful with abundant branches, the envy of all the trees of Eden in the garden of God.

EZEKIEL 31:15

This is what the Sovereign LORD says: On the day it was brought down to the grave I covered the deep springs with mourning for it; I held back its streams, and its abundant waters were restrained. Because of it I clothed Lebanon with gloom, and all the trees of the field withered away.

EZEKIEL 32:13

I will destroy all her cattle from beside abundant waters no longer to be stirred by the foot of man or muddied by the hoofs of cattle.

EZEKIEL 32:15

When I turn Egypt back to the wild and strip her clean of all her abundant produce, when I strike dead all who live there, then they'll realize that I am GOD. (THE MESSAGE)

DANIEL 4:12

Its leaves were beautiful, its fruit abundant, and on it was food for all. Under it the beasts of the field found shelter, and the birds of the air lived in its branches; from it every creature was fed.

DANIEL 4:21

With beautiful leaves and abundant fruit, providing food for all, giving shelter to the beasts of the field, and having nesting places in its branches for the birds of the air.

JOEL 2:23

Be glad, O people of Zion, rejoice in the LORD your God, for he has given you the autumn rains in righteousness. He sends you abundant showers, both autumn and spring rains, as before.

MATTHEW 13:12

"Whoever has will be given more, and he will have an abundance. Whoever does not have, even what he has will be taken from him."

MATTHEW 25:29

"For everyone who has will be given more, and he will have an abundance. Whoever does not have, even what he has will be taken from him."

LUKE 12:15

Then he said to them, "Watch out! Be on your guard against all kinds of greed; a man's life does not consist in the abundance of his possessions."

LUKE 21:4

"For they all gave out of their abundance (their surplus); but she has contributed out of her lack and her want, putting in all that she had on which to live." (AMP)

JOHN 10:10

"The thief comes only in order to steal and kill and destroy. I came that they may have and enjoy life, and have it in abundance (to the full, till it overflows)." (AMP)

JOHN 15:5

"I am the Vine, you are the branches. When you're joined with me and I with you, the relation inti-

mate and organic, the harvest is sure to be abundant. Separated, you can't produce a thing." (THE MESSAGE)

ROMANS 5:17

For if, by the trespass of the one man, death reigned through that one man, how much more will those who receive God's abundant provision of grace and of the gift of righteousness reign in life through the one man, Jesus Christ.

2 CORINTHIANS 9:8

And God is able to make all grace (every favor and earthly blessing) come to you in abundance, so that you may always and under all circumstances and whatever the need be self-sufficient [possessing enough to require no aid or support and furnished in abundance for every good work and charitable donation]. (AMP)

PHILIPPIANS 4:12

I know how to be abased and live humbly in straitened circumstances, and I know also how to enjoy plenty and live in abundance. I have learned in any and all circumstances the secret of facing every situation, whether well-fed or going hungry, having a sufficiency and enough to spare or going without and being in want. (AMP)

1 PETER 1:2

Who have been chosen according to the foreknowledge of God the Father, through the sanctifying work of the Spirit, for obedience to Jesus Christ and sprinkling by his blood: Grace and peace be yours in abundance.

2 PETER 1:2

Grace and peace be yours in abundance through the knowledge of God and of Jesus our Lord.

JUDE 1:2

Mercy, peace and love be yours in abundance.

SCRIPTURE REFERENCES ON WEALTH, RICHES, & PROSPERITY

Wealth

GENESIS 31:1

Jacob Flees from Laban: Now Jacob heard the words of Laban's sons, saying, "Jacob has taken away all that was our father's, and from what was our father's he has acquired all this wealth." (NKJV)

GENESIS 34:29

And all their wealth: All their little ones and their wives they took captive; and they plundered even all that was in the houses. (NKJV)

DEUTERONOMY 8:17

Then you say in your heart, "My power and the might of my hand have gained me this wealth." (NKJV)

DEUTERONOMY 8:18

And you shall remember the LORD your God, for it is He who gives you power to get wealth, that He may establish His covenant which He swore to your fathers, as it is this day. (NKJV)

RUTH 2:1

Ruth Meets Boaz: There was a relative of Naomi's husband, a man of great wealth, of the family of Elimelech. His name was Boaz. (NKJV)

1 KINGS 10:14

Solomon's Great Wealth: The weight of gold that came to Solomon yearly was six hundred and sixty-six talents of gold. (NKJV)

2 KINGS 15:20

And Menahem exacted the money from Israel, from all the very wealthy, from each man fifty shekels of silver, to give to the king of Assyria. So the king of Assyria turned back, and did not stay there in the land. (NKJV)

2 CHRONICLES 1:11

Then God said to Solomon: "Because this was in your heart, and you have not asked riches or wealth or honor or the life of your enemies, nor have you asked long life—but have asked wisdom and knowledge for yourself, that you may judge My people over whom I have made you king." (NKJV)

2 CHRONICLES 1:12

Wisdom and knowledge are granted to you; and I will give you riches and wealth and honor, such as none of the kings have had who were before you, nor shall any after you have the like. (NKJV)

2 CHRONICLES 9:13

Solomon's Great Wealth (see also 1 Kings 10:14–29; 2 Chronicles 1:14–17): The weight of gold that came to Solomon yearly was six hundred and sixty-six talents of gold. (NKJV)

2 CHRONICLES 32:27

Hezekiah's Wealth and Honor (see also 2 Kings 20:12–21; Isaiah 39:1): Hezekiah had very great riches and honor. And he made himself treasuries for silver, for gold, for precious stones, for spices, for shields, and for all kinds of desirable items. (NKJV)

JOB 6:22

Did I ever say, "Bring something to me"? Or, "Offer a bribe for me from your wealth"? (NKJV)

JOB 15:29

He will not be rich, nor will his wealth continue, nor will his possessions overspread the earth. (NKJV)

JOB 20:10

His children will seek the favor of the poor,
And his hands will restore his wealth. (NKJV)

JOB 21:13

They spend their days in wealth,
And in a moment go down to the grave. (NKJV)

JOB 30:1

Job's Wealth Now Poverty: *But now they mock at me, men younger than I, whose fathers I disdained to put with the dogs of my flock.* (NKJV)

JOB 31:25

If I have rejoiced because my wealth was great, and because my hand had gained much. (NKJV)

PSALM 49:6

Those who trust in their wealth, and boast in the multitude of their riches. (NKJV)

PSALM 49:10

For he sees wise men die; likewise the fool and the senseless person perish, and leave their wealth to others. (NKJV)

PSALM 112:3

Wealth and riches will be in his house, and his righteousness endures forever. (NKJV)

PROVERBS 5:10

Lest aliens be filled with your wealth, and your labors go to the house of a foreigner. (NKJV)

PROVERBS 8:21

That I may cause those who love me to inherit wealth, that I may fill their treasuries. (NKJV)

PROVERBS 10:15

The rich man's wealth is his strong city; the destruction of the poor is their poverty. (NKJV)

PROVERBS 13:11

Wealth gained by dishonesty will be diminished, but he who gathers by labor will increase. (NKJV)

PROVERBS 13:22

A good man leaves an inheritance to his children's children, but the wealth of the sinner is stored up for the righteous. (NKJV)

PROVERBS 18:11

The rich man's wealth is his strong city, and like a high wall in his own esteem. (NKJV)

PROVERBS 19:4

Wealth makes many friends, but the poor is separated from his friend. (NKJV)

PROVERBS 29:3

Whoever loves wisdom makes his father rejoice, but a companion of harlots wastes his wealth. (NKJV)

ECCLESIASTES 5:19

As for every man to whom God has given riches and wealth, and given him power to eat of it, to receive his heritage and rejoice in his labor—this is the gift of God. (NKJV)

ECCLESIASTES 6:1

Wealth Is Not the Goal of Life: *There is an evil which I have seen under the sun, and it is common among men.* (NKJV)

ECCLESIASTES 6:2

A man to whom God has given riches and wealth and honor, so that he lacks nothing for himself of all he desires; yet God does not give him power to eat of it, but a foreigner consumes it. This is vanity, and it is an evil affliction. (NKJV)

SONG OF SOLOMON 8:7

Many waters cannot quench love, nor can the floods drown it. If a man would give for love, all the wealth of his house, it would be utterly despised. (NKJV)

ISAIAH 60:5

Then you shall see and become radiant, and your heart shall swell with joy; because the abundance of the sea shall be turned to you, the wealth of the Gentiles shall come to you. (NKJV)

ISAIAH 60:11

Therefore your gates shall be open continually; they shall not be shut day or night, that men may bring to you the wealth of the Gentiles, and their kings in procession. (NKJV)

JEREMIAH 15:13

Your wealth and your treasures, I will give as plunder without price, because of all your sins, throughout your territories. (NKJV)

JEREMIAH 17:3

O My mountain in the field, I will give as plunder your wealth, all your treasures, and your high places of sin within all your borders. (NKJV)

JEREMIAH 20:5

Moreover I will deliver all the wealth of this city, all its produce, and all its precious things; all the treasures of the kings of Judah I will give into the hand of their enemies, who will plunder them, seize them, and carry them to Babylon. (NKJV)

EZEKIEL 29:19

Therefore thus says the Lord GOD: "Surely I will give the land of Egypt to Nebuchadnezzar king of Babylon; he shall take away her wealth, carry off her spoil, and remove her pillage; and that will be the wages for his army." (NKJV)

EZEKIEL 30:4

The sword shall come upon Egypt, and great anguish shall be in Ethiopia, when the slain fall in Egypt, and they take away her wealth, and her foundations are broken down. (NKJV)

HOSEA 12:8

And Ephraim said, "Surely I have become rich, I have found wealth for myself; In all my labors, they shall find in me no iniquity that is sin." (NKJV)

NAHUM 2:9

Take spoil of silver! Take spoil of gold! There is no end of treasure, or wealth of every desirable prize. (NKJV)

ZECHARIAH 14:14

Judah also will fight at Jerusalem. And the wealth of all the surrounding nations shall be gathered together: Gold, silver, and apparel in great abundance. (NKJV)

REVELATION 3:17

Because you say, "I am rich, have become wealthy, and have need of nothing"—and do not know that you are wretched, miserable, poor, blind, and naked. (NKJV)

REVELATION 18:19

They threw dust on their heads and cried out, weeping and wailing, and saying, "Alas, alas, that great city, in which all who had ships on the sea became rich by her wealth! For in one hour she is made desolate." (NKJV)

Rich and Riches

GENESIS 13:2

Abram was very rich in livestock, in silver, and in gold. (NKJV)

GENESIS 14:23

That I will take nothing, from a thread to a sandal strap, and that I will not take anything that is yours, lest you should say, "I have made Abram rich." (NKJV)

GENESIS 49:20

Bread from Asher shall be rich, and he shall yield royal dainties. (NKJV)

EXODUS 30:15

The rich shall not give more and the poor shall not give less than half a shekel, when you give an offering to the LORD, to make atonement for yourselves. (NKJV)

LEVITICUS 25:47

Now if a sojourner or stranger close to you becomes rich, and one of your brethren who dwells by him becomes poor, and sells himself to the stranger or sojourner close to you, or to a member of the stranger's family. (NKJV)

NUMBERS 13:20

Whether the land is rich or poor; and whether there are forests there or not. Be of good courage. And bring some of the fruit of the land. (NKJV)

RUTH 3:10

Then he said, "Blessed are you of the LORD, my daughter! For you have shown more kindness at the end than at the beginning, in that you did not go after young men, whether poor or rich." (NKJV)

1 SAMUEL 2:7

The LORD makes poor and makes rich; He brings low and lifts up. (NKJV)

1 SAMUEL 25:2

Now there was a man in Maon whose business was in Carmel, and the man was very rich. He had three thousand sheep and a thousand goats. And he was shearing his sheep in Carmel. (NKJV)

2 SAMUEL 12:1

Then the LORD sent Nathan to David. And he came to him, and said to him: "There were two men in one city, one rich and the other poor." (NKJV)

2 SAMUEL 12:2

The rich man had exceedingly many flocks and herds. (NKJV)

2 SAMUEL 12:4

And a traveler came to the rich man, who refused to take from his own flock and from his own herd to prepare one for the wayfaring man who had come to him; but he took the poor man's lamb and prepared it for the man who had come to him. (NKJV)

2 SAMUEL 19:32

Now Barzillai was a very aged man, eighty years old. And he had provided the king with supplies while he stayed at Mahanaim, for he was a very rich man. (NKJV)

1 CHRONICLES 4:40

And they found rich, good pasture, and the land was broad, quiet, and peaceful; for some Hamites formerly lived there. (NKJV)

NEHEMIAH 9:25

And they took strong cities and a rich land, and possessed houses full of all goods, cisterns already dug, vineyards, olive groves, and fruit trees in abundance. So they ate and were filled and grew fat, And delighted themselves in your great goodness. (NKJV)

NEHEMIAH 9:35

For they have not served You in their kingdom, or in the many good things that you gave them, or in the large and rich land which You set before them; nor did they turn from their wicked works. (NKJV)

JOB 15:29

He will not be rich, nor will his wealth continue, nor will his possessions overspread the earth. (NKJV)

JOB 27:19

The rich man will lie down, but not be gathered up; he opens his eyes, and he is no more. (NKJV)

JOB 34:19

Yet He is not partial to princes, nor does He regard the rich more than the poor; for they are all the work of His hands. (NKJV)

PSALM 45:12

And the daughter of Tyre will come with a gift; the rich among the people will seek your favor. (NKJV)

PSALM 49:2

Both low and high, rich and poor together. (NKJV)

PSALM 49:16

Do not be afraid when one becomes rich, when the glory of his house is increased. (NKJV)

PSALM 66:12

You have caused men to ride over our heads; we went through fire and through water; but You brought us out to rich fulfillment. (NKJV)

PROVERBS 10:4

He who has a slack hand becomes poor, but the hand of the diligent makes rich. (NKJV)

PROVERBS 10:22

The blessing of the LORD makes one rich, and He adds no sorrow with it. (NKJV)

PROVERBS 11:25

The generous soul will be made rich, and he who waters will also be watered himself. (NKJV)

PROVERBS 13:4

The soul of a lazy man desires, and has nothing; but the soul of the diligent shall be made rich. (NKJV)

PROVERBS 13:7

There is one who makes himself rich, yet has nothing; and one who makes himself poor, yet has great riches. (NKJV)

PROVERBS 14:20

The poor man is hated even by his own neighbor, but the rich has many friends. (NKJV)

PROVERBS 18:23

The poor man uses entreaties, but the rich answers roughly. (NKJV)

PROVERBS 21:17

He who loves pleasure will be a poor man; he who loves wine and oil will not be rich. (NKJV)

PROVERBS 22:2

The rich and the poor have this in common, the LORD is the maker of them all. (NKJV)

PROVERBS 22:7

The rich rules over the poor, and the borrower is servant to the lender. (NKJV)

PROVERBS 22:16

He who oppresses the poor to increase his riches, and he who gives to the rich, will surely come to poverty. (NKJV)

COLOSSIANS 1:27

To them God willed to make known what are the riches of the glory of this mystery among the Gentiles: which is Christ in you, the hope of glory. (NKJV)

COLOSSIANS 2:2

That their hearts may be encouraged, being knit together in love, and attaining to all riches of the full assurance of understanding, to the knowledge of the mystery of God, both of the Father and of Christ. (NKJV)

1 TIMOTHY 6:17

Command those who are rich in this present age not to be haughty, nor to trust in uncertain riches but in the living God, who gives us richly all things to enjoy. (NKJV)

HEBREWS 11:26

Esteeming the reproach of Christ greater riches than the treasures in Egypt; for he looked to the reward. (NKJV)

JAMES 5:2

Your riches are corrupted, and your garments are moth-eaten. (NKJV)

REVELATION 5:12

Saying with a loud voice: "Worthy is the Lamb who was slain To receive power and riches and wisdom, And strength and honor and glory and blessing!" (NKJV)

REVELATION 18:17

"For in one hour such great riches came to nothing." Every shipmaster, all who travel by ship, sailors, and as many as trade on the sea, stood at a distance. (NKJV)

Prosperity

DEUTERONOMY 23:5–6

You shall not seek their peace nor their prosperity all your days forever.

1 SAMUEL 25:5–6

And thus you shall say to him who lives in prosperity: "Peace be to you, peace to your house, and peace to all that you have!"

1 KINGS 10:7

However I did not believe the words until I came and saw with my own eyes; and indeed the half was not told me. Your wisdom and prosperity exceed the fame of which I heard.

EZRA 9:12–13

Now therefore, do not give your daughters as wives for their sons, nor take their daughters to your sons; and never seek their peace or prosperity, that you may be strong and eat the good of the land, and leave it as an inheritance to your children forever.

JOB 15:21

Dreadful sounds are in his ears; In prosperity the destroyer comes upon him.

JOB 21:16

Indeed their prosperity is not in their hand; the counsel of the wicked is far from me.

JOB 30:15

Terrors are turned upon me; They pursue my honor as the wind, And my prosperity has passed like a cloud.

JOB 36:11–12

If they obey and serve Him, they shall spend their days in prosperity, and their years in pleasures. But if they do not obey, they shall perish by the sword, and they shall die without knowledge.

PSALM 25:13

He himself shall dwell in prosperity, and his descendants shall inherit the earth.

PSALM 30:6–7

Now in my prosperity I said, "I shall never be moved." LORD, by Your favor You have made my mountain stand strong; You hid Your face, and I was troubled.

PSALM 35:27

Let them shout for joy and be glad, Who favor my righteous cause; And let them say continually, "Let the LORD be magnified, Who has pleasure in the prosperity of His servant."

PSALM 68:6

God sets the solitary in families; He brings out those who are bound into prosperity; But the rebellious dwell in a dry land.

PSALM 73:3

For I was envious of the boastful, when I saw the prosperity of the wicked.

PSALM 118:25

Save now, I pray, O LORD; O LORD, I pray, send now prosperity.

PSALM 122:7

Peace be within your walls, Prosperity within your palaces.

ECCLESIASTES 7:14

In the day of prosperity be joyful, But in the day of adversity consider: Surely God has appointed the one as well as the other, So that man can find out nothing that will come after him.

JEREMIAH 22:21

I spoke to you in your prosperity, But you said, "I will not hear." This has been your manner from your youth, That you did not obey My voice.

JEREMIAH 33:9

Then it shall be to Me a name of joy, a praise, and an honor before all nations of the earth, who shall hear all the good that I do to them; they shall fear and tremble for all the goodness and all the prosperity that I provide for it.

LAMENTATIONS 3:17–18

You have moved my soul far from peace; I have forgotten prosperity. And I said, "My strength and my hope have perished from the LORD."

DANIEL 4:27

Therefore, O king, let my advice be acceptable to you; break off your sins by being righteous, and your iniquities by showing mercy to the poor. Perhaps there may be a lengthening of your prosperity.

DANIEL 8:25

Through his cunning He shall cause deceit to prosper under his rule; And he shall exalt himself in his heart. He shall destroy many in their prosperity. He shall even rise against the Prince of princes; But he shall be broken without human means.

ZECHARIAH 1:17

Again proclaim, saying, "Thus says the LORD of hosts: 'My cities shall again spread out through prosperity; The LORD will again comfort Zion, And will again choose Jerusalem.'"

ACTS 19:25

He called them together with the workers of similar occupation, and said: "Men, you know that we have our prosperity by this trade."

ACTS 24:2–4

And when he was called upon, Tertullus began his accusation, saying: "Seeing that through you we enjoy great peace, and prosperity is being brought to this nation by your foresight, we accept it always and in all places, most noble Felix, with all thankfulness."

Prosperous

GENESIS 24:2

And the man, wondering at her, remained silent so as to know whether the LORD had made his journey prosperous or not. (NKJV)

GENESIS 26:13

The man began to prosper, and continued prospering until he became very prosperous. (NKJV)

GENESIS 30:4

Thus the man became exceedingly prosperous, and had large flocks, female and male servants, and camels and donkeys. (NKJV)

JOSHUA 1:8

This Book of the Law shall not depart from your mouth, but you shall meditate in it day and night, that you may observe to do according to all that is written in it. For then you will make your way prosperous, and then you will have good success. (NKJV)

JUDGES 18:5

So they said to him, "Please inquire of God, that we may know whether the journey on which we go will be prosperous." (NKJV)

PSALM 22:29

All the prosperous of the earth shall eat and worship; all those who go down to the dust shall bow before Him, even he who cannot keep himself alive. (NKJV)

ZECHARIAH 7:7

Should you not have obeyed the words which the LORD proclaimed through the former prophets when Jerusalem and the cities around it were inhabited and prosperous, and the South and the Lowland were inhabited? (NKJV)

ZECHARIAH 8:12

For the seed shall be prosperous, the vine shall give its fruit, the ground shall give her increase, and the heavens shall give their dew—I will cause the remnant of this people to possess all these. (NKJV)

Prosper

GENESIS 24:40

But he said to me, "The LORD, before whom I walk, will send His angel with you and prosper your way; and you shall take a wife for my son from my family and from my father's house." (NKJV)

GENESIS 24:42

And this day I came to the well and said, "O LORD God of my master Abraham, if you will now prosper the way in which I go." (NKJV)

GENESIS 26:13

The man began to prosper, and continued prospering until he became very prosperous. (NKJV)

GENESIS 39:3

And his master saw that the LORD was with him and that the LORD made all he did to prosper in his hand. (NKJV)

GENESIS 39:23

The keeper of the prison did not look into anything that was under Joseph's authority, because the LORD was with him; and whatever he did, the LORD made it prosper. (NKJV)

DEUTERONOMY 28:29

And you shall grope at noonday, as a blind man gropes in darkness; you shall not prosper in your ways; you shall be only oppressed and plundered continually, and no one shall save you. (NKJV)

DEUTERONOMY 29:9

Therefore keep the words of this covenant, and do them, that you may prosper in all that you do. (NKJV)

DEUTERONOMY 30:5

Then the LORD your God will bring you to the land which your fathers possessed, and you shall possess it. He will prosper you and multiply you more than your fathers. (NKJV)

JOSHUA 1:7

Only be strong and very courageous, that you may observe to do according to all the law which Moses My servant commanded you; do not turn from it to the right hand or to the left, that you may prosper wherever you go. (NKJV)

RUTH 4:11

And all the people who were at the gate, and the elders, said, "We are witnesses. The LORD make the woman who is coming to your house like Rachel and Leah, the two who built the house of Israel; and may you prosper in Ephrathah and be famous in Bethlehem." *(NKJV)*

1 KINGS 2:3

And keep the charge of the LORD your God: to walk in His ways, to keep His statutes, His commandments, His judgments, and His testimonies, as it is written in the Law of Moses, that you may prosper in all that you do and wherever you turn. *(NKJV)*

1 KINGS 22:12

And all the prophets prophesied so, saying, "Go up to Ramoth Gilead and prosper, for the LORD will deliver it into the king's hand." *(NKJV)*

1 KINGS 22:15

Then he came to the king; and the king said to him, "Micaiah, shall we go to war against Ramoth Gilead, or shall we refrain?" And he answered him, "Go and prosper, for the LORD will deliver it into the hand of the king!" *(NKJV)*

1 CHRONICLES 22:11

Now, my son, may the LORD be with you; and may you prosper, and build the house of the LORD your God, as He has said to you. *(NKJV)*

1 CHRONICLES 22:13

Then you will prosper, if you take care to fulfill the statutes and judgments with which the LORD charged Moses concerning Israel. Be strong and of good courage; do not fear nor be dismayed. *(NKJV)*

2 CHRONICLES 13:12

Now look, God Himself is with us as our head, and His priests with sounding trumpets to sound the alarm against you. O children of Israel, do not fight against the LORD God of your fathers, for you shall not prosper! *(NKJV)*

2 CHRONICLES 18:11

And all the prophets prophesied so, saying, "Go up to Ramoth Gilead and prosper, for the LORD will deliver it into the king's hand." *(NKJV)*

2 CHRONICLES 18:14

Then he came to the king; and the king said to him, "Micaiah, shall we go to war against Ramoth Gilead, or shall I refrain?" And he said, "Go and prosper, and they shall be delivered into your hand!" *(NKJV)*

2 CHRONICLES 20:20

So they rose early in the morning and went out into the Wilderness of Tekoa; and as they went out, Jehoshaphat stood and said, "Hear me, O Judah and you inhabitants of Jerusalem: Believe in the LORD your God, and you shall be established; believe His prophets, and you shall prosper." *(NKJV)*

2 CHRONICLES 24:20

Then the Spirit of God came upon Zechariah the son of Jehoiada the priest, who stood above the people, and said to them, "Thus says God: 'Why do you transgress the commandments of the LORD, so that you cannot prosper? Because you have forsaken the LORD, He also has forsaken you.'" *(NKJV)*

2 CHRONICLES 26:5

He sought God in the days of Zechariah, who had understanding in the visions of God; and as long as he sought the LORD, God made him prosper. *(NKJV)*

NEHEMIAH 1:11

"O LORD, I pray, please let Your ear be attentive to the prayer of Your servant, and to the prayer of Your servants who desire to fear Your name; and let Your servant prosper this day, I pray, and grant him mercy in the sight of this man." For I was the king's cupbearer. *(NKJV)*

NEHEMIAH 2:20

So I answered them, and said to them, "The God of heaven Himself will prosper us; therefore we His servants will arise and build, but you have no heritage or right or memorial in Jerusalem." (NKJV)

JOB 8:6

If you were pure and upright, surely now He would awake for you, and prosper your rightful dwelling place. (NKJV)

JOB 12:6

The tents of robbers prosper, and those who provoke God are secure—in what God provides by His hand. (NKJV)

PSALM 1:3

He shall be like a tree planted by the rivers of water, that brings forth its fruit in its season, whose leaf also shall not wither; and whatever he does shall prosper. (NKJV)

PSALM 122:6

Pray for the peace of Jerusalem: May they prosper who love you. (NKJV)

PROVERBS 28:13

He who covers his sins will not prosper, but whoever confesses and forsakes them will have mercy. (NKJV)

ECCLESIASTES 11:6

In the morning sow your seed, and in the evening do not withhold your hand; for you do not know which will prosper, either this or that, or whether both alike will be good. (NKJV)

ISAIAH 48:15

I, even I, have spoken; yes, I have called him, I have brought him, and his way will prosper. (NKJV)

ISAIAH 53:10

Yet it pleased the LORD to bruise Him; he has put Him to grief. When You make His soul an offering for sin, he shall see His seed, He shall prolong His days, and the pleasure of the LORD shall prosper in His hand. (NKJV)

ISAIAH 54:17

"No weapon formed against you shall prosper, and every tongue which rises against you in judgment you shall condemn. This is the heritage of the servants of the LORD, and their righteousness is from Me," says the LORD. (NKJV)

ISAIAH 55:11

So shall My word be that goes forth from My mouth; it shall not return to Me void, but it shall accomplish what I please, and it shall prosper in the thing for which I sent it. (NKJV)

JEREMIAH 2:37

Indeed you will go forth from him with your hands on your head; for the LORD has rejected your trusted allies, and you will not prosper by them. (NKJV)

JEREMIAH 5:28

They have grown fat, they are sleek; yes, they surpass the deeds of the wicked; they do not plead the cause, the cause of the fatherless; yet they prosper, and the right of the needy they do not defend. (NKJV)

JEREMIAH 10:21

For the shepherds have become dull-hearted, and have not sought the LORD; therefore they shall not prosper, and all their flocks shall be scattered. (NKJV)

JEREMIAH 12:1

Righteous are You, O LORD, when I plead with You; yet let me talk with You about Your judgments. Why does the way of the wicked prosper? Why are those happy who deal so treacherously? (NKJV)

JEREMIAH 20:11

But the LORD is with me as a mighty, awesome One. Therefore my persecutors will stumble, and will not *prevail. They will be greatly ashamed, for they will not prosper. Their everlasting confusion will never be forgotten. (NKJV)*

JEREMIAH 22:30

Thus says the Lᴏʀᴅ: "Write this man down as childless, a man who shall not prosper in his days; for none of his descendants shall prosper, sitting on the throne of David, and ruling anymore in Judah." (NKJV)

JEREMIAH 23:5–6

"Behold, the days are coming," says the Lᴏʀᴅ, "That I will raise to David a Branch of righteousness; a King shall reign and prosper, and execute judgment and righteousness in the earth. In His days Judah will be saved, and Israel will dwell safely; now this is His name by which He will be called: THE LORD OUR RIGHTEOUSNESS." (NKJV)

LAMENTATIONS 1:5

Her adversaries have become the master, her enemies prosper; for the Lᴏʀᴅ has afflicted her because of the multitude of her transgressions. Her children have gone into captivity before the enemy. (NKJV)

EZEKIEL 17:15

But he rebelled against him by sending his ambassadors to Egypt, that they might give him horses and many people. Will he prosper? Will he who does such things escape? Can he break a covenant and still be delivered? (NKJV)

DANIEL 8:24

His power shall be mighty, but not by his own power; he shall destroy fearfully, and shall prosper and thrive; he shall destroy the mighty, and also the holy people. (NKJV)

DANIEL 8:25

Through his cunning he shall cause deceit to prosper under his rule; and he shall exalt himself in his heart. He shall destroy many in their prosperity. He shall

even rise against the Prince of princes; but he shall be broken without human means. (NKJV)

DANIEL 11:27

Both these kings' hearts shall be bent on evil, and they shall speak lies at the same table; but it shall not prosper, for the end will still be at the appointed time. (NKJV)

DANIEL 11:36

Then the king shall do according to his own will: he shall exalt and magnify himself above every god, shall speak blasphemies against the God of gods, and shall prosper till the wrath has been accomplished; for what has been determined shall be done. (NKJV)

1 CORINTHIANS 16:2

On the first day of the week let each one of you lay something aside, storing up as he may prosper, that there be no collections when I come. (NKJV)

3 JOHN 1:2

Beloved, I pray that you may prosper in all things and be in health, just as your soul prospers. (NKJV)

SCRIPTURE REFERENCES ON OFFERINGS

Offering

GENESIS 4:3

And in the process of time it came to pass that Cain brought an offering of the fruit of the ground to the LORD.

GENESIS 4:4

Abel also brought of the firstborn of his flock and of their fat. And the LORD respected Abel and his offering,

GENESIS 4:5

But He did not respect Cain and his offering. And Cain was very angry, and his countenance fell.

GENESIS 22:2

And He said, "Take now your son, your only son Isaac, whom you love, and go to the land of Moriah, and offer him there as a burnt offering on one of the mountains of which I shall tell you."

GENESIS 22:3

So Abraham rose early in the morning and saddled his donkey, and took two of his young men with him, and Isaac his son; and he split the wood for the burnt offering, and arose and went to the place of which God had told him.

GENESIS 22:6

So Abraham took the wood of the burnt offering and laid it on Isaac his son; and he took the fire in his hand, and a knife, and the two of them went together.

GENESIS 22:7

But Isaac spoke to Abraham his father and said, "My father!" And he said, "Here I am, my son." Then he said, "Look, the fire and the wood, but where is the lamb for a burnt offering?"

GENESIS 22:8

And Abraham said, "My son, God will provide for Himself the lamb for a burnt offering." So the two of them went together.

GENESIS 22:13

Then Abraham lifted his eyes and looked, and there behind him was a ram caught in a thicket by its horns. So Abraham went and took the ram, and offered it up for a burnt offering instead of his son.

GENESIS 35:14

So Jacob set up a pillar in the place where He talked with him, a pillar of stone; and he poured a drink offering on it, and he poured oil on it.

EXODUS 18:12

Then Jethro, Moses' father-in-law, took a burnt offering and other sacrifices to offer to God. And Aaron came with all the elders of Israel to eat bread with Moses' father-in-law before God.

EXODUS 25:2

Speak to the children of Israel, that they bring Me an offering. From everyone who gives it willingly with his heart you shall take My offering.

EXODUS 25:3

And this is the offering which you shall take from them: gold, silver, and bronze.

EXODUS 29:14

But the flesh of the bull, with its skin and its offal, you shall burn with fire outside the camp. It is a sin offering.

EXODUS 29:18

And you shall burn the whole ram on the altar. It is a burnt offering to the Lord; it is a sweet aroma, an offering made by fire to the Lord.

EXODUS 29:24

And you shall put all these in the hands of Aaron and in the hands of his sons, and you shall wave them as a wave offering before the Lord.

EXODUS 29:25

You shall receive them back from their hands and burn them on the altar as a burnt offering, as a sweet aroma before the Lord. It is an offering made by fire to the Lord.

EXODUS 29:26

Then you shall take the breast of the ram of Aaron's consecration and wave it as a wave offering before the Lord; and it shall be your portion.

EXODUS 29:27

And from the ram of the consecration you shall consecrate the breast of the wave offering which is waved, and the thigh of the heave offering which is raised, of that which is for Aaron and of that which is for his sons.

EXODUS 29:28

It shall be from the children of Israel for Aaron and his sons by a statute forever. For it is a heave offering; it shall be a heave offering from the children of Israel from the sacrifices of their peace offerings, that is, their heave offering to the Lord.

EXODUS 29:36

And you shall offer a bull every day as a sin offering for atonement. You shall cleanse the altar when you make atonement for it, and you shall anoint it to sanctify it.

EXODUS 29:40

With the one lamb shall be one-tenth of an ephah of flour mixed with one-fourth of a hin of pressed oil, and one-fourth of a hin of wine as a drink offering.

EXODUS 29:41

And the other lamb you shall offer at twilight; and you shall offer with it the grain offering and the drink offering, as in the morning, for a sweet aroma, an offering made by fire to the Lord.

EXODUS 29:42

This shall be a continual burnt offering throughout your generations at the door of the tabernacle of meeting before the Lord, where I will meet you to speak with you.

EXODUS 30:9

You shall not offer strange incense on it, or a burnt offering, or a grain offering; nor shall you pour a drink offering on it.

EXODUS 30:10

And Aaron shall make atonement upon its horns once a year with the blood of the sin offering of atonement; once a year he shall make atonement upon it throughout your generations. It is most holy to the Lord.

EXODUS 30:13

This is what everyone among those who are numbered shall give: half a shekel according to the shekel of the sanctuary (a shekel is twenty gerahs). The half-shekel shall be an offering to the Lord.

EXODUS 30:14

Everyone included among those who are numbered, from twenty years old and above, shall give an offering to the Lord.

EXODUS 30:15

The rich shall not give more and the poor shall not give less than half a shekel, when you give an offering to the Lord, to make atonement for yourselves.

EXODUS 30:20

When they go into the tabernacle of meeting, or when they come near the altar to minister, to burn an offering made by fire to the Lord, they shall wash with water, lest they die.

EXODUS 30:28

The altar of burnt offering with all its utensils, and the laver and its base.

EXODUS 31:9

The altar of burnt offering with all its utensils, and the laver and its base.

EXODUS 32:6

Then they rose early on the next day, offered burnt offerings, and brought peace offerings; and the people sat down to eat and drink, and rose up to play.

EXODUS 35:5

Take from among you an offering to the Lord. Whoever is of a willing heart, let him bring it as an offering to the Lord: gold, silver, and bronze.

EXODUS 35:16

The altar of burnt offering with its bronze grating, its poles, all its utensils, and the laver and its base.

EXODUS 35:21

Then everyone came whose heart was stirred, and everyone whose spirit was willing, and they brought the Lord's offering for the work of the tabernacle of meeting, for all its service, and for the holy garments.

EXODUS 35:22

They came, both men and women, as many as had a willing heart, and brought earrings and nose rings, rings and necklaces, all jewelry of gold, that is, every man who made an offering of gold to the Lord.

EXODUS 35:24

Everyone who offered an offering of silver or bronze

brought the Lord's offering. And everyone with whom was found acacia wood for any work of the service, brought it.

EXODUS 35:29

The children of Israel brought a freewill offering to the Lord, all the men and women whose hearts were willing to bring material for all kinds of work which the Lord, by the hand of Moses, had commanded to be done.

EXODUS 36:3

And they received from Moses all the offering which the children of Israel had brought for the work of the service of making the sanctuary. So they continued bringing to him freewill offerings every morning.

EXODUS 36:6

So Moses gave a commandment, and they caused it to be proclaimed throughout the camp, saying, "Let neither man nor woman do any more work for the offering of the sanctuary." And the people were restrained from bringing.

EXODUS 38:1

He made the altar of burnt offering of acacia wood; five cubits was its length and five cubits its width—it was square—and its height was three cubits.

EXODUS 38:24

All the gold that was used in all the work of the holy place, that is, the gold of the offering, was twenty-nine talents and seven hundred and thirty shekels, according to the shekel of the sanctuary.

EXODUS 38:29

The offering of bronze was seventy talents and two thousand four hundred shekels.

EXODUS 40:6

Then you shall set the altar of the burnt offering before the door of the tabernacle of the tent of meeting.

EXODUS 40:10

You shall anoint the altar of the burnt offering and all its utensils, and consecrate the altar. The altar shall be most holy.

EXODUS 40:29

And he put the altar of burnt offering before the door of the tabernacle of the tent of meeting, and offered upon it the burnt offering and the grain offering, as the LORD had commanded Moses.

LEVITICUS 1:2

"Speak to the children of Israel, and say to them: 'When any one of you brings an offering to the LORD, you shall bring your offering of the livestock—of the herd and of the flock.'"

LEVITICUS 1:3

If his offering is a burnt sacrifice of the herd, let him offer a male without blemish; he shall offer it of his own free will at the door of the tabernacle of meeting before the LORD.

LEVITICUS 1:4

Then he shall put his hand on the head of the burnt offering, and it will be accepted on his behalf to make atonement for him.

LEVITICUS 1:6

And he shall skin the burnt offering and cut it into its pieces.

LEVITICUS 1:9

But he shall wash its entrails and its legs with water. And the priest shall burn all on the altar as a burnt sacrifice, an offering made by fire, a sweet aroma to the LORD.

LEVITICUS 1:10

If his offering is of the flocks—of the sheep or of the goats—as a burnt sacrifice, he shall bring a male without blemish.

LEVITICUS 1:13

But he shall wash the entrails and the legs with water. Then the priest shall bring it all and burn it on the altar; it is a burnt sacrifice, an offering made by fire, a sweet aroma to the LORD.

LEVITICUS 1:14

And if the burnt sacrifice of his offering to the LORD is of birds, then he shall bring his offering of turtledoves or young pigeons.

LEVITICUS 1:17

Then he shall split it at its wings, but shall not divide it completely; and the priest shall burn it on the altar, on the wood that is on the fire. It is a burnt sacrifice, an offering made by fire, a sweet aroma to the LORD.

LEVITICUS 2:1

When anyone offers a grain offering to the LORD, his offering shall be of fine flour. And he shall pour oil on it, and put frankincense on it.

LEVITICUS 2:2

He shall bring it to Aaron's sons, the priests, one of whom shall take from it his handful of fine flour and oil with all the frankincense. And the priest shall burn it as a memorial on the altar, an offering made by fire, a sweet aroma to the LORD.

LEVITICUS 2:3

The rest of the grain offering shall be Aaron's and his sons'. It is most holy of the offerings to the LORD made by fire.

LEVITICUS 2:4

And if you bring as an offering a grain offering baked in the oven, it shall be unleavened cakes of fine flour mixed with oil, or unleavened wafers anointed with oil.

LEVITICUS 2:5

But if your offering is a grain offering baked in a pan, it shall be of fine flour, unleavened, mixed with oil.

SCRIPTURE REFERENCES ON OFFERINGS

LEVITICUS 2:6

You shall break it in pieces and pour oil on it; it is a grain offering.

LEVITICUS 2:7

If your offering is a grain offering baked in a covered pan, it shall be made of fine flour with oil.

LEVITICUS 2:8

You shall bring the grain offering that is made of these things to the LORD. And when it is presented to the priest, he shall bring it to the altar.

LEVITICUS 2:9

Then the priest shall take from the grain offering a memorial portion, and burn it on the altar. It is an offering made by fire, a sweet aroma to the LORD.

LEVITICUS 2:10

And what is left of the grain offering shall be Aaron's and his sons'. It is most holy of the offerings to the LORD made by fire.

LEVITICUS 2:11

No grain offering which you bring to the LORD shall be made with leaven, for you shall burn no leaven nor any honey in any offering to the LORD made by fire.

LEVITICUS 2:13

And every offering of your grain offering you shall season with salt; you shall not allow the salt of the covenant of your God to be lacking from your grain offering. With all your offerings you shall offer salt.

LEVITICUS 2:14

If you offer a grain offering of your firstfruits to the LORD, you shall offer for the grain offering of your firstfruits green heads of grain roasted on the fire, grain beaten from full heads.

LEVITICUS 2:15

And you shall put oil on it, and lay frankincense on it. It is a grain offering.

LEVITICUS 2:16

Then the priest shall burn the memorial portion: part of its beaten grain and part of its oil, with all the frankincense, as an offering made by fire to the LORD.

LEVITICUS 3:1

When his offering is a sacrifice of a peace offering, if he offers it of the herd, whether male or female, he shall offer it without blemish before the LORD.

LEVITICUS 3:2

And he shall lay his hand on the head of his offering, and kill it at the door of the tabernacle of meeting; and Aaron's sons, the priests, shall sprinkle the blood all around on the altar.

LEVITICUS 3:3

Then he shall offer from the sacrifice of the peace offering an offering made by fire to the LORD. The fat that covers the entrails and all the fat that is on the entrails.

LEVITICUS 3:5

And Aaron's sons shall burn it on the altar upon the burnt sacrifice, which is on the wood that is on the fire, as an offering made by fire, a sweet aroma to the LORD.

LEVITICUS 3:6

If his offering as a sacrifice of a peace offering to the LORD is of the flock, whether male or female, he shall offer it without blemish.

LEVITICUS 3:7

If he offers a lamb as his offering, then he shall offer it before the LORD.

LEVITICUS 3:8

And he shall lay his hand on the head of his offering, and kill it before the tabernacle of meeting; and Aaron's sons shall sprinkle its blood all around on the altar.

LEVITICUS 3:9

Then he shall offer from the sacrifice of the peace offering, as an offering made by fire to the LORD, its fat and the whole fat tail which he shall remove close to the backbone. And the fat that covers the entrails and all the fat that is on the entrails.

LEVITICUS 3:11

And the priest shall burn them on the altar as food, an offering made by fire to the LORD.

LEVITICUS 3:12

And if his offering is a goat, then he shall offer it before the LORD.

LEVITICUS 3:14

Then he shall offer from it his offering, as an offering made by fire to the LORD. The fat that covers the entrails and all the fat that is on the entrails.

LEVITICUS 3:16

And the priest shall burn them on the altar as food, an offering made by fire for a sweet aroma; all the fat is the LORD's.

LEVITICUS 4:3

If the anointed priest sins, bringing guilt on the people, then let him offer to the LORD for his sin which he has sinned a young bull without blemish as a sin offering.

LEVITICUS 4:7

And the priest shall put some of the blood on the horns of the altar of sweet incense before the LORD, which is in the tabernacle of meeting; and he shall pour the remaining blood of the bull at the base of the altar of the burnt offering, which is at the door of the tabernacle of meeting.

LEVITICUS 4:8

He shall take from it all the fat of the bull as the sin offering. The fat that covers the entrails and all the fat which is on the entrails.

LEVITICUS 4:10

As it was taken from the bull of the sacrifice of the peace offering; and the priest shall burn them on the altar of the burnt offering.

LEVITICUS 4:18

And he shall put some of the blood on the horns of the altar which is before the LORD, which is in the tabernacle of meeting; and he shall pour the remaining blood at the base of the altar of burnt offering, which is at the door of the tabernacle of meeting.

LEVITICUS 4:20

And he shall do with the bull as he did with the bull as a sin offering; thus he shall do with it. So the priest shall make atonement for them, and it shall be forgiven them.

LEVITICUS 4:21

Then he shall carry the bull outside the camp, and burn it as he burned the first bull. It is a sin offering for the assembly.

LEVITICUS 4:23

Or if his sin which he has committed comes to his knowledge, he shall bring as his offering a kid of the goats, a male without blemish.

LEVITICUS 4:24

And he shall lay his hand on the head of the goat, and kill it at the place where they kill the burnt offering before the LORD. It is a sin offering.

LEVITICUS 4:25

The priest shall take some of the blood of the sin offering with his finger, put it on the horns of the altar of burnt offering, and pour its blood at the base of the altar of burnt offering.

LEVITICUS 4:26

And he shall burn all its fat on the altar, like the fat of the sacrifice of the peace offering. So the priest shall

SCRIPTURE REFERENCES ON OFFERINGS

make atonement for him concerning his sin, and it shall be forgiven him.

LEVITICUS 4:28

Or if his sin which he has committed comes to his knowledge, then he shall bring as his offering a kid of the goats, a female without blemish, for his sin which he has committed.

LEVITICUS 4:29

And he shall lay his hand on the head of the sin offering, and kill the sin offering at the place of the burnt offering.

LEVITICUS 4:30

Then the priest shall take some of its blood with his finger, put it on the horns of the altar of burnt offering, and pour all the remaining blood at the base of the altar.

LEVITICUS 4:31

He shall remove all its fat, as fat is removed from the sacrifice of the peace offering; and the priest shall burn it on the altar for a sweet aroma to the Lord. So the priest shall make atonement for him, and it shall be forgiven him.

LEVITICUS 4:32

If he brings a lamb as his sin offering, he shall bring a female without blemish.

LEVITICUS 4:33

Then he shall lay his hand on the head of the sin offering, and kill it as a sin offering at the place where they kill the burnt offering.

LEVITICUS 4:34

The priest shall take some of the blood of the sin offering with his finger, put it on the horns of the altar of burnt offering, and pour all the remaining blood at the base of the altar.

LEVITICUS 4:35

He shall remove all its fat, as the fat of the lamb is removed from the sacrifice of the peace offering. Then the priest shall burn it on the altar, according to the offerings made by fire to the Lord. So the priest shall make atonement for his sin that he has committed, and it shall be forgiven him.

LEVITICUS 5:6

And he shall bring his trespass offering to the Lord for his sin which he has committed, a female from the flock, a lamb or a kid of the goats as a sin offering. So the priest shall make atonement for him concerning his sin.

LEVITICUS 5:7

If he is not able to bring a lamb, then he shall bring to the Lord, for his trespass which he has committed, two turtledoves or two young pigeons: one as a sin offering and the other as a burnt offering.

LEVITICUS 5:8

And he shall bring them to the priest, who shall offer that which is for the sin offering first, and wring off its head from its neck, but shall not divide it completely.

LEVITICUS 5:9

Then he shall sprinkle some of the blood of the sin offering on the side of the altar, and the rest of the blood shall be drained out at the base of the altar. It is a sin offering.

LEVITICUS 5:10

And he shall offer the second as a burnt offering according to the prescribed manner. So the priest shall make atonement on his behalf for his sin which he has committed, and it shall be forgiven him.

LEVITICUS 5:11

But if he is not able to bring two turtledoves or two young pigeons, then he who sinned shall bring for his offering one-tenth of an ephah of fine flour as a sin offering. He shall put no oil on it, nor shall he put frankincense on it, for it is a sin offering.

Leviticus 5:12

Then he shall bring it to the priest, and the priest shall take his handful of it as a memorial portion, and burn it on the altar according to the offerings made by fire to the Lord. It is a sin offering.

Leviticus 5:13

The priest shall make atonement for him, for his sin that he has committed in any of these matters; and it shall be forgiven him. The rest shall be the priest's as a grain offering.

Leviticus 5:15

If a person commits a trespass, and sins unintentionally in regard to the holy things of the Lord, then he shall bring to the Lord as his trespass offering a ram without blemish from the flocks, with your valuation in shekels of silver according to the shekel of the sanctuary, as a trespass offering.

Leviticus 5:16

And he shall make restitution for the harm that he has done in regard to the holy thing, and shall add one-fifth to it and give it to the priest. So the priest shall make atonement for him with the ram of the trespass offering, and it shall be forgiven him.

Leviticus 5:18

And he shall bring to the priest a ram without blemish from the flock, with your valuation, as a trespass offering. So the priest shall make atonement for him regarding his ignorance in which he erred and did not know it, and it shall be forgiven him.

Leviticus 5:19

It is a trespass offering; he has certainly trespassed against the Lord.

Leviticus 6:5

Or all that about which he has sworn falsely. He shall restore its full value, add one-fifth more to it, and give it to whomever it belongs, on the day of his trespass offering.

Leviticus 6:6

And he shall bring his trespass offering to the Lord, a ram without blemish from the flock, with your valuation, as a trespass offering, to the priest.

Leviticus 6:9

Command Aaron and his sons, saying, "This is the law of the burnt offering: The burnt offering shall be on the hearth upon the altar all night until morning, and the fire of the altar shall be kept burning on it."

Leviticus 6:10

And the priest shall put on his linen garment, and his linen trousers he shall put on his body, and take up the ashes of the burnt offering which the fire has consumed on the altar, and he shall put them beside the altar.

Leviticus 6:12

And the fire on the altar shall be kept burning on it; it shall not be put out. And the priest shall burn wood on it every morning, and lay the burnt offering in order on it; and he shall burn on it the fat of the peace offerings.

Leviticus 6:14

This is the law of the grain offering: The sons of Aaron shall offer it on the altar before the Lord.

Leviticus 6:15

He shall take from it his handful of the fine flour of the grain offering, with its oil, and all the frankincense which is on the grain offering, and shall burn it on the altar for a sweet aroma, as a memorial to the Lord.

LEVITICUS 6:17

It shall not be baked with leaven. I have given it as their portion of My offerings made by fire; it is most holy, like the sin offering and the trespass offering.

LEVITICUS 6:20

This is the offering of Aaron and his sons, which they shall offer to the Lord, beginning on the day when he is anointed: one-tenth of an ephah of fine flour as a daily grain offering, half of it in the morning and half of it at night.

LEVITICUS 6:21

It shall be made in a pan with oil. When it is mixed, you shall bring it in. The baked pieces of the grain offering you shall offer for a sweet aroma to the Lord.

LEVITICUS 6:23

For every grain offering for the priest shall be wholly burned. It shall not be eaten.

LEVITICUS 6:25

Speak to Aaron and to his sons, saying, "This is the law of the sin offering: In the place where the burnt offering is killed, the sin offering shall be killed before the Lord. It is most holy."

LEVITICUS 6:30

But no sin offering from which any of the blood is brought into the tabernacle of meeting, to make atonement in the holy place, shall be eaten. It shall be burned in the fire.

LEVITICUS 7:1

Likewise this is the law of the trespass offering (it is most holy).

LEVITICUS 7:2

In the place where they kill the burnt offering they shall kill the trespass offering. And its blood he shall sprinkle all around on the altar.

LEVITICUS 7:5

And the priest shall burn them on the altar as an offering made by fire to the Lord. It is a trespass offering.

LEVITICUS 7:7

The trespass offering is like the sin offering; there is one law for them both: the priest who makes atonement with it shall have it.

LEVITICUS 7:8

And the priest who offers anyone's burnt offering, that priest shall have for himself the skin of the burnt offering which he has offered.

LEVITICUS 7:9

Also every grain offering that is baked in the oven and all that is prepared in the covered pan, or in a pan, shall be the priest's who offers it.

LEVITICUS 7:10

Every grain offering whether mixed with oil, or dry, shall belong to all the sons of Aaron, to one as much as the other.

LEVITICUS 7:13

Besides the cakes, as his offering he shall offer leavened bread with the sacrifice of thanksgiving of his peace offering.

LEVITICUS 7:14

And from it he shall offer one cake from each offering as a heave offering to the Lord. It shall belong to the priest who sprinkles the blood of the peace offering.

LEVITICUS 7:15

The flesh of the sacrifice of his peace offering for thanksgiving shall be eaten the same day it is offered. He shall not leave any of it until morning.

LEVITICUS 7:16

But if the sacrifice of his offering is a vow or a voluntary offering, it shall be eaten the same day that he offers his sacrifice; but on the next day the remainder of it also may be eaten.

Leviticus 7:18

And if any of the flesh of the sacrifice of his peace offering is eaten at all on the third day, it shall not be accepted, nor shall it be imputed to him; it shall be an abomination to him who offers it, and the person who eats of it shall bear guilt.

Leviticus 7:20

But the person who eats the flesh of the sacrifice of the peace offering that belongs to the Lord, while he is unclean, that person shall be cut off from his people.

Leviticus 7:21

Moreover the person who touches any unclean thing, such as human uncleanness, an unclean animal, or any abominable unclean thing, and who eats the flesh of the sacrifice of the peace offering that belongs to the Lord, that person shall be cut off from his people.

Leviticus 7:25

For whoever eats the fat of the animal of which men offer an offering made by fire to the Lord, the person who eats it shall be cut off from his people.

Leviticus 7:29

Speak to the children of Israel, saying: "He who offers the sacrifice of his peace offering to the Lord shall bring his offering to the Lord from the sacrifice of his peace offering."

Leviticus 7:30

His own hands shall bring the offerings made by fire to the Lord. The fat with the breast he shall bring, that the breast may be waved as a wave offering before the Lord.

Leviticus 7:32

Also the right thigh you shall give to the priest as a heave offering from the sacrifices of your peace offerings.

Leviticus 7:33

He among the sons of Aaron, who offers the blood of the peace offering and the fat, shall have the right thigh for his part.

Leviticus 7:34

For the breast of the wave offering and the thigh of the heave offering I have taken from the children of Israel, from the sacrifices of their peace offerings, and I have given them to Aaron the priest and to his sons from the children of Israel by a statute forever.

Leviticus 7:37

This is the law of the burnt offering, the grain offering, the sin offering, the trespass offering, the consecrations, and the sacrifice of the peace offering.

Leviticus 8:2

Take Aaron and his sons with him, and the garments, the anointing oil, a bull as the sin offering, two rams, and a basket of unleavened bread.

Leviticus 8:14

And he brought the bull for the sin offering. Then Aaron and his sons laid their hands on the head of the bull for the sin offering.

Leviticus 8:18

Then he brought the ram as the burnt offering. And Aaron and his sons laid their hands on the head of the ram.

Leviticus 8:21

Then he washed the entrails and the legs in water. And Moses burned the whole ram on the altar. It was a burnt sacrifice for a sweet aroma, an offering made by fire to the Lord, as the Lord had commanded Moses.

Leviticus 8:27

And he put all these in Aaron's hands and in his sons' hands, and waved them as a wave offering before the Lord.

LEVITICUS 8:28

Then Moses took them from their hands and burned them on the altar, on the burnt offering. They were consecration offerings for a sweet aroma. That was an offering made by fire to the LORD.

LEVITICUS 8:29

And Moses took the breast and waved it as a wave offering before the LORD. It was Moses' part of the ram of consecration, as the LORD had commanded Moses.

LEVITICUS 9:2

And he said to Aaron, "Take for yourself a young bull as a sin offering and a ram as a burnt offering, without blemish, and offer them before the LORD."

LEVITICUS 9:3

And to the children of Israel you shall speak, saying, "Take a kid of the goats as a sin offering, and a calf and a lamb, both of the first year, without blemish, as a burnt offering."

LEVITICUS 9:4

Also a bull and a ram as peace offerings, to sacrifice before the LORD, and a grain offering mixed with oil; for today the LORD will appear to you.

LEVITICUS 9:7

And Moses said to Aaron, "Go to the altar, offer your sin offering and your burnt offering, and make atonement for yourself and for the people. Offer the offering of the people, and make atonement for them, as the LORD commanded."

LEVITICUS 9:8

Aaron therefore went to the altar and killed the calf of the sin offering, which was for himself.

LEVITICUS 9:10

But the fat, the kidneys, and the fatty lobe from the liver of the sin offering he burned on the altar, as the LORD had commanded Moses.

LEVITICUS 9:12

And he killed the burnt offering; and Aaron's sons presented to him the blood, which he sprinkled all around on the altar.

LEVITICUS 9:14

And he washed the entrails and the legs, and burned them with the burnt offering on the altar.

LEVITICUS 9:15

Then he brought the people's offering, and took the goat, which was the sin offering for the people, and killed it and offered it for sin, like the first one.

LEVITICUS 9:16

And he brought the burnt offering and offered it according to the prescribed manner.

LEVITICUS 9:17

Then he brought the grain offering, took a handful of it, and burned it on the altar, besides the burnt sacrifice of the morning.

LEVITICUS 9:21

But the breasts and the right thigh Aaron waved as a wave offering before the LORD, as Moses had commanded.

LEVITICUS 9:22

Then Aaron lifted his hand toward the people, blessed them, and came down from offering the sin offering, the burnt offering, and peace offerings.

LEVITICUS 9:24

And fire came out from before the LORD and consumed the burnt offering and the fat on the altar. When all the people saw it, they shouted and fell on their faces.

LEVITICUS 10:12

Then Moses spoke to Aaron, and to Eleazar and Ithamar, his sons who were left: "Take the grain offering that remains of the offerings made by fire to the

L ORD, and eat it without leaven beside the altar; for it is most holy."

LEVITICUS 10:14

The breast of the wave offering and the thigh of the heave offering you shall eat in a clean place, you, your sons, and your daughters with you; for they are your due and your sons' due, which are given from the sacrifices of peace offerings of the children of Israel.

LEVITICUS 10:15

The thigh of the heave offering and the breast of the wave offering they shall bring with the offerings of fat made by fire, to offer as a wave offering before the L ORD. And it shall be yours and your sons' with you, by a statute forever, as the L ORD has commanded.

LEVITICUS 10:16

Then Moses made careful inquiry about the goat of the sin offering, and there it was—burned up. And he was angry with Eleazar and Ithamar, the sons of Aaron who were left.

LEVITICUS 10:17

Why have you not eaten the sin offering in a holy place, since it is most holy, and God has given it to you to bear the guilt of the congregation, to make atonement for them before the L ORD?

LEVITICUS 10:19

And Aaron said to Moses, "Look, this day they have offered their sin offering and their burnt offering before the L ORD, and such things have befallen me! If I had eaten the sin offering today, would it have been accepted in the sight of the L ORD?"

LEVITICUS 12:6

When the days of her purification are fulfilled, whether for a son or a daughter, she shall bring to the priest a lamb of the first year as a burnt offering, and a young pigeon or a turtledove as a sin offering, to the door of the tabernacle of meeting.

LEVITICUS 12:8

And if she is not able to bring a lamb, then she may bring two turtledoves or two young pigeons—one as a burnt offering and the other as a sin offering. So the priest shall make atonement for her, and she will be clean.

LEVITICUS 14:10

And on the eighth day he shall take two male lambs without blemish, one ewe lamb of the first year without blemish, three-tenths of an ephah of fine flour mixed with oil as a grain offering, and one log of oil.

LEVITICUS 14:12

And the priest shall take one male lamb and offer it as a trespass offering, and the log of oil, and wave them as a wave offering before the L ORD.

LEVITICUS 14:13

Then he shall kill the lamb in the place where he kills the sin offering and the burnt offering, in a holy place; for as the sin offering is the priest's, so is the trespass offering. It is most holy.

LEVITICUS 14:14

The priest shall take some of the blood of the trespass offering, and the priest shall put it on the tip of the right ear of him who is to be cleansed, on the thumb of his right hand, and on the big toe of his right foot.

LEVITICUS 14:17

And of the rest of the oil in his hand, the priest shall put some on the tip of the right ear of him who is to be cleansed, on the thumb of his right hand, and on the big toe of his right foot, on the blood of the trespass offering.

LEVITICUS 14:19

Then the priest shall offer the sin offering, and make atonement for him who is to be cleansed from his uncleanness. Afterward he shall kill the burnt offering.

And the priest shall offer the burnt offering and the grain offering on the altar. So the priest shall make atonement for him, and he shall be clean.

But if he is poor and cannot afford it, then he shall take one male lamb as a trespass offering to be waved, to make atonement for him, one-tenth of an ephah of fine flour mixed with oil as a grain offering, a log of oil.

And two turtledoves or two young pigeons, such as he is able to afford: one shall be a sin offering and the other a burnt offering.

And the priest shall take the lamb of the trespass offering and the log of oil, and the priest shall wave them as a wave offering before the LORD.

Then he shall kill the lamb of the trespass offering, and the priest shall take some of the blood of the trespass offering and put it on the tip of the right ear of him who is to be cleansed, on the thumb of his right hand, and on the big toe of his right foot.

And the priest shall put some of the oil that is in his hand on the tip of the right ear of him who is to be cleansed, on the thumb of the right hand, and on the big toe of his right foot, on the place of the blood of the trespass offering.

Such as he is able to afford, the one as a sin offering and the other as a burnt offering, with the grain offering. So the priest shall make atonement for him who is to be cleansed before the LORD.

Then the priest shall offer them, the one as a sin offering and the other as a burnt offering. So the priest shall make atonement for him before the LORD because of his discharge.

Then the priest shall offer the one as a sin offering and the other as a burnt offering, and the priest shall make atonement for her before the LORD for the discharge of her uncleanness.

Thus Aaron shall come into the Holy Place: with the blood of a young bull as a sin offering, and of a ram as a burnt offering.

And he shall take from the congregation of the children of Israel two kids of the goats as a sin offering, and one ram as a burnt offering.

Aaron shall offer the bull as a sin offering, which is for himself, and make atonement for himself and for his house.

And Aaron shall bring the goat on which the LORD's lot fell, and offer it as a sin offering.

And Aaron shall bring the bull of the sin offering, which is for himself, and make atonement for himself and for his house, and shall kill the bull as the sin offering which is for himself.

Then he shall kill the goat of the sin offering, which is for the people, bring its blood inside the veil, do with that blood as he did with the blood of the bull, and sprinkle it on the mercy seat and before the mercy seat.

LEVITICUS 16:24

And he shall wash his body with water in a holy place, put on his garments, come out and offer his burnt offering and the burnt offering of the people, and make atonement for himself and for the people.

LEVITICUS 16:25

The fat of the sin offering he shall burn on the altar.

LEVITICUS 16:27

The bull for the sin offering and the goat for the sin offering, whose blood was brought in to make atonement in the Holy Place, shall be carried outside the camp. And they shall burn in the fire their skins, their flesh, and their offal.

LEVITICUS 17:4

And does not bring it to the door of the tabernacle of meeting to offer an offering to the LORD before the tabernacle of the LORD, the guilt of bloodshed shall be imputed to that man. He has shed blood; and that man shall be cut off from among his people.

LEVITICUS 17:8

"Also you shall say to them: 'Whatever man of the house of Israel, or of the strangers who dwell among you, who offers a burnt offering or sacrifice.'"

LEVITICUS 19:5

And if you offer a sacrifice of a peace offering to the LORD, you shall offer it of your own free will.

LEVITICUS 19:21

And he shall bring his trespass offering to the LORD, to the door of the tabernacle of meeting, a ram as a trespass offering.

LEVITICUS 19:22

The priest shall make atonement for him with the ram of the trespass offering before the LORD for his sin which he has committed. And the sin which he has committed shall be forgiven him.

LEVITICUS 22:18

Speak to Aaron and his sons, and to all the children of Israel, and say to them: "Whatever man of the house of Israel, or of the strangers in Israel, who offers his sacrifice for any of his vows or for any of his freewill offerings, which they offer to the LORD as a burnt offering."

LEVITICUS 22:21

And whoever offers a sacrifice of a peace offering to the LORD, to fulfill his vow, or a freewill offering from the cattle or the sheep, it must be perfect to be accepted; there shall be no defect in it.

LEVITICUS 22:22

Those that are blind or broken or maimed, or have an ulcer or eczema or scabs, you shall not offer to the LORD, nor make an offering by fire of them on the altar to the LORD.

LEVITICUS 22:23

Either a bull or a lamb that has any limb too long or too short you may offer as a freewill offering, but for a vow it shall not be accepted.

LEVITICUS 22:24

You shall not offer to the LORD what is bruised or crushed, or torn or cut; nor shall you make any offering of them in your land.

LEVITICUS 22:27

When a bull or a sheep or a goat is born, it shall be seven days with its mother; and from the eighth day and thereafter it shall be accepted as an offering made by fire to the LORD.

LEVITICUS 23:8

But you shall offer an offering made by fire to the LORD for seven days. The seventh day shall be a holy convocation; you shall do no customary work on it.

LEVITICUS 23:12

And you shall offer on that day, when you wave the

SCRIPTURE REFERENCES ON OFFERINGS

sheaf, a male lamb of the first year, without blemish, as a burnt offering to the LORD.

LEVITICUS 23:13

Its grain offering shall be two-tenths of an ephah of fine flour mixed with oil, an offering made by fire to the LORD, for a sweet aroma; and its drink offering shall be of wine, one-fourth of a hin.

LEVITICUS 23:14

You shall eat neither bread nor parched grain nor fresh grain until the same day that you have brought an offering to your God; it shall be a statute forever throughout your generations in all your dwellings.

LEVITICUS 23:15

And you shall count for yourselves from the day after the Sabbath, from the day that you brought the sheaf of the wave offering: seven Sabbaths shall be completed.

LEVITICUS 23:16

Count fifty days to the day after the seventh Sabbath; then you shall offer a new grain offering to the LORD.

LEVITICUS 23:18

And you shall offer with the bread seven lambs of the first year, without blemish, one young bull, and two rams. They shall be as a burnt offering to the LORD, with their grain offering and their drink offerings, an offering made by fire for a sweet aroma to the LORD.

LEVITICUS 23:19

Then you shall sacrifice one kid of the goats as a sin offering, and two male lambs of the first year as a sacrifice of a peace offering.

LEVITICUS 23:20

The priest shall wave them with the bread of the first-fruits as a wave offering before the LORD, with the two lambs. They shall be holy to the LORD for the priest.

LEVITICUS 23:25

You shall do no customary work on it; and you shall offer an offering made by fire to the LORD.

LEVITICUS 23:27

Also the tenth day of this seventh month shall be the Day of Atonement. It shall be a holy convocation for you; you shall afflict your souls, and offer an offering made by fire to the LORD.

LEVITICUS 23:36

For seven days you shall offer an offering made by fire to the LORD. On the eighth day you shall have a holy convocation, and you shall offer an offering made by fire to the LORD. It is a sacred assembly, and you shall do no customary work on it.

LEVITICUS 23:37

These are the feasts of the LORD which you shall proclaim to be holy convocations, to offer an offering made by fire to the LORD, a burnt offering and a grain offering, a sacrifice and drink offerings, everything on its day.

LEVITICUS 24:7

And you shall put pure frankincense on each row, that it may be on the bread for a memorial, an offering made by fire to the LORD.

LEVITICUS 27:9

If it is an animal that men may bring as an offering to the LORD, all that anyone gives to the LORD shall be holy.

NUMBERS 4:16

The appointed duty of Eleazar the son of Aaron the priest is the oil for the light, the sweet incense, the daily grain offering, the anointing oil, the oversight of all the tabernacle, of all that is in it, with the sanctuary and its furnishings.

Every offering of all the holy things of the children of Israel, which they bring to the priest, shall be his.

Then the man shall bring his wife to the priest. He shall bring the offering required for her, one-tenth of an ephah of barley meal; he shall pour no oil on it and put no frankincense on it, because it is a grain offering of jealousy, an offering for remembering, for bringing iniquity to remembrance.

Then the priest shall stand the woman before the Lord, uncover the woman's head, and put the offering for remembering in her hands, which is the grain offering of jealousy. And the priest shall have in his hand the bitter water that brings a curse.

Then the priest shall take the grain offering of jealousy from the woman's hand, shall wave the offering before the Lord, and bring it to the altar.

And the priest shall take a handful of the offering, as its memorial portion, burn it on the altar, and afterward make the woman drink the water.

And the priest shall offer one as a sin offering and the other as a burnt offering, and make atonement for him, because he sinned in regard to the corpse; and he shall sanctify his head that same day.

He shall consecrate to the Lord the days of his separation, and bring a male lamb in its first year as a trespass offering; but the former days shall be lost, because his separation was defiled.

And he shall present his offering to the Lord: one male lamb in its first year without blemish as a burnt offering, one ewe lamb in its first year without blemish as a sin offering, one ram without blemish as a peace offering.

A basket of unleavened bread, cakes of fine flour mixed with oil, unleavened wafers anointed with oil, and their grain offering with their drink offerings.

Then the priest shall bring them before the Lord and offer his sin offering and his burnt offering.

And he shall offer the ram as a sacrifice of peace offering to the Lord, with the basket of unleavened bread; the priest shall also offer its grain offering and its drink offering.

Then the Nazirite shall shave his consecrated head at the door of the tabernacle of meeting, and shall take the hair from his consecrated head and put it on the fire which is under the sacrifice of the peace offering.

And the priest shall wave them as a wave offering before the Lord; they are holy for the priest, together with the breast of the wave offering and the thigh of the heave offering. After that the Nazirite may drink wine.

This is the law of the Nazirite who vows to the Lord the offering for his separation, and besides that, whatever else his hand is able to provide; according to the vow which he takes, so he must do according to the law of his separation.

NUMBERS 7:3

And they brought their offering before the LORD, *six covered carts and twelve oxen, a cart for every two of the leaders, and for each one an ox; and they presented them before the tabernacle.*

NUMBERS 7:10

Now the leaders offered the dedication offering for the altar when it was anointed; so the leaders offered their offering before the altar.

NUMBERS 7:11

For the LORD *said to Moses, "They shall offer their offering, one leader each day, for the dedication of the altar."*

NUMBERS 7:12

And the one who offered his offering on the first day was Nahshon the son of Amminadab, from the tribe of Judah.

NUMBERS 7:13

His offering was one silver platter, the weight of which was one hundred and thirty shekels, and one silver bowl of seventy shekels, according to the shekel of the sanctuary, both of them full of fine flour mixed with oil as a grain offering.

NUMBERS 7:15

One young bull, one ram, and one male lamb in its first year, as a burnt offering.

NUMBERS 7:16

One kid of the goats as a sin offering.

NUMBERS 7:17

And for the sacrifice of peace offerings: two oxen, five rams, five male goats, and five male lambs in their first year. This was the offering of Nahshon the son of Amminadab.

NUMBERS 7:19

For his offering he offered one silver platter, the weight of which was one hundred and thirty shekels, and one silver bowl of seventy shekels, according to the shekel of the sanctuary, both of them full of fine flour mixed with oil as a grain offering.

NUMBERS 7:21

One young bull, one ram, and one male lamb in its first year, as a burnt offering.

NUMBERS 7:22

One kid of the goats as a sin offering.

NUMBERS 7:23

And as the sacrifice of peace offerings: two oxen, five rams, five male goats, and five male lambs in their first year. This was the offering of Nethanel the son of Zuar.

NUMBERS 7:25

His offering was one silver platter, the weight of which was one hundred and thirty shekels, and one silver bowl of seventy shekels, according to the shekel of the sanctuary, both of them full of fine flour mixed with oil as a grain offering.

NUMBERS 7:27

One young bull, one ram, and one male lamb in its first year, as a burnt offering.

NUMBERS 7:28

One kid of the goats as a sin offering.

NUMBERS 7:29

And for the sacrifice of peace offerings: two oxen, five rams, five male goats, and five male lambs in their first year. This was the offering of Eliab the son of Helon.

NUMBERS 7:31

His offering was one silver platter, the weight of which was one hundred and thirty shekels, and one silver bowl of seventy shekels, according to the shekel of the sanctuary, both of them full of fine flour mixed with oil as a grain offering.

NUMBERS 7:33

One young bull, one ram, and one male lamb in its first year, as a burnt offering.

NUMBERS 7:34

One kid of the goats as a sin offering.

NUMBERS 7:35

And as the sacrifice of peace offerings: two oxen, five rams, five male goats, and five male lambs in their first year. This was the offering of Elizur the son of Shedeur.

NUMBERS 7:37

His offering was one silver platter, the weight of which was one hundred and thirty shekels, and one silver bowl of seventy shekels, according to the shekel of the sanctuary, both of them full of fine flour mixed with oil as a grain offering.

NUMBERS 7:41

And as the sacrifice of peace offerings: two oxen, five rams, five male goats, and five male lambs in their first year. This was the offering of Shelumiel the son of Zurishaddai.

NUMBERS 7:43

His offering was one silver platter, the weight of which was one hundred and thirty shekels, and one silver bowl of seventy shekels, according to the shekel of the sanctuary, both of them full of fine flour mixed with oil as a grain offering.

NUMBERS 7:45

One young bull, one ram, and one male lamb in its first year, as a burnt offering.

NUMBERS 7:46

One kid of the goats as a sin offering.

NUMBERS 7:47

And as the sacrifice of peace offerings: two oxen, five rams, five male goats, and five male lambs in their first year. This was the offering of Eliasaph the son of Deuel.

NUMBERS 7:49

His offering was one silver platter, the weight of which was one hundred and thirty shekels, and one silver bowl of seventy shekels, according to the shekel of the sanctuary, both of them full of fine flour mixed with oil as a grain offering.

NUMBERS 7:51

One young bull, one ram, and one male lamb in its first year, as a burnt offering.

NUMBERS 7:52

One kid of the goats as a sin offering.

NUMBERS 7:53

And as the sacrifice of peace offerings: two oxen, five rams, five male goats, and five male lambs in their first year. This was the offering of Elishama the son of Ammihud.

NUMBERS 7:55

His offering was one silver platter, the weight of which was one hundred and thirty shekels, and one silver bowl of seventy shekels, according to the shekel of the sanctuary, both of them full of fine flour mixed with oil as a grain offering.

NUMBERS 7:57

One young bull, one ram, and one male lamb in its first year, as a burnt offering.

NUMBERS 7:58

One kid of the goats as a sin offering.

NUMBERS 7:59

And as the sacrifice of peace offerings: two oxen, five rams, five male goats, and five male lambs in their *first year. This was the offering of Gamaliel the son of Pedahzur.*

NUMBERS 7:61

His offering was one silver platter, the weight of which was one hundred and thirty shekels, and one silver bowl of seventy shekels, according to the shekel of the sanctuary, both of them full of fine flour mixed with oil as a grain offering.

NUMBERS 7:63

One young bull, one ram, and one male lamb in its first year, as a burnt offering.

NUMBERS 7:64

One kid of the goats as a sin offering.

NUMBERS 7:65

And as the sacrifice of peace offerings: two oxen, five rams, five male goats, and five male lambs in their first year. This was the offering of Abidan the son of Gideoni.

NUMBERS 7:67

His offering was one silver platter, the weight of which was one hundred and thirty shekels, and one silver bowl of seventy shekels, according to the shekel of the sanctuary, both of them full of fine flour mixed with oil as a grain offering.

NUMBERS 7:69

One young bull, one ram, and one male lamb in its first year, as a burnt offering.

NUMBERS 7:70

One kid of the goats as a sin offering.

NUMBERS 7:71

And as the sacrifice of peace offerings: two oxen, five rams, five male goats, and five male lambs in their first year. This was the offering of Ahiezer the son of Ammishaddai.

NUMBERS 7:73

His offering was one silver platter, the weight of which was one hundred and thirty shekels, and one silver bowl of seventy shekels, according to the shekel of the sanctuary, both of them full of fine flour mixed with oil as a grain offering.

NUMBERS 7:75

One young bull, one ram, and one male lamb in its first year, as a burnt offering.

NUMBERS 7:76

One kid of the goats as a sin offering.

NUMBERS 7:77

And as the sacrifice of peace offerings: two oxen, five rams, five male goats, and five male lambs in their first year. This was the offering of Pagiel the son of Ocran.

NUMBERS 7:79

His offering was one silver platter, the weight of which was one hundred and thirty shekels, and one silver bowl of seventy shekels, according to the shekel of the sanctuary, both of them full of fine flour mixed with oil as a grain offering.

NUMBERS 7:81

One young bull, one ram, and one male lamb in its first year, as a burnt offering.

NUMBERS 7:82

One kid of the goats as a sin offering.

NUMBERS 7:83

And as the sacrifice of peace offerings: two oxen, five rams, five male goats, and five male lambs in their first year. This was the offering of Ahira the son of Enan.

NUMBERS 7:87

All the oxen for the burnt offering were twelve young bulls, the rams twelve, the male lambs in their first year twelve, with their grain offering, and the kids of the goats as a sin offering twelve.

NUMBERS 7:88

And all the oxen for the sacrifice of peace offerings were twenty-four bulls, the rams sixty, the male goats sixty, and the lambs in their first year sixty. This was the dedication offering for the altar after it was anointed.

NUMBERS 8:8

Then let them take a young bull with its grain offering of fine flour mixed with oil, and you shall take another young bull as a sin offering.

NUMBERS 8:11

And Aaron shall offer the Levites before the Lord, like a wave offering from the children of Israel, that they may perform the work of the Lord.

NUMBERS 8:12

Then the Levites shall lay their hands on the heads of the young bulls, and you shall offer one as a sin offering and the other as a burnt offering to the Lord, to make atonement for the Levites.

NUMBERS 8:13

And you shall stand the Levites before Aaron and his sons, and then offer them like a wave offering to the Lord.

NUMBERS 8:15

After that the Levites shall go in to service the tabernacle of meeting. So you shall cleanse them and offer them, like a wave offering.

NUMBERS 8:21

And the Levites purified themselves and washed their clothes; then Aaron presented them, like a wave offering before the Lord, and Aaron made atonement for them to cleanse them.

NUMBERS 9:7

And those men said to him, "We became defiled by a human corpse. Why are we kept from presenting the offering of the Lord at its appointed time among the children of Israel?"

NUMBERS 9:13

But the man who is clean and is not on a journey, and ceases to keep the Passover, that same person shall be cut off from among his people, because he did not bring the offering of the Lord at its appointed time; that man shall bear his sin.

NUMBERS 15:3

And you make an offering by fire to the Lord, a burnt offering or a sacrifice, to fulfill a vow or as a freewill offering or in your appointed feasts, to make a sweet aroma to the Lord, from the herd or the flock.

NUMBERS 15:4

Then he who presents his offering to the Lord shall bring a grain offering of one-tenth of an ephah of fine flour mixed with one-fourth of a hin of oil.

NUMBERS 15:5

And one-fourth of a hin of wine as a drink offering you shall prepare with the burnt offering or the sacrifice, for each lamb.

NUMBERS 15:6

Or for a ram you shall prepare as a grain offering two-tenths of an ephah of fine flour mixed with one-third of a hin of oil.

NUMBERS 15:7

And as a drink offering you shall offer one-third of a hin of wine as a sweet aroma to the Lord.

NUMBERS 15:8

And when you prepare a young bull as a burnt offering, or as a sacrifice to fulfill a vow, or as a peace offering to the Lord.

NUMBERS 15:9

Then shall be offered with the young bull a grain offering of three-tenths of an ephah of fine flour mixed with half a hin of oil.

NUMBERS 15:10

And you shall bring as the drink offering half a hin of wine as an offering made by fire, a sweet aroma to the Lord.

NUMBERS 15:13

All who are native-born shall do these things in this manner, in presenting an offering made by fire, a sweet aroma to the Lord.

NUMBERS 15:14

And if a stranger dwells with you, or whoever is among you throughout your generations, and would present an offering made by fire, a sweet aroma to the Lord, just as you do, so shall he do.

NUMBERS 15:19

Then it will be, when you eat of the bread of the land, that you shall offer up a heave offering to the Lord.

NUMBERS 15:20

You shall offer up a cake of the first of your ground meal as a heave offering; as a heave offering of the threshing floor, so shall you offer it up.

NUMBERS 15:21

Of the first of your ground meal you shall give to the Lord a heave offering throughout your generations.

NUMBERS 15:24

Then it will be, if it is unintentionally committed, without the knowledge of the congregation, that the whole congregation shall offer one young bull as a burnt offering, as a sweet aroma to the Lord, with its grain offering and its drink offering, according to the ordinance, and one kid of the goats as a sin offering.

NUMBERS 15:25

So the priest shall make atonement for the whole congregation of the children of Israel, and it shall be forgiven them, for it was unintentional; they shall bring their offering, an offering made by fire to the Lord, and their sin offering before the Lord, for their unintended sin.

NUMBERS 15:27

And if a person sins unintentionally, then he shall bring a female goat in its first year as a sin offering.

NUMBERS 16:15

Then Moses was very angry, and said to the Lord, "Do not respect their offering. I have not taken one donkey from them, nor have I hurt one of them."

NUMBERS 18:9

This shall be yours of the most holy things reserved from the fire: every offering of theirs, every grain offering and every sin offering and every trespass offering which they render to Me, shall be most holy for you and your sons.

NUMBERS 18:11

This also is yours: the heave offering of their gift, with all the wave offerings of the children of Israel; I have given them to you, and your sons and daughters with you, as an ordinance forever. Everyone who is clean in your house may eat it.

NUMBERS 18:17

But the firstborn of a cow, the firstborn of a sheep, or the firstborn of a goat you shall not redeem; they are holy. You shall sprinkle their blood on the altar, and burn their fat as an offering made by fire for a sweet aroma to the Lord.

NUMBERS 18:24

For the tithes of the children of Israel, which they offer up as a heave offering to the Lord, I have given to the Levites as an inheritance; therefore I have said to them, "Among the children of Israel they shall have no inheritance."

NUMBERS 18:26

"Speak thus to the Levites, and say to them: 'When you take from the children of Israel the tithes which I have given you from them as your inheritance, then you shall offer up a heave offering of it to the LORD, a tenth of the tithe.'"

NUMBERS 18:27

And your heave offering shall be reckoned to you as though it were the grain of the threshing floor and as the fullness of the winepress.

NUMBERS 18:28

Thus you shall also offer a heave offering to the LORD from all your tithes which you receive from the children of Israel, and you shall give the LORD's heave offering from it to Aaron the priest.

NUMBERS 18:29

Of all your gifts you shall offer up every heave offering due to the LORD, from all the best of them, the consecrated part of them.

NUMBERS 23:3

Then Balaam said to Balak, "Stand by your burnt offering, and I will go; perhaps the LORD will come to meet me, and whatever He shows me I will tell you." So he went to a desolate height.

NUMBERS 23:15

And he said to Balak, "Stand here by your burnt offering while I meet the LORD over there."

NUMBERS 23:17

So he came to him, and there he was, standing by his burnt offering, and the princes of Moab were with him. And Balak said to him, "What has the LORD spoken?"

NUMBERS 28:2

"Command the children of Israel, and say to them, 'My offering, My food for My offerings made by fire as a sweet aroma to Me, you shall be careful to offer to Me at their appointed time.'"

NUMBERS 28:3

"And you shall say to them, 'This is the offering made by fire which you shall offer to the LORD: two male lambs in their first year without blemish, day by day, as a regular burnt offering.'"

NUMBERS 28:5

And one-tenth of an ephah of fine flour as a grain offering mixed with one-fourth of a hin of pressed oil.

NUMBERS 28:6

It is a regular burnt offering which was ordained at Mount Sinai for a sweet aroma, an offering made by fire to the LORD.

NUMBERS 28:7

And its drink offering shall be one-fourth of a hin for each lamb; in a holy place you shall pour out the drink to the LORD as an offering.

NUMBERS 28:8

The other lamb you shall offer in the evening; as the morning grain offering and its drink offering, you shall offer it as an offering made by fire, a sweet aroma to the LORD.

NUMBERS 28:9

And on the Sabbath day two lambs in their first year, without blemish, and two-tenths of an ephah of fine flour as a grain offering, mixed with oil, with its drink offering.

NUMBERS 28:10

This is the burnt offering for every Sabbath, besides the regular burnt offering with its drink offering.

SCRIPTURE REFERENCES ON OFFERINGS

NUMBERS 28:11

At the beginnings of your months you shall present a burnt offering to the LORD: two young bulls, one ram, and seven lambs in their first year, without blemish.

NUMBERS 28:12

Three-tenths of an ephah of fine flour as a grain offering, mixed with oil, for each bull; two-tenths of an ephah of fine flour as a grain offering, mixed with oil, for the one ram.

NUMBERS 28:13

And one-tenth of an ephah of fine flour, mixed with oil, as a grain offering for each lamb, as a burnt offering of sweet aroma, an offering made by fire to the LORD.

NUMBERS 28:14

Their drink offering shall be half a hin of wine for a bull, one-third of a hin for a ram, and one-fourth of a hin for a lamb; this is the burnt offering for each month throughout the months of the year.

NUMBERS 28:15

Also one kid of the goats as a sin offering to the LORD shall be offered, besides the regular burnt offering and its drink offering.

NUMBERS 28:19

And you shall present an offering made by fire as a burnt offering to the LORD: two young bulls, one ram, and seven lambs in their first year. Be sure they are without blemish.

NUMBERS 28:20

Their grain offering shall be of fine flour mixed with oil: three-tenths of an ephah you shall offer for a bull, and two-tenths for a ram.

NUMBERS 28:22

Also one goat as a sin offering, to make atonement for you.

NUMBERS 28:23

You shall offer these besides the burnt offering of the morning, which is for a regular burnt offering.

NUMBERS 28:24

In this manner you shall offer the food of the offering made by fire daily for seven days, as a sweet aroma to the LORD; it shall be offered besides the regular burnt offering and its drink offering.

NUMBERS 28:26

Also on the day of the firstfruits, when you bring a new grain offering to the LORD at your Feast of Weeks, you shall have a holy convocation. You shall do no customary work.

NUMBERS 28:27

You shall present a burnt offering as a sweet aroma to the LORD: two young bulls, one ram, and seven lambs in their first year.

NUMBERS 28:28

With their grain offering of fine flour mixed with oil: three-tenths of an ephah for each bull, two-tenths for the one ram.

NUMBERS 28:31

Be sure they are without blemish. You shall present them with their drink offerings, besides the regular burnt offering with its grain offering.

NUMBERS 29:2

You shall offer a burnt offering as a sweet aroma to the LORD: one young bull, one ram, and seven lambs in their first year, without blemish.

NUMBERS 29:3

Their grain offering shall be fine flour mixed with oil: three-tenths of an ephah for the bull, two-tenths for the ram.

NUMBERS 29:5

Also one kid of the goats as a sin offering, to make atonement for you.

NUMBERS 29:6

Besides the burnt offering with its grain offering for the New Moon, the regular burnt offering with its grain offering, and their drink offerings, according to their ordinance, as a sweet aroma, an offering made by fire to the Lord.

NUMBERS 29:8

You shall present a burnt offering to the Lord as a sweet aroma: one young bull, one ram, and seven lambs in their first year. Be sure they are without blemish.

NUMBERS 29:9

Their grain offering shall be of fine flour mixed with oil: three-tenths of an ephah for the bull, two-tenths for the one ram.

NUMBERS 29:11

Also one kid of the goats as a sin offering, besides the sin offering for atonement, the regular burnt offering with its grain offering, and their drink offerings.

NUMBERS 29:13

You shall present a burnt offering, an offering made by fire as a sweet aroma to the Lord: thirteen young bulls, two rams, and fourteen lambs in their first year. They shall be without blemish.

NUMBERS 29:14

Their grain offering shall be of fine flour mixed with oil: three-tenths of an ephah for each of the thirteen bulls, two-tenths for each of the two rams.

NUMBERS 29:16

Also one kid of the goats as a sin offering, besides the regular burnt offering, its grain offering, and its drink offering.

NUMBERS 29:18

And their grain offering and their drink offerings for the bulls, for the rams, and for the lambs, by their number, according to the ordinance.

NUMBERS 29:19

Also one kid of the goats as a sin offering, besides the regular burnt offering with its grain offering, and their drink offerings.

NUMBERS 29:21

And their grain offering and their drink offerings for the bulls, for the rams, and for the lambs, by their number, according to the ordinance.

NUMBERS 29:22

Also one goat as a sin offering, besides the regular burnt offering, its grain offering, and its drink offering.

NUMBERS 29:24

And their grain offering and their drink offerings for the bulls, for the rams, and for the lambs, by their number, according to the ordinance.

NUMBERS 29:25

Also one kid of the goats as a sin offering, besides the regular burnt offering, its grain offering, and its drink offering.

NUMBERS 29:27

And their grain offering and their drink offerings for the bulls, for the rams, and for the lambs, by their number, according to the ordinance.

NUMBERS 29:28

Also one goat as a sin offering, besides the regular burnt offering, its grain offering, and its drink offering.

NUMBERS 29:30

And their grain offering and their drink offerings for the bulls, for the rams, and for the lambs, by their number, according to the ordinance.

SCRIPTURE REFERENCES ON OFFERINGS

NUMBERS 29:33

And their grain offering and their drink offerings for the bulls, for the rams, and for the lambs, by their number, according to the ordinance.

NUMBERS 29:36

*You shall present a burnt offering, an offering made by fire as a sweet aroma to the L*ORD*: one bull, one ram, seven lambs in their first year without blemish.*

NUMBERS 29:37

And their grain offering and their drink offerings for the bull, for the ram, and for the lambs, by their number, according to the ordinance.

NUMBERS 31:29

*Take it from their half, and give it to Eleazar the priest as a heave offering to the L*ORD*.*

NUMBERS 31:41

*So Moses gave the tribute which was the L*ORD*'s heave offering to Eleazar the priest, as the L*ORD* commanded Moses.*

NUMBERS 31:52

*And all the gold of the offering that they offered to the L*ORD*, from the captains of thousands and captains of hundreds, was sixteen thousand seven hundred and fifty shekels.*

DEUTERONOMY 12:17

You may not eat within your gates the tithe of your grain or your new wine or your oil, of the firstlings of your herd or your flock, of any of your offerings which you vow, of your freewill offerings, or of the heave offering of your hand.

DEUTERONOMY 16:10

*Then you shall keep the Feast of Weeks to the L*ORD* your God with the tribute of a freewill offering from your hand, which you shall give as the L*ORD* your God blesses you.*

DEUTERONOMY 23:23

*That which has gone from your lips you shall keep and perform, for you voluntarily vowed to the L*ORD* your God what you have promised with your mouth.*

DEUTERONOMY 32:38

Who ate the fat of their sacrifices, and drank the wine of their drink offering? Let them rise and help you, and be your refuge.

JOSHUA 22:26

Therefore we said, "Let us now prepare to build ourselves an altar, not for burnt offering, nor for sacrifice."

JUDGES 11:31

*Whatever comes out of the doors of my house to meet me, when I return in peace from the people of Ammon, shall surely be the L*ORD*'s, and I will offer it up as a burnt offering.*

JUDGES 13:16

*And the Angel of the L*ORD* said to Manoah, "Though you detain Me, I will not eat your food. But if you offer a burnt offering, you must offer it to the L*ORD*." (For Manoah did not know He was the Angel of the L*ORD*.)*

JUDGES 13:19

*So Manoah took the young goat with the grain offering, and offered it upon the rock to the L*ORD*. And He did a wondrous thing while Manoah and his wife looked on.*

JUDGES 13:23

*But his wife said to him, "If the L*ORD* had desired to kill us, He would not have accepted a burnt offering and a grain offering from our hands, nor would He have shown us all these things, nor would He have told us such things as these at this time."*

1 SAMUEL 2:17

Therefore the sin of the young men was very great before the LORD, for men abhorred the offering of the LORD.

1 SAMUEL 2:29

Why do you kick at My sacrifice and My offering which I have commanded in My dwelling place, and honor your sons more than Me, to make yourselves fat with the best of all the offerings of Israel My people?'

1 SAMUEL 3:14

And therefore I have sworn to the house of Eli that the iniquity of Eli's house shall not be atoned for by sacrifice or offering forever.

1 SAMUEL 6:3

So they said, "If you send away the ark of the God of Israel, do not send it empty; but by all means return it to Him with a trespass offering. Then you will be healed, and it will be known to you why His hand is not removed from you."

1 SAMUEL 6:4

Then they said, "What is the trespass offering which we shall return to Him?" They answered, "Five golden tumors and five golden rats, according to the number of the lords of the Philistines. For the same plague was on all of you and on your lords."

1 SAMUEL 6:8

Then take the ark of the LORD and set it on the cart; and put the articles of gold which you are returning to Him as a trespass offering in a chest by its side. Then send it away, and let it go.

1 SAMUEL 6:14

Then the cart came into the field of Joshua of Beth Shemesh, and stood there; a large stone was there. So they split the wood of the cart and offered the cows as a burnt offering to the LORD.

1 SAMUEL 6:17

These are the golden tumors which the Philistines returned as a trespass offering to the LORD: one for Ashdod, one for Gaza, one for Ashkelon, one for Gath, one for Ekron.

1 SAMUEL 7:9

And Samuel took a suckling lamb and offered it as a whole burnt offering to the LORD. Then Samuel cried out to the LORD for Israel, and the LORD answered him.

1 SAMUEL 7:10

Now as Samuel was offering up the burnt offering, the Philistines drew near to battle against Israel. But the LORD thundered with a loud thunder upon the Philistines that day, and so confused them that they were overcome before Israel.

1 SAMUEL 13:9

So Saul said, "Bring a burnt offering and peace offerings here to me." And he offered the burnt offering.

1 SAMUEL 13:10

Now it happened, as soon as he had finished offering the burnt offering, that Samuel came; and Saul went out to meet him, that he might greet him.

1 SAMUEL 13:12

Then I said, "The Philistines will now come down on me at Gilgal, and I have not made supplication to the LORD." Therefore I felt compelled, and offered a burnt offering.

.1 SAMUEL 26:19

Now therefore, please, let my lord the king hear the words of his servant: If the LORD has stirred you up against me, let Him accept an offering. But if it is the children of men, may they be cursed before the LORD, for they have driven me out this day from sharing in the inheritance of the LORD, saying, "Go, serve other gods."

SCRIPTURE REFERENCES ON OFFERINGS

2 SAMUEL 6:18

And when David had finished offering burnt offerings and peace offerings, he blessed the people in the name of the LORD of hosts.

1 KINGS 18:29

And when midday was past, they prophesied until the time of the offering of the evening sacrifice. But there was no voice; no one answered, no one paid attention.

1 KINGS 18:36

And it came to pass, at the time of the offering of the evening sacrifice, that Elijah the prophet came near and said, "LORD God of Abraham, Isaac, and Israel, let it be known this day that You are God in Israel and I am Your servant, and that I have done all these things at Your word.

2 KINGS 3:20

Now it happened in the morning, when the grain offering was offered, that suddenly water came by way of Edom, and the land was filled with water.

2 KINGS 3:27

Then he took his eldest son who would have reigned in his place, and offered him as a burnt offering upon the wall; and there was great indignation against Israel. So they departed from him and returned to their own land.

2 KINGS 5:17

So Naaman said, "Then, if not, please let your servant be given two mule-loads of earth; for your servant will no longer offer either burnt offering or sacrifice to other gods, but to the LORD."

2 KINGS 10:25

Now it happened, as soon as he had made an end of offering the burnt offering, that Jehu said to the guard and to the captains, "Go in and kill them; let no one come out!" And they killed them with the edge of the sword; then the guards and the officers threw them out, and went into the inner room of the temple of Baal.*

2 KINGS 16:13

So he burned his burnt offering and his grain offering; and he poured his drink offering and sprinkled the blood of his peace offerings on the altar.

2 KINGS 16:15

Then King Ahaz commanded Urijah the priest, saying, "On the great new altar burn the morning burnt offering, the evening grain offering, the king's burnt sacrifice, and his grain offering, with the burnt offering of all the people of the land, their grain offering, and their drink offerings; and sprinkle on it all the blood of the burnt offering and all the blood of the sacrifice. And the bronze altar shall be for me to inquire by."

1 CHRONICLES 6:49–50

But Aaron and his sons offered sacrifices on the altar of burnt offering and on the altar of incense, for all the work of the Most Holy Place, and to make atonement for Israel, according to all that Moses the servant of God had commanded.

1 CHRONICLES 16:2

And when David had finished offering the burnt offerings and the peace offerings, he blessed the people in the name of the LORD.

1 CHRONICLES 16:29

Give to the LORD the glory due His name; bring an offering, and come before Him. Oh, worship the LORD in the beauty of holiness!

1 CHRONICLES 16:40

To offer burnt offerings to the LORD on the altar of burnt offering regularly morning and evening, and to do according to all that is written in the Law of the LORD which He commanded Israel.

1 CHRONICLES 21:23

And Ornan said to David, "Take it to yourself, and let my lord the king do what is good in his eyes. Look, I also give you the oxen for burnt offerings, the threshing implements for wood, and the wheat for the grain offering; I give it all."

1 CHRONICLES 21:26

And David built there an altar to the LORD, and offered burnt offerings and peace offerings, and called on the LORD; and He answered him from heaven by fire on the altar of burnt offering.

1 CHRONICLES 21:29

For the tabernacle of the LORD and the altar of the burnt offering, which Moses had made in the wilderness, were at that time at the high place in Gibeon.

1 CHRONICLES 22:1

Then David said, "This is the house of the LORD God, and this is the altar of burnt offering for Israel."

1 CHRONICLES 23:29

Both with the showbread and the fine flour for the grain offering, with the unleavened cakes and what is baked in the pan, with what is mixed and with all kinds of measures and sizes.

2 CHRONICLES 4:6

He also made ten lavers, and put five on the right side and five on the left, to wash in them; such things as they offered for the burnt offering they would wash in them, but the Sea was for the priests to wash in.

2 CHRONICLES 7:1

When Solomon had finished praying, fire came down from heaven and consumed the burnt offering and the sacrifices; and the glory of the LORD filled the temple.

2 CHRONICLES 8:13

According to the daily rate, offering according to the commandment of Moses, for the Sabbaths, the New Moons, and the three appointed yearly feasts—the Feast of Unleavened Bread, the Feast of Weeks, and the Feast of Tabernacles.

2 CHRONICLES 24:14

When they had finished, they brought the rest of the money before the king and Jehoiada; they made from it articles for the house of the LORD, articles for serving and offering, spoons and vessels of gold and silver. And they offered burnt offerings in the house of the LORD continually all the days of Jehoiada.

2 CHRONICLES 29:21

And they brought seven bulls, seven rams, seven lambs, and seven male goats for a sin offering for the kingdom, for the sanctuary, and for Judah. Then he commanded the priests, the sons of Aaron, to offer them on the altar of the LORD.

2 CHRONICLES 29:23

Then they brought out the male goats for the sin offering before the king and the assembly, and they laid their hands on them.

2 CHRONICLES 29:24

And the priests killed them; and they presented their blood on the altar as a sin offering to make an atonement for all Israel, for the king commanded that the burnt offering and the sin offering be made for all Israel.

2 CHRONICLES 29:24

And the priests killed them; and they presented their blood on the altar as a sin offering to make an atonement for all Israel, for the king commanded that the burnt offering and the sin offering be made for all Israel.

2 CHRONICLES 29:27

Then Hezekiah commanded them to offer the burnt offering on the altar. And when the burnt offering began, the song of the LORD also began, with the trumpets and with the instruments of David king of Israel.

SCRIPTURE REFERENCES ON OFFERINGS

2 CHRONICLES 29:28

So all the assembly worshiped, the singers sang, and the trumpeters sounded; all this continued until the burnt offering was finished.

2 CHRONICLES 29:29

And when they had finished offering, the king and all who were present with him bowed and worshiped.

2 CHRONICLES 29:32

And the number of the burnt offerings which the assembly brought was seventy bulls, one hundred rams, and two hundred lambs; all these were for a burnt offering to the LORD.

2 CHRONICLES 29:35

Also the burnt offerings were in abundance, with the fat of the peace offerings and with the drink offerings for every burnt offering. So the service of the house of the LORD was set in order.

2 CHRONICLES 30:22

And Hezekiah gave encouragement to all the Levites who taught the good knowledge of the LORD; and they ate throughout the feast seven days, offering peace offerings and making confession to the LORD God of their fathers.

2 CHRONICLES 35:14

Then afterward they prepared portions for themselves and for the priests, because the priests, the sons of Aaron, were busy in offering burnt offerings and fat until night; therefore the Levites prepared portions for themselves and for the priests, the sons of Aaron.

EZRA 3:5

Afterwards they offered the regular burnt offering, and those for New Moons and for all the appointed feasts of the LORD that were consecrated, and those of everyone who willingly offered a freewill offering to the LORD.

EZRA 6:17

And they offered sacrifices at the dedication of this house of God, one hundred bulls, two hundred rams, four hundred lambs, and as a sin offering for all Israel twelve male goats, according to the number of the tribes of Israel.

EZRA 7:16

And whereas all the silver and gold that you may find in all the province of Babylon, along with the freewill offering of the people and the priests, are to be freely offered for the house of their God in Jerusalem.

EZRA 8:25

And weighed out to them the silver, the gold, and the articles, the offering for the house of our God which the king and his counselors and his princes, and all Israel who were present, had offered.

EZRA 8:28

And I said to them, "You are holy to the LORD; the articles are holy also; and the silver and the gold are a freewill offering to the LORD God of your fathers."

EZRA 8:35

The children of those who had been carried away captive, who had come from the captivity, offered burnt offerings to the God of Israel: twelve bulls for all Israel, ninety-six rams, seventy-seven lambs, and twelve male goats as a sin offering. All this was a burnt offering to the LORD.

NEHEMIAH 10:33

For the showbread, for the regular grain offering, for the regular burnt offering of the Sabbaths, the New Moons, and the set feasts; for the holy things, for the sin offerings to make atonement for Israel, and all the work of the house of our God.

NEHEMIAH 10:34

We cast lots among the priests, the Levites, and the people, for bringing the wood offering into the house of our God, according to our fathers' houses, at the appointed times year by year, to burn on the altar of the LORD our God as it is written in the Law.

NEHEMIAH 10:39

For the children of Israel and the children of Levi shall bring the offering of the grain, of the new wine and the oil, to the storerooms where the articles of the sanctuary are, where the priests who minister and the gatekeepers and the singers are; and we will not neglect the house of our God.

NEHEMIAH 13:9

Then I commanded them to cleanse the rooms; and I brought back into them the articles of the house of God, with the grain offering and the frankincense.

NEHEMIAH 13:31

And to bringing the wood offering and the firstfruits at appointed times. Remember me, O my God, for good!

JOB 42:8

Now therefore, take for yourselves seven bulls and seven rams, go to My servant Job, and offer up for yourselves a burnt offering; and My servant Job shall pray for you. For I will accept him, lest I deal with you according to your folly; because you have not spoken of Me what is right, as My servant Job has.

PSALM 40:6

Sacrifice and offering You did not desire; my ears You have opened; burnt offering and sin offering You did not require.

PSALM 51:16

For You do not desire sacrifice, or else I would give it; You do not delight in burnt offering.

PSALM 51:19

Then You shall be pleased with the sacrifices of righteousness, with burnt offering and whole burnt offering; then they shall offer bulls on Your altar.

PSALM 96:8

Give to the LORD the glory due His name; bring an offering, and come into His courts.

ISAIAH 40:16

And Lebanon is not sufficient to burn, nor its beasts sufficient for a burnt offering.

ISAIAH 53:10

Yet it pleased the LORD to bruise Him; He has put Him to grief. When You make His soul an offering for sin, He shall see His seed, He shall prolong His days, and the pleasure of the LORD shall prosper in His hand.

ISAIAH 57:6

Among the smooth stones of the stream is your portion; they, they, are your lot! Even to them you have poured a drink offering, you have offered a grain offering. Should I receive comfort in these?

ISAIAH 61:8

For I, the LORD, love justice; I hate robbery for burnt offering; I will direct their work in truth, and will make with them an everlasting covenant.

ISAIAH 65:11

But you are those who forsake the LORD, who forget My holy mountain, who prepare a table for Gad, and who furnish a drink offering for Meni.

ISAIAH 66:20

"Then they shall bring all your brethren for an offering to the LORD out of all nations, on horses and in chariots and in litters, on mules and on camels, to My holy mountain Jerusalem," says the LORD, "as the children of Israel bring an offering in a clean vessel into the house of the LORD."

JEREMIAH 11:17

"For the LORD of hosts, who planted you, has pronounced doom against you for the evil of the house of Israel and of the house of Judah, which they have done

SCRIPTURE REFERENCES ON OFFERINGS

against themselves to provoke Me to anger in offering incense to Baal."

JEREMIAH 14:12

"When they fast, I will not hear their cry; and when they offer burnt offering and grain offering, I will not accept them. But I will consume them by the sword, by the famine, and by the pestilence."

EZEKIEL 40:38

There was a chamber and its entrance by the gateposts of the gateway, where they washed the burnt offering.

EZEKIEL 40:39

In the vestibule of the gateway were two tables on this side and two tables on that side, on which to slay the burnt offering, the sin offering, and the trespass offering.

EZEKIEL 40:42

There were also four tables of hewn stone for the burnt offering, one cubit and a half long, one cubit and a half wide, and one cubit high; on these they laid the instruments with which they slaughtered the burnt offering and the sacrifice.

EZEKIEL 40:43

Inside were hooks, a handbreadth wide, fastened all around; and the flesh of the sacrifices was on the tables.

EZEKIEL 42:13

Then he said to me, "The north chambers and the south chambers, which are opposite the separating courtyard, are the holy chambers where the priests who approach the LORD shall eat the most holy offerings. There they shall lay the most holy offerings—the grain offering, the sin offering, and the trespass offering—for the place is holy."

EZEKIEL 43:19

"You shall give a young bull for a sin offering to the priests, the Levites, who are of the seed of Zadok, who approach Me to minister to Me," says the Lord GOD.

EZEKIEL 43:21

Then you shall also take the bull of the sin offering, and burn it in the appointed place of the temple, outside the sanctuary.

EZEKIEL 43:22

On the second day you shall offer a kid of the goats without blemish for a sin offering; and they shall cleanse the altar, as they cleansed it with the bull.

EZEKIEL 43:24

When you offer them before the LORD, the priests shall throw salt on them, and they will offer them up as a burnt offering to the LORD.

EZEKIEL 43:25

Every day for seven days you shall prepare a goat for a sin offering; they shall also prepare a young bull and a ram from the flock, both without blemish.

EZEKIEL 44:11

Yet they shall be ministers in My sanctuary, as gatekeepers of the house and ministers of the house; they shall slay the burnt offering and the sacrifice for the people, and they shall stand before them to minister to them.

EZEKIEL 44:27

"And on the day that he goes to the sanctuary to minister in the sanctuary, he must offer his sin offering in the inner court," says the Lord GOD.

EZEKIEL 44:29

They shall eat the grain offering, the sin offering, and the trespass offering; every dedicated thing in Israel shall be theirs.

EZEKIEL 45:17

"Then it shall be the prince's part to give burnt offerings, grain offerings, and drink offerings, at the feasts, the New Moons, the Sabbaths, and at all the appointed seasons of the house of Israel. He shall prepare the sin offering, the grain offering, the burnt

SCRIPTURE REFERENCES ON OFFERINGS

offering, and the peace offerings to make atonement for the house of Israel."

EZEKIEL 45:19

The priest shall take some of the blood of the sin offering and put it on the doorposts of the temple, on the four corners of the ledge of the altar, and on the gateposts of the gate of the inner court.

EZEKIEL 45:22

And on that day the prince shall prepare for himself and for all the people of the land a bull for a sin offering.

EZEKIEL 45:23

On the seven days of the feast he shall prepare a burnt offering to the LORD, seven bulls and seven rams without blemish, daily for seven days, and a kid of the goats daily for a sin offering.

EZEKIEL 45:24

And he shall prepare a grain offering of one ephah for each bull and one ephah for each ram, together with a hin of oil for each ephah.

EZEKIEL 45:25

In the seventh month, on the fifteenth day of the month, at the feast, he shall do likewise for seven days, according to the sin offering, the burnt offering, the grain offering, and the oil.

EZEKIEL 46:2

The prince shall enter by way of the vestibule of that gateway from the outside, and stand by the gatepost. The priests shall prepare his burnt offering and his peace offerings. He shall worship at the threshold of the gate. Then he shall go out, but the gate shall not be shut until evening.

EZEKIEL 46:4

The burnt offering that the prince offers to the LORD on the Sabbath day shall be six lambs without blemish, and a ram without blemish.

EZEKIEL 46:5

And the grain offering shall be one ephah for a ram, and the grain offering for the lambs, as much as he wants to give, as well as a hin of oil with every ephah.

EZEKIEL 46:7

He shall prepare a grain offering of an ephah for a bull, an ephah for a ram, as much as he wants to give for the lambs, and a hin of oil with every ephah.

EZEKIEL 46:11

At the festivals and the appointed feast days the grain offering shall be an ephah for a bull, an ephah for a ram, as much as he wants to give for the lambs, and a hin of oil with every ephah.

EZEKIEL 46:12

"Now when the prince makes a voluntary burnt offering or voluntary peace offering to the LORD, the gate that faces toward the east shall then be opened for him; and he shall prepare his burnt offering and his peace offerings as he did on the Sabbath day. Then he shall go out, and after he goes out the gate shall be shut."

EZEKIEL 46:13

You shall daily make a burnt offering to the LORD of a lamb of the first year without blemish; you shall prepare it every morning.

EZEKIEL 46:14

And you shall prepare a grain offering with it every morning, a sixth of an ephah, and a third of a hin of oil to moisten the fine flour. This grain offering is a perpetual ordinance, to be made regularly to the LORD.

EZEKIEL 46:15

"Thus they shall prepare the lamb, the grain offering, and the oil, as a regular burnt offering every morning."

EZEKIEL 46:20

And he said to me, "This is the place where the priests shall boil the trespass offering and the sin offering, and where they shall bake the grain offering, so that they do not bring them out into the outer court to sanctify the people."

EZEKIEL 48:8

By the border of Judah, from the east side to the west, shall be the district which you shall set apart, twenty-five thousand cubits in width, and in length the same as one of the other portions, from the east side to the west, with the sanctuary in the center.

JOEL 1:9

The grain offering and the drink offering, have been cut off from the house of the LORD; The priests mourn, who minister to the LORD.

JOEL 1:13

Gird yourselves and lament, you priests; wail, you who minister before the altar; come, lie all night in sackcloth, you who minister to my God; for the grain offering and the drink offering are withheld from the house of your God.

JOEL 2:14

Who knows if He will turn and relent, and leave a blessing behind Him—A grain offering and a drink offering for the LORD your God?

ZEPHANIAH 3:10

From beyond the rivers of Ethiopia, my worshipers, the daughter of My dispersed ones, Shall bring My offering.

MALACHI 1:10

"Who is there even among you who would shut the doors, so that you would not kindle fire on my altar in vain? I have no pleasure in you," says the LORD of hosts, "nor will I accept an offering from your hands."

MALACHI 1:11

For from the rising of the sun, even to its going down, my name shall be great among the Gentiles; in every place incense shall be offered to my name, and a pure offering; for my name shall be great among the nations," says the LORD of hosts.

MALACHI 1:13

"You also say, 'Oh, what a weariness!' And you sneer at it," says the LORD of hosts.

"And you bring the stolen, the lame, and the sick; thus you bring an offering! Should I accept this from your hand?" says the LORD.

MALACHI 2:12

May the LORD cut off from the tents of Jacob, the man who does this, being awake and aware, yet who brings an offering to the LORD of hosts!

MALACHI 2:13

And this is the second thing you do: You cover the altar of the LORD with tears, with weeping and crying; so He does not regard the offering anymore, nor receive it with goodwill from your hands.

MALACHI 3:3

He will sit as a refiner and a purifier of silver; he will purify the sons of Levi, and purge them as gold and silver, that they may offer to the LORD, an offering in righteousness.

MALACHI 3:4

Then the offering of Judah and Jerusalem will be pleasant to the LORD, as in the days of old, as in former years.

LUKE 23:36

The soldiers also mocked Him, coming and offering Him sour wine.

ACTS 21:26

Then Paul took the men, and the next day, having been purified with them, entered the temple to announce the expiration of the days of purification, at which time an offering should be made for each one of them.

ROMANS 15:16

That I might be a minister of Jesus Christ to the Gentiles, ministering the gospel of God, that the offering of the Gentiles might be acceptable, sanctified by the Holy Spirit.

EPHESIANS 5:2

And walk in love, as Christ also has loved us and given Himself for us, an offering and a sacrifice to God for a sweet-smelling aroma.

HEBREWS 10:5

Therefore, when He came into the world, He said: "Sacrifice and offering You did not desire, but a body You have prepared for Me."

HEBREWS 10:10

By that will we have been sanctified through the offering of the body of Jesus Christ once for all.

HEBREWS 10:11

And every priest stands ministering daily and offering repeatedly the same sacrifices, which can never take away sins.

HEBREWS 10:14

For by one offering He has perfected forever those who are being sanctified.

HEBREWS 10:18

Now where there is remission of these, there is no longer an offering for sin.

Offerings

EZEKIEL 43:27

"When these days are over it shall be, on the eighth day and thereafter, that the priests shall offer your burnt offerings and your peace offerings on the altar; and I will accept you," says the Lord GOD.

EZEKIEL 45:15

"And one lamb shall be given from a flock of two hundred, from the rich pastures of Israel. These shall be for grain offerings, burnt offerings, and peace offerings, to make atonement for them," says the Lord GOD.

EZEKIEL 45:17

Then it shall be the prince's part to give burnt offerings, grain offerings, and drink offerings, at the feasts, the New Moons, the Sabbaths, and at all the appointed seasons of the house of Israel. He shall prepare the sin offering, the grain offering, the burnt offering, and the peace offerings to make atonement for the house of Israel.

EZEKIEL 46:2

The prince shall enter by way of the vestibule of that gateway from the outside, and stand by the gatepost. The priests shall prepare his burnt offering and his peace offerings. He shall worship at the threshold of the gate. Then he shall go out, but the gate shall not be shut until evening.

EZEKIEL 46:12

Now when the prince makes a voluntary burnt offering or voluntary peace offering to the LORD, the gate that faces toward the east shall then be opened for him; and he shall prepare his burnt offering and his peace offerings as he did on the Sabbath day. Then he shall go out, and after he goes out the gate shall be shut.

HOSEA 6:6

For I desire mercy and not sacrifice, and the knowledge of God more than burnt offerings.

HOSEA 8:13

For the sacrifices of My offerings they sacrifice flesh and eat it, but the LORD does not accept them. Now He *will remember their iniquity and punish their sins. They shall return to Egypt.*

HOSEA 9:4

They shall not offer wine offerings to the LORD, nor shall their sacrifices be pleasing to Him. It shall be like bread of mourners to them; all who eat it shall be defiled. For their bread shall be for their own life; it shall not come into the house of the LORD.

AMOS 4:5

"Offer a sacrifice of thanksgiving with leaven, proclaim and announce the freewill offerings; for this you love, you children of Israel!" Says the Lord GOD.

AMOS 5:22

Though you offer Me burnt offerings and your grain offerings, I will not accept them, nor will I regard your fattened peace offerings.

AMOS 5:25

Did you offer Me sacrifices and offerings in the wilderness forty years, O house of Israel?

MICAH 6:6

With what shall I come before the LORD, and bow myself before the High God? Shall I come before Him with burnt offerings, with calves a year old?

MALACHI 3:8

"Will a man rob God? Yet you have robbed Me! But you say, 'In what way have we robbed You?' In tithes and offerings."

MARK 12:33

"And to love Him with all the heart, with all the understanding, with all the soul, and with all the strength, and to love one's neighbor as oneself, is more than all the whole burnt offerings and sacrifices."

LUKE 21:4

"For all these out of their abundance have put in offerings for God, but she out of her poverty put in all the livelihood that she had."

ACTS 24:17

Now after many years I came to bring alms and offerings to my nation.

1 CORINTHIANS 9:13

Do you not know that those who minister the holy things eat of the things of the temple, and those who serve at the altar partake of the offerings of the altar?

HEBREWS 10:6

In burnt offerings and sacrifices for sin you had no pleasure.

HEBREWS 10:8

Previously saying, "Sacrifice and offering, burnt offerings, and offerings for sin You did not desire, nor had pleasure in them" (which are offered according to the law).

SCRIPTURE REFERENCES ON OFFERINGS

" The *Family Finance Handbook* from Rich Brott and Frank Damazio provides a well-informed financial and stewardship guide for the individual, classroom, small group, and church stewardship presentation. It's all about biblical principles, practical helps and real life application."

DR. JOHN C. MAXWELL
Founder, The INJOY Group

"I pray that our Heavenly Father will abundantly bless your family with financial health through the reading of this book, so that you may also bless others for His glory."

DR. DAVID YONGGI CHO
Senior Pastor, Yoido Full Gospel Church, Seoul, Korea

"Although it is true that the joy of the Lord is our strength, nothing can rob us of that joy more than financial difficulty. The *Family Finance Handbook* is a tremendous tool to help us manage our resources well and thus stay joyfully strong in Jesus. "

DR. DICK EASTMAN
International President, Every Home for Christ

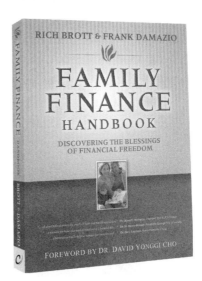

FAMILY FINANCE HANDBOOK

Discovering the Blessings of Financial Freedom

RICH BROTT & FRANK DAMAZIO

With insights gained from twenty-five years in business and ministry, the authors impart to the reader biblical principles of stewardship and financial management. Readers learn how to get out of debt and are carefully guided through the investment process in this comprehensive and well-crafted resource.

Family Life / Finance / Christian Living

Softcover, 288 pages, 7 ½" X 10"
0-914936-60-3

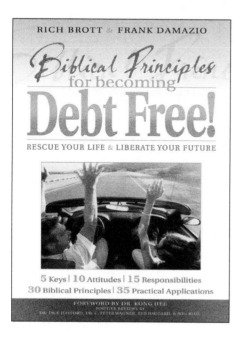

FAMILY FINANCE WORKBOOKS

Discovering the Blessings of Financial Freedom

RICH BROTT
&
FRANK DAMAZIO

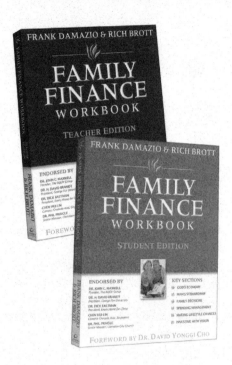

B ased on the contents of the *Family Finance Handbook*, these workbooks assist the student in establishing a solid understanding of the major principles of finances including: God's economy, man's stewardship, decision-making, money management, lifestyle choices, and investing.

Endorsed by Dr. John C. Maxwell, Dr. David Yonggi Cho, Dr. Dick Eastman, Dr. Phil Pringle, and others.

Family Life / Finance / Christian Living

TEACHER EDITION
Softcover, 214 pages, 7 ½" X 10"
1-59383-019-X

STUDENT EDITION
Softcover, 214 pages, 7 ½" X 10"
1-59383-020-3

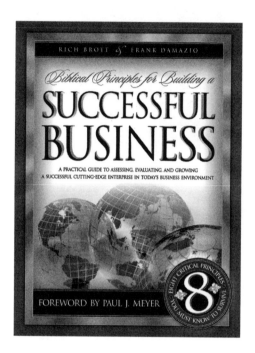

BIBLICAL PRINCIPLES FOR BUILDING A SUCCESSFUL BUSINESS

A Practical Guide to Assessing, Evaluating, and Growing a Successful Cutting-edge Enterprise in Today's Business Environment

RICH BROTT
&
FRANK DAMAZIO

Filled with timeless biblical principles and relevant practical strategies, *Biblical Principles for Building a Successful Business* will equip any new business person or seasoned entrepreneur with the tools necessary for building a thriving, God-honoring business venture.

"This book explains the relationship between good business practices and sound biblical principles. It will provide you with the strongest foundation for pursuing and achieving your dreams and show you how to achieve both success and significance in business."

MARK SANBORN, AUTHOR OF THE FRED FACTOR
(*Wall Street Journal* and *Business Week* best-seller)

Business / Entrepreneurship / Finance / Leadership

Softcover, 477 pages, 7 ½" X 10"
1-59383-027-0

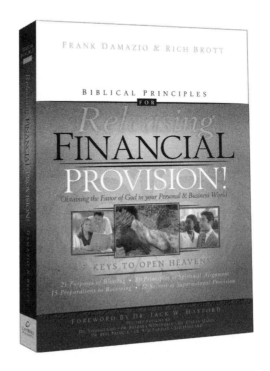